Enduring Critical Acclaim

"Of the many titles which have poured from [Sheen's] pen this may well become the most popular and most influential. In view of the subject matter and its inspiring treatment, it deserves that distinction. . . .

"The most notable feature of all is the author's ability to bring out the dramatic qualities inherent in a scene. This is evident throughout the entire book, but especially in such scenes as the temptation in the desert, the conversation with the Samaritan woman, and above all his account of the Passion. . . .

"But if there is one theme that prevails, it is the theme of the Cross. Since Christ is the heart and core of Christianity, the reader will come away from this book with a deeper insight into the meaning of the Christian life. Preachers especially will find it an abundant source of suggestive ideas for sermons and retreats."—*America*

". . . [a] major work on the entire life of the Savior. Like an evangelist of old, Sheen has put into writing the fruit of years of catechizing, meditating and preaching on the word of God. . . . Unlike most standard lives of Christ, his book places the emphasis on a spiritual, homiletic interpretation rather than on a more precise and scientific exegesis of Scripture, although the latter is not wanting. . . . The author proves himself a master of the paradox in writing of that greatest paradox of all—the God-Man. He restates old truths in new and vivid and appealing ways. All the charm of style, the breadth of vision, the depth of spirituality usually associated with Bishop Sheen's work are found here in abundance. . . .

"We warmly recommend the book to all readers. The laity, religious and priests alike will find it a rich source of material for private meditation and spiritual reading."—*The Critic*

"Although the author is a Roman Catholic, the long work will be of interest to Christians of all denominations."—*Booklist*

"When a gifted author comes to grips with a mighty theme, readers can anticipate a work of unusual merit and value. That anticipation is more than fulfilled in this moving story of the greatest life ever lived as told by one of the most dedicated scholars of our day."—*Chicago Sunday Tribune*

"The Cross and the corollaries of the Cross, such as the life of sacrifice to which the Christian is called, are treated with great power. . . . Life of Christ is a book with many moments of depth and eloquence—the treatment of the Beatitudes and of the Last Supper, to mention two—and the work as a whole is best read as a prolonged hymn of praise."—*New York Herald Tribune*

"Whether or not the reader will hear themes and variations that Bishop Sheen has used before, no one will fail to hear in this synthesis an eloquent voice which is saying again for our times, and in contemporary rhetoric, what the great Fathers of the early Church said for their flocks."—*New York Times*

Other Books by Fulton J. Sheen

The Armor of God
Calvary and the Mass
Characters of the Passion
Christmas Inspirations
Communism and the Conscience
    of the West
The Cross and the Beatitudes
The Cross and the Crisis
A Declaration of Dependence
The Divine Romance
The Divine Verdict
Easter Inspirations
The Eternal Galilean
Footprints in a Darkened Forest
For God and Country
Freedom under God
Go To Heaven
God and Intelligence
God and War
God Love You
Guide to Contentment
Hymn of the Conquered
Jesus, Son of Mary
Liberty, Equality and Fraternity
Life Is Worth Living,
    First Series
Life Is Worth Living,
    Second Series
Thinking Life Through,
    Third Series
Life Is Worth Living,
    Fourth Series
Life Is Worth Living,
    Fifth Series
The Life of All Living
Lift Up Your Heart

Love One Another
Missions and the World Crisis
Moods and Truths
The Moral Universe
The Mystical Body of Christ
Old Errors and New Labels
Peace of Soul
Philosophies at War
Philosophy of Religion
The Philosophy of Science
The Power of Love
Preface to Religion
The Priest Is not His Own
The Rainbow of Sorrow
Religion without God
The Seven Last Words
Seven Pillars of Peace
The Seven Virtues
Seven Words of Jesus and Mary
Seven Words to the Cross
These Are the Sacraments
This Is the Holy Land
This Is the Mass
This Is Rome
Those Mysterious Priests
Thoughts for Daily Living
Three to Get Married
The True Meaning of Christmas
Victory over Vice
Walk with God
The Way of the Cross
Way to Happiness
Way to Inner Peace
Whence Come Wars
The World's First Love

LIFE OF CHRIST

FULTON J. SHEEN, PH.D., D.D.

NATIONAL DIRECTOR,
WORLD MISSION SOCIETY FOR
THE PROPAGATION OF THE FAITH

COMPLETE AND UNABRIDGED

IMAGE BOOKS

A DIVISION OF DOUBLEDAY & COMPANY, INC.

GARDEN CITY, NEW YORK

Image Book edition published September 1977 by special arrangement with the author.

All biblical quotations are from *The New English Bible*, Oxford University Press, New York. © The Delegates of the Oxford University Press and The Syndics of the Cambridge University Press 1961, 1970.

Library of Congress Cataloging in Publication Data

Sheen, Fulton John, Bp., 1895–
   Life of Christ.

   Reprint of the 1958 ed. published by McGraw-Hill, New York.
   Includes index.
   1. Jesus Christ—Biography. 2. Christian biography—Palestine.
I. Title.
BT301.2.S464 1977   232.9
ISBN 0-385-13220-4

DEDICATED
IN FILIAL AFFECTION
TO MARY
THE TRIPLE AUTHOR

FIRST AS MOTHER WHO DIDST GIVE TO THE SON
OF THE LIVING GOD
A BODY WITH WHICH HE BORROWED HUMAN GUILT
AND PAID BACK DEATH WITH LIFE

THEN AS AUTHOR OF THESE WORDS ABOUT THE WORD
FOR ONLY IN DARK HOURS WHEN GALL WITH INK DID MIX
SHE MADE THE WRITER SEE CHRIST AND CRUCIFIX

AND LAST AS AUTHOR WITH THE SPIRIT OF CHRIST
IN EACH READER'S HEART
ACTING ON EACH PAGE AS THE SWEET INCENDIARY
OF THAT LOVE WE FALL JUST SHORT OF
IN ALL LOVE

Preface

Some books are written to answer one's own questions; other books are written to question answers already given. This book was written to find solace in the Cross of Christ, as for about ten years of my life I endured a great trial. The nature of that trial is not important, but what is important is how it was met. Plunging into the Life of Christ what seemed to stare at me from the pages of the Gospel was that Christ, the Son of God, did not come into this world to *live*. He came into it to *die*. Death was the goal of His Life, the gold that He was seeking. You and I come into the world to live. Death is an interruption, as death halted the teaching of Socrates. But for Him, as He told the Greeks, the seed must fall to the ground and die before it springs forth to new life. Unless there is a Good Friday in our lives there will never be an Easter Sunday. The Cross is the condition of the empty tomb, and the crown of thorns is the preface to the halo of light.

When all is said and done, there are only two philosophies of life. One is first the feast, then the hangover; the other, first the fast and then the feast. Deferred joys purchased by sacrifices are always sweetest and most enduring. Christianity begins not with sunshine but with defeat. Sunshine religions that begin with psychic elation, end often in disillusionment and despair. So essential is dying to self the prelude to the true life of self, that there were three monumental attempts to force Christ to abandon His Cross. The Devil offered three short cuts to winning the world at the beginning of His Public Life. Peter, the head of the Apostolic band, also tried to solicit Him from the Cross and was scorched for it by being called "Satan." And finally, at Golgotha, His enemies standing beneath the Cross hurled this challenge—"Come down and we will believe." Apparently they would believe anything He taught if He would only abandon His philosophy that only by losing one's life does one save it.

If we leave the Cross out of the Life of Christ, we have nothing left, and certainly not Christianity. For the Cross is related to our sins. Christ was our "stand-in" on the stage of life. He took our guilt as if He were guilty and thus paid the debt that sin deserved, namely, death. This made possible our resurrection to a "new life" in Him. Christ, therefore, is not just a teacher or a peasant revolutionist, but our Savior. Our modern world does not like the word "sin."

Dr. Karl Menninger, the psychiatrist, has asked, "What Has Happened to Sin?" About the only sin that modern man admits is social sin committed by the State, Government or Capitalists. If he does wrong personally, he is "sick," but he is not a sinner. What is forgotten is that sin is not the worst thing in the world. The worst thing is the denial of sin. If I am blind and deny there is any such thing as light, I shall never see. If I am deaf and deny sound, I shall never hear. And if I deny there is sin, I make forgiveness impossible.

I believe that the whole political and religious situation of the world can be summed up in terms of the divorce of Christ and His Cross. Put the Cross-less Christ on the right side, and the Christ-less Cross on the left. Who picks up the Crossless Christ? Our decadent Western civilization. Christ is weak, effeminate, with no authority to drive buyers and sellers out of temples, and never speaks of self-discipline, restraint and mortification.

Who picks up the Christless Cross? Russia and China, where there is a dedication to a common ideology, the use of discipline and authority to keep peace and order. But neither can heal. The Crossless Christ leaves men burdened with their guilt which festers in a thousand psychoses and neuroses. The Christless Cross cannot save for it ends in Dachau, the Gulag Archipelago and the squeezing of the lives of millions like grapes to make the collective wine of the State. Which will first find Christ with the Cross? The totalitarian states who have the Cross without Love, or the Western world which has love—so often erotic—without sacrifice? We do not know. But we do know that at the end of time, when the great conflict between the forces of good and evil takes place, Satan will appear without the Cross, as the Great Philanthropist and Social Reformer to become the final temptation of mankind.

During those days when my life was backed up against the Cross, I began to know and to love it more. Out of it came this book. The point I sought to stress most clearly and most strongly was that the shadow of the Cross fell over every detail of the Life of Christ from the beginning. It fell across His Crib. His Baptism was not just a call to teach, but to be the Victim prophesied by Isaiah; it was the whole burden of Satan's temptation on the Mount; it was hinted in the cleansing of the Temple when He challenged His enemies to destroy the Temple of His Body on Good Friday and He would rebuild it on Easter; it was hidden in the title of "Savior" He accepted when He forgave a prostitute's sins; it was implied in the Beatitudes, for anyone who would practice the Beatitudes in this world would be crucified; it was prophesied clearly three times as He gave details of His Death and Resurrection; it was hidden in the seven times He used the word "Hour" in contrast to "Day" which stood for His conquest of evil.

Finally, the Cross met its defeat when the earth received its most serious wound—the empty Tomb. To create the world cost God nothing; to save it from sin cost His Life-Blood. It is hoped that the sweet intimacy with the Crucified Christ, during what I now know were the most blessed days of my life, will break through these pages and give to the reader the lesson I learned—that every tribulation is, "The Shade of His Hand outstretched caressingly."

Contents

LIFE OF CHRIST

1. *The Only Person Ever Pre-announced*

History is full of men who have claimed that they came from God, or that they were gods, or that they bore messages from God—Buddha, Mohammed, Confucius, Christ, Lao-tze, and thousands of others, right down to the person who founded a new religion this very day. Each of them has a right to be heard and considered. But as a yard-stick external to and outside of whatever is to be measured is needed, so there must be some permanent tests available to all men, all civilizations, and all ages, by which they can decide whether any of these claimants, or all of them, are justified in their claims. These tests are of two kinds: *reason* and *history*. Reason, because everyone has it, even those without faith; history, because everyone lives in it and should know something about it.

Reason dictates that if any one of these men actually came from God, the least thing that God could do to support His claim would be to pre-announce His coming. Automobile manufacturers tell their customers when to expect a new model. If God sent anyone from Himself, or if He came Himself with a vitally important message for all men, it would seem reasonable that He would first let men know when His messenger was coming, where He would be born, where He would live, the doctrine He would teach, the enemies He would make, the program He would adopt for the future, and the manner of His death. By the extent to which the messenger conformed with these announcements, one could judge the validity of his claims.

Reason further assures us that if God did not do this, then there would be nothing to prevent any impostor from appearing in history and saying, "I come from God," or "An angel appeared to me in the desert and gave me this message." In such cases there would be no objective, historical way of testing the messenger. We would have only his word for it, and of course he could be wrong.

If a visitor came from a foreign country to Washington and said he was a diplomat, the government would ask him for his passport and other documents testifying that he represented a certain government. His papers would have to antedate his coming. If such proofs of identity are asked from delegates of other countries, reason certainly ought to do so with messengers who claim to have come from God. To each claimant reason says, "What record was there before you were born that you were coming?"

With this test one can evaluate the claimants. (And at this preliminary stage, Christ is no greater than the others.) Socrates had no one to foretell his birth. Buddha had no one to pre-announce him and his message or tell the day when he would sit under the tree. Confucius did not have the name of his mother and his birthplace recorded, nor were they given to men centuries before he arrived so that when he did come, men would know he was a messenger from God. But, with Christ it was different. Because of the Old Testament prophecies, His coming was not unexpected. There were no predictions about Buddha, Confucius, Lao-tze, Mohammed, or anyone else; but there were predictions about Christ. Others just came and said, "Here I am, believe me." They were, therefore, only men among men and not the Divine in the human. Christ alone stepped out of that line saying, "Search the writings of the Jewish people and the related history of the Babylonians, Persians, Greeks, and Romans." (For the moment, pagan writings and even the Old Testament may be regarded only as historical documents, not as inspired works.)

It is true that the prophecies of the Old Testament can be best understood in the light of their fulfillment. The language of prophecy does not have the exactness of mathematics. Yet if one searches out the various Messianic currents in the Old Testament, and compares the resulting picture with the life and work of Christ, can one doubt that the ancient predictions point to Jesus and the kingdom which he established? God's promise to the patriarchs that through them all the nations of the earth would be blessed; the prediction that the tribe of Juda would be supreme among the other Hebrew tribes until the coming of Him Whom all nations would obey; the strange yet undeniable fact that in the Bible of the Alexandrian Jews, the Septuagint, one finds clearly predicted the *virgin* birth of the Messiah; the prophecy of Isaiah 53 about the patient sufferer, the Servant of the Lord, who will lay down his life as a guilt-offering for his people's offenses; the perspectives of the glorious, everlasting kingdom of the House of David —in whom but Christ have these prophecies found their fulfillment? From an historical point of view alone, here is uniqueness which sets Christ apart from all other founders of world religions. And once the fulfillment of these prophecies did historically take place in the person of Christ, not only did all prophecies cease in Israel, but there was discontinuance of sacrifices when the true Paschal Lamb was sacrificed.

Turn to pagan testimony. Tacitus, speaking for the ancient Romans, says, "People were generally persuaded in the faith of the ancient prophecies, that the East was to prevail, and that from Judea was to come the Master and Ruler of the world." Suetonius, in his account of the life of Vespasian, recounts the Roman tradition thus, "It was an old and constant belief throughout the East, that by indubitably certain prophecies, the Jews were to attain the highest power."

China had the same expectation; but because it was on the other side of the world, it believed that the great Wise Man would be born in the *West*. The Annals of the Celestial Empire contain the statement:

> In the 24th year of Tchao-Wang of the dynasty of the Tcheou, on the 8th day of the 4th moon, a light appeared in the South-west which illumined the king's palace. The monarch, struck by its splendor, interrogated the sages. They showed him books in which this prodigy signified the appearance of the great Saint of the West whose religion was to be introduced into their country.

The Greeks expected Him, for Aeschylus in his *Prometheus* six centuries before His coming, wrote, "Look not for any end, moreover, to this curse until God appears, to accept upon His Head the pangs of thy own sins vicarious."

How did the Magi of the East know of His coming? Probably from the many prophecies circulated through the world by the Jews as well as through the prophecy made to the Gentiles by Daniel centuries before His birth.

Cicero, after recounting the sayings of the ancient oracles and the Sibyls about a "King whom we must recognize to be saved," asked in expectation, "To what man and to what period of time do these predictions point?" The Fourth Eclogue of Virgil recounted the same ancient tradition and spoke of "a chaste woman, smiling on her infant boy, with whom the iron age would pass away."

Suetonius quoted a contemporary author to the effect that the Romans were so fearful about a king who would rule the world that they ordered all children born that year to be killed—an order that was not fulfilled, except by Herod.

Not only were the Jews expecting the birth of a Great King, a Wise Man and a Savior, but Plato and Socrates also spoke of the *Logos* and of the Universal Wise Man "yet to come." Confucius spoke of "the Saint"; the Sibyls, of a "Universal King"; the Greek dramatist, of a savior and redeemer to unloose man from the "primal eldest curse." All these were on the Gentile side of the expectation. What separates Christ from all men is that first He was expected; even the Gentiles had a longing for a deliverer, or redeemer. This fact alone distinguishes Him from all other religious leaders.

A second distinguishing fact is that once He appeared, He struck history with such impact that He split it in two, dividing it into two periods: one before His coming, the other after it. Buddha did not do this, nor any of the great Indian philosophers. Even those who deny God must date their attacks upon Him, A.D. so and so, or so many years after His coming.

A third fact separating Him from all the others is this: *every other person who ever came into this world came into it to live. He came into it to die.* Death was a stumbling block to Socrates—it interrupted his teaching. But to Christ, death was the goal and fulfillment of His life, the gold that He was seeking. Few of His words or actions are intelligible without reference to His Cross. He presented Himself as a Savior rather than merely as a Teacher. It meant nothing to teach men to be good unless He also gave them the power to be good, after rescuing them from the frustration of guilt.

The story of every human life begins with birth and ends with death. In the Person of Christ, however, *it was His death that was first and His life that was last.* The Scripture describes Him as "the Lamb slain as it were, from the beginning of the world." He was slain in intention by the first sin and rebellion against God. It was not so much that His birth cast a shadow on His Life and thus led to His death; it was rather that the Cross was first, and cast its shadow back to His birth. His has been the only life in the world that was ever lived backward. As the flower in the crannied wall tells the poet of nature, and as the atom is the miniature of the solar system, so too, His birth tells the mystery of the gibbet. He went from the known to the known, from the reason of His coming manifested by His name "Jesus" or "Savior" to the fulfillment of His coming, namely, His death on the Cross.

John gives us His eternal prehistory; Matthew, His temporal prehistory, by way of His genealogy. It is significant how much His temporal ancestry was connected with sinners and foreigners! These blots on the escutcheon of His human lineage suggest a pity for the sinful and for the strangers to the Covenant. Both these aspects of His compassion would later on be hurled against Him as accusations: "He is a friend of sinners"; "He is a Samaritan." But the shadow of a stained past foretells His future love for the stained. Born of a woman, He was a man and could be one with all humanity; born of a Virgin, who was overshadowed by the Spirit and "full of grace," He would also be outside that current of sin which infected all men.

A fourth distinguishing fact is that He does not fit, as the other world teachers do, into the established category of a *good man*. Good men do not lie. But if Christ was not all that He said He was, namely, the Son of the living God, the Word of God in the flesh, then He was not "just a good man"; then He was a knave, a liar, a charlatan and the greatest deceiver who ever lived. If He was not what He said He was, the Christ, the Son of God, He was the anti-Christ! If He was only a man, then He was not even a "good" man.

But He was *not only* a man. He would have us either worship Him or despise Him—despise Him as a mere man, or worship Him as true God and true man. That is the alternative He presents. It may very well be that the Communists, who are so anti-Christ, are closer to Him than those who see Him as a sentimentalist and a vague moral reformer. The Communists have at least decided that if He wins, they lose; the others are afraid to consider Him either as winning or losing, because they are not prepared to meet the moral demands which this victory would make on their souls.

If He is what He claimed to be, a Savior, a Redeemer, then we have a virile Christ and a leader worth following in these terrible times; One Who will step into the breach of death, crushing sin, gloom and despair; a leader to Whom we can make totalitarian sacrifice without losing, but gaining freedom, and Whom we can love even unto death. We need a Christ today Who will make cords and drive the buyers and sellers from our new temples; Who will blast the unfruitful fig tree; Who will talk of crosses and sacrifices and Whose voice will be like the voice of the raging sea. But He will not allow us to pick and choose among His words, discarding the hard ones, and accepting the ones that please our fancy. We need a Christ Who will restore moral indignation, Who will make us hate evil with a passionate intensity, and love goodness to a point where we can drink death like water.

2. Early Life of Christ

Every civilization has had a tradition of a golden age in the past. A more precise Jewish record tells of a fall from a state of innocence and happiness through a woman tempting a man. If a woman played such a role in the fall of mankind, should she not play a great role in its restoration? And if there was a lost Paradise in which the first nuptials of man and woman were celebrated, might there not be a new Paradise in which the nuptials of God and man would be celebrated?

In the fullness of time an Angel of Light came down from the great Throne of Light to a Virgin kneeling in prayer, to ask her if she was willing to give God a human nature. Her answer was that she "knew not man" and, therefore, could not be the mother of the "Expected of the Nations."

There never can be a birth without love. In this the maiden was right. The begetting of new life requires the fires of love. But besides the human passion which begets life, there is the "passionless passion and wild tranquility" of the Holy Spirit; and it was this that overshadowed the woman and begot in her Emmanuel or "God with us." At the moment that Mary pronounced *Fiat* or "Be it done," something greater happened than the *Fiat lux* (Let there be light) of creation; for the light that was now made was not the sun, but the Son of God in the flesh. By pronouncing *Fiat* Mary achieved the full role of womanhood, namely, to be the bearer of God's gifts to man. There is a passive receptiveness in which woman says *Fiat* to the cosmos as she shares its rhythm, *Fiat* to a man's love as she receives it, and *Fiat* to God as she receives the Spirit.

Children come into the world not always as a result of a distinct act of love of man and woman. Though the love between the two be willed, the fruit of their love, which is the child, is not willed in the same way as their love one for another. There is an undetermined element in human love. The parents do not know whether the child will be a boy or a girl, or the exact time of its birth, for conception is lost in some unknown night of love. Children are later accepted and loved by their parents, but they were never directly willed into being by them. But in the Annunciation, the Child was not accepted in any unforeseen way; *the Child was willed.* There was a collaboration between a woman and the Spirit of Divine Love. The consent was voluntary under the *Fiat*; the physical cooperation was freely offered by the same word. Other mothers become conscious of motherhood through physical changes within them; Mary became conscious through a spiritual change wrought by the Holy Spirit. She probably received a spiritual ecstasy far greater than that given to man and woman in their unifying act of love.

As the fall of man was a free act, so too the Redemption had to be free. What is called the Annunciation was actually God asking the free consent of a creature to help Him to be incorporated into humanity.

Suppose a musician in an orchestra freely strikes a sour note. The conductor is competent, the music is correctly scored and easy to play, but the musician still exercises his freedom by introducing a discord which immediately passes out into space. The director can do one of two things: he can either order the selection to be replayed, or he can ignore the discord. Fundamentally, it makes no difference which he does, for that false note is traveling out into space at the rate of more than a thousand feet per second; and as long as time endures, there will be discord in the universe.

Is there any way to restore harmony to the world? It can be done only by someone coming in from eternity and stopping the note in its wild flight. But will it still be a false note? The harmony can be destroyed on one condition only. If that note is made the first note in a new melody, then it will become harmonious.

This is precisely what happened when Christ was born. There had been a false note of moral discord introduced by the first man which infected all humanity. God could have ignored it, but it would have been a violation of justice for Him to do so, which is, of course, unthinkable. What He did, therefore, was to ask a woman, representing humanity, freely to give Him a human nature with which He would start a new humanity. As there was an old humanity in Adam, so there would be a new humanity in Christ, Who was God made man through the free agency of a human mother. When the angel appeared to Mary, God was announcing this love for the new humanity. It was the beginning of a new earth, and Mary became "a flesh-girt Paradise to be gardened by the Adam new." As in the first garden Eve brought destruction, so in the garden of her womb, Mary would now bring Redemption.

For the nine months that He was cloistered within her, all the food, the wheat, the grapes that she consumed served as a kind of natural Eucharist, passing into Him Who later on was to declare that He was the Bread and Wine of Life. After her nine months were over, the fitting place for Him to be born was Bethlehem, which meant "House of Bread." Later on He would say:

> The bread that God gives comes down from heaven and brings life to the world. *John 6:33*

> I am the bread of life. Whoever comes to me shall never be hungry.
> *John 6:35*

When the Divine Child was conceived, Mary's humanity gave Him hands and feet, eyes and ears, and a body with which to suffer. Just as the petals of a rose after a dew close on the dew as if to absorb its energies, so too, Mary as the Mystical Rose closed upon Him Whom the Old Testament had described as a dew descending upon the earth. When finally she did give Him birth, it was as if a great ciborium had opened, and she was holding in her fingers the Guest Who was also the Host of the world, as if to say, "Look, this is the Lamb of God; this is He Who takes away the sins of the world."

THE VISITATION

Mary was given a sign that she would conceive by the Holy Ghost. Her elderly cousin Elizabeth had already conceived a son in her old age, and was now in her sixth month. Mary, now bearing the Divine Secret within her, journeyed several days from Nazareth to the city of Hebron, which, according to tradition, rested over the ashes of the founders of the people of God—Abraham, Isaac, and Jacob. Elizabeth, in some mysterious way, knew that Mary was bearing within herself the Messiah. She asked:

> Who am I, that the mother of my Lord should visit me? *Luke 1:43*

This salutation came from the mother of the herald to the mother of the King Whose path the herald was destined to prepare. John the Baptist, still cloistered in his mother's womb, on his mother's testimony leaped with joy at the mother who brought the Christ to her home.

Mary's response to this salutation is called the *Magnificat*, a song of joy celebrating what God had done for her. She looked back over history, back to Abraham; she saw the activity of God preparing for this moment from generation to generation, she looked also into an indefinite future when all peoples and all generations would call her "Blessed." Israel's Messiah was on His way, and God was about to manifest Himself on earth and in the flesh. She even prophesied the qualities of the Son Who was to be born of her as full of justice and mercy. Her poem ends by acclaiming the revolution He will inaugurate with the unseating of the mighty and the exaltation of the humble.

THE PREHISTORY OF CHRIST

The Lord to be born of Mary is the only Person in the world Who ever had a prehistory; a prehistory to be studied not in the primeval slime and jungles, but in the bosom of the Eternal Father. Though He appeared as the Cave Man in Bethlehem, since He was born in a stable hewn out of rock, His beginning in time as man was without beginning as God in the agelessness of eternity. Only progressively did He reveal His Divinity; and this was not because He grew in the consciousness of Divinity; it was due rather to His intent to be slow in revealing the purpose of His coming.

St. John at the beginning of his Gospel relates His prehistory as the Son of God:

> When all things began, the Word already was. The Word dwelt with God, and what God was, the Word was. The Word, then, was with God at the beginning, and through him all things came to be; no single thing was created without him. *John 1:1–3*

"In the beginning was the Word." Whatever there is in the world, is made according to the thought of God, for all things postulate thought. Every bird, every flower, every tree was made according to an idea existing in the Divine Mind. Greek philosophers held that thought was abstract. Now, the Thought or Word of God is revealed as Personal. Wisdom is vested in Personality. Prior to His earthly existence, Jesus Christ is eternally God, the Wisdom, the Thought of the Father. In His earthly existence, He is that Thought or Word of God speaking to men. The words of men pass away when they have been conceived and uttered, but the Word of God is eternally uttered and can never cease from utterance. By His Word, the Eternal Father expresses all that He understands, all that He knows. As the mind holds converse with itself by its own thought, and sees and knows the world by means of this thought, so does the Father see Himself, as in a mirror, in the Person of His Word. Finite intelligence needs many words in order to express ideas; but God speaks once and for all within Himself—one single Word which reaches the abyss of all things that are known and can be known. In that Word of God are hidden all the treasures of wisdom, all the secrets of sciences, all the designs of the arts, all the knowledge of mankind. But this knowledge, compared to the Word, is only the feeblest broken syllable.

In the agelessness of eternity, the Word was with God. But there was a moment in time when He had not come forth from the Godhead, as there is a moment when a thought in the mind of man is not yet uttered. As the sun is never without its beam, so the Father is never without His Son; and as the thinker is not without a thought, so in an infinite degree, the Divine Mind is never without His Word. God did not spend the everlasting ages in sublime solitary activity. He had a Word with Him equal to Himself.

> The Word, then, was with God at the beginning, and through him all things came to be; no single thing was created without him. All that came to be was alive with his life, and that life was the light of men. The light shines on in the dark, and the darkness has never mastered it. *John* 1:3–5

Everything in space and time exists because of the creative Power of God. Matter is not eternal; the universe has an intelligent Personality back of it, an Architect, a Builder, and a Sustainer. Creation is the work of God. The sculptor works on marble, the painter on canvas, the machinist on matter, but none of them can create. They bring existings into new combinations, but nothing else. Creation belongs to God alone.

God writes His name on the soul of every man. Reason and conscience are the God within us in the natural order. The Fathers of the early Church were wont to speak of the wisdom of Plato and Aristotle as the unconscious Christ within us. Men are like so many books issuing from the Divine press, and if nothing else be written on them, at least the name of the Author is indissolubly engraved on the title page. God is like the watermark on paper, which may be written over without ever being obscured.

BETHLEHEM

Caesar Augustus, the master bookkeeper of the world, sat in his palace by the Tiber. Before him was stretched a map labeled *Orbis Terrarum, Imperium Romanum.* He was about to issue an order for a census of the world; for all the nations of the civilized world were subject to Rome. There was only one capital in this world: Rome; only one official language: Latin; only one ruler: Caesar. To every outpost, to every satrap and governor, the order went out: every Roman subject must be enrolled in his own city. On the fringe of the Empire, in the little village of Nazareth, soldiers tacked up on walls the order for all the citizens to register in the towns of their family origins.

Joseph, the builder, an obscure descendant of the great King David, was obliged by that very fact to register in Bethlehem, the city of David. In accordance with the edict, Mary and Joseph set out from the village of Nazareth for the village of Bethlehem, which lies about five miles on the other side of Jerusalem. Five hundred years earlier the prophet Micheas had prophesied concerning that little village:

> Bethlehem in the land of Judah, you are far from least in the eyes of the rulers of Judah; for out of you shall come a leader to be the shepherd of my people Israel. *Matthew 2:6*

Joseph was full of expectancy as he entered the city of his family, and was quite convinced that he would have no difficulty in finding lodgings for Mary, particularly on account of her condition. Joseph went from house to house only to find each one crowded. He searched in vain for a place where He, to Whom heaven and earth belonged, might be born. Could it be that the Creator would not find a home in creation? Up a steep hill Joseph climbed to a faint light which swung on a rope across a doorway. This would be the village inn. There, above all other places, he would surely find shelter. There was room in the inn for the soldiers of Rome who had brutally subjugated the Jewish people; there was room for the daughters of the rich merchants of the East; there was room for those clothed in soft garments, who lived in the houses of the king; in fact, there was room for anyone who had a coin to give the innkeeper; but there was no room for Him Who came to be the Inn of every homeless heart in the world. When finally the scrolls of history are completed down to the last words in time, the saddest line of all will be: "There was no room in the inn."

Out to the hillside to a stable cave, where shepherds sometimes drove their flocks in time of storm, Joseph and Mary went at last for shelter. There, in a place of peace in the lonely abandonment of a cold windswept cave; there, under the floor of the world, He Who is born without a mother in heaven, is born without a father on earth.

Of every other child that is born into the world, friends can say that it resembles his mother. This was the first instance in time that anyone could say that the mother resembled the Child. This is the beautiful paradox of the Child Who made His mother; the mother, too, was only a child. It was also the first time in the history of this world that anyone could ever think of heaven as being anywhere else than "somewhere up there"; when the Child was in her arms, Mary now looked down to Heaven.

In the filthiest place in the world, a stable, Purity was born. He, Who was later to be slaughtered by men acting as beasts, was born among beasts. He, Who would call Himself the "living Bread descended from Heaven," was laid in a manger, literally, a place to eat. Centuries before, the Jews had worshiped the golden calf, and the Greeks, the ass. Men bowed down before them as before God. The ox and the ass now were present to make their innocent reparation, bowing down before their God.

There was no room in the inn, but there was room in the stable. The inn is the gathering place of public opinion, the focal point of the world's moods, the rendezvous of the worldly, the rallying place of the popular and the successful. But the stable is a place for the outcasts, the ignored, the forgotten. The world might have expected the Son of God to be born—if He was to be born at all—in an inn. A stable would be the last place in the world where one would have looked for Him. *Divinity is always where one least expects to find it.*

No worldly mind would ever have suspected that He Who could make the sun warm the earth would one day have need of an ox and an ass to warm Him with their breath; that He Who, in the language of Scriptures, could stop the turning about of Arcturus would have His birthplace dictated by an imperial census; that He, Who clothed the fields with grass, would Himself be naked; that He, from Whose hands came planets and worlds, would one day have tiny arms that were not long enough to touch the huge heads of the cattle; that the feet which trod the everlasting hills would one day be too weak to walk; that the Eternal Word would be dumb; that Omnipotence would be wrapped in swaddling clothes; that Salvation would lie in a manger; that the bird which built the nest would be hatched therein —no one would have ever suspected that God coming to this earth would ever be so helpless. And that is precisely why so many miss Him. *Divinity is always where one least expects to find it.*

If the artist is at home in his studio because the paintings are the creation of his own mind; if the sculptor is at home among his statues because they are the work of his own hands; if the husband-man is at home among his vines because he planted them; and if the father is at home among his children because they are his own, then surely, argues the world, He Who made the world should be at home in it. He should come into it as an artist into his studio, and as a father into his home; but, for the Creator to come among His creatures and be ignored by them; for God to come among His own and not be received by His own; for God to be homeless at home—that could only mean one thing to the worldly mind: the Babe could not have been God at all. And that is just why it missed Him. *Divinity is always where one least expects to find it.*

The Son of God made man was invited to enter His own world through a back door. Exiled from the earth, He was born under the earth, in a sense, the first Cave Man in recorded history. There He shook the earth to its very foundations. Because He was born in a cave, all who wish to see Him must stoop. To stoop is the mark of humility. The proud refuse to stoop and, therefore, they miss Divinity. Those, however, who bend their egos and enter, find that they are not in a cave at all, but in a new universe where sits a Babe on His mother's lap, with the world poised on His fingers.

The manger and the Cross thus stand at the two extremities of the Savior's life! He accepted the manger because there was no room in the inn; He accepted the Cross because men said, "We will not have this Man for our king." Disowned upon entering, rejected upon leaving, He was laid in a stranger's stable at the beginning, and a stranger's grave at the end. An ox and an ass surrounded His crib at Bethlehem; two thieves were to flank His Cross on Calvary. He was wrapped in swaddling bands in His birthplace, He was again laid in swaddling clothes in His tomb—clothes symbolic of the limitations imposed on His Divinity when He took a human form.

The shepherds watching their flocks nearby were told by the angels:

> And this is your sign: you will find a baby lying wrapped in his swaddling clothes, in a manger. *Luke 2:12*

He was already bearing His Cross—the only cross a Babe could bear, a cross of poverty, exile and limitation. His sacrificial intent already shone forth in the message the angels sang to the hills of Bethlehem:

> Today in the city of David a deliverer has been born to you—the Messiah, the Lord. *Luke 2:11*

Covetousness was already being challenged by His poverty, while pride was confronted with the humiliation of a stable. The swathing of Divine power, which needs to accept no bounds, is often too great a tax upon minds which think only of power. They cannot grasp the idea of Divine condescension, or of the "rich man becoming poor that through His poverty, we might be rich." Men shall have no greater sign of Divinity than the absence of power as they expect it—the spectacle of a Babe Who said He would come in the clouds of heaven, now being wrapped in the cloths of earth.

He, Whom the angels call the "Son of the most High," descended into the red dust from which we all were born, to be one with weak, fallen man in all things, save sin. And it is the swaddling clothes which constitute His "sign." If He Who is Omnipotence had come with thunderbolts, there would have been no sign. There is no sign unless something happens contrary to nature. The brightness of the sun is no sign, but an eclipse is. He said that on the last day, His coming would be heralded by "signs in the sun," perhaps an extinction of light. At Bethlehem the Divine Son went into an eclipse, so that only the humble of spirit might recognize Him.

Only two classes of people found the Babe; the shepherds and the Wise Men; the simple and the learned; those who knew that they knew nothing, and those who knew that they did not know everything. He is never seen by the man of one book; never by the man who thinks he knows. Not even God can tell the proud anything! Only the humble can find God!

As Caryll Houselander put it, "Bethlehem is the inscape of Calvary, just as the snowflake is the inscape of the universe." This same idea was expressed by the poet who said that if he knew the flower in a crannied wall in all its details, he would know "what God and man is." Scientists tell us that the atom comprehends within itself the mystery of the solar system.

It was not so much that His birth cast a shadow on His life, and thus led to His death; it was rather that the Cross was there from the beginning, and it cast its shadow backward to His birth. Ordinary mortals go from the known to the unknown submitting themselves to forces beyond their control; hence we can speak of their "tragedies." But He went from the known to the known, from the reason for His coming, namely, to be "Jesus" or "Savior," to the fulfillment of His coming, namely, the death on the Cross. Hence, there was no tragedy in His life; for, tragedy implies the unforseeable, the uncontrollable, and the fatalistic. Modern life is tragic when there is spiritual darkness and unredeemable guilt. But for the Christ Child there were no uncontrollable forces; no submission to fatalistic chains from which there could be no escape; but there was an "inscape"—the microcosmic manger summarizing, like an atom, the macrocosmic Cross on Golgotha.

In His First Advent, He took the name of Jesus, or "Savior"; it will be in His Second Advent that He will take the name of "Judge." Jesus was not a name He had before He assumed a human nature; it properly refers to that which was united to His Divinity, not that which existed from all eternity. Some say "Jesus taught" as they would say "Plato taught," never once thinking that His name means "Savior from sin." Once He received this name, Calvary became completely a part of Him. The Shadow of the Cross that fell on His cradle also covered His naming. This was "His Father's business"; everything else would be incidental to it.

PREHISTORY NOW HISTORY

"The Word became Flesh." The Divine Nature, which was pure and holy, entered as a renovating principle into the corrupted line of Adam's race, without being affected by corruption. Through the Virgin Birth, Jesus Christ became operative in human history without being subject to the evil in it.

> So the Word became flesh; he came to dwell among us, and we saw his glory, such glory as befits the Father's only Son, full of grace and truth. *John 1:14*

Bethlehem became a link between heaven and earth; God and man met here and looked each other in the face. In the taking of human flesh, the Father prepared it, the Spirit formed it, and the Son assumed it. He Who had an eternal generation in the bosom of the Father now had a temporal generation in time. He Who had His birth in Bethlehem came to be born in the hearts of men. For, what would it profit if He was born a thousand times in Bethlehem unless He was born again in man?

> But to all who did receive him, to those who have yielded him their allegiance, he gave the right to become children of God. *John 1:12*

Now man need not hide from God as Adam did; for He can be seen through Christ's human nature. Christ did not gain one perfection more by becoming man, nor did He lose anything of what He possessed as God. There was the Almightiness of God in the movement of His arm, the Infinite Love of God in the beatings of His human heart and the Unmeasured Compassion of God to sinners in His eyes. God is now manifest in the flesh; this is what is called the Incarnation. The whole range of the Divine attributes of power and goodness, justice, love, beauty, were in Him. And when Our Divine Lord acted and spoke, God in His perfect nature became manifest to those who saw Him and heard Him and touched Him. As He told Philip later on:

> Anyone who has seen me has seen the Father. *John 14:9*

No man can love anything unless he can get his arms around it, and the cosmos is too big and too bulky. But once God became a Babe and was wrapped in swaddling clothes and laid in a manger, men could say, "This is Emmanuel, this is God with us." By His reaching down to frail human nature and lifting it up to the incomparable prerogative of union with Himself, human nature became dignified. So real was this union that all of His acts and words, all of His agonies and tears, all of His thoughts and reasonings, resolves and emotions, while being properly human, were at the same time the acts and words, agonies and tears, thoughts and reasonings, resolves and emotions of the Eternal Son of God.

What men call the Incarnation is but the union of two natures, the

Divine and the human in a single Person Who governs both. This is not difficult to understand; for what is man but a sample, at an immeasurably lower level, of a union of two totally different substances, one material and the other immaterial, one the body, the other the soul, under the regency of a single human personality? What is more remote from one another than powers and capacities of flesh and spirit? Antecedent to their unity, how difficult it would be ever to conceive of a moment when body and soul would be united in a single personality. That they are so united is an experience clear to every mortal. And yet it is an experience at which man does not marvel because of its familiarity.

God, Who brings together body and soul into one human personality, notwithstanding their difference of nature, could surely bring about the union of a human body and a human soul with His Divinity under the control of His Eternal Person. This is what is meant by the

So the Word became flesh; he came to dwell among us. *John 1:14*

The Person which assumed human nature was not created, as is the case of all other persons. His Person was the pre-existent Word or *Logos.* His human nature, on the other hand, was derived from the miraculous conception by Mary, in which the Divine overshadowing of the Spirit and the human *Fiat* or the consent of a woman, were most beautifully blended. This is the beginning of a new humanity out of the material of the fallen race. When the Word became flesh, it did not mean that any change took place in the Divine Word. The Word of God proceeding forth did not leave the Father's side. What happened was not so much the conversion of the Godhead into flesh, as the taking of a manhood into God.

There was continuity with the fallen race of man through the manhood taken from Mary; there is discontinuity through the fact that the Person of Christ is the pre-existent *Logos.* Christ thus literally becomes the second Adam, the Man through whom the human race starts all over. His teaching centered on the incorporation of human natures to Him, after the manner in which the human nature that He took from Mary was united to the Eternal Word.

It is hard for a human being to understand the humility that was involved in the Word becoming flesh. Imagine, if it were possible, a human person divesting himself of his body, and then sending his soul into the body of a serpent. A double humiliation would follow: first, accepting the limitations of a serpentine organism, knowing all the while his mind was superior, and that fangs could not adequately articulate thoughts no serpent ever possessed. The second humiliation would be to be forced as a result of this "emptying of self" to live in the companionship of serpents. But all this is nothing compared to the emptying of God, by which He took on the form of man and accepted the limitations of humanity, such as hunger and persecution; not trivial either was it for the Wisdom of God to condemn Himself to association with poor fishermen who knew so little. But this humiliation which began in Nazareth when He was conceived in the Virgin Mary was only the first of many to counteract the pride of man, until the final humiliation of death on the Cross. If there were no Cross, there would have been no crib; if there had been no nails, there would have been no straw. But He could not *teach* the lesson of the Cross as payment for sin; He had to *take* it. God the Father did not spare His Son—so much did He love mankind. That was the secret wrapped in the swaddling bands.

THE NAME "JESUS"

The name "Jesus" was a fairly common one among the Jews. In the original Hebrew, it was "Josue." The angel told Joseph that Mary would:

> She will bear a son; and you shall give him the name Jesus (Saviour), for he will save his people from their sins. *Matthew 1:21*

This first indication of the nature of His mission on earth does not mention His teaching; for the teaching would be ineffective, unless there was first salvation.

He was given another name at the same time, the name "Emmanuel."

> The virgin will conceive and bear a son, and he shall be called Emmanuel, a name which means God is with us. *Matthew 1:23*

This name was taken from the prophecy of Isaiah and it assured something besides a Divine presence; together with the name "Jesus," it meant a Divine presence which delivers and saves. The angel also told Mary:

> You shall conceive and bear a son, and you shall give him the name Jesus. He will be great; he will bear the title Son of the Most High; the Lord God will give him the throne of his ancestor David, and he will be king over Israel for ever; his reign shall never end.
> *Luke 1:31–33*

The title "Son of the Most High" was the very one that was given to the Redeemer by the evil spirit which possessed the youth in the land of the Gerasenes. The fallen angel thus confessed Him to be what the unfallen angel said He was:

> What do you want with me, Jesus, son of the Most High God?
>
> *Mark* 5:7

The salvation that is promised by the name "Jesus" is not a social salvation, but rather a spiritual one. He would not save people necessarily from their poverty, but he would save them from their sins. To destroy sin is to uproot the first causes of poverty. The name "Jesus" brought back the memory of their great leader, who had brought them out of Egypt to rest in the promised land. The fact that He was prefigured by Josue indicates that He had the soldierly qualities necessary for the final victory over evil, which would come from the glad acceptance of suffering, unwavering courage, resoluteness of will and unshakable devotion to the Father's mandate.

The people enslaved under the Roman yoke were seeking deliverance; hence they felt that any prophetic fulfillment of the ancient Josue would have something to do with politics. Later on, the people would ask Him when He was going to deliver them from the power of Caesar. But here, at the very beginning of His life, the Divine Soldier affirmed through an angel that he had come to conquer a greater enemy than Caesar. They must still render to Caesar the things that were Caesar's; His Mission was to deliver them from a far greater bondage, namely, that of sin. All through His life people would continue to materialize the concept of salvation, thinking that deliverance was to be interpreted only in terms of the political. The name "Jesus" or Savior was not given to Him after He had wrought salvation, but at the very moment He was conceived in the womb of His mother. The foundation of His salvation was from eternity and not from time.

"FIRSTBORN"

> She gave birth to a son, her first-born. *Luke* 2:7

The term "firstborn" did not mean that Our Lady was to bear other children according to the flesh. There was always a position of honor assigned in law to the firstborn, even if there were not any other children. It could very well be that Luke employs the term here in view of the account which he later on is to give of the Blessed Mother presenting her Child in the temple "as the firstborn Son." The other brethren of Our Lord mentioned by Luke were not sons of Mary; they were either half brothers, sons of Joseph by a possible former marriage, or else His cousins. Mary had no other children in the flesh. But "firstborn" could mean Our Lady's relation to other children she would have according to the Spirit. In this sense, her Divine Son called John her "son" at the foot of the Cross. Spiritually, John was her "second son." St. Paul later on used the term "firstborn" in time to parallel Our Lord's Eternal Generation as the Only Begotten of the Father. It was only to His Divine Son that God said:

> Thou art my Son; today I have begotten thee, or again, I will be father to him, and he shall be my son. Again, when he presents the first-born to the world, he says, Let all the angels of God pay him homage. *Hebrews 1:5–6*

CHRIST'S FAMILY TREE

Though His Divine nature was from eternity, His human nature had a Jewish background. The blood that flowed in His veins was from the royal house of David through His mother who, though poor, belonged to the lineage of the great king. His contemporaries called Him the "Son of David." The people would never have consented to regard as a Messiah any pretender who did not fulfill this indispensable condition. Nor did Our Blessed Lord Himself ever deny His Davidic origin. He only affirmed that His Davidic affiliation did not explain the relations which He possessed with the Father in His Divine Personality.

The opening words of the Gospel of Matthew suggest the Genesis of Our Lord. The Old Testament begins with the Genesis of heaven and earth through God making all things. The New Testament had another kind of Genesis, in the sense that it describes the making of all things new. The genealogy that is given implies that Christ was "a Second Man," and not merely one of the many that had sprung from Adam. Luke, who directed his Gospel to the Gentiles, traced Our Lord's descent back to the first man, but Matthew, who directed His Gospel to the Jews, set Him forth as "Son of David and the Son of Abraham." The difference in the genealogy between Luke and Matthew is due to the fact that Luke, writing for the Gentiles, was careful to give a natural descent; while Matthew, writing for the Jews, verged from the natural after the time of David, in order to make it clear to the Jews that Our Lord was the Heir to the Kingdom of David.

Luke is concerned about the Son of Man; Matthew about the King of Israel. Hence Matthew opens his Gospel:

> A table of the descent of Jesus Christ, son of David, son of Abraham.
> *Matthew 1:1*

Matthew pictures the generations from Abraham to Our Lord as having passed through three cycles of fourteen each. This does not, however, represent a complete genealogy. Fourteen are mentioned from Abraham to David, fourteen from David to the Babylonian captivity, and fourteen from the Babylonian captivity to Our Blessed Lord. The genealogy goes beyond the Hebrew background to include a few non-Jews. There may have been a very good reason for this, as well as for the inclusion of others who had not the best reputations in the world. One was Rahab, who was a foreigner and a sinner; another was Ruth, a foreigner though received into the nation; a third was the sinner Bethsabee whose sin with David cast shame upon the royal line. Why should there be blots on the royal escutcheon, such as Bethsabee, whose womanly purity was tainted; and Ruth who, though morally good, was an introducer of alien blood into the stream? Possibly it was in order to indicate Christ's relationship to the stained and to the sinful, to harlots and sinners, and even to the Gentiles who were included in His Message and Redemption.

In some translations of Scripture, the word that is used to describe the genealogy is the word "begot"; for example, "Abraham begot Isaac, Isaac begot Jacob"; in other translations there is the expression "was the father of"; for example, "Jechonias was the father of Salathiel." The translation is unimportant; what stands out is that this monotonous expression is used throughout forty-one generations. But it is omitted when the forty-second generation is reached. Why? Because of the Virgin Birth of Jesus.

> Jacob of Joseph, the husband of Mary, who gave birth to Jesus called Messiah. *Matthew* 1:16

Matthew, drawing up the genealogy, knew that Our Lord was not the Son of Joseph. Hence on the very first pages of the Gospel, Our Lord is presented as connected with the race which nevertheless did not wholly produce Him. That He came into it, was obvious; yet He was distinct from it.

If there was a suggestion of the Virgin Birth in the genealogy of Matthew, so there was a suggestion of it in the genealogy of Luke. In Matthew, Joseph is not described as having begotten Our Lord, and in Luke, Our Lord is called:

> The son, as people thought, of Joseph. *Luke* 2:34

He meant that Our Lord was popularly supposed to be the Son of Joseph. Combining the two genealogies; in Matthew, Our Lord is the Son of David and of Abraham; He is, in Luke, the Son of Adam and the seed of the woman God promised would crush the head of the serpent. Men who are not moral, by God's Providence, are made the instruments of His policy; David, who murdered Urias, nevertheless is the channel through which the blood of Abraham floods into the blood of Mary. There were sinners in the family tree, and He would *seem* to be the greatest sinner of all when He would hang upon the family tree of the Cross, making men adopted sons of the Heavenly Father.

CIRCUMCISION

> Eight days later the time came to circumcise him, and he was given the name of Jesus, the name given by the angel before he was conceived. *Luke 2:21*

Circumcision was the symbol of the covenant between God and Abraham and his seed, and took place on the eighth day. Circumcision presumed that the person circumcised was a sinner. The Babe was now taking the sinner's place—something He was to do all through His Life. Circumcision was a sign and token of membership in the body of Israel. Mere human birth did not bring a child into the body of God's chosen people. Another rite was required, as recorded in the Book of Genesis:

> God said to Abraham, For your part, you must keep my covenant, you and your descendants after you, generation by generation. This is how you shall keep my covenant between myself and you and your descendants after you: circumcise yourselves, every male among you.
> *Genesis 17:9-11*

Circumcision in the Old Testament was a prefiguring of Baptism in the New Testament. Both symbolize a renunciation of the flesh with its sins. The first was done by wounding of the body; the second, by cleansing the soul. The first incorporated the child into the body of Israel; the second incorporates the child into the body of the new Israel or the Church. The term "Circumcision" was later used in the Scriptures to reveal the spiritual significance of applying the Cross to the flesh through self-discipline. Moses, in the Book of Deuteronomy clearly spoke of circumcising the heart. Jeremiah also used the same expression. St. Stephen, in his last address before being killed, told his hearers that they were uncircumcised in heart and ears. By submitting to this rite, which He need not have done because He was sinless, the Son of God made man satisfied the demands of His nation, just as He was to keep all the other Hebrew regulations. He kept the Passover; He observed the Sabbath; He went up to the Feasts; He obeyed the Old Law until the time came for Him to fulfill it by realizing and spiritualizing its shadowy prefigurements of God's dispensation.

In the Circumcision of the Divine Child there was a dim suggestion and hint of Calvary, in the precocious surrendering of blood. The shadow of the Cross was already hanging over a Child eight days old. He would have seven bloodsheddings of which this was the first, the others being the Agony in the Garden, the Scourging, the Crowning with Thorns, the Way of the Cross, the Crucifixion, and the Piercing of His Heart. But whenever there was an indication of Calvary, there was also some sign of glory; and it was at this moment when He was anticipating Calvary by shedding His blood that the name of Jesus was bestowed on Him.

A Child only eight days old was already beginning the blood-shedding that would fulfill His perfect manhood. The cradle was tinged with crimson, a token of Calvary. The Precious Blood was beginning its long pilgrimage. Within an octave of His birth, Christ obeyed a law of which He Himself was the Author, a law which was to find its last application in Him. There had been sin in human blood, and now blood was already being poured out to do away with sin. As the East catches at sunset the colors of the West, so does the Circumcision reflect Calvary.

Must He begin redeeming all at once? Cannot the Cross wait? There will be plenty of time for it. Coming straight from the Father's arms to the arms of His earthly mother, He is carried in her arms to His first Calvary. Many years later He will be taken from her arms again, after the bruising of the flesh on the Cross, when the Father's work is done.

PRESENTATION IN THE TEMPLE

At Bethlehem He had been an exile; at the Circumcision, an anticipated Savior; now at the Presentation, He became a sign to be contradicted. As Jesus was circumcised, so Mary was purified, though He needed not the first because He was God, and she needed not the second because she was conceived without sin.

> Then, after their purification had been completed in accordance with the Law of Moses, they brought him up to Jerusalem to present him to the Lord (as prescribed in the law of the Lord). *Luke 2:22*

The fact of sin in human nature is underlined not only by the necessity of enduring pain to expiate for it in circumcision, but also by the need for purification. Ever since Israel had been delivered from the bondage of the Egyptians, after the firstborn of the Egyptians had been slain, the firstborn of the Jews had always been looked upon as one dedicated to God. Forty days after His birth, which was the appointed time for a male child according to the Law, Jesus was brought to the temple. Exodus decreed that the firstborn belonged to God. In the Book of Numbers, the tribe of Levi was set apart for the priestly function, and this priestly dedication was understood as a substitute for the sacrifice of the firstborn, a rite which was never practiced. But when the Divine Child was taken to the temple by Mary, the law of the consecration of the firstborn was observed in its fullness; for this Child's dedication to the Father was absolute, and would lead Him to the Cross.

We find here another instance of how God in the form of man shared the poverty of mankind. The traditional offerings for purification were a lamb and a turtledove if the parents were rich, and two doves or two pigeons if they were poor. Thus the mother who brought the Lamb of God into the world had no lamb to offer—except the Lamb of God. God was presented in the temple at the age of forty days. About thirty years later He would claim the temple and use it as the symbol of His Body in which dwelt the fulness of Divinity. Here it was not the Firstborn of Mary alone Who was presented, but the Firstborn of the Eternal Father. As the Only Begotten of the Father, He was now presented as the Firstborn of a restored humanity. A new race began in Him.

The character of the man in the temple whose name was Simeon and who received the Child, is described simply as:

> This man was upright and devout, one who watched and waited for the restoration of Israel, and the Holy Spirit was upon him.
>
> *Luke* 2:25

It was revealed to him by the Holy Spirit:

> It had been disclosed to him by the Holy Spirit that he would not see death until he had seen the Lord's Messiah. *Luke* 2:26

His words seem to imply that as soon as one sees Christ, the sting of death departs. The old man, taking the Child in his arms, exclaimed with joy:

> This day, Master, thou givest thy servant his discharge in peace;
>   now thy promise is fulfilled.
> For I have seen with my own eyes
> the deliverance which thou had made ready in full view of all the nations:
>   a light that will be a revelation to the heathen,
>   and glory to thy people Israel. *Luke* 2:29–33

Simeon was like a sentinel whom God had sent to watch for the Light. When the Light finally appeared, he was ready to sing his *Nunc Dimittis*. In a poor Child brought by poor people making a poor offering, Simeon discovered the riches of the world. As this old

man held the Child in his arms, he was not like the aged of whom
Horace speaks. He did not look back, but forward, and not only to the
future of his own people but to the future of all the Gentiles of all
the tribes and nations of the earth. An old man at the sunset of his
own life spoke of the sunrise of the world; in the evening of life he told
of the promise of a new day. He had seen the Messiah before by faith;
now his eyes could close, for there was nothing more beautiful to look
upon. Some flowers open only in the evening. What he had seen now
was "Salvation"—not salvation from poverty, but salvation from sin.

Simeon's hymn was an act of adoration. There are three acts of adoration described in the early life of the Divine Child. The shepherds
adored; Simeon, and Anna the prophetess, adored; and the heathen
Magi adored. The song of Simeon was like a sunset in which a shadow
heralds a substance. It was the first hymn by men in the life of Christ.
Simeon, though addressing Mary and Joseph, did not address the
Child. It would not have been fitting to give his blessing to the Son of
the Highest. He blessed them; but he did not bless the Child.

After his hymn of praise he addressed himself only to the mother;
Simeon knew that she, and not Joseph, was related to the Babe in his
arms. He saw furthermore that there were sorrows in store for her, not
for Joseph. Simeon said:

> This child is destined to be a sign which men reject; and you too shall
> be pierced to the heart. Many in Israel will stand or fall because of
> him. *Luke 2:34*

It was as if the whole history of the Divine Child were passing before the eyes of the old man. Every detail of that prophecy was to be
fulfilled within the lifetime of the Babe. Here was a hard fact of the
Cross, affirmed even before the tiny arms of the Babe could stretch
themselves out straight enough to make the form of a cross. The
Child would create terrible strife between good and evil, stripping the
masks from each, thus provoking a terrible hatred. He would be at
once a stumbling block, a sword that would divide evil from good, and
a touchstone that would reveal the motives and dispositions of human
hearts. Men would no longer be the same once they had heard His
name and learned of His life. They would be compelled either to accept Him, or reject Him. About Him there would be no such thing as
compromise: only acceptance or rejection, resurrection or death. He
would, by His very nature, make men reveal their secret attitudes toward God. His mission would be not to put souls on trial, but to
redeem them; and yet, because their souls were sinful, some men
would detest His coming.

It would henceforth be His fate to encounter fanatical opposition from mankind even unto death itself, and this would involve Mary in cruel distress. The angel had told her, "Blessed art thou among women," and Simeon was now telling her that in her blessedness she would be the *Mater Dolorosa*. One of the penalties of original sin was that a woman should bring forth her child in sorrow; Simeon was saying that she would continue to live in the sorrow of her Child. If He was to be the Man of Sorrows, she would be the Mother of Sorrows. An unsuffering Madonna to the suffering Christ would be a loveless Madonna. Since Christ loved mankind so much that He wanted to die to expiate its guilt, then He would also will that His mother should be wrapped in the swaddling bands of His own grief.

From the moment she heard Simeon's words, she would never again lift the Child's hands without seeing a shadow of nails on them; every sunset would be a blood-red image of His Passion. Simeon was throwing away the sheath that hid the future from human eyes, and letting the blade of the world's sorrow flash in front of her eyes. Every pulse that she would feel in the tiny wrist would be like an echo of an oncoming hammer. If He was dedicated to salvation through suffering, so was she. No sooner was this young life launched than Simeon, like an old mariner, talked of shipwreck. No cup of the Father's bitterness had yet come to the lips of the Babe, and yet a sword was shown to His mother.

The nearer Christ comes to a heart, the more it becomes conscious of its guilt; it will then either ask for His mercy and find peace, or else it will turn against Him because it is not yet ready to give up its sinfulness. Thus He will separate the good from the bad, the wheat from the chaff. Man's reaction to this Divine Presence will be the test: either it will call out all the opposition of egotistic natures, or else galvanize them into a regeneration and a resurrection.

Simeon was practically calling Him the "Divine Disturber," Who would provoke human hearts either to good or evil. Once confronted with Him, they must subscribe to light or darkness. Before everyone else they can be "broadminded"; but His Presence reveals their hearts to be either fertile ground or hard rock. He cannot come to hearts without clarifying them and dividing them; once in His Presence, a heart discovers both its own thoughts about goodness and its own thoughts about God.

This could never be so if He were just a humanitarian teacher. Simeon knew this well, and He told Our Lord's mother that her Son must suffer because His life would be so much opposed to the complacent maxims by which most men govern their lives. He would act on one soul in one way, and on another in another way, as the sun shines on wax and softens it, and shines on mud and hardens it. There is no difference in the sun, only in the objects on which it shines. As the Light of the World, He would be a joy to the good and the lovers of light; but He would be like a probing searchlight to those who were evil and preferred to live in darkness. The seed is the same, but the soil is different, and each soil will be judged by the way it reacts to the seed. The will of Christ to save is limited by the free reaction of each soul either to accept or reject. That was what Simeon meant by saying:

The secret thoughts of many will be laid bare. *Luke* 2:35

An Eastern fable tells of a magic mirror that remained clear when the good looked upon it, and became sullied when the impure gazed at it. Thus the owner could always tell the character of those who used it. Simeon was telling His mother that her Son would be like this mirror: men would either love or hate Him, according to their own reflections. A light falling on a sensitive photographic plate registers a chemical change that cannot be effaced. Simeon was saying that the Light of this Babe falling on Jew and Gentile would stamp on each the ineffaceable vestige of its presence.

Simeon also said that the Babe would disclose the true inner dispositions of men. He would test the thoughts of all who were to encounter Him. Pilate would temporize and then weaken; Herod would mock; Judas would lean to a kind of greedy social security; Nicodemus would sneak in darkness to find the Light; tax collectors would become honest; prostitutes, pure; rich young men would reject His poverty; prodigals would return home; Peter would repent; an Apostle would hang himself. From that day to this, He continues to be a sign to be contradicted. It was fitting, therefore, that He should die on a piece of wood in which one bar contradicted the other. The vertical bar of God's will is negated by the horizontal bar of the contradicting human will. As the Circumcision pointed to the shedding of blood, so the Purification foretold His Crucifixion.

After saying that He was a sign to be contradicted, Simeon turned to the Mother, adding:

And you too shall be pierced to the heart. *Luke* 2:35

She was told that He would be rejected by the world, and with His Crucifixion there would be her transfixion. As the Child willed the Cross for Himself, so He willed the Sword of Sorrow for her. If He chose to be a Man of Sorrows, He also chose her to be a Mother of Sorrows! God does not always spare the good from grief. The Father spared not the Son, and the Son spared not the mother. With His Passion there must be her compassion. An unsuffering Christ Who did not freely pay the debt of human guilt would be reduced to the level of an ethical guide; and a mother who did not share in His sufferings would be unworthy of her great role.

Simeon not only unsheathed a sword; he also told her where Providence had destined it to be driven. Later on, the Child would say, "I came to bring the sword." Simeon told her that she would feel it in her heart while her Son was hanging on the sign of contradiction and she was standing beneath it transfixed in grief. The spear that would physically pierce His heart would mystically be run into her own heart. The Babe came to die, not to live, for His name was "Savior."

MAGI AND THE SLAUGHTER OF THE INNOCENTS

Simeon had foretold that the Divine Babe would be a Light to the Gentiles. They were already on the march. At His birth there were the Magi, or the scientists of the East; at His death, there would be the Greeks, or the philosophers of the West. The Psalmist had foretold that the kings of the East would come to do homage to Emmanuel. Following a star, they came to Jerusalem to ask Herod where the King had been born.

> Jesus was born at Bethlehem in Judea during the reign of Herod. After his birth astrologers from the east arrived in Jerusalem, asking, Where is the child who is born to be king of the Jews? We observed the rising of his star, and we have come to pay him homage.
>
> *Matthew 2:1–2*

It was a star that led them. God spoke to the Gentiles through nature and philosophers; to the Jews, through prophecies. The time was ripe for the coming of the Messiah and the whole world knew it. Though they were astrologers, the slight vestige of truth in their knowledge of the stars led them to the Star out of Jacob, as the "Unknown God" of the Athenians later on would be the occasion for Paul preaching to them the God Whom they knew not, but dimly desired. Though coming from a land that worshiped stars, they surrendered that religion as they fell down and worshiped Him Who made the stars. The Gentiles in fulfillment of the prophecies of Isaiah and Jeremiah "came to Him from the ends of the earth." The Star, which disappeared during the interrogation of Herod, reappeared and finally stood over the place where the Child was born.

> At the sight of the star they were overjoyed. Entering the house, they saw the child with Mary his mother, and bowed to the ground in homage to him; then they opened their treasures and offered him gifts: gold, frankincense, and myrrh. *Matthew 2:10–11*

Isaiah had prophesied:

> Camels in droves shall cover the land,
>   dromedaries of Midian and Ephah,
> all coming from Sheba
> laden with golden spice and frankincense,
>   heralds of the Lord's praise. *Isaiah* 60:6

They brought three gifts: gold to honor His Kingship, frankincense to honor His Divinity, and myrrh to honor His Humanity which was destined for death. Myrrh was used at His burial. The crib and the Cross are related again, for there is myrrh at both.

When the Magi came from the East bringing gifts for the Babe, Herod the Great knew that the time had come for the birth of the King announced clearly to the Jews, and apprehended dimly in the aspirations of the Gentiles. But like all carnal-minded men, he lacked a spiritual sense, and therefore felt certain that the King would be a political one. He made inquiries as to where Christ was to be born. The chief priests and learned men told him, "At Bethlehem in Judea, for so it has been written by the prophet." Herod said that he wanted to worship the Babe. But his actions proved that he really meant, "If this is the Messiah, I must kill Him."

> When Herod saw how the astrologers had tricked him he fell into a passion, and gave orders for the massacre of all children in Bethlehem and its neighbourhood, of the age of two years or less, corresponding with the time he had ascertained from the astrologers.
>
> *Matthew* 2:16

Herod will forever be the model of those who make inquiries about religion, but who never act rightly on the knowledge they receive. Like train announcers, they know all the stations, but never travel. Head knowledge is worthless, unless accompanied by submission of the will and right action.

Totalitarians are fond of saying that Christianity is the enemy of the State—a euphemistic way of saying an enemy of themselves. Herod was the first totalitarian to sense this; he found Christ to be his enemy before He was two years old. Could a Babe born under the earth in a cave shake potentates and kings? Could He, Who as yet had no *demos* or people following Him, be a dangerous enemy of the *demos-cratos* or democracy, the rule of the people? No mere human baby could ever provoke such violence by a State. The Czar did not fear Stalin, the son of a cobbler, when he was two years old; he did not drive the cobbler's son and his mother into exile for fear that he would one day be a menace to the world. Similarly, no swords hung over the head of the infant Hitler, nor did the government move against Mao Tse-tung while he was still in swaddling clothes because it feared that he would some day deliver China to the murderous sickle. Why then were the soldiers summoned against this Infant? It must surely have been because those who possess the spirit of the world conceal an instinctive hatred and jealousy of God Who reigns over human hearts. The hatred the second Herod would show Christ at His death had its prologue in the hatred of his father, Herod the Great, for Christ as a Babe.

Herod was fearful that He Who came to bring a heavenly crown would steal away his own tinsel one. He pretended that he wanted to bring gifts, but the only gift he wanted to bring was death. Wicked men sometimes hide their evil designs under an appearance of religion: "I am a religious man, but. . . ." Men can make inquiries about Christ for two reasons, either to worship or to harm. Some would even make use of religion for their evil designs, as Herod made use of the Wise Men. Inquiries about religion do not produce the same results in all hearts. *What* men ask about Divinity is never as important as *why* they ask it.

Before Christ was two years of age, there was a shedding of blood for His sake. It was the first attempt on His life. A sword for the Babe; stones for the Man; the Cross at the end. That was how His own received Him. Bethlehem was the dawn of Calvary. The law of sacrifice that would wind itself around Him and His Apostles, and around so many of His followers for centuries to come, began its work by snatching these young lives which are so happily commemorated in the Feast of the Holy Innocents. An upended cross for Peter, a push from a steeple for James, a knife for Bartholomew, a cauldron of oil followed by long waiting for John, a sword for Paul, and many swords for the innocent babies of Bethlehem. "The world will hate you," Christ promised all those who were signed with His seal. These Innocents died for the King Whom they had never known. Like little lambs, they died for the sake of the Lamb, the prototypes of a long procession of martyrs—these children who never struggled, but were crowned. In the Circumcision He shed His own Blood; now His coming heralds the shedding of the blood of others for His sake. As circumcision was the mark of the Old Law, so persecution would be the mark of the New Law. "For My name's sake," He told His Apostles they would be hated. All things around Him speak of His death, for that was the purpose of His coming. The very entrance door over the stable where He was born was marked with blood, as was the threshold of the Jews in Egypt. Innocent lambs in the Passover bled for

Him in centuries past; now innocent children without spot, little
human lambs, bled for Him.

But God warned the Wise Men not to return to Herod,

> They returned home another way.   *Matthew 2:12*

No one who ever meets Christ with a good will returns the same way
as he came. Baffled in his design to kill the Divine, the enraged tyrant
ordered the indiscriminate slaughter of all male children under two
years of age. There are more ways than one of practicing birth control.

Mary was already prepared for a Cross in the life of her Babe, but
Joseph moving on a lower level of awareness needed the revelation of
an angel, telling him to take the Child and His mother into Egypt.

> Rise up, take the child and his mother and escape with them to
> Egypt, and stay there until I tell you; for Herod is going to search
> for the child to do away with him. So Joseph rose from sleep, and
> taking mother and child by night he went away with them to Egypt,
> and there he stayed till Herod's death.   *Matthew 2:13*

Exile was to be the lot of the Savior, otherwise the millions of exiles
from persecuted lands would be without a God Who understood the
agony of homelessness and frantic flight. By His Presence in Egypt,
the Infant Savior consecrated a land that had been the traditional
enemy of His own people, and thus gave hope to other lands which
would later reject Him. The Exodus was reversed, as the Divine Child
made Egypt His temporary home. Mary now sang as Miriam had
done, while a second Joseph guarded the Living Bread for which
human hearts were starving. The murder of the Innocents by Herod
recalls Pharaoh's slaughter of the Hebrew children; and what
happened when Herod died recalled the original Exodus. When Herod
the Great died, an angel charted the course of Joseph, bidding him to
return to Galilee. He came and settled there in fulfillment of what had
been said by the prophets, "He shall be a Nazarene."

> When they had done everything prescribed in the law of the Lord,
> they returned to Galilee to their own town of Nazareth.   *Luke 2:39*

The term "Nazarene" signified contempt. The little village was off
the main roads at the foot of the mountains; nestling in a cup of hills,
it was out of reach of the merchants of Greece, the legions of Rome,
and the journeys of the sophisticated. It is not mentioned in ancient
geographies. It deserved its name, for it was just a "netzer," a sprout
that grows on the stump of a tree. Centuries before, Isaiah had foretold that a "branch," or "sprout," or "netzer," would grow out of the
roots of the country; it would seem to be of little value and many

would despise it, but it would ultimately have dominion over the earth. The fact that Christ took up His residence in a despised village was a prefigurement of the obscurity and ignominy that would ever plague Himself and His followers. The name "Nazareth" would be nailed over His Head on the "sign of contradiction" as a scornful repudiation of His claims. Before that, when Philip told Nathanael:

> We have met the man spoken of by Moses in the Law, and by the prophets: it is Jesus son of Joseph, from Nazareth. *John* 1:45

Nathanael would retort:

> Nazareth! Can anything good come from Nazareth? *John* 1:46

The big cities are sometimes thought to contain all the wisdom, while the little towns are looked upon as backward and unprogressive. Christ chose the insignificant Bethlehem for the glory of His birth; the ridiculed Nazareth for His youth; but the glorious, cosmopolitan Jerusalem for the ignominy of His death. "Can anything good come out of Nazareth?" is but the prelude to "Can anything redemptive come from a man who dies on a cross?"

Nazareth would be a place of humiliation for Him, a training ground for Golgatha. Nazareth was in Galilee, and the whole of Galilee was a despised region in the eyes of the more cultured people of Judea. Galilean speech was supposed to be crude and rude, so much so that when Peter denied Our Lord, the maidservant reminded him that his speech betrayed him; he had been with the Galilean. No one would ever look to Galilee, therefore, for a teacher; and yet the Light of the World was the Galilean. God chooses the foolish things of the world to confound the selfwise and proud. Nathanael merely gave expression to an evil prejudice probably as old as humanity itself; people and their power to teach are judged by the places whence they come. Worldly wisdom comes from where we expect it, in the bestsellers, the "standard brands" and the universities. Divine Wisdom comes from the unsuspected quarters, which the world holds in derision. The ignominy of Nazareth would hang about Him later on. His hearers would taunt:

> How is it, they said, that this untrained man has such learning? *John* 7:15

While this was a reluctant tribute to His learning, it was also a sneer at His "backwoods" village. . . . How did He know? They did not suspect the true answer; namely, that in addition to the knowledge of His human intellect, He had a Wisdom that was not school-taught, nor self-taught, nor even God-taught, in the sense in which the prophets were God-taught. He learned from His mother and the village synagogue; but the secrets of His knowledge must be found in His oneness with the Heavenly Father.

OBEDIENCE AND THE CHILD AT THE TEMPLE

On the first Passover after Jesus had passed His twelfth year, His parents took Him to Jerusalem with the other men of Nazareth. The Law required the attendance of all Jewish men at the three great feasts: Passover, Pentecost, and the Tabernacles. When the Divine Child went up to the temple, He probably followed as usual all the injunctions of the Jewish Law. At three, He had been given a tasseled garment; at five, He learned under His mother's direction portions of the Law which were written out on scrolls; at twelve, He began to wear phylacteries, which the Jews always put on for the recital of daily prayer. It took several days to travel the narrow roads between Nazareth and the Holy City. Like all pilgrims, the Holy Family probably chanted the processional Psalms en route, Psalm 121 being sung when the walls of the temple first came in sight.

Joseph must have gone to the temple to kill the Paschal lamb. Since the Child was of legal age for the temple ceremonies, He must have watched the lamb's blood pour forth from the wound, to be scattered at the foot of the altar in the four directions of the earth. The Cross was once more before His eyes. The Child would also have seen the carcass of the lamb being prepared for supper. This was done, according to the Law, by running two skewers of wood through the body, one through the breast, and the other through the forelegs, so that the lamb had the appearance of being on a cross.

After fulfilling the rites, the men and women left in separate caravans, to meet again at night. But the Boy Jesus, unknown to His parents, stayed behind in Jerusalem. They, thinking that He was among their traveling companions, had gone a day's journey before they missed Him. It was thus that Jesus was "lost" for three days. All through His infancy there was talk of "contradiction," "swords," "no room," "exile," "slaughter," and now there was "loss." In those three days, Mary came to know one of the effects of sin, namely, the loss of God. Though she was without sin, nevertheless she knew the fears and the loneliness, the darkness and the isolation which every sinner experiences when he loses God. It was a kind of glorified hide-and-seek. He was hers; that was why she sought Him. He was on the business of redemption; that was why He left her and went to the temple. She had her *dark night* of the body in Egypt; she would now have her *dark night* of the soul in Jerusalem. Mothers must be trained to bear crosses. Not only her body, but also her soul would have to pay dearly for the privilege of being His mother. She would later suffer another three-day loss from Good Friday to Easter Sunday. This first loss was part of her preparation.

Christ is always found in unexpected places; in a manger by the Wise Men; in a small town, despised even by the Apostles. His parents now found Him unexpectedly in the temple. It was three days before they found Him, just as it would be the third day before Mary would find Him again after Calvary. The temple had great fascination for Him, since it was the little figure or model of heaven; the Father's house was His home and in it He felt at home.

There was a school in the temple, in which a number of Rabbis taught; the gentle Hillel was perhaps still alive and may have been present in the temple to join in the discussion of the Divine Child. Hillel's son, Rabbi Simeon and his even greater grandson, Gamaliel, the future teacher of St. Paul, may have been of the number— although Gamaliel at that time would have been only about the same age as the Divine Child. Annas had just been appointed high priest, and certainly he must have heard about the Divine Child, if he were not actually present.

It was in this school of Rabbis that Mary and Joseph found Him.

> After three days they found him sitting in the temple surrounded by the teachers, listening to them and putting questions; and all who heard him were amazed at his intelligence and the answers he gave.
>
> *Luke 2:47–48*

The fact that He was sitting in the midst of the doctors would indicate that they received Him not just as a learner, but as a professor. There is a restraint manifested in the Gospel concerning this scene which contrasts strongly with certain apocryphal writings. The Gospel of Thomas, which belongs to the second century and which is not an accredited gospel, describes Our Lord on this occasion as a professor. An Arabic gospel of a later period actually makes the instructions touch on metaphysics and astronomy. The revealed Gospels, however, always show powerful restraint to the point of understatement in describing the life of Our Lord.

> His parents were astonished to see him there. *Luke 2:48*

They were probably astonished because of the learning which He displayed. The Psalmist had suggested that He had more understanding than His teachers because the testimonies of God were His study. The astonishment may also have derived from the fact that it is sometimes difficult for a mother to realize that a son grows quickly into man's estate and asserts his own individual purpose in life.

In a land where the authority of the father was supreme, it was not Joseph the foster father, but Mary, who spoke:

> My son, why have you treated us like this? Your father and I have been searching for you in great anxiety. *Luke 2:48*

The virgin Birth was implied in her questioning. Her question implied that the emphasis was more on the fact that He was *her* Son than upon the fact that He was also the Son of God. This distinction is further underlined by the fact that she added a note about fatherhood, saying, "Thy father and I."

The Divine Child answered by making a distinction between the one whom He honored as a father on earth and the Eternal Father. This answer affirmed a parting of the ways; it did not diminish the filial duty that He owed to Mary and Joseph, for He became immediately subject to them again, but it decisively put them in a second place.

These are the first recorded words of Jesus in the Gospels, and they are in the form of a question:

> What made you search? he said. Did you not know that I was bound to be in my Father's house? *Luke 2:49*

This is an evident reference to Mary's words "Thy father and I." When He said that His mother should have known He was about His Father's business, He was evidently referring to what she had learned at the Annunciation when the Angel said to her:

> The Holy Spirit will come upon you, and the power of the Most High will overshadow you; and for that reason the holy child to be born will be called Son of God. *Luke 1:35*

His relationship with His own mother He would take up again at the Marriage Feast of Cana; here He established the nature of His relationship to His foster father. He disowned physical paternity, by claiming His Divine paternity, that of His Heavenly Father. At Cana He would say to His Mother:

> Your concern, mother, is not mine. *John 2:4*

Then he was implying a motherhood other than that of the flesh, as now He implied a fatherhood other than that which was exercised by Joseph. Never again does Joseph appear in the Gospels.

In the temple, Our Lord alienated Himself from the claim of His foster father, just as later at Cana He would alienate Himself from the claims of His mother. His supreme business was to be a Savior; but for the moment that included obedience to His earthly guardians.

The Child was implying that there was something in history which ought to be known to His mother and His foster father, something that justified His being where He was, and forbade their anxiety about Him. It was because of that that He asked, "What reason had you to search for Me?" And added, "Could you not tell that I must needs be in the place which belongs to My Father?" He was saying that He must be in the temple of His own Father. This was the first of many "musts" that Our Blessed Lord uttered during His life to indicate that He was under a mandate, under obedience to be a ransom. The very fact that He associated the word "must" with His Heavenly Father meant that Sonship implied obedience. At the age of twelve, He was girding Himself for something that would be irksome to His human nature, but His whole nature was bent on the accomplishment of a Divine "must."

If there is anything that dispels the false assumption that His consciousness of a union with the Father developed gradually, it is this text in which He, as a Boy of twelve, hinted at His mysterious origin and at the peculiar foster character of His father, as well as at His perfectly conscious unity with the Godhead; the Divine constraints which swayed His life were already profoundly realized by Him. He often used the word "must."

I *must* preach the Kingdom of God.
I *must* abide in thy house.
I *must* do the works of Him Who sent Me.
The Son of Man *must* suffer many things.
The Son of Man *must* be lifted up.
The Son of Man *must* suffer to enter into His glory.
The Son of Man *must* rise again.

He always talked as one under orders. Free from the compulsions of heredity, circumstances or family, this Boy of twelve said that He was bound by heaven's commission. Therefore, He asked why they had searched for Him. He was surprised that any explanation other than that He was obeying His Father's will should even have occurred to them. The imperative of Divine Love was manifested in His "I must." There was no fundamental difference between the Boy in the temple and the Man Who was to say that He "must be lifted up" on the Cross. He would have to die because He wanted to save. His filial obedience to His Father coincided with His pity for men. It would not be a tragedy, for the "Son of Man must rise again after three days." His plan was gradually revealed to the minds of men; but there was no gradual revelation in His mind, no new understanding, of why He had come.

His Father's business at the end of the three days in the temple was no different from His Father's business at the end of three days in the grave. Like all other incidents in His infancy, this one bore witness to the Mission of the Cross. All men are born to live; He was born to do the Father's business, which was to die, and thereby to save. These first recorded words seem like the buds of a passion flower. On Easter Sunday Mary would find Him again in the temple—the temple of His glorified Body.

The sword was already coming to Mary before the Cross had come to her Son, for she was already feeling the cutting separation. On the Cross, He would, in His human nature, utter the cry of His greatest agony, "My God! My God! Why hast Thou forsaken Me?" But Mary uttered it while He was still a Boy, lost in the temple. The most penetrating sorrows of the soul are those which God imposes, as Jesus imposed this one on His mother. Creatures can hurt one another only on the outside, but God's purifying flame can enter their souls like a two-edged sword. Both His natures were teaching her to prepare her for His sorrowful life: His human nature by hiding the loveliness of His Face from her during those three days, better called three nights; His Divine nature by proclaiming that the Father had sent Him to earth to do heaven's business, which was to open it to mankind by paying the debt of mankind's sins.

NAZARETH

This is the only incident of His boyhood told in the Scriptures. For the next eighteen years, He stayed in Nazareth.

> Then he went back with them to Nazareth, and continued to be under their authority; his mother treasured up all these things in her heart. As Jesus grew up he advanced in wisdom and in favour with God and men. *Luke 2:51*

If there ever was a Son Who might have been expected to claim personal independence (especially after His powerful affirmation in the temple), it was He. And yet to sanctify and exemplify human obedience, and to make up for the disobedience of men, He lived under a humble roof, obedient to His parents. For eighteen uneventful years He fixed the flat roofs of Nazarene homes and mended the wagons of the farmers. Every mean and lowly task was part of the Father's business. Human development of the God-man unfolded in the village so naturally that not even the townspeople were conscious of the greatness of Him Who dwelled in their midst. It was indeed a going "down" in the sense that it was a self-denial and a self-abnegation for Him to submit Himself to His own creatures. He evidently followed the trade of a carpenter, for eighteen years later, the townspeople were to ask:

Is not this the carpenter, the son of Mary? *Mark 6:3*

Justin Martyr, basing himself on tradition, says that during this time Our Lord made plows and yokes, and taught men righteousness through the products of His peaceful toil.

The growth in wisdom that is spoken of in the Divine Child was not, as we have seen, a growth in His consciousness of Divinity. Inasmuch as He was a man, He was subject to all the laws which regulate human growth; having a human intellect and a human will, it was natural for these faculties to unfold in a human way. In the development of His experimental knowledge, the influence of His environment is to be particularly noted. Many of the comparisons which He used in parables were borrowed from the world in which He had lived. It was through the influence of His parents that He learned the common language of Aramaic, and, without doubt, also the liturgical language of Hebrew. Very likely, He learned Greek since it was spoken to some extent in Galilee and was also apparently the language of at least two of His relatives, James the Minor and Jude, who later wrote their Epistles in Greek.

He also learned the trade of carpentry which involved a further development of the human intellect. Later on, He was accorded the title of Rabbi because of His profound knowledge of the Scriptures and the Law. He often introduced discussions with the words, "Have you not read," thus demonstrating His knowledge of the Scriptures. His family, the synagogue, His surroundings, nature itself—all contributed a little to His human intellect and will. He had both a human intellect and a human will. Without the first, He could not have grown in human experimental knowledge; without the second, He could not have been obedient to a higher will. Furthermore, both were essential to Him as man. He had created knowledge as man; as God, He went beyond human knowledge. This is what John describes as the "Word," which signifies the Wisdom or the Thought or the Intelligence of God.

When all things began, the Word already was. The Word dwelt with God, and what God was, the Word was . . . through him all things came to be; no single thing was created without him . . . So the Word became flesh; he came to dwell among us. *John 1:1,3,14*

The intimate relations which He had with His Father in heaven were not just those that came from prayer and meditation; these any human being may establish. They came rather from the identity of nature with the Godhead.

Inasmuch as the most general sin of mankind is pride or the exaltation of the ego, it was fitting that in atoning for that pride, Christ should practice obedience. He was not like one who is obedient for the sake of a reward, or in order to build up his character for the future; rather, being the Son, He already enjoyed the love of the Father to the full. It was out of this very fullness that there flowed a childlike surrender to His Father's will. He gave this as the reason for His surrender to the Cross. Within an hour or so before going into His Agony in the Garden, He would say:

> The world must be shown that I love the Father, and do exactly as he commands. *John 14:30–31*

The only acts of Christ's childhood which are recorded are acts of obedience—obedience to His Heavenly Father and to His earthly parents. The foundation of obedience to man, He taught, is obedience to God. The elders who serve not God find that the young serve them not. His whole life was submission. He submitted to John's baptism, though He did not need it; He submitted to the temple tax, though as the Son of the Father, He was exempt from it; and He bade His own followers to submit to Caesar. Calvary cast its shadow over Bethlehem; so now it darkened the obedient years at Nazareth. In being subject to creatures, though He was God, He prepared Himself for that final obedience—obedience to the humiliation of the Cross.

For the next eighteen years, after the three-day loss, He Who had made the universe played the role of a village carpenter, a maker in wood. The familiar nails and crossbeams in the shop would later on become the instruments of His own torture; and He would Himself be hammered to a tree. One wonders why this long preparation for such a brief ministry of three years. The reason might very well be that He waited until the human nature which He had assumed had grown in age to full perfection, that He might then offer the perfect sacrifice to His Heavenly Father. The farmer waits until the wheat is ripe before cutting it and subjecting it to the mill. So He would wait until His human nature had reached its most perfect proportions and its peak of loveliness, before surrendering it to the hammer of the crucifiers and the sickle of those who would cut down the Living Bread of Heaven. The newborn lamb was never offered in sacrifice, nor is the first blush of the rose cut to pay tribute to a friend. Each thing has its hour of perfection. Since He was the Lamb that could set the hour for His own sacrifice, since He was the Rose that could choose the moment of its cutting, He waited patiently, humbly and obediently, while He grew in age and grace and wisdom before God and man. Then He would say: "This is your Hour." Thus the choicest wheat and the reddest wine would become the worthiest elements of sacrifice.

JOHN THE BAPTIST

The awful silence of thirty years was interrupted only by the brief scene in the temple. The time was now coming to move from privacy to publicity. Because the event was to be world-shaking, Luke connects the appearance of the herald of Our Lord, John the Baptist, with the reign of the tyrant Tiberius, the ruler of Rome. Pliny, who was later on to write as a Roman historian about Christ, was now a child of four; Vespasian, who later on would conquer Jerusalem with his son Titus, was nineteen. One of the very important marriages in Rome at that time was that of the daughter of Germanicus, who nine years later was to give birth to the great persecutor of Christ's followers, Nero. In the midst of this relative Roman peace:

> The word of God came to John son of Zechariah in the wilderness.
>
> *Luke* 3:2

John was living in solitude in the desert, clothed in camel's hair with a leather girdle about his loins. His food consisted of locusts and wild honey. His costume was probably meant to resemble that of Elijah, in whose spirit John was to go before Christ. Since he preached mortification, he practiced it also. If he was to prepare for Christ, he must also evoke a penitent consciousness of sin. John was a severe ascetic, moved by a deep conviction of sin in the world. The heart of his message to soldiers, public officials, farmers, and anyone else who would listen was "Repent." The first note of warning in the New Testament tells all men to change. The Sadducees must lay aside their worldliness, the Pharisees their hypocrisy and self-righteousness; all who come to Christ must repent.

With the country under a Roman yoke, it would have been a more certain route to popularity for John to promise that the One Who was to come, the One Whom he announced, would be a political liberator. That would have been the way of men; but instead of a call to arms, John gave a call to reparation for sin. And those who claim descent from Abraham must not glory in it, because if God willed, He could raise up children of Abraham from the very stones.

> Who warned you to escape from the coming retribution? Then prove your repentance by the fruit it bears; and do not begin saying to yourselves, We have Abraham for our father. I tell you that God can make children for Abraham out of these stones here. *Luke* 3:7–9

Many centuries before, Isaiah had foretold that the Messiah would be preceded by a messenger.

> Here is my herald whom I send on ahead of you, and he will prepare your way. A voice crying aloud in the wilderness, Prepare a way for the Lord; clear a straight path for him. *Mark* 1:2–4

About three hundred years after Isaiah, the prophet Malachi prophesied that the herald Isaiah had promised he would come in the spirit of Elijah.

> Look, I will send you the prophet Elijah. *Malachi* 4:5–6

Now, after centuries had whirled away into space, there appeared in the wilderness this great man leading the same kind of life as Elijah.

In all countries, when the head of a government wishes to visit another government, he sends messengers "before his face." So, John the Baptist was sent to prepare the way of Christ, to announce the conditions of His reign and government. John, despite the prophecies that were made about him, disclaimed that he was the Messiah, and said that he was only:

> I am a voice crying aloud in the wilderness. *John* 1:23

Even before he met the Messiah, Who was his own cousin, he announced the superiority of Christ:

> After me comes one who is mightier than I. I am not fit to unfasten his shoes. *Mark* 1:7–8

John considered himself unworthy to untie the shoes of Our Lord, but Our Lord would surpass him in humility as He would wash the feet of the Apostles. The greatness of John consisted in the fact that to him was given the privilege of running before the chariot of the King and saying, "Christ has come."

John used symbols as well as words. The chief symbol of the washing away of sin was a cleansing by water. John had been baptizing in the Jordan, as a token of repentance, but he knew that his baptism did not regenerate or quicken the dead soul. That is why he made a contrast between his baptism and the baptism that later on Christ Himself would confer; speaking of the latter, he said:

> He will baptize you with the Holy Spirit and with fire. *Matthew* 3:12

The day on which John and Jesus met in the Jordan, there awakened in John the deepest and most reverent humility. John felt the need of a Redeemer, but when Our Lord asked him to baptize

Him, John was reluctant to do so. John immediately recognized the incongruity of submitting Our Lord to a rite which professed repentance and promised cleansing:

> Do you come to me? he said; I need rather to be baptized by you.
> *Matthew 3:14*

How could he baptize One Who had no sin? His refusal to baptize Jesus was recognition of His sinlessness.

> Jesus replied, Let it be so for the present; we do well to conform in this way with all that God requires. *Matthew 3:15*

The object of His baptism was the same as the object of His birth, namely, to identify Himself with sinful humanity. Had not Isaiah foretold that He would be "numbered with the transgressors?" In effect, Our Lord was saying, "Suffer this to be done; it does not seem fitting to you, but in reality, it is in complete harmony with the purpose of My coming." Christ was not being this as a private Person but as a representative of sinful humanity, though Himself without sin.

Every Israelite who came to John made a confession of his sins. It is evident that Our Blessed Lord did not make any such confession, and John himself admitted that He had no need of it. He had no sin to repent of and no sin to be washed away. But He was identifying Himself with sinners all the same. When He went down into the river Jordan to be baptized, He made Himself one with sinners. The innocent can share the burdens of the guilty. If a husband is guilty of a crime, it is pointless to tell his wife not to worry about it, or that it is no concern of hers. It is equally absurd to say that Our Lord should not have been baptized because He had no personal guilt. If He was to be identified with humanity, so much so as to call Himself the "Son of Man," then He had to share the guilt of humanity. And this was the meaning of the baptism by John.

Many years before, He had said that He must be about His Father's business; now He was revealing what His Father's business was: the salvation of mankind. He was expressing His relationship to His people, on whose behalf He had been sent. In the temple at the age of twelve, it had been His origin that He emphasized; now in the Jordan, it was the nature of His mission. In the temple He had spoken of His Divine mandate. Under the cleansing hands of John, He made clear His oneness with humanity.

Later on, Our Blessed Lord would say:

> Until John, it was the Law and the Prophets. *Luke 16:16*

He meant that long centuries had borne faithful witness to the coming of the Messiah, but now a new page was turned, a new chapter written. From now on, He was to be merged with the sinful population. He was committed henceforth to live among, and minister unto, the victims of sin; to be betrayed into the hands of sinners and to be accused of sin though He knew no sin. As in His infancy He was circumcised, as if His nature were sinful, so now He was baptized, although He had no need of purification.

There were three rites in the Old Testament which were "baptisms" of sorts. First was a "baptism" of water. Moses brought Aaron and his son to the doors of the tabernacle and washed them with water. This was followed by a "baptism" of oil, when Moses poured oil upon Aaron's head in order to sanctify him. The final "baptism" was one of blood. Moses took the blood of the ram of consecration and put it upon Aaron's right ear and upon the thumb of his right hand and upon the great toe of his right foot. This ritual implied a gradual consecration. These baptisms would have their counterpart in the Jordan, the Transfiguration, and Calvary.

The baptism of Jordan was a prelude to the baptism of which He would later speak, the baptism of His passion. Twice afterward did He refer to His baptism. The first time was when James and John asked Him if they could sit on either side of Him in His Kingdom. In answer, He asked them if they were ready to be baptized with the baptism which He was going to receive. Thus His baptism of water looked forward to His baptism of blood. The Jordan flowed into the red rivers of Calvary. The second time He referred to His baptism was when He said to His Apostles:

> I have a baptism to undergo, and what constraint I am under until the ordeal is over! *Luke 12:50*

In the waters of the Jordan He was identified with sinners; in the baptism of His Death, He would bear the full burden of their guilt. In the Old Testament, the Psalmist speaks of "entering into deep water" as a symbol of suffering which is manifestly the same imagery. There was a fitness in describing agony and death as a kind of baptism.

The Cross must have been looming up in His thoughts now with increasing vividness. It was no afterthought in His mind. He was temporarily immersed in the waters of the Jordan only to emerge again. So would He be immersed by the death on the Cross and the burial in the tomb, only to emerge triumphantly in the Resurrection. He had proclaimed His mission from the Father at the age of twelve; now He was preparing Himself for oblation.

> After baptism Jesus came up out of the water at once, and at that moment heaven opened; he saw the Spirit of God descending like a dove to alight upon him; and a voice from heaven was heard saying, This is my Son, my Beloved, on whom my favour rests. *Matthew 3:16*

The sacred humanity of Christ was the connecting link between heaven and earth. The voice from heaven which declared Him to be the Beloved Son of the Eternal Father was not announcing a new fact or a new Sonship of Our Blessed Lord. It was merely making a solemn declaration of that Sonship, which had existed from all eternity, but which was now beginning to manifest itself publicly as Mediator between God and man. The Father's good pleasure, in the original Greek, is recorded in the aorist tense, to denote the eternal act of loving contemplation with which the Father regards the Son.

The Christ Who came out of the water, as the earth had come out of the water at creation and after the Flood, as Moses and his people had come out of the waters of the Red Sea, was now glorified by the Holy Spirit appearing in the form of a Dove. The Spirit of God never appears in the figure of a Dove anywhere save here. The Book of Leviticus mentions offerings which were made according to the economic and social position of the giver. A man who could afford it would bring a bullock, and a poorer man would offer a lamb; but the poorest of all had the privilege of bringing doves. When the mother of Our Lord brought Him to the temple, her offering was a dove. The dove was the symbol of gentleness and peacefulness, but above all it was the type of sacrifice possible to the lowliest people. Whenever a Hebrew thought of a lamb or a dove, he immediately thought of a sacrifice for sin. Therefore, the Spirit descending upon Our Lord was for them a symbol of submission to sacrifice. Christ had already united Himself symbolically with man in baptism, in anticipation of His submergence into the waters of suffering; but now He was also crowned, dedicated, and consecrated to that sacrifice through the coming of the Spirit. The waters of the Jordan united Him with men, the Spirit crowned Him and dedicated Him to sacrifice, and the Voice attested that His sacrifice would be pleasing to the Eternal Father.

The seeds of the doctrine of the Trinity which were planted in the Old Testament began here to unfold. They would become clearer as time went on: the Father; the Creator, the Son, the Redeemer; and the Holy Spirit, the Sanctifier. The very words the Father spoke here,

"Thou art My Son," had been prophetically addressed to the Messiah a thousand years before, in the second psalm.

> You are my son, he said; this day I become your father. *Psalm* 2:7

Our Blessed Lord would tell Nicodemus later on:

> In truth I tell you, no one can enter the kingdom of God without being born from water and spirit. *John* 3:5,6

The baptism in the Jordan closed Our Lord's private life and began His public ministry. He had gone down into the water known to most men only as the son of Mary; He came out ready to reveal Himself as what He had been from all eternity, the Son of God. He was the Son of God in the likeness of man in all things, save sin. The Spirit was anointing Him not just for teaching, but for redeeming.

3. The Three Short Cuts from the Cross

Immediately after the baptism, Our Blessed Lord withdrew into seclusion. The wilderness would be His school, just as it had been the school of Moses and Elijah. Retirement is a preparation for action. It would later serve the same purpose for Paul. All human consolation was left behind as "He lodged with the beasts." And for forty days, He ate nothing.

Since the purpose of His coming was to do battle with the forces of evil, His first encounter was not a debate with a human teacher, but a contest with the prince of evil himself.

> Jesus was then led away by the Spirit into the wilderness, to be tempted by the devil. *Matthew 4:1*

Temptation was a negative preparation for His ministry, as baptism had been a positive preparation. In His baptism, He had received the Spirit and a confirmation of His mission; in His temptations, He received the strengthening which comes directly from trial and testing. There is a law written across the universe, that no one shall be crowned unless he has first struggled. No halo of merit rests suspended over those who do not fight. Icebergs that float in the cold streams of the north do not command our respectful attention, just for being icebergs; but if they were to float in the warm waters of the Gulf Stream without dissolving, they would command awe and wonderment. They might, if they did it on purpose, be said to have character.

The only way one can ever prove love is by making an act of choice; mere words are not enough. Hence, the original trial given to man has been given again to all men; even the angels have passed through a trial. Ice deserves no credit for being cold, nor fire for being hot; it is only those who have the possibility of choice that can be praised for their acts. It is through temptation and its strain that the depths of character are revealed. Scripture says:

> Happy the man who remains steadfast under trial, for having passed that test he will receive for his prize the gift of life promised to those who love God. *James 1:12*

The defenses of the soul are seen at their strongest when the evil which has been resisted is also strong. The presence of temptation does not necessarily imply moral imperfection on the part of the one who is tempted. In that case, Our Divine Lord could not have been tempted at all. An inward tendency toward evil, such as man has, is not a necessary condition for an onslaught of temptation. The temptation of Our Blessed Lord came only from without, and not from within as ours so often do. What was at stake in the trial of Our Lord was not the perversion of natural appetites to which the rest of men are tempted; rather, it was an appeal to Our Lord to disregard His Divine Mission and His Messianic work. The temptation that comes from without does not necessarily weaken character; indeed, when conquered, it affords an opportunity for holiness to increase. If He was to be the Pattern Man, He would have to teach us how to gain holiness by overcoming temptation.

> For since he himself has passed through the test of suffering, he is able to help those who are meeting their test now. *Hebrews 2:18*

This is illustrated in the character of Angelo in *Measure for Measure:*

> 'Tis one thing to be tempted,
> Another thing to fall.

The tempter was sinful, but the One tempted was innocent. The entire history of the world revolves around two persons, Adam and Christ. Adam was given a position to maintain, and he failed. Therefore his loss was humanity's loss; for he was its head. When a ruler declares war, the citizens declare war also, although they do not make an explicit declaration themselves. When Adam declared war against God, man declared war too.

Now, with Christ, everything was at stake again. There was a repetition of the temptation of Adam. If God had not taken upon Himself a human nature, He could not have been tempted. Though His Divine and human natures were united in one Person, the Divine nature was not diminished by His humanity, nor was the humanity swollen out of proportion through union with His Divinity. Because He had a human nature He could be tempted. If He were to become like us in all things, He would have to undergo the human experience of withstanding temptation. That is why, in the Epistle to the Hebrews, we are reminded of how closely bound He was to humanity by His trials:

> For ours is not a high priest unable to sympathize with our weaknesses, but one who, because of his likeness to us, has been tested every way, only without sin. *Hebrews 4:15*

It is part of the discipline of God to make His loved ones perfect through trial and suffering. Only by carrying the Cross can one reach the Resurrection. It was precisely this part of Our Lord's Mission that the devil attacked. The temptations were meant to divert Our Lord from His task of salvation through sacrifice. Instead of the Cross as a means of winning the souls of men, Satan suggested three short cuts to popularity: an economic one, another based on marvels, and a third, which was political. Very few people believe in the devil these days, which suits the devil very well. He is always helping to circulate the news of his own death. The essence of God is existence, and He defines Himself as: "I am Who am." The essence of the devil is the lie, and he defines himself as: "I am who am not." Satan has very little trouble with those who do not believe in him; they are already on his side.

The temptations of man are easy enough to analyze, because they always fall into one of three categories: they either pertain to the flesh (lust and gluttony), or to the mind (pride and envy), or to the idolatrous love of things (greed). Though man is buffeted all through life by these three kinds of temptation, they vary in intensity from age to age. It is during youth that man is most often tempted against purity and inclined to the sins of the flesh; in middle age, the flesh is less urgent and temptations of the mind begin to predominate, e.g. pride and the lust for power; in the autumn of life, temptations to avarice are likely to assert themselves. Seeing that the end of life is near, man strives to banish doubts about eternal security or salvation, by piling up the goods of earth and redoubling his economic security. It is a common psychological experience that those who have given way to lust in youth are often those who sin by avarice in their old age.

Good men are not tempted in the same way as evil men, and the Son of God, Who became man, was not tempted in the same way as even a good man. The temptations of an alcoholic to "return to his vomit," as Scripture puts it, are not the same as the temptations of a saint to pride, though they are, of course, no less real.

In order to understand the temptations of Christ, it must be recalled that at the baptism of John, when He Who had no sins identified Himself with sinners, the heavens opened, and the Heavenly Father declared Christ to be His Beloved Son. Then Our Lord went up into the mountain and fasted for forty days, after which, the Gospel says, "He was hungry"—a typical understatement. Satan tempted Him by pretending to help Him find an answer to the question: How could He best fulfill His high destiny among men? The problem was to win men. But how? Satan had a satanic suggestion, namely, to bypass the moral problem of guilt and its need of expiation, and to concentrate purely on worldly factors. All three temptations sought to woo Our Lord from His Cross and, therefore, from

Redemption. Peter would tempt Our Lord later on, in the same way, and for that reason would be called "Satan."

The human flesh, which He had taken upon Himself, was not for leisure, but for battle. Satan saw in Jesus an extraordinary human being Whom he suspected of being the Messiah and the Son of God. Hence he prefaced each of the temptations with the conditional "if." If he had been sure that he was speaking to God, he would not indeed have tried to tempt Him. But if Our Lord was merely a man whom God had chosen for the work of salvation, then he would do everything in his power to lead Him into ways of dealing with the sins of mankind other than the ways that God Himself would choose.

THE FIRST TEMPTATION

Knowing that Our Lord was hungry, Satan pointed down to some little black stones that resembled round loaves of bread, and said:

> If you are the Son of God, tell these stones to become bread.
>
> *Matthew 4:3*

The first temptation of Our Blessed Lord was to become a kind of social reformer, and to give bread to the multitudes in the wilderness who could find nothing there but stones. The vision of social amelioration without spiritual regeneration has constituted a temptation to which many important men in history have succumbed completely. But to Him, this would not be adequate service of the Father; there are deeper needs in man than crushed wheat; and there are greater joys than the full stomach.

The evil spirit was saying, "Start with the primacy of the economic! Forget about sin!" He still says this today in different words, "My Commissar goes into classrooms and asks children to pray to God for bread. And when their prayers are not answered, my Commissar feeds them. The Dictator gives bread; God does not, because there is no God, there is no soul; there is only the body, pleasure, sex, the animal, and when we die, that is the end." Satan was here trying to make Our Lord feel the terrific contrast between the Divine greatness He claimed and His actual destitution. He was tempting Him to reject the ignominies of human nature, the trials and the hunger, and to use the Divine power, if He really possessed it, to save His human nature and also to win the mob. Thus, he was appealing to Our Lord to stop acting as a man, and in the name of man, and to use His supernatural powers to give His human nature ease, comfort, and immunity from trial. What could be more foolish than for God to be hungry, when He had once spread a miraculous table in the desert for Moses and his people? John had said that He could raise up children of Abraham

from the very stones; why, then, could He not make bread of them
for Himself? The need was real; the power, if He was God, was also
real; why then was He submitting His human nature to all the ills and
sufferings to which mankind is heir? Why was God accepting such
humiliation just to redeem His own creatures? "If You are the Son of
God, as you claim to be, and You are here to undo the destruction
wrought by sin, then save Yourself." It was exactly the same kind of
temptation men would hurl at Him in the hour of His Crucifixion.

> Come down from the cross and save yourself, if you are indeed the
> Son of God. *Matthew* 27:40

The answer of Our Blessed Lord was that even while accepting
human nature with all its failings and trials and self-denials, He nevertheless was not without Divine help.

> Scripture says, Man cannot live on bread alone; he lives on every
> word that God utters. *Matthew* 4:4

The words quoted were taken from the Old Testament account of
the miraculous feeding of the Jews in the desert when manna fell to
them from heaven. He refused to satisfy Satan's burning curiosity as
to whether He was, or was not, the Son of God; but He affirmed that
God can feed men by something greater than bread. Our Lord would
not use miraculous powers to provide food for Himself, as He would
not use miraculous powers, later on, to come down from the Cross.
Men in all ages would be hungry, and He was not going to dissociate
Himself from His starving brethren. He had become man and He was
willing to submit Himself to all of the ills of man until the moment
of His glory would at last arrive.

Our Lord was not denying that men must be fed, or that social justice much be preached; but He was asserting that these things are not
first. He was, in effect, saying to Satan, "You tempt Me to a religion
which would relieve want; you want Me to be a baker, instead of a
Savior; to be a social reformer, instead of a Redeemer. You are tempting Me away from My Cross, suggesting that I be a cheap leader of
people, filling their bellies instead of their souls. You would have Me
begin with security instead of ending with it; you would have Me
bring outer abundance instead of inner holiness. You and your materi-
alist followers say, 'Man lives by bread alone,' but I say to you, 'Not
by bread alone.' Bread there must be, but remember even bread gets
all its power to nourish mankind from Me. Bread without Me can
harm man; and there is no real security apart from the Word of God.
If I give bread alone, then man is no more than an animal, and dogs
might as well come first to My banquet. Those who believe in Me

must hold to that faith, even when they are starved and weak; even when they are imprisoned and scourged.

"I know about human hunger! I have gone without food Myself for forty days. But I refuse to become a mere social reformer who caters only to the belly. You cannot say that I am unconcerned with social justice, for I am feeling at this moment the hunger of the world. I am One with every poor, starving member of the human race. That is why I have fasted: so that they can never say that God does not know what hunger is. Begone, Satan! I am not just a social worker who has never been hungry Himself, but One who says, 'I reject any plan which promises to make men richer without making them holier.' Remember! I Who say, 'Not by bread alone,' have not tasted bread for forty days!"

THE SECOND TEMPTATION

Satan, having failed to win Our Lord away from His Cross and Redemption by turning Him into a "Communist Commissar" who promises nothing but bread, now turned the attack directly upon His Soul. Seeing that Our Lord refused to subscribe to the belief that man is an animal or a mere stomach, Satan now tempted Him to pride and egotism. Satan displayed his own kind of vanity by taking Him to a lofty impressive pinnacle of the temple, and saying:

> Throw yourself down. *Matthew 4:6*

Then he continued by quoting Scripture:

> He will put his angels in charge of you, and they will support you in their arms, for fear you should strike your foot against a stone.
> *Matthew 4:6*

Satan was here saying, "Why take the long and tedious way to win mankind, through the shedding of blood, the mounting of a Cross, through being despised and rejected, when You can take a short cut by performing a prodigy? You have already affirmed Your trust in God. Very well! If You really trust God, I dare You to do something heroic! Prove Your faith, not by struggling up Calvary in obedience to God's will, but by flinging Yourself down. You will never win people to Yourself by preaching sublime truths from steeples, pinnacles and crucifixes. The masses cannot follow You; they are too far below. Clothe Yourself with wonders instead. Throw Yourself down from the pinnacle, then stop just before You hit bottom; that is something they can appreciate. It is the spectacular that people want, not the Divine. People are always bored! Relieve the monotony of their lives and stimulate their jaded spirits, but leave their guilty consciences alone!"

The second temptation was to forget the Cross and replace it with an effortless display of power, which would make it easy for everyone to believe in Him. Having heard Our Blessed Lord quote Scripture, the devil now quoted it too. The Savior had said in answer to the first temptation, that God could give Him bread if He asked for it, but He would not ask for it if it meant a surrendering of His Divine Mission. Satan retorted that if Our Lord really trusted so much in the Father, He should prove it by doing a daring deed and giving the Father an opportunity to protect Him. In the desert, there was no one to see Him perform a miracle by making bread from stones; but in the great city there were plenty of spectators. If one were to be the Messiah, the people would have to be won; and what could win them more quickly than a display of wonders?

The truth that would answer this temptation was that faith in God must never contradict reason. The unreasonable venture never has the assurance of the Divine protection. Satan wanted to make God the Father do something for Our Lord that Our Lord refused to do for Himself; namely, to make Him an object of special care, exempt from obedience to natural laws which were already the laws of God. But Our Blessed Lord, Who came to show us the Father, knew that the Father was not just a mechanical, impersonal Providence which would protect anyone, even someone who surrendered a Divinely ordained mission for the sake of winning a mob. The answer of Our Lord to the second temptation was:

> Scripture says again, You are not to put the Lord your God to the test. *Matthew* 4:8

Our Blessed Lord was to have that same temptation later on in His public life when a mob would stand around Him demanding a miracle, any miracle, just to prove His powers and to make it easy for them to believe.

> With the crowds swarming round him he went on to say: This is a wicked generation. It demands a sign. *Luke* 11:29

If He did show such signs, He would certainly have all men running after Him; but what would it profit them if sin was still on their souls?

In answer to modern requests for signs and wonders, Our Lord might say, "You repeat Satan's temptation, whenever you admire the wonders of science, and forget that I am the Author of the Universe and its science. Your scientists are the proofreaders, but not the authors of the Book of Nature; they can see and examine My handiwork, but they cannot create one atom themselves. You would tempt

Me to prove Myself omnipotent by meaningless tests; you have even pulled watches on Me and said, 'I challenge You to strike me dead within five minutes.' Know you not that I have mercy on fools? You tempt Me after you have wilfully destroyed your own cities with bombs by shrieking out, 'Why does God not stop this war?' You tempt Me, saying that I have no power, unless I show it at your beck and call. This, if you remember, is exactly how Satan tempted Me in the desert.

"I have never had many followers on the lofty heights of Divine truth, I know; for instance, I have hardly had the intelligentsia. I refuse to perform stunts to win them, for they would not really be won that way. It is only when I am seen on the Cross that I really draw men to Myself; it is by sacrifice, and not by marvels, that I must make My appeal. I must win followers not with test tubes, but with My blood; not with material power, but with love; not with celestial fireworks, but with the right use of reason and free will. No sign shall be given to this generation but the sign of Jonas, namely, the sign of someone rising up from below, not of someone flinging Himself down from the pinnacles.

"I want men who will believe in Me, even when I do not protect them; I will not open the prison doors where My brethren are locked; I will not stay the murderous Red sickle or the imperial lions of Rome, I will not halt the Red hammer that batters down My tabernacle doors; I want My missionaries and martyrs to love Me in prison and death as I love them in My own suffering. I never worked any miracles to save Myself! I will work few miracles even for My saints. Begone, Satan! Thou shalt not tempt the Lord, thy God."

THE THIRD TEMPTATION

The final assault took place on the mountaintop. It was the third attempt to divert Him from His Cross, this time by a plea for coexistence between good and evil. He had come to establish a kingdom on earth by acting as the Lamb going to sacrifice. Why could He not choose a much quicker way of establishing His kingdom, by striking up a treaty, which would give Him all He desired, namely the world, but without the Cross?

> Next the devil led him up and showed him in a flash all the kingdoms of the world. All this dominion will I give to you, he said, and the glory that goes with it; for it has been put in my hands and I can give it to anyone I choose. You have only to do homage to me and it shall all be yours. *Luke* 4:5–7

The words of Satan seem, indeed, very boastful. Had the kingdoms of the world really been delivered to him? Our Lord called Satan the "prince of the world," but it was not God that had delivered any of the kingdoms of the world to him; mankind had done so, by sin. But even if Satan did, so to speak, rule the kingdoms of the earth by popular consent, it was not really within his power to give them to whomsoever he pleased. Satan was lying in order to tempt Our Lord again from the Cross, by way of a short cut. He was offering Our Lord the world on one condition: that He worship Satan. Worship, of course, would imply service. The service would be this: that inasmuch as the kingdom of the world was under the power of sin, the new Kingdom which Our Lord would establish must be only a continuation of the old one. In short, He could have the earth, provided He promised not to change it. He could have mankind, as long as He promised not to redeem it. It was a kind of temptation that Our Blessed Lord would face later on, when the people attempted to make Him an earthly king.

> Jesus, aware that they meant to come and seize him to proclaim him king, withdrew again to the hills by himself. *John 6:15*

And before Pilate, He said that He would establish another Kingdom, but that it would not be one of the kingdoms that Satan could offer. When Pilate asked Him, "Art Thou a King?"

> Jesus replied, My kingdom does not belong to this world. If it did, my followers would be fighting to save me from arrest by the Jews. My kingly authority comes from elsewhere. *John 18:36*

The kingdom that Satan offered was of the world, and not of the Spirit. It would still be a kingdom of evil and the hearts of His subjects would not be regenerated.

Satan was saying in effect, "You have come, O Christ, to win the world, but the world is already mine; I will give it to You, if You will compromise and worship me. Forget Your Cross, Your Kingdom of Heaven. If You want the world, it is at Your feet. You will be hailed with louder hosannas than Jerusalem ever sang to its kings; and You will be spared the pains and sorrows of the Cross of contradiction."

Our Lord, knowing that those kingdoms could be won only by His suffering and death, said to Satan:

> Begone, Satan! Scripture says, You shall do homage to the Lord your God and worship him alone. *Matthew 4:10*

We can conjecture how these terse, uncompromising words must have sounded to Satan, "Satan, you want worship; but to worship you is to serve you, and to serve you is slavery. I do not want your world, so long as it bears the terrible burden of guilt. In all the kingdoms which you claim as yours, the hearts of your citizens still long for something you cannot give them, namely, peace of soul and unselfish love. I do not want your world, which you do not even own yourself.

"I am a revolutionist too, as My mother sang in her *Magnificat*. I am in revolt against you, the prince of the world. But My revolution is not by the sword thrust outward to conquer by force, but inward against sin and all the things that make war among men. I will first conquer evil in the hearts of men, and then I shall conquer the world. I will conquer your world by going into the hearts of your dishonest tax collectors, your false judges, your Commissars, and I will redeem them from guilt and sin, and send them back clean to their professions. I shall tell them that it profits them nothing to win the whole world if they lose their immortal souls. You may keep your kingdoms for the moment. Better the loss of all your kingdoms, of the whole world even, than the loss of a single soul! The kingdoms of the world must be elevated to the Kingdom of God; the Kingdom of God will not be dragged down to the level of the kingdoms of the world. All I now want of this earth is a place large enough to erect a Cross; there I shall let you unfurl Me before the crossroads of your world! I shall let you nail Me in the name of the cities of Jerusalem, Athens, and Rome, but I will rise from the dead, and you will discover that you, who seemed to conquer, have been crushed, as I march with victory on the wings of the morning! Satan, you are asking Me to become anti-Christ. Before this blasphemous request, patience must give way to just anger. 'Get thee behind Me, Satan.'"

Our Lord came down from that mountain as poor as when He ascended it. When He had finished His earthly life and had risen from the dead, He would speak to His Apostles on another mountain:

> The eleven disciples made their way to Galilee, to the mountain where Jesus had told them to meet him. When they saw him, they fell prostrate before him, though some were doubtful. Jesus then came up and spoke to them. He said: Full authority in heaven and on earth has been committed to me. Go forth therefore and make all nations my disciples; baptize men everywhere in the name of the Father and the Son and the Holy Spirit, and teach them to observe all that I have commanded you. And be assured, I am with you always, to the end of time. *Matthew 28:16–20*

4. *The Lamb of God*

Now that Our Lord had mastered the supreme temptation to become the King of men by filling their stomachs, by thrilling them with scientific wonders, and by making a political deal with the prince of darkness, He was ready to go before the world as a sacrificial victim for sin. After the long fast and trial, angels came and ministered unto Him. Then He returned to the Jordan and mingled, for a while unnoticed, in the crowd that surrounded the Baptist. On the previous day, John had spoken of Our Lord to a deputation of priests and Levites from the temple of Jerusalem, who had come to ask, "Who art thou?" They knew the time was ripe for the coming of Christ or the Messiah, hence their pointed query. But John told them "he was not the Christ." He was merely the Voice announcing the Word. As Christ refused titles of external power, so also John refused title which the Pharisees were willing to confer on him, even the greatest, that he was the One sent by God.

The next day Our Lord was in the crowd, and John saw Him at a distance. Immediately, John reached back into the Jewish heritage of symbol and prophecy, known to all his hearers.

> Look, there is the Lamb of God; it is he who takes away the sin of the world. *John 1:29*

John was affirming that we must not look first for a teacher, a giver of moral precepts, or a worker of miracles. First we must look for One Who had been appointed as a sacrifice for the sins of the world. The Passover was approaching, and the highways were filled with people driving or carrying their one-year-old lambs to the temple to be sacrificed. In full view of those lambs, John pointed out the Lamb Who, when sacrificed, would end all sacrifices in the temple, because He would take away the sins of the world.

John was the parting voice of the Old Testament, in which the lamb played such an important role. In Genesis, we find Abel offering a lamb, the firstling of his flock, in a bloody sacrifice for the expiation of sin. Later on, God asked Abraham to sacrifice his son Isaac—a prophetic symbol of the Heavenly Father sacrificing His own Son. When Isaac asked, "Where is the lamb?" Abraham said:

> God will provide himself with a young beast for a sacrifice, my son. *Genesis 22:8*

The answer to the question, "Where is the lamb of sacrifice?" asked in the beginning of Genesis, was now answered by John the Baptist as he pointed to Christ and said, "Here is the Lamb of God." God had at last provided a Lamb. The Cross that had been defended in the wilderness during the temptations was now showing itself over the Jordan.

Every family sought to have its own Paschal Lamb; and those who were now taking their lambs to Jerusalem, where the Lamb of God said that He must be sacrificed, knew that the lamb was a symbol of Israel's deliverance from the political slavery of Egypt. John was saying that it was also a symbol of deliverance from the spiritual slavery of sin.

The Lamb would come in the form of a man; for the prophet Isaiah had foretold:

> The Lord laid upon him
> the guilt of us all.
> He was afflicted, he submitted to be struck down
> and did not open his mouth;   *Isaiah 53:7*

The lamb was most often used as a victim of sacrifice, because of its innocence and mildness; therefore, it was an emblem most suited to the character of the Messiah. The fact that John the Baptist called Him the Lamb of God is most significant; He was neither the peoples' lamb, nor the lamb of the Jews, nor the lamb of any human owner, but the Lamb of God. When the Lamb was finally sacrificed, it was not because He was a victim of those who were stronger than Himself, but rather because He was fulfilling His willing duty of love for sinners. It was not man who offered this sacrifice, although it was man who slew the victim; it was God Who gave Himself.

Peter, who was a disciple of John and who probably was there that day, would later on make clearer the meaning of "the Lamb" when he wrote:

> Well you know that it was no perishable stuff, like gold or silver, that bought your freedom from the empty folly of your traditional ways. The price was paid in precious blood, as it were of a lamb without mark or blemish—the blood of Christ.   *I Peter 1:18*

After the Resurrection and Ascension, the Deacon Philip encountered a courier of the Queen of Ethiopia. The courier had been reading a passage from the prophet Isaiah which foretold the Lamb:

> The passage he was reading was this: He was led like a sheep to be slaughtered; and like a lamb that is dumb before the shearer, he does not open his mouth.   *Acts 8:32*

Philip explained to him that this Lamb had just been sacrificed and had risen from the dead and ascended into heaven. St. John the Evangelist, who too was at the Jordan that day (for he was one of John the Baptist's disciples), later stood at the foot of the Cross when the Lamb was sacrificed. Years later, he wrote that the Lamb slain on Calvary was by intent slain from the beginning of the world. The Cross was not an afterthought.

> The Lamb that was slain keeps in his roll of the living, written there since the world was made. *Apocalypse 13:8*

This means that the Lamb was slain, as it were, by Divine decree from all eternity, though the temporal fulfillment had to await Calvary. His death was according to God's eternal plan and God's determinate counsel. But the principle of self-sacrificing love was eternal. Redemption was in the mind of God before the foundation of the world was laid. God, Who is outside time, saw from all eternity mankind falling, and being redeemed. The earth itself would be the stage for this great event. The lamb was the eternal antetype of every sacrifice. When the Hour of the Cross came and the centurion ran his spear into Our Lord's side, then was fulfilled the Old Testament prophecy.

> They shall look on me, on him whom they have pierced.
> *Zachariah 12:10*

The phrase which John the Baptist used to describe how the Lamb of God would "take away" the sins of the world is one which is parallel in Hebrew and in Greek; Leviticus describes the scapegoat which

> Shall carry all their iniquities upon itself into some barren waste and the man shall let it go, there in the wilderness. *Leviticus 16:22*

As the scapegoat on which sins were laid was driven out of the city, so the Lamb of God Who really took away sins would be driven from the City of Jerusalem.

Thus, the Lamb which God promised to provide Abraham for his sacrifice, and all the subsequent lambs and goats offered by Jews and pagans throughout history, derived their value from the Lamb of God Who stood before John. Here it was not Our Lord who was prophesying the Cross; rather it was the Old Testament through John, declaring Him to be a Divinely appointed sacrifice for sin and the only remover of human guilt.

The Israelites had long realized that forgiveness of sin was in some way connected with sacrificial offerings; therefore, they came to suppose that there was some inherent virtue in the victim. Sin was in the blood; hence, blood had to be shed. No wonder then, that when the Victim had been offered on Calvary and had risen from the dead, He reaffirmed how necessary it was for Him to suffer. To apply the merits of that redemptive blood to ourselves became the theme of the New Testament. In the Old Testament, when the lambs were sacrificed, some of the blood was sprinkled on the people. When the Lamb of God came to be sacrificed, some asked again for the sprinkling of the blood, in a horribly ironical way!

> His blood be on us, and on our children. *Matthew 27:26*

But millions of others would also find glory because of the sprinkling of the Blood of the Lamb. John the Evangelist later on described them in eternal glory.

> Then as I looked I heard the voices of countless angels. These were all round the throne and the living creatures and the elders. Myriads upon myriads there were, thousands upon thousands, and they cried aloud:
>
> > Worthy is the Lamb, the Lamb that was slain, to receive all power and wealth, wisdom and might, honour and glory and praise!
>
> Then I heard every created thing in heaven and on earth and under the earth and in the sea, all that is in them, crying:
>
> > Praise and honour, glory and might, to him who sits on the throne and to the Lamb for ever and ever! *Apocalypse 5:11–14*

5. The Beginning of "The Hour"

Throughout the gospels whenever there is a warning, like thunder, of the Cross, there is an accompanying flash of the glory of the Resurrection; whenever there is the approaching shadow of redemptive suffering, there is also the light of spiritual freedom that will come after it. That counterpoint of joy and sorrow in the life of Christ is found again in His first miracle which took place in the village of Cana. It is part of His pattern, that He Who came to preach a crucifixion of disordered flesh, should have begun His Public Life by assisting at a marriage feast.

In the Old Testament, the relation between God and Israel was compared to the relation between a bridegroom and his bride. Our Lord suggested that the same relation would henceforth exist between Himself and the new spiritual Israel, which He was going to found. He would be the Bridegroom, His Church would be the bride. And since He came to establish this kind of union between Himself and redeemed humanity, it was fitting that He should commence His public ministry by assisting at a marriage. St. Paul was not introducing a new idea when he wrote to the Ephesians later on that the union of man and woman was the symbol of the union of Christ and His Church.

> Husbands, love your wives, as Christ also loved the church and gave himself up for it. *Ephesians 5:25*

A marriage feast is an occasion for much joy; and wine is served as a symbol of that joy. At the feast of Cana, which had such symbolic importance, the Cross did not cast a shadow over the joy; rather the joy came first, and then the Cross. But when the joy had been accomplished the shadow of the Cross cast itself over the feast.

Our Lord had already been affirmed as the Lamb of God in the river Jordan; He had also chosen five disciples from among the followers of John the Baptist; John the Evangelist, Andrew, Peter, Philip, and Nathanael. These He brought to the wedding feast which was already in progress and which altogether lasted several days. In those days, fathers of the bride had greater burdens than today. For the rejoicings and the expenses could continue for eight days. One of the probable reasons for the wine giving out was that Our Lord had brought in so many uninvited guests. Since the great excitement at the Jordan, when the heavens opened to affirm that He was the Son of God, His presence had been attracting hundreds of stray followers, who also came to the feast. He was coming to the marriage not just as the village carpenter, but as the Christ or the Messiah. Before the rejoicings came to an end, it would be revealed that He had a rendezvous with the Cross.

Mary, His Blessed Mother, was present at the wedding feast. This is the only occasion in the life of Our Lord where Mary is mentioned before her Son. Mary was to be the instrument of His first miracle, or sign, that He was what He claimed to be, the Son of God. She had already been an instrument for the sanctification of John the Baptist in his mother's womb; now, by her intercession, she sounded the trumpet for a long procession of miracles—an intercession so strong that it has inspired souls in all ages to invoke her name for other miracles of nature and grace.

John the Evangelist, who had already been chosen to be a disciple, was present at the feast; and it was he who was both an eye-and-ear witness to what Mary did at Cana. He was also with her at the foot of the Cross, and he recorded both events faithfully in his Gospel. In the temple and in the Jordan, Our Lord received His Father's blessing and sanction to begin His work of Redemption. At Cana, He received the assent of His human parent. Later, in the terrible isolation of Calvary, there would come a dark moment when His Father would seemingly withdraw from Him and He would quote the psalm that begins:

My God, my God, why hast thou forsaken me? *Psalm 21:1*

Another moment would come when He would seem to withdraw from His Mother:

Mother, there is your son. *John 19:26*

When the wine gave out at Cana, it is interesting to note that Mary was more concerned with the guests than was the wine-steward; for it was she, and not he, who noticed their need of wine. Mary turned to her Divine Son in a perfect spirit of prayer. Completely confident in Him and trusting in His mercy, she said:

They have no wine left. *John 2:3*

It was not a personal request; she was already a mediatrix for all who were seeking the fulness of joy. She has never been just a spectator, but a full participant willingly involving herself in the needs of others. The mother used the special power which she had as a mother over her Son, a power generated by mutual love. He answered her with apparent hesitation:

> Your concern, mother, is not mine. My hour has not yet come.
>
> *John 2:4*

First, consider the words, "What is that to Me and to thee?" This is a Hebrew phrase which is difficult to translate into English. St. John rendered it very literally into Greek, and the Vulgate preserved this literalism in *Quid mihi et tibi,* which means, "What to Me and to thee?" The word "that" is not represented in the original phrase; it has been added in the English translation to make the idea more understandable. Knox translates it freely, "Why dost thou trouble Me with that?"

In order to understand His meaning more fully, consider the words, "My Hour is not yet come." The "Hour" obviously refers to His Cross. Whenever the word "Hour" is used in the New Testament, it is used in relation to His Passion, death, and glory. References to this "Hour" are made seven times in John alone, some of which are noted here.

> At this they tried to seize him, but no one laid a hand on him because his appointed hour had not yet come. *John 7:30*

> These words were spoken by Jesus in the treasury as he taught in the temple. Yet no one arrested him, because his hour had not yet come.
>
> *John 8:20*

> Then Jesus replied: The hour has come for the Son of Man to be glorified. *John 12:23*

> Now my soul is in turmoil, and what am I to say? Father, save me from this hour. No, it was for this that I came to this hour.
>
> *John 12:27*

> Look, the hour is coming, has indeed already come, when you are all to be scattered, each to his home, leaving me alone. Yet I am not alone, because the Father is with me. *John 16:32*

> After these words Jesus looked up to heaven and said:
>   Father, the hour has come. Glorify thy Son, that the Son may glorify thee. *John 17:1*

The "Hour," therefore, referred to His glorification through His Crucifixion, Resurrection and Ascension. At Cana, Our Lord was referring to Calvary and saying that the time appointed for beginning the task of Redemption was not yet at hand. His mother was asking for a miracle; He was implying that a miracle worked as a sign of His Divinity would be the beginning of His Death. The moment He showed Himself before men as the Son of God, He would draw down upon Himself their hatred, for evil can tolerate mediocrity, but not supreme goodness. The miracle she was asking for would be unmistakably related to His Redemption.

There were, in His life, two occasions when His human nature seemed to show an unwillingness to take on His burden of suffering. In the Garden, He asked His Father if it be possible to take away His chalice of woe. But He immediately afterward acquiesced in His Father's will: "Not My will, but Thine be done." The same apparent reluctance was also manifested in the face of the will of His mother. Cana was a rehearsal for Golgotha. He was not questioning the wisdom of beginning His Public Life and going to death at this particular point in time; it was rather a question of submitting His reluctant human nature to obedience to the Cross. There is a striking parallel between His Father's bidding Him to His public death and His mother's bidding Him to His public life. Obedience triumphed in both cases; at Cana, the water was changed into wine; at Calvary, the wine was changed into blood.

He was telling His mother that she was virtually pronouncing a sentence of death over Him. Few are the mothers who send their sons to battlefields; but here was one who was actually hastening the hour of her Son's mortal conflict with the forces of evil. If He agreed to her request, He would be beginning His hour of death and glorification. To the Cross He would go with double commission, one from His Father in heaven, the other from His mother on earth.

As soon as He had consented to begin His "Hour," He proceeded immediately to tell her that her relations with Him would be henceforth changed. Until then, during His hidden life, she had been known as the mother of Jesus. But now that He was launched on the work of Redemption, she would no longer be just His mother, but also the mother of all His human brethren whom He would redeem. To indicate this new relationship, He now addressed her, not as "Mother" but as the "Universal Mother" or "Woman." What a ring those words had to people who lived in the light of the Old Testament. When Adam fell, God spoke to Satan and foretold that He would put enmity between his seed and "the Woman," for goodness would have a progeny as well as evil. The world would have not only the City of Man which Satan claimed as his own, but also the City of God. The "Woman" did have a seed, and it was her Seed that was standing now at the marriage feast, the Seed that would fall to the ground and die and then spring forth unto new life.

The moment the "Hour" began, she became "the Woman"; she

would have other children too, not according to the flesh, but according to the spirit. If He was to be the new Adam, the founder of a redeemed humanity, she would be the new Eve and the mother of that new humanity. As Our Lord was a man, she was His mother; and as He was a Savior, she was also the mother of all whom He would save. John, who was present at that wedding, was also present at the climax of the "Hour" on Calvary. He heard Our Lord calling her "Woman" from the Cross and then saying to her, "Behold thy son." It was as if he, John, was now the symbol of her new family. When Our Lord raised the son of the widow of Naim from the dead, He said, "Give him back to his mother." On the Cross, He consoled His mother by giving her another son, John, and with him the whole of redeemed humanity.

At the Resurrection He gave Himself back to her, to show that while she had gained new children, she had not lost Him. At Cana the prophecy that Simeon had made to her in the temple was confirmed: henceforth, whatever involved her Son would involve her, too; whatever happened to Him would happen to her. If He was destined to go to the Cross, so was she; and if He was now beginning His Public Life, then she would begin a new life too, no longer as just the mother of Jesus, but as the mother of all whom Jesus the Savior would redeem. He called Himself "Son of Man," a title embracing all humanity; she would be henceforth the "Mother of Men." Just as she was at His side as He began His Hour, so would she be at His side at its climactic finish. When she took Him away from the temple as a boy of twelve, it was because she sensed that His Hour had not yet come; He obeyed her then and returned to Nazareth with her. Now, He told her that His Hour had not yet come, but she bade Him begin it, and He obeyed. At Cana, she gave Him as a Savior to sinners; on the Cross He gave her as a refuge to sinners.

When He suggested that His first miracle would lead unerringly to His Cross and death, and that she would become henceforth a Mother of Sorrows, she turned at once to the winesteward and said:

Do whatever he tells you. *John* 2:5

What a magnificent valedictory! She never speaks again in Scripture. Seven times she had spoken in the Scriptures, but now that Christ had shown Himself, like the sun in the full brilliance of His Divinity, Our Lady was willingly overshadowed like the moon, as John later on described her.

The six waterpots were filled, making about one hundred and twenty gallons, and in the beautiful language of Richard Crashaw, "the conscious water saw its God and blushed." The first miracle was something like creation itself; it was done by the power of "the Word." The wine He created was so good that the bridegroom was reproached by the steward with the words:

> Everyone serves the best wine first, and waits until the guests have drunk freely before serving the poorer sort; but you have kept the best wine till now. *John 2:10*

Truly the best wine was kept. Up until then in the unfolding of revelation, the poor wine had been the prophets, judges, and kings, Abraham, Isaac, Jacob, Moses, Josue—all were like the water awaiting the miracle of the Expected of the Nations. The world generally gives its best pleasures first; afterward come the dregs and the bitterness. But Christ reversed the order and gave us the feast after the fast, the Resurrection after the Crucifixion, the joy of Easter Sunday after the sorrow of Good Friday.

> This deed at Cana-in-Galilee is the first of the signs by which Jesus revealed his glory and led his disciples to believe in him. *John 2:11*

The Cross is everywhere. When a man stretches out his arms in relaxation, he unconsciously forms the image of the reason for the Son of Man's coming. So too at Cana, the shadow of the Cross was thrown across a "Woman," and the first stroke of the "Hour" was sounded like a bell of execution. In all the other incidents of His life, the Cross came first, then the joy. But at Cana, it was the joy of the nuptials that came first—the nuptials of the Bridegroom and the Bride of redeemed humanity; only after that are we reminded that the Cross is the condition of that ecstasy.

Thus He did at a marriage feast what He would not do in a desert; He worked in the full gaze of men what He had refused to do before Satan. Satan asked Him to turn stones into bread in order that He might become an economic Messiah; His mother asked Him to change water into wine that He might become a Savior. Satan tempted Him *from* death; Mary "tempted" Him *to* death and Resurrection. Satan tried to lead Him *from* the Cross; Mary sent Him *toward* it. Later on, He would take hold of the bread that Satan had said men needed, and the wine that His mother had said the wedding guests needed, and He would change them both into the memorial of His Passion and His death. Then He would ask that men renew that memorial, even "unto the consummation of the world." The antiphon of His life continues to ring: *Everyone else came into the world to live; He came into the world to die.*

6. The Temple of His Body

A temple is a place where God dwells. Where then was the true temple of God? Was the great temple in Jerusalem with all its physical grandeur the true temple? The answer to this question must have seemed obvious to the Jews; but Our Lord was just about to suggest that there was another temple. Pilgrims were going up to Jerusalem for the Passover feast, and among them was Our Lord and His first disciples, after a brief stay in Capharnaum. The temple was a truly magnificent sight, particularly since Herod had almost completed rebuilding and adorning it. A year later, the Apostles themselves, on Mount Olivet, would be so struck by its glittering appearance as it shone in the morning sunlight that they would ask Our Lord to look at it and admire its beauty.

It was naturally a problem for anyone who came to offer sacrifice to get hold of the materials of sacrifice; then too, the sacrificial victims had to be tested and judged according to Levitical standards. Accordingly, there was a flourishing trade in sacrificial animals of all degrees. Gradually, the sellers of sheep and doves had been pushing themselves closer and closer to the temple, choking the avenues that led to it, until some of them, particularly the sons of Annas, actually gained entrance to Solomon's porch, where they sold their doves and cattle and changed money. Every visitor to the feasts was obliged to pay half a shekel to help defray the expenses of the temple; since no foreign money was accepted, the sons of Annas, so Josephus tells us, trafficked in the exchange of coins, presumably at highly profitable rates. A couple of doves were sold at one time for a gold coin which in American money would be worth about $2.50. This abuse, however, was corrected by the grandson of the great Hillel, who reduced the price to about one-fiftieth of the above price. All kinds of currency from Tyre, Syria, Egypt, Greece, and Rome circulated around the temple, thus leading to a thriving black market among the money-changers. The situation was bad enough for Christ to call the temple a "den of thieves"; in fact, the Talmud itself protested against those who had so defiled this holy place.

Considerable interest was aroused among the pilgrims when Our Lord first entered the sacred enclosure. This was both His first public appearance before the nation and His first to the temple as the Messiah. He had already worked His first miracle at Cana; now He came into His Father's house to claim a Son's right. Our Blessed Lord, finding Himself in this incongruous scene, where prayers were mingled with the blasphemous bidding of the merchants, and where the clinking of money chimed in with the braying of cattle, was filled with zeal for His Father's house. Out of some cords lying around, which were probably used as leashes around the necks of the cattle, He made a small scourge. With this, He proceeded to drive out the cattle and the profiteers. The unpopularity of the exploiters and their fear of public scandal probably prevented them from putting up any real resistance to the Savior. A wild scene ensued with the cattle rushing hither and thither, and the money-changers grabbing what coins they could as the Savior upset their tables. He opened the cages of the doves and released them.

> Take them out, he said; you must not turn my Father's house into a market. *John 2:16*

Even those most friendly to Him must have wondered as they saw Him, with uplifted scourge and flaming eyes, driving forth men and beasts as He said:

> My house shall be called a house of prayer for all the nations? But you have made it a robbers' cave. *Mark 11:17*

> His disciples recalled the words of Scripture, Zeal for thy house will destroy me. *John 2:17*

The part of the temple out of which Our Lord drove the traders was known as the Porch of Solomon, the eastern side of the Court of the Gentiles. This section should have served as a symbol showing that all the nations of the world were welcome; but the traders were defiling it. He was now making it clear that the temple was meant for all nations, not for Jerusalem alone; it was a house of prayer for the Magi, as well as for the shepherds, for the foreign missions as well as for the home missions.

He called the temple "My Father's house," affirming at the same moment His own filial relationship to the Heavenly Father. Those who were driven out of the temple did not lay hands on Him, nor did they reprove Him as if He had done something wrong. They merely asked for a sign or a warrant which would justify His actions. As He stood in lonely dignity, among the scattered coins and scurrying cattle with the pigeons flying this way and that, they asked Him:

> What sign, they asked, can you show as authority for your action?
> *John 2:18*

They were bewildered by His capacity for righteous indignation (which was the other side of the joy-bringing character manifested at Cana), and they demanded a sign. He had already given them a sign that He was God, for He told them that they had profaned *His Father's house*. To ask for another sign was like asking for a light to see a light. But He gave them a second sign:

> Destroy this temple, Jesus replied, and in three days I will raise it again. *John 2:19*

The people who heard these words never forgot them. Three years later, at the trial, they would bring them up again in a slightly distorted form, accusing Him of saying:

> I will pull down this temple, made with human hands, and in three days I will build another, not made with hands. *Mark 14:58*

They remembered His words again as He hung on the Cross:

> Aha! they cried, wagging their heads, you would pull the temple down, would you, and build it in three days? Come down from the cross and save yourself! *Mark 15:29*

They were still haunted by His words when they asked Pilate to take precautions in guarding His grave. They understood by then that He had been referring not just to their temple of stone, but to His Body.

> Next day, the morning after that Friday, the chief priests and the Pharisees came in a body to Pilate. Your Excellency, they said, we recall how that impostor said while he was still alive, I am to be raised again after three days. So will you give orders for the grave to be made secure until the third day? Otherwise his disciples may come, steal the body. *Matthew 28:63–64*

The theme of the temple was echoed again in the trial and martyrdom of Stephen, when the persecutors charged that

> This man is for ever saying things against this holy place and against the Law. *Acts 6:13*

He was actually throwing down a challenge when He said to them: "Destroy!" He did not say, "If you destroy. . . ." He was challenging them directly to test His kingly and priestly power by a Crucifixion, and He would answer it with a Resurrection.

It is important to note that in the Original Greek of the Gospel, Our Lord did not use the word *hieron*, which was the usual Greek name for the temple, but rather *naos*, which meant the Holy of Holies of the temple. He was saying in effect, "The temple is the place where God dwells. You have profaned the old temple; but there is now another Temple. Destroy this new Temple, by crucifying Me, and in three days I shall raise it up. Though you will destroy My Body, which is the house of My Father, by My Resurrection I shall put all nations in possession of the new Temple." It is very likely that Our Blessed Lord pointed to His own Body when He spoke in this way. Temples can be constructed of flesh and bone as well as of stone and wood. Christ's Body was a Temple, because the fullness of God was dwelling in Him corporally. His challengers immediately responded by asking:

> It has taken forty-six years to build this temple. Are you going to raise it again in three days? *John 2:21*

They may have been referring to the temple of Zorobabel which had taken forty-six years to build. It was begun in the first year of the reign of Cyrus in 559 B.C., completed in 513, the ninth year of Darius. It is also possible that they may have been referring to the alterations of Herod, which had perhaps been going on for forty-six years at that point. The alterations had begun about the year 20 B.C., they were not completed until A.D. 63. But as John wrote:

> The temple he was speaking of was his body. After his resurrection his disciples recalled what he had said. *John 2:22*

The first temple of Jerusalem was associated with great kings, like David who prepared for it, and Solomon who built it. The second temple harked back to the great leaders of the return from captivity; this restored temple with its costly magnificence was linked with the royal house of Herod. All of these shadows of temples were to be superseded by the true Temple, which they would destroy on Good Friday. The moment that it was destroyed, the veil that hung over the Holy of Holies would be rent from top to bottom; and the veil of His flesh would also be rent, revealing the true Holy of Holies, the Sacred Heart of the Son of God.

He would use the same figure of the temple on another occasion when talking to the Pharisees:

> I tell you, there is something greater than the temple here.
> *Matthew 12:6*

This was how He answered their request for a sign. The sign was to be His death and His Resurrection. Later on to the Pharisees He would promise the same sign, under the symbol of Jonas. His authority would not be proved by His death alone; it would be proved by His death and His Resurrection. The death would be brought about both by the evil heart of man and by His own willingness; the Resurrection by the almighty power of God alone.

At this moment, He was calling the temple His own Father's house. When He left it for the last time three years later, He did not call it His Father's house any more, because the people had disowned Him; rather He said:

Look, look! there is your temple, forsaken by God. *Matthew 23:28*

It was no longer His Father's house, it was their house. The earthly temple ceases to be God's dwelling place when it becomes the center of mercenary interests. Without Him, it was not a temple at all.

Here, as elsewhere, Our Blessed Lord was proving Himself to be the only One Who came into the world to die. The Cross was not something that came at the end of His life; it was something that hung over Him from the very beginning. He said to them: "Destroy," and they said to him, "Crucify." No Temple was ever more systematically destroyed than was His Body. The dome of the Temple, His head, was crowned with thorns; the foundations of it, His sacred feet, were riven with nails; the transepts, His hands, were stretched out in the form of a Cross; the Holy of Holies, His Heart, was pierced with a lance.

Satan tempted Him to an apparent sacrifice by asking Him to fling Himself down from the pinnacle of the temple. Our Lord rejected this spectacular form of sacrifice. But when those who had polluted His Father's house asked Him for a sign, He offered them the sign of a different kind, that of His sacrifice on the Cross. Satan asked Him to cast Himself down; now Our Blessed Lord was saying that He would, indeed, be cast down to the obloquy of death; His sacrifice, however, would not be a piece of pointless exhibitionism, but an act of redemptive self-humiliation. Satan proposed that He expose His Temple to possible ruin for the sake of exhibitionism, for the sake of display; but Our Lord exposed the Temple of His Body to certain ruin for the sake of salvation and atonement. At Cana, He said that He was going to His "Hour"; in the temple He said that that Hour of the Cross would lead to His Resurrection. His public life would fulfill the pattern of these prophecies.

7. Nicodemus, the Serpent, and the Cross

Not having received a welcome in the temple which was His Father's house, Jesus did not force the issue. That earthly temple would fade away and He, the true Temple wherein God dwells, would rise again in glory. For the moment, He limited Himself to proving that He was the Messiah by teaching and miracles. During these few days, He worked many more miracles than are recorded; and the Gospel states that many, seeing the miracles He wrought, believed in Him. One of the members of the Sanhedrin admitted not only that the miracles were authentic but also that God had to be with Him Who worked these signs.

> There was one of the Pharisees named Nicodemus, a member of the Jewish Council, who came to Jesus by night. *John 3:1*

By all worldly standards Nicodemus was a wise man; he was well versed in the Scriptures, a religious man, inasmuch as he belonged to one of the sects, the Pharisees, that insisted on the minutiae of external rites. But Nicodemus was not, at least in the beginning, a fearless man, for he chose to talk with Our Blessed Lord at a time when the mantle of darkness hid him from the eyes of men.

Nicodemus is the "night character" of the Gospel, for whenever we meet him, it is in darkness. This first visit is definitely described as being at night. Later on at night, as a member of the Sanhedrin, it was he who spoke in defense of Our Lord, saying that no man should be judged before having a hearing. On Good Friday in the darkness after the Crucifixion, Joseph of Arimathea came:

> He was joined by Nicodemus (the man who had first visited Jesus by night), who brought with him a mixture of myrrh and aloes, more than half a hundredweight. *John 19:39*

Despite the fact that there were social impediments to discourage his showing any interest in Our Divine Lord, he nevertheless did come to see Him when He was in Jerusalem for the Passover. He came to do reverence to Christ, and he learned quickly that this kind of reverence was not enough. Nicodemus said to Him:

> Rabbi, he said, we know that you are a teacher sent by God; no one could perform these signs of yours unless God were with him.
>
> *John 3:2*

But though Nicodemus had seen the miracles he was not yet ready to confess the Divinity of Him Who worked them. He was still holding back a little, for he veiled his personality under the official "we." This is a trick intellectuals sometimes use to escape personal responsibility; it is meant to imply that if a change is needed it must be for society at large, rather than for their own hearts. Later on, during this night conversation, Our Lord chided Nicodemus as a "teacher" for still being ignorant of many prophecies. In this, Our Lord was showing Himself to be a Teacher too. But before the dawn had broken on their long discussion, Our Lord proclaimed that though He was a Teacher, He was not merely that; He was first and foremost a Redeemer. He affirmed that not human truth in the mind, but a rebirth of the soul, purchased through His death, was essential for being one with Him. Nicodemus began by calling Him a teacher; by the end of their meeting Our Lord had proclaimed Himself a Savior.

The Cross reflected itself back over every incident in His life; it never shone so brilliantly on one who knew the Old Testament as it did this night. This Pharisee had thought Him to be only a Master or a Rabbi, but he discovered in the end that there was healing in what had always been thought up to then to be a curse; namely, a Crucifixion.

Our Blessed Lord, in answer, bade him to leave the order of worldliness.

> In truth, in very truth I tell you, unless a man has been born over again he cannot see the kingdom of God. *John* 3:3

The idea that stood out in the beginning of the discussion between Nicodemus and Our Lord was that spiritual life was different from physical or intellectual life. The difference between spiritual life and physical life, Jesus was telling him, was greater than that between a crystal and a living cell. Spiritual life is not a push from below; it is a gift from above. A man does not really become less selfish and more liberal-minded until he becomes a follower of Christ. There must be a new birth generated from above. Every person in the world has a first birth from the flesh. But Jesus said that a second birth from above is necessary for the spiritual life. So necessary is it, that a man "cannot" enter the Kingdom of God without it; He did not say "will not," for the impossibility is real. As one cannot lead a physical life unless born to it, so neither can one lead a Divine life unless born of God. The first birth makes us children of our parents; the second makes us children of God. The emphasis is not on self-development, but on regeneration; not on improving our present state, but on completely changing our status.

Overcome by the loftiness of the idea suggested to him, Nicodemus asked for greater clarity. He could understand a man's *being* what he is, but he could not understand a man's *becoming* what he is not. Nicodemus understood about redecorating the old man, but not about creating an entirely new man. Hence the question:

> But how is it possible for a man to be born when he is old? Can he enter his mother's womb a second time and be born? *John 3:4*

Nicodemus did not deny the doctrine of the new birth. He was a literalist; he doubted the exactness of the term "born."

Our Blessed Lord answered the difficulty:

> In truth I tell you, no one can enter the kingdom of God without being born from water and spirit. Flesh can give birth only to flesh; it is spirit that gives birth to spirit. You ought not to be astonished, then, when I tell you that you must be born over again. *John 3:5–7*

The illustration of Nicodemus was inadequate. It only applied to the realm of flesh. Nicodemus could not enter into his mother's womb a second time to be born. But what is impossible for the flesh is possible for the spirit. Nicodemus had expected instruction and teaching, but instead, he was being offered regeneration and rebirth. The Kingdom of God was presented as a new creation. When a man issues from the womb of his mother he is only a *creature* of God, as a table is the creation, in a lesser degree, of the carpenter. No man in the natural order can call God "Father"; to do this man would have to become something he is not. He must by a Divine gift share in the nature of God, as he presently shares in the nature of his parents. Man makes that which is unlike him; but he begets that which is like him. An artist paints a picture, but it is unlike the artist in nature; a mother begets a child and the child is like her in nature. Our Lord here suggests that over and above the order of making or creation, is the order of begetting, regeneration, and rebirth by which God becomes our Father.

Evidently, Nicodemus was startled out of his purely intellectual approach to religion, for Our Blessed Lord said to him, "Do not be surprised." Nicodemus wondered how this effect of regeneration could be produced. Our Lord explained that the reason why Nicodemus did not understand this second birth was that he was ignorant of the work of the Holy Spirit. A few moments later, He suggested that just as His death would reconcile mankind to the Father, so would mankind be regenerated by the agency of His Holy Spirit. The new birth Our Lord hinted at would escape the senses and is known only by its effects on the soul.

Our Blessed Lord used an illustration of this mystery, "You cannot understand the blowing of the wind, but you obey its laws and thus harness its force; so also with the Spirit. Obey the law of the wind, and it will fill your sails and carry you onward. Obey the law of the Spirit and you will know the new birth. Do not postpone relationship with this law simply because you cannot fathom its mystery intellectually."

> The wind blows where it wills; you hear the sound of it, but you do not know where it comes from, or where it is going. So with everyone who is born from spirit. *John 3:8*

The Spirit of God is free and always acts freely. His movements cannot be anticipated by any human calculations. One cannot tell when grace is coming or how it will work on the soul; whether it will come as a result of a disgust with sin, or of a yearning for a higher goodness. The voice of the Spirit is within the soul; the peace which It brings, the light which It sheds, and the strength which It gives, are unmistakably there. The regeneration of man is not directly discernible to the human eye.

Though Nicodemus was a sophisticated scholar, he was, nevertheless, perplexed by the sublimity of the doctrine that he was hearing from the One Whom he called Master. His interest as a Pharisee had been not in personal holiness, but in the glory of an earthly kingdom. He now asked the question:

> How is this possible? *John 3:9*

Nicodemus saw that the Divine life in man is not just a question of *being*; it also involves the problem of *becoming*, through a power that is not in man but only in God Himself.

Our Lord explained that His teaching was something that no mere human could ever have thought out. There was, therefore, some excuse for the ignorance of the Pharisee. After all, no man had ever gone up to heaven to learn the heavenly secrets and had then returned to earth to make them known. The only one who could know them was He Who had descended from heaven, He Who as God had become man, and was now speaking to Nicodemus. Our Lord for the first time referred to Himself as the Son of Man. At the same time, He was implying that He was something more than that; He was also the only-begotten Divine Son of the Heavenly Father. He was, in fact, affirming His Divine and human natures.

> No one ever went up into heaven except the one who came down from heaven, the Son of Man whose home is in heaven. *John 3:13*

This was not the only time that Our Lord spoke of His reascension into heaven or of the fact that He had come down from heaven. To one of His Apostles He said:

> In truth, in very truth I tell you all, you shall see heaven wide open, and God's angels ascending and descending upon the Son of Man.
>
> *John* 1:51

> I have come down from heaven, not to do my own will, but the will of him who sent me. *John* 6:38

> He who comes from above is above all others; he who is from the earth belongs to the earth and uses earthly speech. He who comes from heaven bears witness to what he has seen and heard, yet no one accepts his witness. *John* 3:31

> They said, Surely this is Jesus son of Joseph; we know his father and mother. How can he now say, I have come down from heaven?
>
> *John* 6:42

> What if you see the Son of Man ascending to the place where he was before? *John* 6:63

Our Lord never spoke of His Heavenly, or Risen Glory without bringing in the ignominy of the Cross. Sometimes He spoke of the glory first as He was doing now with Nicodemus, but the Crucifixion had to be its condition. Our Lord lived both a heavenly life and an earthly life; a heavenly life as the Son of God, and earthly life as the Son of Man. While continuing to be one with His Father in Heaven, He gave Himself up for men on earth. To Nicodemus, He affirmed that the condition on which man's salvation depended would be His own Passion and death. He made this clear by referring to the most famous foreshadowing of the Cross in the Old Testament.

> This Son of Man must be lifted up as the serpent was lifted up by Moses in the wilderness, so that everyone who has faith in him may in him possess eternal life. *John* 3:14–15

The Book of Numbers relates that when the people murmured rebelliously against God, they were punished with a plague of fiery serpents, so that many lost their lives. When they repented, Moses was told by God to make a brazen serpent and set it up for a sign, and all those bitten by the serpents who looked upon that sign would be healed. Our Blessed Lord was now declaring that He was to be lifted up, as the serpent had been lifted up. As the brass serpent had the appearance of a serpent and yet lacked its venom, so too, when He would be lifted up upon the bars of the Cross, He would have the appearance of a sinner and yet be without sin. As all who looked upon the brass serpent had been healed of the bite of the serpent, so all who looked upon Him with love and faith would be healed of the bite of the serpent of evil.

It was not enough that the Son of God should come down from the heavens and appear as the Son of Man, for then He would have been only a great teacher and a great example, but not a Redeemer. It was more important for Him to fulfill the purpose of the coming, to redeem man from sin while in the likeness of human flesh. Teachers change men by their lives; our Blessed Lord would change men by His death. The poison of hate, sensuality, and envy which is in the hearts of men could not be healed simply by wise exhortations and social reforms. The wages of sin is death, and therefore it was to be by death that sin would be atoned for. As in the ancient sacrifices the fire symbolically burned up the imputed sin along with the victim, so on the Cross the world's sin would be put away in Christ's sufferings, for He would be upright as a priest and prostrate as a victim.

The two greatest banners that were ever unfurled were the uplifted serpent and the uplifted Savior. And yet there was an infinite difference between them. The theater of one was the desert, and the audience was a few thousand Israelites; the theater of the other was the universe and the audience, the whole of mankind. From the one came a bodily healing, soon to be undone again by death; from the other flowed soul-healing, unto life everlasting. And yet one was the prefiguration of the other.

But though He came to die, He insisted that it would be voluntary, and not because He would be too weak to defend Himself from His enemies. The only cause for His death would be love; as He told Nicodemus:

> God loved the world so much that he gave his only Son, that every-
> one who has faith in him may not die but have eternal life.
>
> *John 3:16*

On this night, when an old man came to see the Divine Master Who had startled the world with His miracles, Our Lord told the story of His life. It was a life that began not in Bethlehem, but existed from all eternity in the Godhead. He Who is the Son of God became the Son of Man because the Father sent Him on a mission of redeeming man through love.

If there is anything that every good teacher wants, it is a long life in which to make his teaching known, and to gain wisdom and experience. Death is always a tragedy to a great teacher. When Socrates was given the hemlock juice, his message was cut off once and for all. Death was a stumbling block to Buddha and his teaching of the eightfold way. The last breath of Lao-tze rang down the curtain on his doctrine concerning the *Tao* or "doing nothing," as against aggressive self-determination. Socrates had taught that sin was due to ignorance and that, therefore, knowledge would make a good and perfect world. The Eastern teachers were concerned about man being caught up in some great wheel of fate. Hence the recommendation of Buddha that men be taught to crush their desires and thus find peace. When Buddha died at eighty, he pointed not to himself but to the law he had given. Confucius' death stopped his moralizings about how to perfect a State by means of kindly reciprocal relations between prince and subject, father and son, brothers, husband and wife, friend and friend.

Our Blessed Lord in His talk with Nicodemus proclaimed Himself the Light of the World. But the most astounding part of His teaching was that He said no one would understand His teaching while He was alive and that His Death and Resurrection would be essential to understanding it. No other teacher in the world ever said that it would take a violent death to clarify his teachings. Here was a Teacher Who made His teachings so secondary that He could say that the only way that He would ever draw men to Himself would be *not by His doctrine, not by what He said, but by His Crucifixion.*

> When you have lifted up the Son of Man you will know that I am what I am. *John 8:28*

He did not say that it would even be His teaching that they would understand; it would rather be His Personality that they would grasp. Only then would they know, after they had put Him to death, that He spoke the Truth. His death, then, instead of being the last of a series of failures, would be a glorious success, the climax of His mission on earth.

Hence, the great difference in the statues and pictures of Buddha and Christ. Buddha is always seated, eyes closed, hands folded across a fat body. Christ is never seated; He is always lifted up and enthroned. His person and His death are the heart and soul of His lesson. The Cross, and all it implies, is once again central in His life.

8. *Savior of the World*

After Our Lord had cleansed the temple, wrought miracles in Jerusalem, and told Nicodemus that He had come to die for those who were bitten by the serpent of sin, He left Jerusalem, which had rejected Him, and went into "Galilee of the Gentiles." The usual route between Judea in the south and Galilee in the north was through Perea. The Jews took this route to avoid passing through the land of the Samaritans. But Our Lord did not take it. He had declared that the temple was for all nations; He was called to minister to all races and peoples.

> He had to pass through Samaria. *John 4:4*

The Gospel speaks of His death and Redemption as a "must." What had happened in Samaria was related to that other—that He should offer His life vicariously for mankind.

Separating the two provinces of Judea and Galilee was a strip of country inhabited by a mongrel semi-alien race, the Samaritans. Between them and the Jews there was a long-standing feud. The Samaritans were a hybrid race, formed centuries before, when the Israelites were brought into bondage. The Assyrians sent some of their own people among them to mix with them, thus creating a new race. The first colonists of Samaria brought idolatry with them, but later on, there was an introduction of a spurious Judaism. The Samaritans accepted the five books of Moses and some of the prophecies; but all other historical books were rejected because these recounted the story of the Jews whom they despised. Their worship was performed in a temple on Mount Garizim.

No Jew would ever pronounce the word "Samaritan," so hateful was it. Hence, when the lawyer was asked who was the neighbor, he used a circumlocution. On the other hand, the most offensive term the Jews could apply to anyone was to call him a "Samaritan," as they once called Our Lord, Who ignored the charge. But later on, in the story of the Good Samaritan, Jesus represented Himself as a "certain Samaritan," indicating the humiliation and the scorn heaped upon Him on His coming to earth.

Our Blessed Lord did not avoid these people. The Maker of all worlds must needs pass through the abode of "foreign" humanity on

His way to the heavenly throne. A Sovereign Love laid this necessity upon Him. The time was noon, and Our Blessed Lord was "wearied with His journey"; so He sat down at Jacob's well. But along with this weakness, there appeared His Omniscience, and He read the heart of a woman. Christ was weary in His work, not of it. Two of the greatest converts that Our Blessed Lord ever made, the Syro-Phoenician woman and this woman, were both made when He was tired. When He seemed most unfit to do His Father's business, He did it most effectively. St. Paul was taken from work to prison; but he converted some of his jailers and wrote his Epistles. The willing heart always creates its own opportunities.

> A Samaritan woman came to draw water. *John* 4:7

It was rather unusual for a woman in the East to come in the heat of day in order to draw water. The reason for this unusual conduct is to be discovered a little later. Nothing in an earthly sense was more accidental than a woman carrying a waterpot to a well; and yet, it was one of those ordinary everyday providences of God, which help unravel the riddle of a soul. The great benefit which lay in ambush for her, she knew not. He was there first. As Isaiah wrote:

> I was there to be sought by a people who did not ask,
> to be found by men who did not seek me. *Isaiah* 65:1

Our Lord found Zaccheus; not Zaccheus Him; Paul too, was found when he was not searching for his Lord. The drawing power of Divinity the Master emphasized later:

> No man can come to me unless he is drawn by the Father who sent me. *John* 6:44

As she filled her pitcher, she must have already sought to avoid Our Blessed Lord, for she recognized in Him the features of Jewish physiognomy with which the Samaritans had nothing in common. But to her surprise, the Stranger beside the well addressed her with a request,

> Give me a drink. *John* 4:7

Whenever Our Lord wished to do a favor, He always began by asking for one. He did not begin with a reproof, but with a request. His first was "Give!" There must always be an emptying of the human before there can be a filling with the Divine, as the Divine emptied Himself to fill the human. The water, a subject uppermost in her thoughts, became the common denominator between the Sinless and a sinner.

> What! You, a Jew, ask a drink of me, a Samaritan woman? *John* 4:9

In this long conversation between the two, there was a progression of spiritual development which finally ended in her coming to the knowledge of Christ, the Savior. Imperfect understanding at first sneered at Him as a member of a certain race or people. At first, He was only "a Jew." The answer of Our Lord implied that He actually was not the receiver but the giver. She had erred in thinking that it was He who needed her help, when in reality it was she that needed him.

> If only you knew what God gives, and who it is that is asking you for a drink, you would have asked him and he would have given you living water. *John 4:10,11*

He set forth Himself under the image of water, as a little later on, when men would ask for bread that nourishes, He would set forth Himself under the appearance of bread. Though He spoke of Himself as the Gift of God, the woman saw in Him only a weary travel-stained man of another race. Her eye could not penetrate beneath the outward form to the Divine nature enshrined within. She saw the Jew, but not the Son of God; the weary man, but not the rest of weary souls; the thirsty pilgrim, but not the One Who could quench the world's thirst. The penalty of those who live too close to the flesh is never to understand the spiritual. But she grows in respect for Him as she adds:

> You have no bucket and this well is deep. How can you give me living water? Are you a greater man than Jacob our ancestor, who gave us the well, and drank from it himself, he and his sons, and his cattle too? *John 4:11,12*

He was now called not a "Jew" but a "man." The woman suspected, though she could not quite understand His words, that He, being a Jew, was casting some aspersions upon the traditions of her people. He answered that He was greater than Jacob:

> Everyone who drinks this water will be thirsty again, but whoever drinks the water that I shall give him will never suffer thirst any more. The water that I shall give him will be an inner spring always welling up for eternal life. *John 4:13,14*

Here was His philosophy of life. All the human satisfactions of the cravings of body and soul have one defect; they do not satisfy forever. They only serve to deaden the present want; but they never extinguish it. The want always revives again. The waters the world gives fall back to earth again; but the water of life which He gives is a supernatural impulse, and pushes onward even to heaven itself.

Our Blessed Lord did not attempt to dislodge the world's broken cisterns without offering something better. He did not condemn the earthly streams nor forbid them; He merely said that if she restricted herself to the wells of human happiness, she would never be completely satisfied.

She could not understand grace or heavenly power under the analogy of water for the body; for she had long slaked her thirst at the muddiest pools of sensual gratification. She continues:

> Sir, give me that water, and then I shall not be thirsty, nor have to come all this way to draw. *John 4:15*

He was no longer "Jew" or "man," but "Sir." Confusion was still in her mind, for she imagined that His promise would exempt her from the toil of coming to the well. Our Lord spoke from the top of spiritual apprehension; the woman, from the depths of sensuous knowledge. The windows of her soul had become so dirty with sin that she could not see spiritual significance in the material universe.

Our Blessed Lord, seeing that she failed to comprehend the spiritual lesson, now brought home to her why she did not understand His meaning: her life was immoral. He got into her conscience with rather an abrupt turn of conversation:

> Go home, call your husband and come back. *John 4:16*

He intended to bring out her sense of shame and sin. "Go . . . , come. . . . Go and face the truth of the life you live; *come* and receive the waters of life." The woman answered:

> I have no husband. *John 4:17*

This was an honest and truthful confession as far as it went; but it did not go far enough. She had asked for living water, but she did not yet know that the well must first be dug. In the depth of her spirit there was a potency for His gift; but the waters of grace could not flow because of the hard rocks of sin, the many layers of transgression, the habits formidable as clay, and the multiple deposits of carnal thoughts. All these had to be dug before she could have the living water. Sin had to be confessed before salvation could be obtained. Conscience must be aroused. With master skill Our Lord was exposing her whole wanton career, and like a lightning flash, fastening a sense of guilt upon her conscience.

Our Lord answered:

> You are right in saying that you have no husband. *John 4:18*

He commended the woman's honest confession. An unskillful physician of souls would probably have rebuked her sharply for concealing the truth. Our Lord on the contrary said, "True enough." But then He continued:

> You have had five husbands, the man with whom you are now living is not your husband; you told me the truth there. *John 4:18*

The man with whom she was living was not a husband; she had fallen so deep into degradation that she did not go through the legal sanction of marriage which in other times she would have done.

The woman felt Our Lord was "meddling." He was probing into her morals and behavior and implying that she could not receive His gift because of the way she lived. She then did what millions of people have done ever since when religion demands a reformation in their conduct: *she changed the subject*. She was willing to make religion a matter of discussion, but she did not want to make it a matter of decision. Our Blessed Lord had brought the discussion around to the moral order, namely, the way she had conducted herself personally before God and her conscience. To avoid the moral problem, she first tried flattery, then introduced a speculative problem:

> Sir, I can see that you are a prophet. *John 4:19*

She, who at first called Him "Jew," then "man," then "Sir," now called Him a "Prophet." She dropped the subject of religion down to the purely intellectual plane, in order that it might not affect her morally. And she added:

> Our fathers worshiped on this mountain, but you Jews say that the temple where God should be worshipped is in Jerusalem. *John 4:20*

The woman made a wild attempt to get off the hook. She tried to pull a red herring across the road by bringing up the old religious squabble. The Jews worshiped in Jerusalem; the Samaritans on Mount Garizim. She sought to turn aside the arrow directed to her conscience by introducing a speculative subject. This would distract her soul from its evil.

But He answered:

> Believe me, the time is coming when you will worship the Father neither on this mountain, nor in Jerusalem. You Samaritans worship without knowing what you worship, while we worship what we know. It is from the Jews that salvation comes. But the time approaches, indeed it is already here, when those who are real worshippers will worship the Father in spirit and in truth. *John 4:21–24*

He was telling her that the little local disputes would vanish very soon. The controversy between Jerusalem and Samaria would be superseded; for, as Simeon had foretold, He would be a Light to the Gentiles. Our Lord did, however, vindicate the Jews by saying:

> It is from the Jews that salvation comes. *John* 4:22

Indeed the Messiah, the Son of God and Savior, would rise from among them and not from the Samaritans. "Salvation" is equivalent to the Savior, for Simeon, while holding the Babe, had declared that his eyes had seen "Salvation." Israel was the channel through which the salvation of God would be conveyed to the world. It was the tree which had been watered for centuries, and which had now brought forth the consummate flower: the Messiah and Savior.

The words of Our Lord carried the poor sinner into deeper waters than she could conquer, and transported her into a realm of truth too great for her understanding. But one thing that He said, about an hour coming when there would be true worship of the Father, she dimly grasped, for the Samaritans themselves had some belief in the Messiah. She answered:

> I know that Messiah (that is Christ) is coming. When he comes, he will tell us everything. *John* 4:25

She did not yet give Him the title of "Messiah," but she would make the acknowledgment in a moment. The Samaritans had enough of the Old Testament to know that God would send His Anointed One; but in their perverted religion, He was merely a prophet, just as He was to the Jews, in their perverted understanding, a political king. But her statement was tantamount to saying that she awaited the One promised by God. In answer to her feeble belief, Our Lord answered:

> I am he, I who am speaking to you now. *John* 4:26

It was settled now; it was no longer Jerusalem or Mount Garizim in which worship must be centered, but in Christ Himself.

At this moment the disciples returned from the city, whereupon the woman left the well. But in her excitement she left her water bucket. Any time would do for water. Acting impulsively, she hastened into the city to tell the men:

> Come and see a man who has told me everything I ever did. Could this be the Messiah? *John* 4:29

Here was a new title given to Our Lord. Now He was the "Christ." She began with a pressing invitation. She did not say that He had told her all the things that pertained to the worship of God; but all the things that she had done, even her own faults which she had shunned. The sun no sooner rises than it shines; the fire is no sooner kindled than it burns; so grace acts as soon as the soul cooperates. She became one of the first home missionaries in the history of Christianity.

She told what one would have expected her to withhold. She came to draw water, and when she found the True Well, she left behind her waterpot, as the Apostles had abandoned their nets.

Our Lord, too, on this occasion forgot His hunger, as the Apostles pressed Him to eat, for He told them He had a meat whereof they knew not.

It is worth noting that the Samaritan woman told the men of her meeting with Christ. It may well have been that the women in the city would not allow her to associate with them. That is why she came to the well at noon; the other women came in the cool of the morning or in the evening. Apparently because the women had shunned her, she gave her first message to the men. And evidently she worked effectively in the village; for the Gospel tells us:

> Many Samaritans of that town came to believe in him because of the woman's testimony: He told me everything I ever did. *John* 4:39

The woman did not say, "You must believe what I say," rather she told them, "Come and see for yourselves." Make an investigation; shake off prejudice. Her earnest manner convinced the men. A few hours later, she ran out to the well again, the men trailing behind her; but this time for a different purpose—the pursuit of salvation.

> So when these Samaritans had come to him they pressed him to stay with them; and he stayed there two days. Many more became believers because of what they heard from his own lips. *John* 4:40,41

After seeing Our Lord, they said to the woman:

> It is no longer because of what you said that we believe, for we have heard him ourselves; and we know that this is in truth the Saviour of the world. *John* 4:42

This was the first time the phrase "Savior of the world" was used to describe Our Lord. Her spiritual growth was now complete. At first Christ was to her a "Jew," then a "man," then "Sir," then a "Prophet," then "the Messiah," and at last the "Savior of the world" and "Redeemer from sin." Conversion might be rapid in some, but it was not complete in this woman until she saw that Our Lord came to save not the just, but sinners. No physical miracle was performed; no healing, nor opening of blind eyes. The wonder wrought was in a sinful soul. Out of release from sin came the most glorious title. The Cross was not mentioned, but the One Who hung upon it was clearly denominated: "Savior of the world." The Cross was everywhere in His life long before He mounted it.

In contrast to this woman were the Pharisees. They denied sin, but they had all the effects of sin: terror, anguish, fear, unhappiness, and emptiness; by denying the cause, they made the cure impossible. If the starving deny famine, then who shall be the bearer of bread? If the sinners deny sin and guilt, then who can be their Savior? Of those conceited, proud Pharisees, Our Lord said:

It is not the healthy that need a doctor, but the sick. *Luke* 5:31

Two classes of people make up the world: those who have found God, and those who are looking for Him—thirsting, hungering, seeking! And the great sinners come closer to Him than the proud intellectuals! Pride swells and inflates the ego; gross sinners are depressed, deflated and empty. They, therefore, have room for God. God prefers a loving sinner to a loveless "saint." Love can be trained; pride cannot. The man who thinks that he knows will rarely find truth; the man who knows he is a miserable, unhappy sinner, like the woman at the well, is closer to peace, joy and salvation than he knows.

Millions in this world have *white* grace in their souls; they feel the Divine Presence. Millions of others have *black* grace; they feel not God's Presence, but His *absence*. The Samaritan woman who first felt His absence, came to feel His Presence. But if she had never sinned, she never could have called Christ "Savior." He had come not with a book in His hand only to read to those who wanted to be taught; He did more: He came with Blood in His Body to pour it out in full acquittal of a debt man could never pay.

9. The First Public Announcement of His Death

The story of each man is told in two brief items: born—such a date; died—such a date. In the life of only One of all who have lived on this earth, death was first in the sense that dying was the reason for His coming. As Browning put it:

> I think this is the authentic sign and seal
>   of Godship; that it ever waxes glad,
> And more glad, until gladness blossoms, bursts
>   Into a rage to suffer for mankind.

Though He came to die, it was not for the sake of dying. Hence, whenever there is suffering, death, or even a humiliation mentioned, there is always the counterpoint of glory, victory or exaltation. Divinity shines forth whenever His human nature is humbled. This intrinsic relationship runs all through His life. If He was born of a humble maid in a stable, there were angels of heaven to announce His glory; if He lowered Himself to companionship with an ox and an ass in a manger, there was a shining star to lead Gentiles to Him as King; if He was hungry and tempted in the wilderness, there were angels to minister unto Him; if His Blood poured forth in Gethsemane it was because His Heavenly Father reached Him a cup; if He was arrested because His Hour had come, there were twelve legions of angels to liberate Him if He did not will to offer His life for men; if He humbled Himself as a sinner to receive the baptism of John, there was a Voice from Heaven to proclaim the glory of the Eternal Son Who needed no purification; if there were townspeople to reject Him and throw Him over a cliff, there was the Divine power to walk through the midst of them unharmed; if He was nailed to a Cross, there was a sun to hide its face in shame and an earth to quake in rebellion against what creatures did to its Creator; if He was laid in a tomb, there were angels to herald His Resurrection.

What makes the life of Christ unique is that He conditioned the establishment of His reign on earth and in heaven, on His suffering and death. His victory over evil, by absorbing the worst that evil could do, had for Him a representative and vicarious character. Quoting Isaiah, He said that He came to be "counted among the malefactors."

But His victory over evil, through His Cross, would pass on to men who would reproduce the experience of cross-bearing in their lives.

The Cross was everywhere in His Life. He could not speak too openly about it, for when He did, even His closest friends, the Apostles, did not grasp its meaning. The first public announcement that He came to die was occasioned by the Pharisees as they discussed with Him the subject of fasting. The Pharisees had complained to the disciples that Our Lord ate and drank in very questionable company. Joining themselves for the moment with the fasting practices of John the Baptist, they complained that Our Lord and His disciples were eating while John's disciples were fasting. The devout person in Israel fasted twice a week, namely, on Mondays and Fridays, which were thought to be the days when Moses went up to Sinai. Our Blessed Lord apparently was not fasting with His disciples in the same way that John the Baptist fasted. This gave occasion later on for the Pharisees to complain that He was a glutton and a winebibber. The answer Our Blessed Lord gave to their question why His disciples did not fast, was much more profound than seems at first sight.

> Can you expect the bridegroom's friends to fast while the bridegroom is with them? As long as they have the bridegroom with them, there can be no fasting. *Mark 2:19*

He calls Himself "the Bridegroom." The Pharisees, who knew the Old Testament well, were familiar with that idea. The relation between God and Israel was always that of Bridegroom and Bride. Over seven centuries before, the prophet Hosea heard God speak to Israel:

> I will betroth you to myself for ever, betroth you in lawful wedlock with unfailing devotion and love; I will betroth you to myself to have and to hold, and you shall know the Lord. *Hosea 2:19*

The prophecy of Isaiah among others also spoke of the relation between God and Israel in the terms of the Bridegroom and the Bride:

> Your husband is your maker, whose name is the Lord of Hosts;
>   your ransomer is the Holy One of Israel
> who is called God of all the earth. *Isaiah 54:5*

His listeners knew what He was saying, namely, that He was God; He was the Lord to Whom Israel was espoused. He stepped into the place of the God of the Old Testament, claiming the same rights and privileges. Our Lord made other references to Himself as Bridegroom in the parable of the banquet for the king's son, and in the parable of the ten virgins where the Bridegroom who cometh was Himself. John the Baptist earlier, when he saw Our Lord, also recognized Christ under that Old Testament figure of the Bridegroom, as he said:

> I am not the Messiah; I have been sent as his forerunner. It is the bridegroom to whom the bride belongs. The bridegroom's friend, who stands by and listens to him, is overjoyed at hearing the bridegroom's voice. This joy, this perfect joy, is now mine. *John* 3:29

John was only the friend of the Bridegroom, or the "best man," at the marriage, or the forerunner of the Messiah. But Christ Himself was the Bridegroom, because by taking a human nature in Bethlehem without ever being a human person, He potentially espoused all humanity. Until the hour when sin would be vanquished and the Bridegroom would take as His Bride regenerated humanity, or the Church, John would prepare for the nuptials. Paul would later on describe himself as playing a role like John the Baptist's, except that his would be in relation to the Church of Corinth:

> I betrothed you to Christ, thinking to present you as a chaste virgin to her true and only husband. *II Corinthians* 11:2

The old Israel that was the Bride would become the new Israel, or the Church, and at the end of time, the glorious nuptials between the Bridegroom and the Bride would be celebrated in heaven:

> For the wedding-day of the Lamb has come! His bride has made herself ready, and for her dress she has been given fine linen, clean and shining. *Apocalypse* 19:7
> (Now the fine linen signifies the righteous deeds of God's people.)

The answer to the question of the Pharisees was that the disciples of Our Lord did not fast because they were not sad; in fact, they were happy, because God was walking the earth with them. While He was with them, there could be only joy. But, it would not always be thus on earth. He came to die. Once again, there is that inseparable connection between the Cross and glory. He then proceeded to speak of His death.

> But the time will come when the bridegroom will be taken away from them, and on that day they will fast. *Mark* 2:20

The Bridegroom will be crucified; He will go to war against the forces of evil and then will claim His Bride. From the joy of the feast they would pass to the sorrowful gloom of the fast when the Bridegroom would be smitten.

This was the first public announcement of His death. His primary purpose in answering the Pharisees was not to emphasize the practice of fasting, but to announce the removal of the Bridegroom. He implied furthermore that His death would be no stroke of fate, but an essential part of His mission. That moment when Our Blessed Lord was speaking of the joy of a marriage feast, He looked down into the abyss of His Cross and saw Himself hanging there. The shadow of the Cross was never off Him, even when He rejoiced as a Bridegroom. Good Friday and Easter were here again united, but in reverse. It was from joy that He looked to the Cross in His first announcement of Himself as the Bridegroom.

10. The Choosing of the Twelve

Our Lord's great command was: "Follow Me!" By calling others to Himself, He introduced the idea that man should have charge over man. It was a prolongation of the principle of His Incarnation: He Who is God would teach and redeem and sanctify through the human nature which He had taken from Mary. But He would work also through other human natures, starting with those first twelve whom He called to be His followers. It was not to be the angels who would administer to men: the government of the Father would be placed in the hands of human beings. Such is the meaning of His apostolic call to the twelve.

One is struck at once by the gigantic aim he proposed for His followers, namely, the moral conquest of the whole world; they were to be the "light of the world," the "salt of the earth," and the "city that cannot be hid." He bade rather insignificant men to take an almost cosmic view of their mission, for on them would He build His Kingdom. These chosen lights were to cast their rays over the rest of humanity, in all nations.

In his essay *The Twelve Men*, dealing with the British jury system, G. K. Chesterton wrote, "Whenever our civilization wants a library to be catalogued, or a solar system discovered, or any other trifle of this kind, it uses up its specialists. But when it wishes anything done which is really serious, it collects twelve of the ordinary men standing around. The same thing was done, if I remember right, by the Founder of Christianity."

It is evident that from the beginning, Our Blessed Lord intended to prolong His teaching, and His reign and His very life "unto the consummation of the world"; but in order to do this He had to call to Himself a body of men to whom He would communicate certain powers that He had brought with Him to earth. This body would not be a social body such as a club, united only for the sake of pleasure and convenience; nor would it be a political body, held together by common material interests; it would be truly spiritual, the cement of which would be charity and love and the possession of His Spirit. If the society or Mystical Body Our Lord wanted to found was to have continuity, it would need a head and members. If it was a vineyard, as He declared in one of His parables, it would need laborers; if it was a net, it would need fishermen; if it was a field, it would need sowers and reapers; if it was a herd, or a flock, it would need shepherds.

> During this time he went out one day into the hills to pray, and spent the night in prayer to God. When day broke he called his disciples to him, and from among them he chose twelve and named them Apostles: Simon, to whom he gave the name of Peter, and Andrew his brother, James and John, Philip and Bartholomew, Matthew and Thomas, James son of Alphaeus, and Simon who was called the Zealot, Judas son of James, and Judas Iscariot who turned traitor.
>
> *Luke 6:12*

The night before the choice He spent praying on the mountainside that they who were in the heart of the Father would also be in His own. When morning broke, He came down to where His disciples were gathered and, man by man, called those whom He had chosen. Of Peter the most is known. Peter is mentioned 195 times; the rest of the Apostles only 130 times. The one mentioned next in frequency to Peter is John, to whom there are 29 references. Peter's original name was Simon, but it was changed by Our Blessed Lord to Cephas. When he was brought to Our Blessed Lord:

> He brought Simon to Jesus, who looked at him and said, You are Simon son of John. You shall be called Cephas (that is, Peter, the Rock). *John 1:42*

The word Cephas meant "rock"; we do not get the full flavor of it in English, because Peter, the proper name, is not the same as our word "rock." The words were identical in the Aramaic which Our Blessed Lord spoke, just as they are in French, where the proper name Pierre is the same as *pierre*, or rock. In Scripture, whenever God changed the name of a man, it was to raise him to a higher dignity and role in the community to which he belonged. Our Lord might have been saying to Peter, "you are impulsive and fickle and unreliable, but one day all this will be changed; you will be called by a name that no one would dare give you now—Rock Man." Whenever he is called "Simon" in the Gospels, it is a reminder of the Apostle's uninspired and unregenerate humanity; for example, when he was sleeping in the garden, Our Blessed Lord addressed him:

> Asleep, Simon? *Mark 14:37*

Peter had by nature great qualities of leadership. For example, after the Resurrection when he said, "I go a fishing," the other Apostles followed suit. His moral courage was manifested when he left his business and his home for the Master; that same courage, expressed impetuously, made him smite off the ear of Malchus when the leaders came to arrest Our Lord. He was boastful too, for he swore that though others would betray the Master, he would not. He had a deep sense of sin, and he begged the Lord to depart from him because of his unworthiness. His very faults endear him. He was deeply attached to his Divine Master. When other disciples left, he maintained there was no one else to whom they could go. He had courage, for he left his wife and his business to follow Our Lord. To the credit of all mothers-in-law, it must be said that Peter showed no regret when Our Lord cured her of a serious illness. He was impulsive to an extreme degree, guided more by feeling than by reason. He wanted to walk on the waters and, given the power, became frightened and screamed in fear—he a man of the sea. He was an emphatic man, swinging swords, cursing, protesting against the Savior washing his feet; though named head of the Church, he had none of the ambition of James and John. But through the power of his Divine Master this impetuous man, as fluid as water, was turned into the rock on which Christ built His Church. The Divine Savior constantly linked Himself verbally with His Heavenly Father; but the only human being He ever united with Himself and spoke of Himself and that one as "we," was Peter. From that day on, Peter and his successors have always used "we" to indicate the unity between the invisible Head of the Church and its visible head. But this same Peter, who is always tempting Our Lord from the Cross, proves to be a rock of fidelity, for later on in his life the constant theme of his letters was the Cross of Christ.

> It gives you a share in Christ's suffering, and that is cause for joy; and when his glory is revealed, your joy will be triumphant. *I Peter 4:13*

Andrew, the brother of Peter, is referred to eight times in the New Testament. After being called from his nets and his boats to be a "fisher of men" along with his brother Peter, Andrew is seen next on the occasion of the feeding of the five thousand, telling Our Lord that there was a boy present with five loaves and two fishes. Toward the end of the public ministry, Andrew is met with again when some Gentiles, probably Greeks, came to Philip asking to see Our Lord. Philip then consulted Andrew and they both came to the Lord. At the very first meeting of Andrew and Our Blessed Lord, Jesus asked him:

> What are you looking for? *John 1:38*

Andrew had been a friend of John the Baptist. When he met Our Lord, to whom John the Baptist had pointed, he immediately went and told Peter that he had found the Messiah. Andrew is always spoken of as Simon Peter's brother. He was an "introducer" because he brought his brother Peter to Our Lord; he introduced the lad with the barley loaves and fishes to Our Lord; and finally with Philip, came to introduce the Greeks to Our Lord. When it is a question of dispensing some benefits of the Lord or bringing others to the Lord, Philip and Andrew are mentioned together. Andrew was rather silent, being overshadowed by his brother Peter, but apparently he was never jealous. There was room for envy when Peter, James, and John were selected on three occasions for intimacy with the Divine Master, but he accepted his humble place; sufficient it was to him to have found the Christ.

Like Peter and Andrew, James and John were brothers and fishermen. They worked together for their father Zebedee. Their mother Salome was apparently not lacking in ambition; for it was she who, one day, thinking that the Kingdom that Our Blessed Lord had come to establish would be without a Cross, asked that her two sons be picked to sit at the left and right side of Our Lord in His Kingdom. To her credit, however, it must be added that we find her again on Calvary, at the foot of the Cross. Our Blessed Lord gave her sons a nickname—Boanerges or "sons of thunder." This happened when the Samaritans refused to receive Our Blessed Lord because He had set His Face towards Jerusalem and His death. The two Apostles, discovering this, manifested their intolerance to Our Lord:

> Lord, may we call down fire from heaven to burn them up? But he turned and rebuked them, and they went on to another village.
>
> *Luke 9:54–56*

The two "sons of thunder" did not fail to drink deeply of the chalice of suffering. John was later plunged in boiling oil, which he survived only through a miracle. James was the first of all of the Apostles to suffer martyrdom for Christ. John described himself as "the disciple whom Jesus loved," and to him was accorded the guardianship of the mother of Our Lord after the Crucifixion. John was known to the High Priest probably because of his cultural refinement which justified his name, which in the original Hebrew means "favored of God." His Gospel revealed him truly as an eagle who soared to heaven to understand the mysteries of the Word. No one better understood the heart of Christ; no one penetrated more deeply into the significance of His words. He too was the only one of the Apostles to be found at the foot of Christ; he is the one who tells us that "Jesus wept," and he gives the New Testament definition of God as "Love." James his brother, who is called "the Greater" belonged, together with Peter and John, to that "special committee" which witnessed the

Transfiguration, the raising of the daughter of Jairus from the dead, and the agony of Gethsemane.

The Apostle Philip came from Bethsaida and was a fellow townsman of Andrew and Peter. Philip was the curious enquirer; and his enquiry was crowned by the joy of discovery when he found Christ.

> Philip went to find Nathanael, and told him, We have met the man spoken of by Moses in the Law, and by the prophets: it is Jesus son of Joseph, from Nazareth. Nazareth! Nathanael exclaimed; can anything good come from Nazareth? Philip said, Come and see. *John* 1:45,46

Philip declined all controversy with a man who was so prejudiced as to believe that a prophet could not come out of a despised village. Philip is not met again until the multiplication of the loaves and the fishes, and again he was enquiring:

> Twenty pounds would not buy enough bread for every one of them to have a little. *John* 6:7

Philip made a last enquiry on the night of the Last Supper, when he asked Our Lord to show him the Father.

Philip brought Bartholomew, or Nathanael as he was also called, to Our Blessed Lord. As soon as He saw him, Our Divine Savior read his soul and described him as follows:

> Here is an Israelite worthy of the name; there is nothing false in him. Nathanael asked him, How do you come to know me? Jesus replied, I saw you under the fig-tree before Philip spoke to you. *John* 1:47,48

Then Nathanael answered Him:

> Rabbi, you are the Son of God; you are king of Israel. Jesus answered, Is this the ground of your faith, that I told you I saw you under the fig-tree? You shall see greater things than that. Then he added, In truth, in very truth I tell you all, you shall see heaven wide open, and God's angels ascending and descending upon the Son of Man.
>
> *John* 1:49–51

When Our Lord told him that He had seen him under a fig tree, Bartholomew was willing immediately to make the affirmation that Christ was the Son of God. His first contact with Our Lord had already lighted the lamp of faith within him, but Our Lord quickly assured him that there would be greater experiences in store; in particular, the great vision which had come to Jacob would be realized in Him.

Our Lord said that Nathanael belonged to the true Israel. Israel was the name given to Jacob. He, however, was very shrewd, and full of guile. Nathanael is characterized as a true Israelite, or one without guile. A sudden transition from the plural to the singular happens when Our Lord says: "You will see heaven opening"; Jacob had seen the heavens opened and angels ascending and descending on the ladder, bringing the things of man to God and the things of God to men. Jesus was now telling Nathanael that he would see even greater things. The implication was that He Himself would henceforth be the Mediator between heaven and earth, God and man; in Him, all the traffic between time and eternity would meet as at a crossroad.

This prophecy of Our Lord to Bartholomew shows that the incarnation of the Son of God would be the basis of communion between man and God. Nathanael had called Him the "Son of God"; Our Lord called Himself the "Son of Man": "Son of God" because He is eternally Divine; "Son of Man" because He is related humbly to all humanity. This title, used in close relationship with another title that had been given to Our Lord, namely, the "King of Israel," still carried with it a Messianic meaning; but it took it out of the limited context of one people and one race, into the sphere of universal humanity.

Of Matthew or Levi, the publican, there is a record of his vocation and how he responded to it. The great and imperishable glory of Matthew is his Gospel. Matthew was a publican under the government of Herod, a vassal of Rome. A publican was one who sold out his own people and collected taxes for the invader, retaining for himself a fairly large percentage. Very understandably, because a publican was a kind of Quisling, he was held in contempt by his fellow men; yet he knew at the same time that he had the power and legal authority of the Roman government behind him. The particular place where we first meet Matthew is at the head of the lake, near Capharnaum where he was gathering in the taxes. His calling demanded that he should be a careful recorder of the accounts. His submission to the Savior was immediate. The Gospel relates:

> As he passed on from there Jesus saw a man named Matthew at his
> seat in the custom-house, and said to him, Follow me; and Matthew
> rose and followed him. *Matthew 9:9*

He who had been wealthy would now have nothing to look forward to but poverty and persecution; and yet, he accepted this condition at the first summons. "Come," says the Savior to a despised man, and he follows immediately. His response was all the more remarkable because he had been immersed in a trade which attracted mostly the unscrupulous and the unethical. It was bad enough that the tribute of homage from Israel should be collected by a Roman, but for it to be collected by a Jew was to make him one of the most despised of men.

And yet, this Quisling who had forfeited all love of country, and who had completely suffocated the virtue of patriotism in his lust for gain, ended by becoming one of the most patriotic of his own people. The Gospel which he wrote might be described as the gospel of patriotism. A hundred times in his Gospel, he goes back into the history of the past, quoting from Isaias, Jeremias, Micheas, David, Daniel and all the prophets; after piling them one upon the other in a great cumulative argument, he says to his people in effect: "This is the glory of Israel, this is our hope, we have begotten the Son of the Living God; we have given to the world the Messiah." His country, which had yesterday meant nothing at all to him, became in his Gospel of the highest importance. He was declaring himself a son of Israel, ready to lavish on her all his praise. As men love God, they will also love their country.

Thomas was the pessimist of the Apostles, and probably his pessimism had something to do with his scepticism. When Our Lord tried to console His Apostles, on the night of the Last Supper by assuring them that He would prepare the way for them in heaven, Thomas responded by saying that he wanted to believe but could not. Later on, when the news was brought to Our Lord that Lazarus was dead:

> Thomas, called the Twin, said to his fellow-disciples, Let us also go, that we may die with him. *John* 11:16

Thomas was called Didymus, which is merely the Greek translation of a Hebrew name and means "twin"; Thomas was a twin in another sense, for in him lived side-by-side the twins of unbelief and faith, each contending for mastery. There was faith, because he believed it was better to die with the Lord than to forsake Him; there was unbelief, for he could not help believing that death would be the end of whatever work the Lord had a mind to accomplish.

Chrysostom says of him that while he would hardly venture to go with Jesus as far as the neighboring town of Bethany, Thomas would travel without Him after Pentecost, to farthest India to implant the Faith; even to this day, the faithful in India still call themselves "St. Thomas Christians."

Two of the Apostles were relatives of Our Lord, namely, James and Jude. They are called "brethren" of Our Lord, but in Aramaic and Hebrew this word often means cousins or distant relatives. We know that Mary had no other children but Jesus. The phrase "my dear brethren," as used so often in the pulpit, does not imply that all the members of the congregation have the same mother. Scripture often uses "brethren" in the wide sense. For example, Lot is called the "brother" of Abraham, whereas he was actually his nephew; Laban is called the "brother" of Jacob, but he was his uncle. The sons of Oziel

and Aaron, the sons of Cis and the daughters of Eleazar are called
"brothers," but they were cousins. So it is with the "brethren" of Our
Lord. These two Apostles, James the Less and Jude, were probably the
sons of Cleophas, who was married to Our Lady's sister.

Jude had three names. Having the same name as Judas the traitor,
he is always described negatively as "not the Iscariot." The night of
the Last Supper, he questioned Our Lord about the Holy Spirit, or
how He would be invisible and yet manifest Himself after His Resurrection. There had always been lurking in the minds of many of the
Apostles a desire to see some great flashing Messianic glory that
would open blind eyes and capture every intelligence.

> Judas asked him—the other Judas, not Iscariot—Lord, what can have
> happened, that you mean to disclose yourself to us alone and not to
> the world?   *John 14:22*

The answer of Our Lord to Jude was that when our responsive love
melts into obedience, then God makes His dwelling within us. Later
on, Jude, sometimes called Thaddeus, wrote an Epistle beginning with
words which reflected the answer he received on Holy Thursday
night:

> From Jude, servant of Jesus Christ and brother of James, to those
> whom God has called, who live in the love of God the Father and
> in the safe keeping of Jesus Christ.
> Mercy, peace, and love be yours in fullest measure.   *Jude 1:1–3*

Another Apostle was James the Just, also called James the Less, to
distinguish him from the son of Zebedee. We know he had a good
mother for she was one of the women who stood at the foot of the
Cross. Like his brother Jude he wrote an Epistle which was addressed
to the twelve tribes of the dispersion, that is, to the Jewish Christians
who were scattered throughout the Roman world. It began:

> From James, a servant of God and the Lord Jesus Christ.
> Greetings to the Twelve Tribes dispersed throughout the world.
>   *James 1:1*

James who like all the other Apostles failed to understand the Cross
when Our Lord foretold it, afterward came like the others to make
the Cross the condition of glory.

> My brothers, whenever you have to face trials of many kinds, count
> yourselves supremely happy . . . Happy the man who remains stead-
> fast under trial, for having passed that test he will receive for his prize
> the gift of life promised to those who love God.   *James 1:2,12*

Simon the Zealot is one of the twelve Apostles about whom we know the least. His Aramaic name meaning "Zealot" suggests that he was a partisan to a sect which would use violence to overthrow the foreign yoke. This name had been given to him before his conversion. He belonged to a band of patriots who were so zealous for the overthrow of Roman rule that they revolted against Caesar. Perhaps the Lord chose him because of his wholehearted enthusiasm for a cause; but a Niagara of purification would be needed before he would understand the Kingdom in terms of a Cross instead of a sword. Imagine Simon the Zealot, an Apostle with Matthew the publican! One was an extreme nationalist, while the other was by profession virtually a traitor to his own people. And yet both were made one by Christ, and later on they would both be martyrs for His Kingdom. The twelfth Apostle was Judas, "the son of perdition," who will be treated later.

The number twelve is symbolic. The Book of the Apocalypse speaks of the twelve foundations of the Church. There were twelve patriarchs in the Old Testament, and also twelve tribes in Israel; there were twelve spies who explored the promised land; there were twelve stones on the breast of the High Priest; when Judas failed, a twelfth Apostle had to be named. The Apostles are most often referred to in the Gospels as "the twelve," that title being attributed to them thirty-two times. In choosing these twelve, it was evident that Our Lord was preparing them for a work after His Ascension; that the Kingdom He came to found was not only invisible but visible; not only Divine but human. But they had so much to learn before they could be the twelve gates of the Kingdom of God. Their first lesson would be the Beatitudes.

11. *Beatitudes*

Two mounts are related as the first and second acts in a two-act drama: the Mount of the Beatitudes and the Mount of Calvary. He who climbed the first to preach the Beatitudes must necessarily climb the second to practice what He preached. The unthinking often say the Sermon on the Mount constitutes the "essence of Christianity." But let any man put these Beatitudes into practice in his own life, and he too will draw down upon himself the wrath of the world. The Sermon on the Mount cannot be separated from His Crucifixion, any more than day can be separated from night. The day Our Lord taught the Beatitudes, He signed His own death warrant. The sound of nails and hammers digging through human flesh were the echoes thrown back from the mountainside where He told men how to be happy or blessed. Everybody wants to be happy; but His ways were the very opposite of the ways of the world.

One way to make enemies and antagonize people is to challenge the spirit of the world. The world has a spirit, as each age has a spirit. There are certain unanalyzed assumptions which govern the conduct of the world. Anyone who challenges these worldly maxims, such as, "you only live once," "get as much out of life as you can," "who will ever know about it?" "what is sex for if not for pleasure?" is bound to make himself unpopular.

In the Beatitudes, Our Divine Lord takes those eight flimsy catchwords of the world—"Security," "Revenge," "Laughter," "Popularity," "Getting Even," "Sex," "Armed Might," and "Comfort"—and turns them upside down. To those who say, "You cannot be happy unless you are rich," He says, "Blessed are the poor in spirit." To those who say, "Don't let him get away with it," He says, "Blessed are the patient." To those who say, "Laugh and the world laughs with you," He says, "Blessed are those who mourn." To those who say: "If nature gave you sex instincts you ought to give them free expression, otherwise you will become frustrated," He says, "Blessed are the clean of heart." To those who say, "Seek to be popular and well known," He says, "Blessed are you when men revile you and persecute you and speak all manner of evil against you falsely because of Me." To those who say, "In time of peace prepare for war," He says, "Blessed are the peacemakers."

The cheap clichés around which movies are written and novels composed, He scorns. He proposes to burn what they worship; to conquer errant sex instincts instead of allowing them to make slaves of man; to tame economic conquests instead of making happiness consist in an abundance of things external to the soul. All false beatitudes which make happiness depend on self-expression, license, having a good time, or "Eat, drink, and be merry for tomorrow you die," He scorns because they bring mental disorders, unhappiness, false hopes, fears, and anxieties.

Those who would escape the impact of the Beatitudes say that Our Divine Savior was a creature of His time, but not of ours, and that, therefore, His Words do not apply to us. He was not a creature of His time nor of any time; but we are! Mohammed belonged to his time; hence he said a man could have concubines in addition to four wives at one time. Mohammed belongs even to our time, because moderns say that a man can have many wives, if he drives them in tandem style, one after another. But Our Lord did not belong to His day, any more than He belonged to ours. To marry one age is to be a widow in the next. Because He suited no age, He was the model for all ages. He never used a phrase that depended on the social order in which He lived; His Gospel was no easier then than it is now. As He put it:

> So long as heaven and earth endure, not a letter, not a stroke, will disappear from the Law until all that must happen has happened.
>
> *Matthew* 5:18

The key to the Sermon on the Mount is the way He used two expressions: one was, "You have heard"; the other was the short, emphatic word, "But." When He said, "You have heard," He reached back to what human ears had heard for centuries and still hear from ethical reformers—all those rules and codes and precepts which are half measures between instinct and reason, between local customs and the highest ideals. When He said, "You have heard," He included the Mosaic Law, Buddha with his eightfold way, Confucius with his rules for being a gentleman, Aristotle with his natural happiness, the broadness of the Hindus, and all the humanitarian groups of our day, who would translate some of the old codes into their own language and call them a new way of life. Of all these compromises, He said, "You have heard."

"You have heard that it was said, 'Thou shalt not commit adultery.'" Moses had said it; pagan tribes suggested it; primitive peoples respected it. Then came the terrible and awful BUT: "But I tell you. . . ." "But I tell you that he who casts his eye on a woman so as to lust after her, has already committed adultery with her in his own heart." Our Lord went into the soul, and laid hold of thought, and branded even the *desire* for sin as a sin. If it was wrong to do a certain thing, it was wrong to think about that thing. He would say, "Away with your hygiene which tries to keep hands clean after they have stolen, and bodies free from disease after they have ravished another." He went into the depths of the heart, and branded even the intention to sin a sin. He did not wait for the evil tree to bear evil fruits. He would prevent the very sowing of the evil seed. Wait not until your hidden sins come out as psychoses and neuroses and compulsions. Get rid of them at their sources. Repent! Purge! Evil that can be put into statistics, or that can be locked in jails, is too late to remedy.

Christ affirmed that when a man married a woman, he married both her body and her soul; he married the whole person. If he got tired of the body, he might not thrust her body away for another, since he was still responsible for her soul. So He thundered, "You have heard." In that expression He summarized the jargon of every decaying civilization. "You have heard, 'Get a divorce; God does not expect you to live without happiness' "; then came the BUT.

> But what I tell you is this: If a man divorces his wife for any cause other than unchastity he involves her in adultery; and anyone who marries a divorced woman commits adultery. *Matthew* 5:32

What matters if the body is lost? The soul is still there, and that is worth more than the thrill a body can give, more even than the universe itself. He would keep men and women pure, not from contagion, but from desire of another; to imagine a betrayal is in itself a betrayal. So He declared:

> What God has joined together, man must not separate. *Mark* 10:9

No man! No judge! No nation!

Next, Christ laid hold of all those social theories which would say that sin was due to environment: to Grade B milk, to insufficient dance halls, to not enough spending money. Of them all He said, "You have heard." Then came the BUT: "But I tell you." He affirmed that sins, selfishness, greed, adultery, crime, theft, bribery, political corruption—all these come from man himself. The offenses result from our own will, and not from our glands; we cannot excuse our lust because our grandfather had an Oedipus complex, or because we inherited an Electra complex from our grandmother. Sin, He said, is conveyed to the soul through our body, and the body is moved by the will. In war against all false self-expressions, He thundered out His recommendations of self-operation: "Cut it off," and "cut it out."

> If your right eye is your undoing, tear it out and fling it away; it is better for you to lose one part of your body than for the whole of

it to be thrown into hell. And if your right hand is your undoing, cut it off and fling it away; it is better for you to lose one part of your body than for the whole of it to go to hell.   *Matthew 5:29,30*

Men will cut off their legs and arms to save the body from gangrene or poisoning. But here Our Lord transferred circumcision of the flesh to circumcision of the heart, and advocated letting out the lifeblood of beloved lusts and hewing passions to tatters, rather than be separated from the love of God which is in Him, Christ Jesus.

Next He talked of revenge, hatred, violence, expressed in those sayings of everybody, "Get even," "Sue him," "Don't be a fool." He knew them all, and of all of them He said:

You have learned that they were told, "Eye for eye, tooth for tooth."
Matthew 5:38

Then comes the awful BUT:

But what I tell you is this: Do not set yourself against the man who wrongs you. If someone slaps you on the right cheek, turn and offer him your left. If a man wants to sue you for your shirt, let him have your coat as well. If a man in authority makes you go one mile, go with him two.   *Matthew 5:38–41*

Why turn the other cheek? Because hate multiplies like a seed. If one preaches hate and violence to ten men in a row, and tells the first man to strike the second, and the second to strike the third, the hatred will envelope all ten. The only way to stop this hate is for one man (say the fifth in line), to turn his other cheek. Then the hatred ends. It is never passed on. Absorb violence for the sake of the Savior, Who will absorb sin and die for it. The Christian law is that the innocent shall suffer for the guilty.

Thus He would have us do away with adversaries, because when no resistance is offered, the adversary is conquered by a superior moral power; such love prevents the infection of the wound of hate. To endure for a year the bore who afflicts you for a week; to write a letter of kindness to the man who calls you dirty names; to offer gifts to the man who would steal from you; never to answer back with hatred the man who lies and says you are disloyal to your country or tells the worse lie, that you are against freedom—these are the hard things which Christ came to teach, and they no more suited His time than they do ours. They suit only the heroes, the great men, the saints, the holy men and women who will be the salt of the earth, the leaven in the mass, the elite among the mob, the kind who will transform the world. If certain people are not lovable, one puts love into them and they will become lovable. Why is anyone lovable—if it be not that God put His love into each of us?

The Sermon on the Mount is so much at variance with all that our world holds dear that the world will crucify anyone who tries to live up to its values. Because Christ preached them, He had to die. Calvary was the price He paid for the Sermon on the Mount. Only mediocrity survives. Those who call black black, and white white, are sentenced for intolerance. Only the grays live.

Let Him Who says, "Blessed are the poor in spirit," come into the world that believes in the primacy of the economic; let Him stand in the market place where some men live for collective profit, or where others say men live for individual profit, and see what happens. He will be so poor that during life He will have nowhere to lay His head; a day will come when He will die without anything of economic worth. In His last hour He will be so impoverished that they will strip Him of His garments and even give Him a stranger's grave for His burial, as He had a stranger's stable for His birth.

Let Him come into the world which proclaims the gospel of the strong, which advocates hating our enemies, which condemns Christian virtues as the "soft" virtues, and say to that world, "Blessed are the patient," and He will one day feel the scourges of the strong barbarians laid across His back; He will be struck on the cheek by a mocking fist during one of His trials; He will see men take a sickle and cut the grass from a hill on Calvary, and then use a hammer to pinion Him to a Cross to test the patience of One Who endures the worst that evil has to offer, that having exhausted itself it might eventually turn to Love.

Let Him come into our world which ridicules the idea of sin as morbidity, considers reparation for past guilt as a guilt complex and preach to that world, "Blessed are they who mourn" for their sins; and He will be blindfolded and mocked as a fool. They will take His Body and scourge it, until His bones can be numbered; they will crown His head with thorns, until He begins to weep not salt tears but crimson beads of blood, as they laugh at the weakness of Him Who will not come down from the Cross.

Let Him come into the world which denies Absolute Truth, which says that right and wrong are only questions of point of view, that we must be broadminded about virtue and vice, and let Him say to them, "Blessed are they who hunger and thirst after holiness," that is, after the Absolute, after the Truth which "I am"; and they will in their broadmindedness give the mob the choice of Him or Barabbas; they will crucify Him with thieves, and try to make the world believe that God is no different from a batch of robbers who are His bedfellows in death.

Let him come into a world which says that "my neighbor is hell," that all which is opposite me is nothing, that the ego alone matters, that my will is supreme law, that what I decide is good, that I must forget others and think only of myself, and say to them, "Blessed are the merciful." He will find that He will receive no mercy; they will open five streams of blood out of His Body; they will pour vinegar and gall into His thirsting mouth; and, even after His death, be so merciless as to plunge a spear into His Sacred Heart.

Let Him come into a world which tries to interpret man in terms of sex; which regards purity as coldness, chastity as frustrated sex, self-containment as abnormality, and the union of husband and wife until death as boredom; which says that a marriage endures only so long as the glands endure, that one may unbind what God binds and unseal what God seals. Say to them, "Blessed are the pure"; and He will find Himself hanging naked on a Cross, made a spectacle to men and angels in a last wild crazy affirmation that purity is abnormal, that the virgins are neurotics, and that carnality is right.

Let Him come into a world which believes that one must resort to every manner of chicanery and duplicity in order to conquer the world, carrying doves of peace with stomachs full of bombs, say to them, "Blessed are the peacemakers," or "Blessed are they who eradicate sin that there may be peace"; and He will find Himself surrounded by men engaged in the silliest of all wars—a war against the Son of God; making violence with steel and wood, pinions and gall and then setting a watch over His grave that He who lost the battle might not win the day.

Let Him come into a world that believes that our whole life should be geared to flattering and influencing people for the sake of utility and popularity, and say to them: "Blessed are you when men hate, persecute, and revile you"; and He will find Himself without a friend in the world, an outcast on a hill, with mobs shouting His death, and His flesh hanging from Him like purple rags.

The Beatitudes cannot be taken alone: they are not ideals; they are hard facts and realities inseparable from the Cross of Calvary. What He taught was self-crucifixion: to love those who hate us; to pluck out eyes and cut off arms in order to prevent sinning; to be clean on the inside when the passions clamor for satisfaction on the outside; to forgive those who would put us to death; to overcome evil with good; to bless those who curse us; to stop mouthing freedom until we have justice, truth and love of God in our hearts as the condition of freedom; to live in the world and still keep oneself unpolluted from it; to deny ourselves sometimes legitimate pleasures in order the better to crucify our egotism—all this is to sentence the old man in us to death.

Those who heard Him preach the Beatitudes were invited to stretch themselves out on a cross, to find happiness on a higher level by death to a lower order, to despise all the world holds sacred, and to venerate as sacred all the world regards as an ideal. Heaven is happiness; but it is too much for man to have two heavens, an *ersatz* one below, and a real one above. Hence the four "woes" He immediately added to the Beatitudes.

> But alas for you who are rich; you have had your time of happiness.
> Alas for you who are well-fed now; you shall go hungry.
> Alas for you who laugh now; you shall mourn and weep.
> Alas for you when all speak well of you; just so did their fathers treat
> the false prophets. *Luke 6:24–26*

Crucifixion cannot be far away when a Teacher says "woe" to the rich, the satiated, the gay and the popular. Truth is not in the Sermon on the Mount alone; it is in the One Who lived out the Sermon on the Mount on Golgotha. The four woes would have been ethical condemnations, if He had not died full of the opposite of the four woes: poor, abandoned, sorrowful, and despised. On the Mount of the Beatitudes, He bade men hurl themselves on the cross of self-denial; on the Mount of Calvary, He embraced that very cross. Though the shadow of the Cross would not fall across the place of the skull until three years later, it was already in His Heart the day He preached on "How to be Happy."

12. *The Intruder Who Was a Woman*

While visiting the Galilean towns early in His public life and before open hostility had broken out, a rich Pharisee named Simon invited Our Lord to his home for a meal. He had heard of the acclaim given Our Lord by the people and was anxious to determine for himself whether He was really a prophet or a teacher. Curiously enough, there was someone else in the vicinity who was also anxious to meet Our Lord, but her interests were higher. She had a burden on her conscience, and wanted to see Him as Savior from her guilt. Great as was her shame, she did not permit it to hold her back even in the face of those who might condemn her. Our Lord thus found Himself between one who was curious about Him as a Teacher and another who was penitent before Him as a Savior.

When Our Lord arrived, there was little enthusiasm in the welcome of Simon who coldly omitted the usual courtesies and attentions paid to a guest. In those days, to enter a house except with bare feet was much the same thing as entering a house today without taking off one's hat. Shoes and sandals were removed at the threshold. The visitor was always greeted with a kiss on the cheek by the master of the house with the invocation, "The Lord be with you." Then the guest was shown to a couch where a servant would bring water to wash his feet and assure ceremonial cleanliness. Next, the host or at least one of the servants anointed the head and beard of the visitor with fragrant oil. In the case of Our Blessed Lord, there was no water for His weary feet, and no kiss of welcome to His cheek; no perfume for His hair—nothing but an unceremonious gesture indicating a vacant place at the table. Perhaps Simon knew he was watched by other Pharisees and hence omitted these courtesies. The guests in those days did not sit at table, but reclined on couches, the unsandaled feet stretched out at full length.

Access to the dining room was very easy, probably because of the universal prevalence of the law of hospitality so common among the peoples of the East. While the meal was being served, an untoward incident happened. Simon looked up, and what he saw brought a blush to his cheek. He would not have minded it if anyone else had been there, but This Man! What would He think of it? The intruder was a woman; her name was Mary; her profession, a sinner, a common woman of the streets. She moved slowly across the floor, not brushing back her hair, for it acted as a screen against the gaze of the Pharisee. She stood at the feet of Our Blessed Lord, and let fall upon those sandaled harbingers of peace, like the first drops of warm summer rain, a few tears. Then, ashamed of what she had done, she bent lower as if to hide her shame, but the fountain of tears would not be stilled. Emboldened because unreproved, she cast herself on her knees and began to wipe the tears from His feet with her long disheveled hair. To anoint the head was the usual course, but she would not venture on such an honor, but would make bold in her humility to anoint only His feet. Taking from her veil a vessel of precious perfume, she did not pour it out drop by drop, slowly, as if to indicate by the very slowness of giving the generosity of the giver. She broke the vessel and gave everything, for love knows no limits. She was not paying tribute to a sage; she was unburdening her heart of her sins. She had certainly seen and heard Him before, and she was certain that somehow He might give her new hope. There was love in her boldness, repentance in her tears, sacrifice and surrender of self in her ointment.

But the Pharisee was horrified that the Master should have allowed such a disreputable woman of the streets to approach Him, and contrary to all traditions of the strict Pharisees, to pour out tears at His feet. Simon would not speak the words aloud, but merely thought within himself:

> If this fellow were a real prophet, he would know who this woman is that touches him, and what sort of woman she is, a sinner.
>
> *Luke 7:39*

How did he know she was a woman of the streets? In judging another he judged himself. In Simon's eyes she was a sinner and she would always be accounted a sinner. To him there was abomination in her touch, sin in her tears, and a lie in her ointment. The Pharisee made no inquiries, indulged in no hopes. It was all one to him whether it was a depraved will, vanity, starvation, or the lusts of men that drove her to her ruin. It was one to him whether she arose at night because of her troubled conscience and condemned herself a thousand times for doing that which she knew would bring her no peace. And as for Christ, if He had any insight into human character He would know she was a prostitute.

Our Lord then read Simon's thoughts as He will one day read the souls of the living and the dead. He said to him:

> Simon, I have something to say to you.

Simon said:

> Speak on, Master.

Our Lord continued:

> Two men were in debt to a money-lender: one owed him five hun-
> dred silver pieces, the other fifty. As neither had anything to pay with
> he let them both off. Now, which will love him most?   *Luke 7:41,42*

The implication of the story was that God is a creditor Who trusts us
with His goods until a day is set for the payment of that debt and the
rendering of an account of our stewardship. Some are indebted more
than others; some, because they have sinned more; others, because
they have greater gifts; some receive ten talents, others five, still others
one. It could have been that the woman's sins were like a debt of five
hundred pieces of silver, while Simon's were only like a debt of fifty.
But in the end, both were debtors, and neither could pay the debt.
The meaning of the parable was clear. God is the creditor Who trusts
man with His gifts of wealth, intelligence, influence. But a day is
finally set for the payment. Though no man in strict justice can pay
the debt he owes to God through sin, God is nevertheless willing to
forgive all debtors, great or small. What this forgiveness costs in strict
justice, Our Lord did not here discuss. But He prepared Simon to understand that He had come to bring remission of sins.

Our Lord now asks:

> Now, which will love him most?
> Simon replied, I should think the one that was let off most. You are
> right, said Jesus. Then turning to the woman, he said to Simon, You
> see this woman? I came to your house: you provided no water for my
> feet; but this woman has made my feet wet with her tears and wiped
> them with her hair. You gave me no kiss; but she has been kissing my
> feet ever since I came in. You did not anoint my head with oil; but
> she has anointed my feet with myrrh.   *Luke 7:43–46*

What did Our Lord mean when He said to Simon, "Dost thou see
this woman?" He meant that Simon could not see the woman as she
really was, but only as the woman that she used to be, or the woman
he thought she was. Simon had said within himself that if Our Lord
were a prophet He would know she was a sinner. Now Our Blessed
Lord turned the phrase and asked Simon, "Do you see her, Simon?
The trouble with your tribe of self-righteous people is that you judge
yourselves virtuous, because you find someone else who is vicious. You
never see. You think you see, but you do not. Guilt is always in the
neighbor, never in self."

Our Lord then went on to describe the common courtesies which had been neglected, but which this woman showed Him. "She has washed My feet with tears." The garment that is deeply soiled cannot without much rubbing and pouring of water become clean. When there is a deep pollution of sin, there must not be only a washing but a soaking and bathing with the tears of contrition. Then she wiped His feet with her hair. In true repentance there is always a converting of those things which have been abused in the service of sin to the service of God. The best ornament of the body, in the judgment of the penitent, was not too good to be employed in the most menial service toward Our Blessed Lord.

The courtesies which Simon omitted in the order of nature, his Divine visitor now contrasts with the higher courtesies and the order of grace. The marks of honor are then traced to their source, her desire for forgiveness. In all the conventional civilities of life there is some root of affection and love. Simon thought he showed enough honor to a carpenter's Son by inviting Him to table; but the woman's love He traced to her deep sense of forgiven sin:

> And so, I tell you, her great love proves that her many sins have been forgiven; where little has been forgiven, little love is shown.
>
> *Luke* 7:47

It would be very wrong to deduce that it would be well to have sinned much, or to have run up a bigger debt in order that the sinner might have more forgiven. Rather the lesson is that flagrant sinners are much more likely to discover that they are sinners than those who think they are good. As in a hospital, a patient who is a mass of sores and bruises solicits more pity than one less injured, so too, admitted guilt is not an obstacle, but an argument in favor of Divine mercy. The love of this woman grew in proportion to her gratitude for pardon. It was not the quantity of sin, but rather the consciousness of it and the mercy extended in its forgiveness, which manifested the great love of this penitent woman. Much was forgiven her; therefore she loved much.

Nothing so much brings one person in contact with another as the confession of sin. When a friend tells of his success, he stands at a distance from our heart; when he tells of his guilt with tears, he is very near. Actually, when a person has a consciousness of his sin, he does not very much distinguish between whether his sins belong in the five hundred pieces of silver category, or the fifty. What troubles him is the fact that he has hurt someone that he loves. St. Paul considered himself the chief of sinners, but he was not a great sinner except in his bigotry and persecution. He who makes light of sin will make light of forgiveness. He who makes light of really serious wounds will never appreciate the power of the physician.

Simon had something to learn; so he invited a teacher; the woman had something to be forgiven, so she poured out her contrite tears on the Divine Creditor Who proved to be her Savior. Simon had not denied the existence of guilt; but he felt himself relatively innocent when he saw the woman who was a sinner. Guilt is not just the breaking of a love; it is the wounding of someone who is loved. The seriousness of sin rises in proportion as Christ is approached. Standing close to the Cross and feeling the agonies of Him Whose death was necessary for sin's atonement, could make Paul, the Pharisee of the Pharisees, call himself the "greatest of sinners."

The lesson was over and the woman was dismissed with the words:

> Your sins are forgiven. *Luke 7:48*

The man whom Simon thought might be a teacher, was not formalizing a code; He was forgiving sins. But who can forgive sins except God? That was the thought running through the minds of everyone at table:

> The other guests began to ask themselves, Who is this, that he can forgive sins? *Luke 7:49*

This was their question as they arose from their couches. Couches would come back as a symbol of a guiltless world nineteen centuries later. Men would rise from them with their guilt explained away. But such souls would not have the inner joy of the woman, who heard One more than a prophet say to her:

> Your faith has saved you; go in peace. *Luke 7:50*

Her faith had told her that God loves purity, goodness, and holiness. And before her stood He Who alone could restore her to that holiness. But the price He would pay for that peace would come only after a war—the war against evil. The forgiveness the woman received was not merely that of being "let off"; it was one in which justice itself was satisfied. Peter, who was there at the dinner, later on recorded the price that was paid:

> In his own person he carried our sins to the gibbet, so that we might cease to live for sin and begin to live for righteousness. By his wounds you have been healed. *I Peter 2:24*

The guests at table wondered how He could forgive sins. Right they were, who could forgive sins but God? The purpose of His coming to this earth as the Son of Man was once more revealed: He would be identified with sinners in taking their guilt; He would be separate from sinners in offering Himself for their salvation and, therefore, could forgive their sins. On the one hand, identification:

He was counted among the outlaws.   *Luke* 22:37

On the other hand, separation:

—devout, guileless, undefiled, separated from sinners . . .
Hebrews 7:26

These are complementary truths. The first referred to the price He had to pay to forgive sins, such as those of the woman; the second to His Divine life which gave His sufferings infinite value. The woman before Him had her debt of sin blotted out, but she had no idea how much it cost Him. All the tokens of tenderness the sinful woman showed Him, He would receive again in another form. A kiss would come from Judas; the washing of His feet would be reversed as He would gird Himself with a towel and wash the feet of His disciples; and for the oil on His head there would be the crown of thorns as He would pour out the perfume of His own Blood.

13. *The Man Who Lost His Head*

The redemptive purpose of God's coming to earth was revealed under many symbols and figures; one of the most striking was foretold in what happened to John the Baptist. Although John sought no earthly honor, he received it; for he was sought out by King Herod Antipas, the son of the blood-thirsty Herod who had tried to take the life of Our Lord when He was not yet two years of age. "Herod feared John," knowing that he was a "just and holy man." The wicked fear the good, because the good are a constant reproach to their consciences. The ungodly like religion in the same way that they like lions, either dead or behind bars; they fear religion when it breaks loose and begins to challenge their consciences.

Herod was typical of all worldlings who sent for what they call "learned men of the cloth" (as Felix sent for Paul); they love their brilliance, their turn of phrase, their abstract wisdom; but as soon as these men begin to make the teachings of Christ concrete and personal, they are dismissed at once with the words "too intense," "intolerant," or "Do you know, he actually tried to convert me?" Herod, always looking for new stimulations and excitements, invited the court to hear this thrilling preacher who was all the rage at the time. What text would John the Baptist choose? Would he talk about brotherly love (without the Fatherhood of God), or about the necessity of reducing armies, or about the great need of economic reform in Galilee? John knew that all these were important, but he knew that something else was more important still; so he decided to address himself to consciences.

Herod probably looked at him with a half-smile of satisfaction; Herodias, his wife, must have glared out of the corner of her eye; the others were curious, but not really interested. Herod and Herodias had both been married before, she to Herod's brother. It was one of those nasty, festering messes which become commonplace in a nation that is beginning to rot. Herod had been married previously to the daughter of Aretas, who left him when he began to be involved with Herodias, the wife of his brother Philip. Herodias had a daughter Salome by her previous marriage to Philip.

If there was one subject that, from a worldly point of view, John would have been wise to avoid in that court, it was this situation. But

John was bent on pleasing God, not men; he resolved to talk against
such lustful living. He was too kind to excuse Herod's sin, too interested in moral health to leave the wound unprobed, too loving to have
any thought except to save Herod's soul.

John followed Our Divine Lord's teaching that marriage was holy
and indivisible: "What God has joined together let no man put
asunder." He cut straight into the quick with words that were clear,
decisive, and abrupt. Pointing his finger at Herod and his wife seated
on their golden thrones, he said:

> You have no right to your brother's wife. *Mark 6:18*

Herodias winced. She knew that John was recalling the fact that she
had seduced Herod, who was already in her power. One look from her
was enough for Herod. Before John could finish the next sentence,
iron chains were thrown about his wrists and guards began dragging
him from the court to throw him into the black dungeon below. The
preacher was imprisoned, but his words were not—they would echo in
conscience long after the voice had been silenced.

For months John was kept in the dark dungeon of Machaerus. Did
this enforced inactivity cause him to doubt the Messiah and Lamb of
God of Whom he had spoken? Did his faith waver a little in the
darkness of the dungeon? Perhaps he was impatiently longing for God
to punish those who had refused to receive His message. In any case:

> Summoning two of their number he sent them to the Lord with this
> message: Are you the one who is to come, or are we to expect some
> other? *Luke 7:19*

The very way John put the question indicated that he had faith both
in the great Messianic promise and in Him Whom he was questioning.

When the question was brought to Him, Our Lord did not answer
it with a promise that John would be released from prison, or that He
Himself would destroy his enemies. He answered only by pointing to
His own work of healing, comforting, and teaching.

> Go, he said, and tell John what you have seen and heard: how the
> blind recover their sight, the lame walk, the lepers are made clean, the
> deaf hear, the dead are raised to life, the poor are hearing the good
> news—and happy is the man who does not find me a stumbling-block.
> *Luke 7:22,23*

Divinity and its ways will always be a scandal to men. The poverty
and worldly insignificance of Our Savior had been the earliest objection to His gospel. This prejudice arose from a very false conception

of the power and the majesty of God, as if the achievement of His purposes really depended upon the means which the world associates with success. In effect, Christ was giving a two-fold answer to John's disciples, pointing to both His works and His word, His miracles and His teachings. His miracles would not just be things to wonder at; rather they would be signs of a Divine Kingdom of righteousness and mercy; and the power by which He worked them would be a power outside nature, which could control nature. His teaching, in particular, would be another proof of His Divinity: the poor would have the Gospel preached to them.

This was especially significant, because poverty is only another word for human imperfection and weakness. The strong in body and the keen in intellect and those who possess the bounties of earth receive their reward in this world; but the poor and the weak often hunger and suffer. Christ was saying that in the Kingdom of Heaven there would be a gospel for the poor. God has another world in which to redress the inequalities of this one. While the rich man is told that if he wants to go to heaven he must part with his riches for Christ's sake, the poor man is told that his weariness and suffering, toil and disappointment, united with the Cross, will bring their own inner peace and reward.

When the messengers had left, Our Lord began to praise John. John had borne witness to Him. He would now bear witness to John. He answered those who might have been judging John by a message that was sent in an hour of trial. He contrasted the multitude who hung upon the words of the messengers with John himself—the fickleness of the crowd was the stability of the prophet. It was not John that was weak; it was their own hearts. It was not doubt that had made John send the enquiry, nor was it a fear of bodily consequences. Using three figures of speech, Our Lord rose to John's defense. The first figure was the reed that used to wave in the breeze beside the strong rapid stream of the Jordan, where they had heard John preach; the second figure was the soft garments of those who lived in the house of Herod; the third figure was a sign from heaven and a reference to all the men who have gone through the portals of the flesh in human birth.

> After John's messengers had left, Jesus began to speak about him to the crowds: What was the spectacle that drew you to the wilderness? A reed-bed swept by the wind? No? Then what did you go out to see? A man dressed in silks and satins? Surely you must look in palaces for grand clothes and luxury. But what did you go out to see? A prophet? Yes indeed, and far more than a prophet. He is the man of whom Scripture says,

Here is my herald, whom I send on ahead of you,
and he will prepare your way before you.
I tell you, there is not a mother's son greater than John, and yet the
least in the kingdom of God is greater than he.   *Luke 7:24–28*

Three times Our Blessed Lord asked, "What was it you went out to
see?" This was their error; professing a desire to know the will of God,
they had really been bent on sights and spectacles, on enjoying the
wonders and popularity of the messenger. They went out just to *see*
someone, not to *hear* someone; to satisfy the concupiscence of their
eyes, but not to imitate the temperance and self-denial of the Baptist.
Our Lord was telling the mob that St. John did not ask his question
from prison simply because he was a reed shaken by the wind of public opinion, or because he was one who cared for his bodily well-being,
as did the courtiers in the house of Herod. John was no frivolous reed
shaken by every breath of popular applause. He delivered his rebukes
with fearlessness; he was not only severe on others, he was even more
severe on himself. He might have dwelt in the houses of kings, and
yet he made the desert his home. In his relation to God, he was a
prophet, and more than a prophet—the precursor and forerunner of
the Messiah and the Son of God.

Greatness is of two kinds: the earthly and the heavenly. If John's
greatness had been of the earth, he would have lived in palaces, his
garments would have been gaudy, and his opinions would probably
have been variable like a reed, blown toward one popular philosophy
one day and another the next. But his greatness was of the Divine
order, and his superiority was not just in his person, but in his
unchanging work and mission, namely, to announce the Lamb of
God.

Some months later, the time came for Herod's birthday to be celebrated with a great feast. To this Balthasarian banquet were invited
all Herod's lords and ladies, the military personnel, and various
hangers-on from Galilee. It was evening, and the castle was softly
lighted. Faces were painted to look their best in the dim flattering
candlelight. The noise of music, the blare of horns, and the shouts of
revelry resounded through the stony castle of Machaerus, even
reaching down to the narrow dark dungeon below, where for ten
months John the Baptist had languished. Nevertheless, the guests
were probably bored to distraction; for nothing is more sickening than
the organized joy of the jaded.

Herod's voice rang out in this first great night club of the Christian
Era, calling for a sensuous dance to stimulate their weary spirits. The
dancer would be Salome, the fair young daughter of the king's wife by
her first husband. This maiden, who was a descendant of the noble

Maccabees but who had been utterly debased and corrupted by the connivance of a degenerate mother, danced her way on to the floor. The revelers were charmed, and Herod, following her every movement of grace, soon became as much aroused by the dance as by the wine. When with one last fling, Salome threw herself into his lap, he blurted out in a burst of passion:

Ask what you like and I will give it you. And he swore an oath to her. Whatever you ask I will give you, up to half my kingdom.

Mark 6:22,23

Salome did not know what to ask, so she turned to her mother. Herod had already forgotten that unfortunate sermon of John the Baptist; but a woman does not forget so easily. Those ten months while John was in the prison below, he was also in the soul of Herodias, troubling it, disturbing her sleep, torturing her conscience, and haunting her dreams. She now resolved to get rid of him, thinking that if she could just do away with this moral representative of God, she could sin with impunity for the rest of her life. With one word to Salome, she would silence her own conscience, and her husband's, forever. She whispered her answer into her daughter's ear. Salome approached Herod. The shrill music stopped; silence fell over the assembly; the food became tasteless, and even their hearts were sickened as the young girl asked Herod:

Give me here on a dish the head of John the Baptist. *Matthew* 14:8

Herod was thrown into confusion because of his oath. He thought of all his past respect for the prophet; but at the same time, he was afraid of the taunts and the whispered jests of the guests if they should see him draw back from his promise. Unfaithful to God, to conscience, to himself, not ashamed of any crime but ashamed of public opinions, he decided to be faithful to his drunken oath. Above all, he trembled at the wrath of his second wife.

Herod called forward a few slaves. Torches were lighted. No one spoke as they heard the slaves descending the stairs, deeper and deeper, the sound growing fainter; then they heard the fumblings of keys in dungeon doors, the creaking of hinges. There was silence for a few seconds, broken by a sickening thud; then a slow march up the stairs, louder and louder, in rhythm with the beating of their hearts. The slaves approached Herodias with the gory gift. She went to Salome, and Salome carried it across the dance floor and gave it to Herod on a golden platter, the bearded head of the Prophet of Fire.

On that dark night, at the bidding of the child of an adulteress, Herod had murdered the forerunner of Christ.

After that, Herod was haunted by fears, as Nero was haunted by the ghost of his mother whom he had murdered. The Emperor Caligula could not sleep because he too was haunted by the faces of his victims; the historian Suetonius says that "he sat up in bed," or else walked around in the long porticos of the palace, looking for the approach of day.

Herod, hearing of Our Divine Lord some time later, thought that He was John the Baptist, risen from the dead. Herod did not believe in a future life; no sensual man does. Belief in immortality dies easily in those who live in such a way that they cannot face the prospect of a judgment. A future life is denied not so much by the way one thinks as by the way one lives. Herod had convinced himself that the door was closed at death; but now, once he heard that Our Lord was preaching, he began to think that John had risen from the dead. Scepticism is never certain of itself, being less a firm intellectual position than a pose to justify bad behavior. As a Sadducee, Herod rejected the next life; but he feared his conscience after all. And hearing of the wonders and miracles of Our Lord, "he sought to see Him." And he did see Him. Less than two years later, Pilate would send Our Lord to him:

> Having heard about him, he had long been wanting to see him, and had been hoping to see some miracle performed by him.   *Luke* 23:8

Herod had never seen the face of Jesus until that last hour; he never before had heard His voice. When the moment came, Our Lord refused to speak to him.

After the Transfiguration, the Apostles, who had seen Moses and Elijah speaking with Our Lord, began asking questions about Elijah. Our Lord told them that Elijah had already been among them in spirit; they had seen him in the dweller of lonely places, the man clothed in camel's hair who lived on a meagre fare. Then He dragged the Cross before their eyes again. He showed them that the death of John the Baptist was a prefigurement of His own death. As the people who had seen John believed him not, so neither would they believe Our Lord:

> They failed to recognize him, and worked their will upon him; and in the same way the Son of Man is to suffer at their hands.
>
> *Matthew* 17:12

Through His comment on the Baptist's fate, Jesus foretold His own suffering and death. He was endeavoring to make the Apostles familiar with the idea of a dying as well as a conquering Messiah. As people blundered in blindness by failing to welcome the Baptist when he came in the spirit of a penitential Elijah, so they would miss the Messiah when He came among them as One bearing their guilt, to ransom it on the tree of the Cross. The Apostles were told that such a destiny was foretold of the Son of Man:

> That he is to endure great sufferings and to be treated with contempt.
>
> *Mark 9:11*

The Psalms and the Prophets had alluded to His suffering as the Son of Man. Just as Our Lord did not save John the Baptist from the cruelty of Herod, neither would He save Himself from that same Herod. The herald had suffered the lot of the One Whom he heralded; the messenger received violence because he had announced the Message. And once again, the Mount of Calvary looked down, this time across the valleys to the foot of the Mount of the Transfiguration. Everything in His life told of His Cross, including the violent death of John.

14. *The Bread of Life*

Two banquets were held in Galilee in the course of a year: one in the court of Herod at which John the Baptist preached; the other, a banquet in the open air served by Our Lord. He had crossed over the Sea of Galilee, probably to avoid the fury of Herod who had just murdered the Baptist and

> A large crowd of people followed who had seen the signs he performed in healing the sick. *John* 6:2

Their motives for following Him were somewhat confused; but there was a growing idea that He was the Christ. Greatly disappointed were they when He retired to the mountain with His disciples. The Gospel chariot was stopped briefly for the sake of a little rest for those who drove it. Because the Passover was near and many were on their way to Jerusalem, the crowd swelled to five thousand (not counting women and children).

> For they had no leisure even to eat, so many were coming and going. *Mark* 6:31

The little town to which they came was six miles across the water from Capharnaum. When Our Blessed Lord got out of the boat as it touched the shore, the multitudes were there to meet Him. They had brought their sick with them, and they were hungry in more ways than one. They gave Him no repose, not because they believed Him to be the Son of God, but because they regarded Him as a magician who could do wonders, or a physician who could heal the sick.

> His heart went out to them, because they were like sheep without a shepherd. *Mark* 6:34

He arranged the crowds in rows of a hundred and fifty, each row seated a little higher than the one below. In the center of them all stood Our Lord. Testing Philip, He asked:

> Where are we to buy bread to feed these people? *John* 6:5

Philip made a rapid calculation that it would take two hundred pennyworth to feed the multitude. Jesus did not ask, "How much money is needed?" but "Whence would come the bread?" Philip should have answered that He Who had raised the dead and healed the sick could supply the bread. Andrew then pointed to a boy who had five barley loaves and two fishes. Andrew, too, did a little arithmetic and asked:

> But what is that among so many? *John* 6:9

In the Old Testament, God was pleased to use trivial and insignificant things to fulfill His purposes, like the flag on the cradle of a babe which won the heart of Pharaoh's daughter, or the shepherd's stick of Moses which worked miracles in Egypt, or the slingshot of David which overthrew the Philistines. Because bread was now involved, there was even a kind of a parallel to the gestures that were later used at the Last Supper.

> Then, taking the five loaves and the two fishes, he looked up to heaven, said the blessing, broke the loaves, and gave them to the disciples to distribute. *Mark* 6:41

As a grain of wheat slowly multiplies in the ground, so the bread and fishes, by a Divinely hastened process were multiplied until everyone had his fill. If He had given money, no one would have had his fill. Nature was to go as far as it could, then God supplied the rest. He ordered that the fragments be gathered up; they filled twelve baskets. In the reckoning of men there is always a deficit; in the arithmetic of God, there is always a surplus.

The effect of the miracle on the multitude was stupendous. There was no denying the fact that Christ had Divine power; He showed it in multiplying the bread. It brought their minds back immediately to Moses, who had given their forefathers manna in the desert. And had not Moses said that he was the prefigure of Christ or the Messiah?

> The Lord your God will raise up a prophet from among you like myself, and you shall listen to him. *Deuteronomy* 18:15

If Moses had authenticated or sealed himself by bread in the desert, was not This the One to Whom Moses had pointed, since He too gave bread miraculously? Who, then, could be a better King for them to throw off the yoke of the Romans and make them free? Here was a Deliverer, greater than Josue, and here were five thousand men ready to take up arms; here was a King greater than David or Solomon, Who could rebel against the tyrants and set the people free. They had already acknowledged Him as a Prophet and Teacher; now they would proclaim Him as King. But the Reader of hearts knew how worldly were their ambitions for Him:

> Jesus, aware that they meant to come and seize him to proclaim him king, withdrew again to the hills by himself. *John* 6:15

They could not *make* Him King; He was *born* a King. The Wise Men knew this as they asked:

> Where is the child who is born to be king of the Jews? We observed the rising of his star, and we have come to pay him homage.
>
> *Matthew* 2:2

His Kingship would come through the Divine "must" of the Cross, and not through popular force. This was the second time that He declined a crown; the first was when Satan offered Him the kingship of the world, if He would fall down and adore him. "My Kingdom is not of this world," He would tell Pilate later on. But the crowd would push Him to a throne; He said He would not be pushed; He would be "lifted up" to it and the throne would be the Cross, and His Kingship would be over hearts.

It might have been this very flight from political kingship that put doubts into the mind of Judas; for it was in connection with this miracle and the speech of Our Lord which followed that Judas was first described as a traitor. Since Our Lord would not accept a temporal sovereignty such as Satan offered Him, He must prepare Himself to hear later on, "We have no King, but Caesar."

Our Lord, knowing what was in the hearts of the populace, withdrew into the mountain alone. No unclean hands would put a crown on His head—except a crown of thorns. But in order to teach His Apostles that they, too, were not to "cash in" on cheap popularity, He constrained them to take a ship and go to the other side of the lake, a distance of five or six miles. But He did not go with them.

Between the hours of three and six in the morning, as they were shivering, wet and weary in the boat, a storm arose. This was the second storm which found them on the lake after having been called to be Apostles; the first was on the occasion of an earlier visit of Our Lord. Both storms came at night and both were violent. It must have been a particularly strong tempest to have affected these men whose lives had been spent on that particular sea. Perhaps it was not only the storm at sea that troubled them, but also the fact that their Master had refused to be a King. It is very likely that they also doubted the power of the One Who had multiplied the bread, and then sent them across the lake the night of a storm. If He could multiply bread, why could He not prevent storms?

For Our Lord to leave them and then quickly return in the midst of the sea, was to them just as impossible as if He should be dead and then rise again. But suddenly, while they were toiling at the oars, they saw Him coming to them across the waters. They were afraid and troubled. He spoke to them:

> It is I; do not be afraid. Then they were ready to take him aboard, and immediately the boat reached the land they were making for.
> *John 6:20*

The solitary crew were not as solitary as they thought. The same rhythm of joy and sorrow that ran through His life was present here; for it was in the midst of darkness, storm, and danger that Christ came, planting His feet on the white crests of the raging sea. Now that He had shown His power:

> And the men in the boat fell at his feet, exclaiming, Truly you are the Son of God. *Matthew 14:33*

They acknowledged that He was not only the Messiah Who was expected but also the Son of God. Some of the men in that boat had been disciples of John the Baptist, and had heard the Father say during Our Lord's baptism that this was the Son of God. It is also very likely that some of them had been present when the demon declared Him to be the Son of God. Nathanael had already given Him this title.

It was on this occasion that Peter, when he first saw Our Lord and before He came into the boat, asked if he might walk upon the waters and come to Him. The Lord bade Peter come; but after a few moments Peter began to sink. Why? Because he took account of the winds; because he concentrated on natural difficulties; because he trusted not in the power of the Master and failed to keep his eyes on Him.

> But when he saw the strength of the gale he was seized with fear; and beginning to sink, . . . *Matthew 14:30*

He finally cried out to the Lord for help:

> Save me, Lord. Jesus at once reached out and caught hold of him, and said, Why did you hesitate? How little faith you have!
> *Matthew 14:31*

The deliverance was first; then the gentle rebuke; and that probably with a smile on His face and love in His voice. But this was not the only time that poor Peter would doubt the Master Whom he loved so well. He who then asked to walk upon the waters in order to come quickly to the Lord was the one who would later swear that he was ready to go to prison and even to death for Him. Courageous in the boat but timid in the waters, he would later on be bold at the Last

Supper, but cowardly the night of the trial. The scene at the lake was a rehearsal for another fall of Peter.

The people were still bent on making Our Lord King when they found Him the following day at Capharnaum. To their inquiry as to how He came thither, His answer was one which reprimanded those who thought religion had to do primarily with bread lines and soup kitchens.

> In very truth I know that you have not come looking for me because you saw signs, but because you ate the bread and your hunger was satisfied. *John* 6:26

They had not taken the miracle as a sign of His Divinity; they were looking *for* Him instead of *to* Him. Job saw Him in His loss as well as His gain; they saw Him only as a means of satisfying their bread-hunger, not soul-hunger. Excitement is not religion; if it was, an "Alleluia" on Sunday could become a "Crucify" on Friday.

Our Lord then told them:

> You must work, not for this perishable food, but for the food that lasts, the food of eternal life.
> This food the Son of Man will give you, for he it is upon whom God the Father has set the seal of his authority. *John* 6:27

He was setting two kinds of bread before them: the bread that could perish, and the bread that could endure unto life everlasting. He cautioned them against following Him as a donkey following the master who holds a carrot. To lift their carnal minds to Eternal Food, He suggested that they seek the Heavenly Bread the Father authorized or sealed. Oriental bread was often sealed with the official mark or name of the baker. In fact, the Talmudic word for "baker" is related to the word "seal." As hosts used in the Mass have a seal upon them (such as a lamb, or a cross), so Our Lord was implying that the Bread they should seek was the Bread affirmed by His Father, therefore Himself.

They wanted some further proof that the Father had authorized Him; He gave bread, yes, but it was not stupendous enough. After all, had not Moses given bread from heaven? Their argument was: what proof had they that He was greater than Moses? Thus, they minimized the miracle of the day before, by comparing Him to Moses, and the bread He gave to the manna of the desert. Our Lord had fed the multitude only once, and Moses had fed them for forty years. In the desert the people always called bread "manna," meaning "What is it?" But on one occasion, when they despised the manna, they had called it "light bread." So they now made light of this gift. Our Lord took up the challenge; He said that the manna that they had received from Moses was not Heavenly Bread, nor had it come from heaven; furthermore, it nourished only one nation for a brief space of time. More important still, it was not Moses who gave the manna; it was His Father; finally, the Bread which He would give would nourish unto life everlasting. When He told them that the true Bread came down from heaven, they asked:

Give us this bread now and always.

He answered:

I am the bread of life. *John 6:35*

This was the third time that Our Blessed Lord used an instance from the Old Testament to symbolize Himself. The first was when He likened Himself to the ladder that Jacob saw, thus revealing Himself as a Mediator between heaven and earth. In His discourse with Nicodemus, He compared Himself to the brazen serpent, a healer of the sin-stricken and poisoned world. Now He referred to the manna of the desert, and claimed that He was the true Bread of which the manna had been only the prefigurement. He Who would say:

I am the light of the world. *John 8:12*

I am the door of the sheepfold. *John 10:7–9*

I am the good shepherd. *John 10:11–14*

I am the resurrection and I am life. *John 11:25*

I am the way; I am the truth and I am life. *John 14:6*

I am the real vine. *John 11:25*

now called Himself three times:

I am the bread of life. *John 6:35,41,48,51*

Once again, He makes the shadow of the Cross appear. Bread must be broken; and He Who had come from God must be a sacrificial Victim that men might truly feed on Him. Hence, it would be a Bread that would result from the voluntary offering of His own flesh to rescue the world from the slavery of sin unto the newness of life.

How can this man give us his flesh to eat? they said. Jesus replied, In truth, in very truth I tell you, unless you eat the flesh of the Son of Man and drink his blood you can have no life in you. Whoever eats my flesh and drinks my blood possesses eternal life. *John 6:52–54*

He not only pictured Himself as One Who had come down from heaven but as One Who had come down to *give* Himself, or to die. It would only be in the slain Christ that they would come to understand the glory of a Bread that nourishes unto eternity. He was here referring to His death; for the word "giving" expressed the sacrificial act. The Flesh and Blood of the Incarnate Son of God, which would be severed in death, would become the source of everlasting life. When He said, "My Flesh," He meant His human nature, as "The Word became Flesh" meant that God the Word or the Son assumed to Himself a human nature. But it was only because that human nature would be linked to a Divine Personality for all eternity that He could give eternal life to those who received it. And when He said that He would give that for the life of the world, the Greek word used meant "all mankind."

His words became more poignant because this was the season of the Passover. Though the Jews looked on blood in an awesome manner, they were leading their lambs at that time to Jerusalem, where blood would be sprinkled to the four directions of the earth. The strangeness of the utterance about giving His Body and Blood diminished against the background of the Passover; He meant that the shadow of the animal lamb was passing, and that its place was being taken by the true Lamb of God. As they had communion with the flesh and blood of the Paschal Lamb, so they would now have communion with the Flesh and Blood of the true Lamb of God. He, Who was born in Bethlehem, the "House of Bread" and was laid in a manger, a place of food for lower animals, would now be to men, so inferior to Him, their Bread of Life. Everything in nature has to have communion in order to live; and through it what is lower is transformed into what is higher: chemical into plants, plants into animals, animals into man. And man? Should he not be elevated through communion with Him Who "came down" from heaven to make man a partaker of the Divine nature? As a Mediator between God and man, He said that, as He lived by the Father, so they would live by Him:

> As the living Father sent me, and I live because of the Father, so he who eats me shall live because of me. *John 6:58*

How carnal was the eating of the manna, and how spiritual was the eating of the flesh of Christ! It was a far more intimate living by Him than a baby's living by the nourishment supplied by the mother. Every mother to every child at her breast can say, "Eat, this is my body; this is my blood." But actually the comparison ends there; for in the mother-child relationship, both are on the same level. In the Christ-human relationship, the difference is that of God and man, heaven and earth. Furthermore, no mother ever has to die and take on a more glorious existence in her human nature before she can be the nourishment of her offspring. But Our Lord said that He would have to "give" His life, before He would be the Bread of Life to believers. The plants which nourish animals do not live on another planet; the animals which nourish man do not live in another world. If Christ then was to be the "Life of the World," He must be tabernacled among men as Emmanuel or "God with us," supplying a life for the soul as earthly bread is the life of the body.

But the mind of His hearers rose no higher than the physical, as they asked:

How can this man give us his flesh to eat? *John* 6:52

It was madness for any man to offer his flesh to eat. But they were not left long in the dark as Our Lord corrected them, saying that not a mere man, but "the Son of Man" would give it. As usual, that title referred to the expiatory sacrifice He would offer. Not the dead Christ would believers feed upon, but the Glorified Christ in Heaven Who died, rose from the dead, and ascended into heaven. The mere eating of the flesh and blood of a man would profit nothing; but the glorified Flesh and Blood of the Son of Man would profit unto life everlasting. As man died spiritually by physically eating in the Garden of Eden, so he would live again spiritually through eating the fruit of the Tree of Life.

Christ's words were too literal, and He cleared up too many false interpretations, for any of His hearers to claim that the Eucharist (or Body and Blood He would give) was a mere type or symbol, or that its effects depended upon the subjective dispositions of the receiver. It was Our Lord's method whenever anyone *misunderstood* what He said to correct the misunderstanding, as He did when Nicodemus thought "born again" meant re-entering his mother's womb. But, whenever anyone correctly understood what He said, but found fault with it, He *repeated* what He said. And in this discourse, Our Lord repeated five times what He had said about His Body and Blood. The full meaning of these words did not become evident until the night before He died. In His last will and testament, He left that which on dying no other man has ever been able to leave, namely, His Body, Blood, Soul, and Divinity, for the life of the world.

15. The Refusal to Be a Bread King

The announcement of the Eucharist produced one of the greatest crises in His life. His promise to give His Body, Blood, Soul, and Divinity for the souls of men caused Him to lose much that He had gained. Until now He had almost everyone behind Him: first, the masses or the common people; next, the elite, the intellectuals, and the spiritual leaders; and finally, His own Apostles. But this lofty spiritual doctrine was too much for them. The announcement of the Eucharist cracked His followers wide open. No wonder there has been such a division of sects in Christianity when each man decides for himself whether he will accept a segment of the circle of Christ's truth or the whole circle. Our Lord Himself was responsible for this; He asked a faith too much for most men; His doctrine was too sublime. If He had been only a little more worldly-minded, if He had only allowed His words to be treated as figures of speech, and if He had only been less imperative He might have been more popular.

But He rocked all His followers. Calvary would be the hot war against Him; this was the beginning of the cold war. Calvary would be the physical Crucifixion; this was the social Crucifixion.

He lost the masses;

He created a schism among His disciples;

He even weakened His apostolic band.

He lost the masses: The masses were generally interested only in wonders and in security. When He multiplied the loaves and fishes, He startled their eyes. When He filled their stomachs, He satisfied their sense of social justice. That was the kind of king they wanted, a bread king. "What else can religion do for man, anyway, except give him social security?" they seemed to ask. The masses tried to force Him to become a king. That is what Satan wanted, too! Fill gullets, turn stones into bread, and promise prosperity—this is the end of living to most mortals.

But Our Lord would have no kingship based on the economics of plenty. To make Him King was His Father's business, not theirs: His Kingship would be of hearts and souls, not digestive tracts. So the Gospel tells us He fled into the mountains Himself alone, to escape their tinsel crown and tin sword.

How close the masses were to salvation! They wanted life; He wanted to give *life*. The difference was in their interpretation of life. Is it the business of Christ to win followers by elaborate social programs? This is one form of life. Or is it the business of Christ to be willing to lose all the stomach-minded at the cost of reaching the few with faith, to whom will be given the Bread of Life and the Wine that germinates virgins? From that day on, Christ never won the masses; within twenty months they would shout, "Crucify!" as Pilate would say, "Behold your King." Christ cannot keep everybody united with Him: it is His fault; He is too Divine, too interested in souls, too spiritual for most men.

He also lost a second group that day, namely, the elite, or the intellectual and religious leaders. They would accept Him as a meek, gentle Reformer Who would not extinguish the burning flax; but when it came to saying that He would give His very life, more intimately than a mother gives life to a child at her breast, that was too much. So the Gospel tells us:

> Many of his disciples on hearing it exclaimed, This is more than we can stomach! Why listen to such talk? *John* 6:61

> From that time on, many of his disciples withdrew and no longer went about with him. *John* 6:67

Our Blessed Lord would certainly never have permitted them to leave if they had not understood what He had said, namely, that He would give us His very life as our life. It could only be that understanding it correctly, they could not swallow it. And He permitted them to leave. As they left He said to them:

> Does this shock you? What if you see the Son of Man ascending to the place where he was before? *John* 6:63

Of course, it tried their faith. Do not men have reason? What was He expecting them to believe? That He was God? That every word He said was Absolute Truth? That He would be able to give hungry souls the same Divine life that they saw before their eyes now? Why not forget this Bread of Life and make it a figure of speech? So Our Lord watched them leave; and they never came back. One day they would be found stirring up the masses against Him; for although they did not leave Him for the same reason, they were agreed that they should take leave of Him.

Christ lost both the chaff and the wheat when He spoke of Himself as the Bread of Life. But now came the break which caused Him the greatest of all sorrow—a sorrow so great that, a thousand years before, it had been prophesied as one of those human rents which would torture His soul—the loss of Judas. Many wonder why Judas broke with

Our Lord; they think it was only at the end of Our Lord's life, and
that it was only love of money that forced the break. Avarice, indeed
it was; but the Gospel tells us the astounding story that Judas broke
with Our Divine Lord the day He announced the giving of His Flesh
for the life of the world. In the midst of this long story of the Body
and Blood of Christ, the Gospel tells us that Our Lord knew who it
was that would betray Him. Showing Judas that He knew, He said:

> Have I not chosen you, all twelve? Yet one of you is a devil.
>
> *John 6:71*

At this promise of the Heavenly Bread, Judas cracked; and at the giving of the Eucharist on the night of the Last Supper, Judas split wide
open and betrayed.

Our Lord now marched practically alone. There would be only 120
awaiting His Spirit on Pentecost. He had lost all three types: He saw
the masses abandon, the elite walk away, and Judas prepare to betray
Him. So He turned to the one whom He had associated so intimately
with Himself, the man whose name He had changed, from Simon to
Peter or Rock, and said to him:

> Do you also want to leave me? Simon Peter answered him, Lord, to
> whom shall we go? Your words are words of eternal life. We have
> faith, and we know that you are the Holy One of God.
>
> *John 6:67–69*

But the Heart of Christ already had a Cross in it. One of His own
twelve was a traitor. The elite, who were divided among themselves,
would now unite against Him. And the five thousand that had been
in contact with His hand refused to be in contact with His Heart.
The forces were shaping up for "the Hour."

16. Purity and Property

At the beginning of His public life Our Lord's object was by miracles, teachings, and the fulfillment of prophecies, so to attach His Apostles to Himself as to forestall outside pressure and the natural rebellion of the flesh against Himself as the Suffering Servant. But even when they had become devoted to Him and had accepted Him as the Messiah and the Son of God, they shrank from the idea of the Crucifixion, even when He said it would be followed by the Resurrection. They were all like little Indians, each one wanting to be the chief. The darkness into which His death cast them was another proof of how little prepared they were for the scandal of the Cross. It was no wonder that Our Lord did not speak more often about His Cross; for the little they did hear, they did not want to hear or else they misunderstood.

> There is still much that I could say to you, but the burden would be too great for you now. *John 16:12*

To prepare their souls for His lifework and also to indicate the conditions under which others would enter into His Kingdom, the Savior among other subjects dilated particularly on purity and poverty. Unregulated sex could become lust; unregulated desire for property could become avarice.

PURITY

The subject was occasioned by the Pharisees who came to ask Him if it was right for a man to put away his wife for any reason whatsoever. The reason why the Pharisees presented this question was because of a dispute between two rival schools of Jewish theology, namely, the school of Hillel and that of Shannai. One school held that divorce could be granted on trivial grounds; the other required evidence of serious sin before it would approve of divorce. The question was further complicated by the fact that divorce in those days was becoming very common; the Romans, who were masters of the country, practiced it openly and flagrantly. Furthermore, Herod, the ruler of the country under Rome, was living with his brother's wife and had murdered John the Baptist.

The Divine Savior in answer to their enquiry reaffirmed what He had already said on the Mount, and also what was held from the beginning as regards husband and wife.

It follows that they are no longer two individuals: they are one flesh.
What God has joined together, man must not separate.

> *Matthew 19:6*

When the disciples had heard the full remarks of Our Blessed Lord
on this subject—though some perhaps were married, including Peter
for certain—they went to the opposite extreme and concluded:

It is better not to marry. *Matthew 19:11*

Here the Savior answered that because there were infidelities in some
marriages, there must be others which would balance the excesses by
self-denial. If there are excesses of the flesh, there must be those who
will forgo even the legitimate pleasures of the flesh; if there are deor-
dinations in the pursuit of property, there must be some who will
voluntarily practice poverty; if there are some who are proud, there
must be others who will not even insist upon their own rights, but
will make reparation for acts of pride by humility.

Our Lord told the Apostles that it ought not be thought that it was
better not to marry. Rather He said:

> That is something which not everyone can accept, but only those for
> whom God has appointed it. For while some are incapable of mar-
> riage because they were born so, or were made so by men, there are
> others who have themselves renounced marriage for the sake of the
> kingdom of Heaven. Let those accept it who can. *Matthew 19:11,12*

Celibacy is recommended as a wiser way, but is not required of the
majority. Later on, Peter left his wife in order to preach the Gospel.
When Our Blessed Lord recommended celibacy, it was very likely
that the disciples were not thinking of it as applied to themselves, but
rather were objecting to the severity of the Master's teaching on the
ground that it would deter men from entering marriage. His answer
shows that they understood His meaning. Their error was in failing to
realize to what sacrificial heights He would summon men for the sake
of His Kingdom. He Who founded society and Who knew the compulsions of the sex instinct, nevertheless made room for a few who
would be celibates. Some are born eunuchs; others, like Origen, have
wrongly made themselves eunuchs; but there is a third class, those
who, not by any physical act, but by an act of willful self-denial and
self-abnegation, have set aside the pleasure of the flesh for the joys of
the spirit; it is these He called eunuchs for the Kingdom of Heaven.
Later on, St. Paul, hearing of this doctrine, wrote:

> I want you to be free from anxious care. The unmarried man cares
> for the Lord's business; his aim is to please the Lord. But the married
> man cares for worldly things; his aim is to please his wife; and he has
> a divided mind. *I Corinthians 7:32,33*

Marriage is honorable; at no point did Our Savior say that it blotted out the spiritual sense, or man's relations with God; but in celibacy or virginity the soul chooses Him as its exclusive Lover.

PROPERTY

Just as sex is a God-given instinct for the prolongation of the human race, so the desire for property as a prolongation of one's ego is a natural right sanctioned by natural law. A person is free on the inside because he can call his soul his own; he is free on the outside because he can call property his own. Internal freedom is based upon the fact that "I am"; external freedom is based on the fact that "I have." But just as the excesses of flesh produce lust, for lust is sex in the wrong place, as dirt is matter in the wrong place, so there can be a deordination of the desire for property until it becomes greed, avarice, and capitalistic aggression.

In order to atone, repair, and make up for excess of avarice and selfishness, Our Blessed Lord now gave a second lesson in self-sacrifice to His Apostles. The occasion of the first lesson on purity was a pharisaical question about marriage; the occasion of the second was an enquiring young man. Our Blessed Lord had a chance to win him as a follower; but when He spoke of the Cross, He lost him. The young man wanted the prize, but the cost was too great. The youth who came was rich and also a synagogue official. The desire to be associated with Our Lord was manifested by the fact that he came running to Him and fell at His feet. As regards the uprightness of the youth there could be no doubt; his question to Our Lord was:

Master, what good must I do to gain eternal life? *Matthew 19:16*

Unlike Nicodemus, he did not come at night, but openly avowed the goodness of the Master. The youth believed that he was not very far from the great attainment of eternal life; but all that he needed was just some further instruction and enlightenment. The Savior pointed to the fact that men knew enough, but they did not always do enough. And lest the young man rest in some imperfect idea of goodness, the Lord asked:

Why do you call me good? No one is good except God alone.
Mark 10:18

Our Lord was not objecting to being called good, but to being taken merely as a good teacher. The young man had addressed Him as a great teacher, but still as a man; he had admitted goodness, but still on the level of human goodness. If He were merely a man the title of essential goodness would not belong to Him. There was hidden in His answer an affirmation of His Deity; God alone is good. He was, therefore, inviting the young man to cry out, "Thou art Christ, the Son of the Living God."

The young man admitted that he had kept the commandments since his youth. With that Our Lord fastened His eyes on him and conceived a love for him.

When the young man asked:

> Where do I still fall short? *Matthew* 19:20

Our Lord answered:

> If you wish to go the whole way, go, sell your possessions, and give to the poor, and then you will have riches in heaven; and come, follow me. *Matthew* 19:21

There was no condemnation of wealth here as there was no condemnation of marriage in the previous enquiry; but there was a higher perfection than the human. As a man might leave his wife, so also a man might leave his property. The Cross would demand that souls give up what they loved most and be content with the treasure in God's hands. One may ask why did the Lord ask for such a sacrifice? The Savior allowed Zacchaeus the tax collector to keep half his goods; Joseph of Arimathea, after the Crucifixion, was described as rich; the property of Ananias was his own; Our Lord ate in the home of His wealthy friends in Bethany. But here it was a question of a young man who asked what was still wanting in the way of perfection. When the Lord proposed to him the ordinary way of salvation, namely, keeping the commandments, the youth was dissatisfied. He sought for something more perfect; but when the perfect way was proposed to him, namely, renunciation:

> When the young man heard this, he went away with a heavy heart; for he was a man of great wealth. *Matthew* 19:22

There are degrees in the love of God, one common and the other heroic. The common was the keeping of the commandments; the heroic was renouncement, the taking-up of the cross of voluntary poverty. The earnestness of the youth vanished; he kept his possessions and he lost the One Who would give him the Cross. Though the young man kept his possessions, he is described as going away "sorrowful."

When the young man left, Our Lord said to His Apostles:

> How hard it will be for the wealthy to enter the kingdom of God!
>   . . . It is easier for a camel to pass through the eye of a needle than for a rich man to enter the kingdom of God.
>   *Mark* 10:23–25

Our Lord then turned to His followers whom He had called to the perfect way, and made use of this incident to speak to them of the virtues of poverty. Just as the disciples before had wondered if anyone should ever marry, now they wondered how anyone could ever be saved. The disciples were "astonished" and asked:

> They were more astonished than ever, and said to one another, Then who can be saved? *Mark 10:26*

One wonders what thoughts circulated in the brain of one of the disciples, who was even then pilfering from the bag what was intended for the poor. The disciples were those who had at least implicitly associated riches with the blessings of heaven, just as in modern history there have not been wanting those who held Divine favor was always known by economic prosperity. The rich come to the top because God has blessed them, it is said, and the poor go to the bottom because God does not favor them. Now, to be told that wealth was a hindrance to the Kingdom of God, was in another form the "scandal of the Cross." The Apostles knew that they had given up their boats and their fishing nets, little enough though they were; but still they did not quite feel themselves sufficiently free from avarice to be safe. It was this Divine prodding of their conscience that made them wonder about salvation, as on the night of the Last Supper everyone would ask: "Is it I?" As the Divine eyes were fixed on them, they wondered about the state of their souls. The Divine Master did not tell them they were judging themselves too strictly. In answer to their question about salvation:

> Jesus looked at them, and said, For men this is impossible; but everything is possible for God. *Matthew 19:26*

Because a camel cannot pass through the eye of a needle, it would be too severe to say that the same impossibility stands in the way of a man's salvation; for there is always the Divine possibility.

Peter, once again acting as spokesman of the Apostles, demanded some further elucidation of this economic problem of giving up property. He had heard Our Lord speak of the greatness of the reward reserved for those who followed Him. Knowing that they had left their business by the sea in order to follow Him, Peter asked:

> We here have left everything to become your followers. What will there be for us? *Matthew 19:27*

The Apostles evidently had not left as much as the rich young man would have abandoned; but it is not the quantity that one leaves that matters, but rather the fact that one has left all. Charity is to be measured, not by what one has given away, but by what one has left. In both cases, neither would have had anything left. Those who choose Christ must choose Him for His own sake, and not for the sake of a reward. It was only after they had completely committed themselves to following Him that He spoke of compensation. He had recommended the Cross; now He would speak of the glory which would be its inevitable consequence:

> I tell you this: in the world that is to be, when the Son of Man is seated on his throne in heavenly splendour, you my followers will have thrones of your own, where you will sit as judges of the twelve tribes of Israel. *Matthew 19:28*

He bade them look forward to a great regeneration, to a Divine new order of things. The Son of Man Who would have the Cross on earth would have His glory in heaven.

As for them, they were to be the foundation stones of this new order. Israel had been founded out of the twelve sons of Jacob; so too His new order was to be founded on these twelve Apostles, who left all for Him. In this new Kingdom, a peculiar glory would be given to them as patriarchs of the new order. John, who was among them at the moment, later on would write:

> The city wall had twelve foundation-stones, and on them were the names of the twelve apostles of the Lamb. *Apocalypse 21:14*

Elaborating on the idea of reward for those who gave up their possessions, Jesus said:

> I tell you this: there is no one who has given up home, brothers or sisters, mother, father or children, or land, for my sake and for the Gospel, who will not receive in this age a hundred times as much— houses, brothers and sisters, mothers and children, and land—and persecutions besides; and in the age to come eternal life.
> *Mark 10:29-31*

"Persecution" was thrown into the account of the rewards, not as if it were a loss, but a gain. The hundredfold reward would come not so much in spite of persecution, as on account of it. If they were faithful unto death, they would receive the crown of life; for the afflictions of this world were not to be compared with the joys to come. Thus did the Master brand Calvary into their flesh and their possessions, telling the Apostles to forsake that which others desired to keep. Peter, who had asked what he would get out of giving up his boats, had already been told that he would be the helmsman of the bark of Peter, or the

Church. But that day, when Our Lord spoke of blessings and tossed in "persecution" as good measure, Peter never forgot. Later, in the midst of joys and persecutions, he wrote it down:

> It gives you a share in Christ's sufferings, and that is cause for joy; and when his glory is revealed, your joy will be triumphant.
>
> *I Peter 4:14*

17. Our Lord's Testimony Concerning Himself

The closer a person approaches God, the less worthy he feels. A painting under candlelight shows fewer defects than under the brilliance of the sun; so too the souls who are some distance from God feel more certain of their moral integrity than those who are very close to Him. Those who have left the lights and glamours of the world, and for years have been irradiated by His countenance, have been the foremost to acknowledge themselves as freighted down with the great burden of sin. St. Paul, who has been such an edification to men, called himself "the chief of sinners." In the presence of the holiest of creatures, the soul becomes self-accusing and broken-hearted with the weight of its defects. As evil men feel their guilt more in the presence of an innocent babe than in the companionship of those who are wicked like themselves, so he who loves God is the most deeply burdened with the sense of his own unworthiness.

But Our Blessed Lord, Who claimed oneness with God, never once confessed a sin or an imperfection. In vain can this be attributed to moral dullness, since His analysis of sin in others was so penetrating. What man is there in the world who could boldly stand up before great crowds and say:

> Which of you can prove me in the wrong? *John 8:46*

Though Our Blessed Lord associated Himself with sinners, there never existed the least suspicion against His spotless innocence. He told His disciples to pray, "Forgive us our trespasses," but not even in His last agony did He have to utter such a prayer. He forgave the sins of others, in *His name:* "Thy sins are forgiven thee," and yet never asked for pardon. He issued the challenge: "If you cannot detect a moral blot on My escutcheon, then credit Me with truth." Because He was sinless, He asserted His position in such a way as to make claims upon all mankind, such as calling Himself "the Light" of a darkened world:

> I am the light of the world. No follower of mine shall wander in the dark; he shall have the light of life. *John 8:12*

Note, it is not His teaching that is the Light of the World, but rather His Person. As there is only one sun to light a world physically, so He was asserting that He was the only Light for the world spiritually; without Him every soul would be wrapped in darkness. As dust in the room cannot be seen until the light is let in, so no man can know himself until this Light shows him his true condition. He who was only a good man could never claim to be the Light of the World; for there would cling to him some of the trappings and faults of even the best human nature. Buddha wrote a code which he said would be useful to guide men in darkness, but he never claimed to be the Light of the World. Buddhism was born with a disgust for the world, when a prince's son deserted his wife and child, turning from the pleasures of existence to the problems of existence. Burnt by the fires of the world, and already weary with it, Buddha turned to ethics.

But Our Divine Lord never had this feeling of disgust. If He was the Light, it was not because He had injured Himself stumbling in the darkness. Mohammed admitted at his death that he was no Light of the World, but said, "Fearful, beseeching, seeking for shelter, weak and in need of mercy, I confess my sin before Thee, presenting my supplication as the poor supplicate the rich." Confucius was so overshadowed by the darkness of sin, that he never made such a claim. He admitted:

> that I have not been able to practice virtue aright, that I have not been able to utter or pursue aright what I have learned, that I have been unable to change that which was wrong—these are my sorrows. . . . In knowledge perhaps I am equal to other men, but I have not been able to transform the essence of what is noble into deed.

Before his death, Buddha said to Ananda, his favorite disciple, "The doctrines and the laws, O Ananda, which I have taught and proclaimed unto you, *they* shall be your master when I have left you."

Our Blessed Lord left the world without leaving any written message. His doctrine was Himself. Ideal and History were identified in Him. The truth that all other ethical teachers proclaimed, and the light that they gave to the world, was not *in* them, but *outside* them. Our Divine Lord, however, identified Divine Wisdom with Himself. It was the first time in history that it was ever done, and it has never been done since.

This identification of His Personality with Wisdom He broadened when He said:

> I am the way; I am the truth and I am life; no one comes to the Father except by me. If you knew me you would know my Father too. *John 14:6,7*

This is equivalent to saying that without the Way there is no going; without the Truth, there is no knowing; without the Life, there is no living. The Way becomes lovable, not when it is in abstract codes and commandments, but when it is Personal. As Plato once said, "The Father of the world is hard to discover, and when discovered cannot be communicated." Our Lord's answer to Plato would have been that the Father is hard to discover unless He is revealed through the Person of His Son.

There is no such thing as seeking first the truth and then finding Christ, any more than there is any point in lighting tapers to find the sun. As scientific truths put us in an intelligent relation with the cosmos, as historic truth puts us in temporal relation with the rise and fall of civilizations, so does Christ put us in intelligent relation with God the Father; for He is the only possible Word by which God can address Himself to a world of sinners.

> Everything is entrusted to me by my Father; and no one knows the Son but the Father, and no one knows the Father but the Son and those to whom the Son may choose to reveal him. *Matthew* 11:27

Life is resident in Him in virtue of an eternal communication from the Father. All who came before Him, and who will come after Him, and who offer any other way than Himself, He compares with thieves and robbers of mankind.

> I am the door of the sheepfold. The sheep paid no heed to any who came before me, for these were all thieves and robbers. I am the door; anyone who comes into the fold through me shall be safe. He shall go in and out and shall find pasturage. *John* 10:7–10

No one else ever made His personality the condition of securing peace or eternal life. Our Blessed Lord, however, identified Personality with a door; it is an emblem of separation because on the one side is the world and on the other side the home; but also it is a sign of protection, hospitality, and relationship. As the old city of Troy had but one gate, so Our Blessed Lord said that He is the only Gate to salvation. Being united with Him He called a trysting place, where He and souls meet in the ecstasy of love. "Come and go at will," would seem to indicate a union of both the contemplative and the actual life; for the combination of an interior union with Christ is here combined with practical obedience in the world of action.

Not only did Our Lord identify all Truth and Life with Himself, but He put forth His claim to judge the world—something no mere man would ever do. He said that as the Judge of all He would return again seated on a throne of glory and attended by the angels, to judge all men according to their works. Imagination recoils at the thought of any human being able to penetrate into the depths of all consciences, to ferret out all the hidden motives, and to pass judgment on them for all eternity. But this final judgment was a long way off and hidden from the eyes of men. There would be a symbol or rehearsal of the final judgment which would be the destruction of Jerusalem and which would be accomplished before the end of the actual generation of Christ's day. It would also be a prelude to the final destruction at the end of the world, when the Kingdom of God would be established in its eternal and glorious phase. Speaking of the end of the world, He said:

> Then will appear in heaven the sign that heralds the Son of Man. All the peoples of the world will make lamentation, and they will see the Son of Man coming on the clouds of heaven with great power and glory. With a trumpet blast he will send out his angels, and they will gather his chosen from the four winds, from the farthest bounds of heaven on every side. *Matthew 24:30,31*

When He comes to judge it will not be merely the circumscribed area of the earth in which He labored and revealed Himself; rather it will be all the nations and the empires of the world. The time of His second coming He knows not as man, but only as God. He will not tell it except in warning that it will be sudden, like lightning. He came as a "Man of Sorrows"; then He shall come in His glory. The attributes of His suffering humanity will be necessary for His identification. Hence, after His Resurrection, He kept the scars. With Him will be the angels, and all the nations will be divided into two classes: sheep and goats. As He divided men on earth into two classes, namely, those who hated and those who loved Him, so He would divide them then. "I am the Good Shepherd," He said of Himself. The title He would vindicate on the last day by a separation of His flock of sheep from the goats.

The sheep will hear themselves commended for loving service to Him, even when it was unconscious service. There are many more people loving and serving Him than one suspects. It would seem that the most surprised of all will be the social workers who will ask, "When was it that we saw Thee hungry? Was it case #643?" The wicked, on the other hand, will find themselves refusing Him when they refused to do anything for their fellow man in His name.

> When the Son of Man comes in his glory and all the angels with him, he will sit in state on his throne, with all the nations gathered before him. He will separate men into two groups, as a shepherd separates the sheep from the goats, and he will place the sheep on his right

hand and the goats on his left. Then the king will say to those on his right hand, You have my Father's blessing; come, enter and possess the kingdom that has been ready for you since the world was made. For when I was hungry, you gave me food; when thirsty, you gave me drink; when I was a stranger you took me into your home, when naked you clothed me; when I was ill you came to my help, when in prison you visited me. Then the righteous will reply, Lord, when was it that we saw you hungry and fed you, or thirsty and gave you drink, a stranger and took you home, or naked and clothed you? When did we see you ill or in prison, and come to visit you? And the king will answer, I tell you this: anything you did for one of my brothers here, however humble, you did for me. Then he will say to those on his left hand, The curse is upon you; go from my sight to the eternal fire that is ready for the devil and his angels. For when I was hungry you gave me nothing to eat, when thirsty nothing to drink; when I was a stranger you gave me no home, when naked you did not clothe me; when I was ill and in prison you did not come to my help. And they too will reply, Lord when was it that we saw you hungry or thirsty or a stranger or naked or ill or in prison, and did nothing for you? And he will answer, I tell you this: anything you did not do for one of these, however humble, you did not do for me. And they will go away to eternal punishment, but the righteous will enter life.

Matthew 25:31–46

His words even imply that philanthropy has deeper depths than is generally realized. The great emotions of compassion and mercy are traced to Him; there is more to human deeds than the doers are aware. He identified every act of kindness as an expression of sympathy with Himself. All kindnesses are either done explicitly or implicitly in His name, or they are refused explicitly or implicitly in His name. Mohammed said that alms had to be given, but not in *his name.* Our Lord made that the condition, but as a mere man, it would have been foolishness. Furthermore, only an Omniscient Will could ever judge the motives behind all philanthropy to decide when it was charity, and when it was self-praise. That He claimed He would do and with such finality that the repercussions would be eternal. He Who was the Redeemer said that He would also be the Judge. It is a beautiful arrangement of Providence that the Judge and the Redeemer meet in the same Person.

When one takes into account also His reiterated assertions about His Divinity—such as asking us to love Him above parents, to believe in Him even in the face of persecution, to be ready to sacrifice our bodies in order to save our souls in union with Him—to call Him just a good man ignores the facts. No man is good unless he is humble; and humility is a recognition of truth concerning oneself. A man who thinks he is greater than he actually is is not humble, but a vain and boastful fool. How can any man claim prerogatives over conscience, and over history, and over society and the world, and still claim he is "meek and humble of heart"? But if He is God as well as man, His language falls into place and everything that He says is intelligible. But if He is not what He claimed to be, then some of His most precious sayings are nothing but bombastic outbursts of self-adulation that breathe rather the spirit of Lucifer than the spirit of a good man. What avails Him to proclaim the law of self-renouncement, if He Himself renounces truth to call Himself God? Even His sacrifice on the Cross becomes a suspect and a dated thing, when it goes hand in hand with delusions of grandeur and infernal conceit. He could not be called even a sincere teacher, for no sincere teacher would allow anyone to construe his claims to share the rank and the name of the Great God in heaven.

The choice that lies before men is either the hypothesis of culpable insincerity or the fact that He spoke the literal truth and, therefore, must be taken at His word. It is easier to believe that God has achieved His Works of Wonder and Mercy in His Divine Son on earth than to close the moral eye to the brightest spot that meets it in human history, and thus lapse into despair. No human could be good, aye! he would be arrogant and blasphemous, to have made the assertions He did concerning Himself. Instead of being above His moral followers who call themselves Christians, He would have been infinitely below the level of the worst of them. It is easier to believe what He said about Himself, namely, that He is God, than to explain how the world could ever have taken as a model such an unmitigated liar, such a contemptuous boaster. It is only because Jesus is God that the human character of Jesus is a manifestation of the Divine.

We must either lament His madness or adore His Person, but we cannot rest on the assumption that He was a professor of ethical culture. Rather, one can say with Chesterton, "Expect the grass to wither and the birds to drop dead out of the air, when a strolling carpenter's apprentice says calmly and almost carelessly, like one looking over his shoulder: 'Before Abraham was, I am.'" The Roman sergeant, who had his own gods and was hardened both to war and death, came to the answer during the Crucifixion, when both his reason and his conscience affirmed the truth:

Truly this man was a son of God. *Matthew 27:54*

18. *Transfiguration*

Three important scenes of Our Lord's life took place on mountains. On one, He preached the Beatitudes, the practice of which would bring a Cross from the world; on the second, He showed the glory that lay beyond the Cross; and on the third, He offered Himself in death as a prelude to His glory and that of all who would believe in His name.

The second incident took place within a few weeks, at most, of Calvary, when He took with Him to a high mountain Peter, James, and John—Peter the Rock; James destined to be the first Apostle-martyr; and John the visionary of the future glory of the Apocalypse. These three were present when He raised from the dead the daughter of Jairus. All three needed to learn the lesson of the Cross and to rectify their false conceptions of the Messiah. Peter had vehemently protested against the Cross, while James and John had been throne-seekers. All three would later on sleep in the Garden of Gethsemane during His agony. To believe in His Calvary, they must see the glory that shone beyond the scandal of the Cross.

On the mountaintop, after praying, He became transfigured before them as the glory of His Divinity flashed through the threads of His earthly raiment. It was not so much a light that was shining from without as the beauty of the Godhead that shone from within. It was not the full manifestation of Divinity which no man of earth could see; nor was His body glorified, for He had not risen from the dead, but it possessed a quality of glory. His crib, His carpenter trade, His bearing opprobrium from enemies were a humiliation; fittingly there should also be epiphanies of glory, as the angels' song at His birth and the voice of the Father during the baptism.

Now as He nears Calvary, a new glory surrounds Him. The voice again invests Him in the robes of the priesthood, to offer sacrifice. The glory that shone around Him as the Temple of God was not something with which He was outwardly invested, but rather a natural expression of the inherent loveliness of "Him who came down from heaven." The wonder was not this momentary radiance around Him; it was rather that at all other times it was repressed. After Moses, after communing with God, put a veil over his face to hide it from the people of Israel, so Christ had veiled His glory in humanity. But for this brief moment, He turned it aside so that men might see it; the outgoing of these rays was the transitory proclamation to every human eye of the Son of Righteousness. As the Cross came nearer, His glory became greater. So it may be that the coming of the anti-Christ or the final crucifixion of the good will be preceded by an extraordinary glory of Christ in His members.

In man, the body is a kind of cage of the soul. In Christ, the Body was the Temple of Divinity. In the Garden of Eden, we know that man and woman were naked but not ashamed. This is because the glory of the soul before sin shone through the body and became a kind of a raiment. Here too in the Transfiguration, the Divinity shone through humanity. This was probably much more natural than for Christ to be seen in any other pose, namely, without that glory. It took restraint to hide the Divinity that was in Him.

> And while he was praying the appearance of his face changed and his clothes became dazzling white. Suddenly there were two men talking with him; these were Moses and Elijah, who appeared in glory and spoke of his departure, the destiny he was to fulfil in Jerusalem.
>
> *Luke 9:30,31*

The Old Testament was coming to meet the New. Moses the publisher of the Law, Elijah the chief of the Prophets—both of them were seen shining in the Light of Christ Himself Who, as the Son of God, gave the Law and sent the Prophets. The subject of conversation of Moses, Elijah and Christ was not what he had taught, but His sacrificial death; it was His duty as Mediator which fulfilled the Law, the Prophets and the Eternal Decrees. Their work done, they pointed to Him to see the Redemption accomplished.

Thus did He keep before Him the goal of being "numbered with the transgressors," as Isaiah had foretold. Even in this moment of glory, the Cross is the theme of the discourse with the celestial visitors. But it was death conquered, sin atoned and the grave despoiled. The light of glory which enveloped the scene was joy like the "Now let me die," which Jacob said on seeing Joseph, or like the *Nunc Dimittis* which Simeon uttered on seeing the Divine Babe. Aeschylus, in his *Agamemnon*, describes a soldier returning to his native land after the Trojan War and in his joy saying that he was willing to die. Shakespeare puts the same joyful words on the lips of Othello after the perils of voyage:

> If it were now to die
> 'Twere now to be most happy; for, I fear,
> My soul hath her content so absolute
> That not another comfort like to this
> Succeeds in unknown fate.

But in the case of Our Lord, it was as St. Paul said, "Having joy set before Him, He endured the Cross."

What the Apostles noticed as particularly beautiful and glorified were His face and His garments—the face which later would be splattered with blood flowing from a crown of thorns; and the garments, which would be a robe of scorn with which sneering Herod would dress Him. The gossamer of light which now surrounded Him would be exchanged for nakedness when He would be stripped on a hill.

While the Apostles were standing at what seemed to be the very vestibule of heaven, a cloud formed, overshadowing them:

> While he was still speaking, a bright cloud suddenly overshadowed them, and a voice called from the cloud: This is my Son, my Beloved, on whom my favour rests; listen to him. *Matthew 17:6*

When God sets up a cloud it is a manifest sign that there are bonds which man dare not break. At His baptism, the heavens were opened; now at the Transfiguration they opened again to install Him in His office as Mediator, and to distinguish Him from Moses and the Prophets. It was heaven itself that was sending Him on His mission not the perverse will of men. At the baptism, the voice from heaven was for Jesus Himself; on the Hill of the Transfiguration it was for the disciples. The shouts of "Crucify" would be too much for their ears if they did not know that it behooved the Son to suffer. It was not Moses nor Elijah they were to hear, but Him who apparently would die like any other teacher, but was more than a prophet. The voice testified to the unbroken and undivided union of Father and Son; it recalled also the words of Moses that in due time God would raise up from Israel One like Himself Whom they should hear.

The Apostles, awakening at the brilliance of what they had seen, found their spokesman, as almost always, in Peter.

> And as these were moving away from Jesus, Peter said to him, Master, how good it is that we are here! Shall we make three shelters, one for you, one for Moses, and one for Elijah?; but he spoke without knowing what he was saying. *Luke 9:33,34*

A week before, Peter was trying to find a way to glory without the Cross. Now he thought the Transfiguration a good short cut to salvation by having a Mount of the Beatitudes or a Mount of the Transfiguration without the Mount of Calvary. It was Peter's second attempt to dissuade Our Lord from going to Jerusalem to be crucified. Before Calvary he was the spokesman for all those who would enter into glory without purchasing it by self-denial and sacrifice. Peter in his impetuosity here felt that the glory which God brought down from the heavens, and of which the angels sang at Bethlehem, could be tabernacled among men without a war against sin. Peter forgot that as the dove rested his foot only after the deluge, so true peace comes only after the Crucifixion.

Like a child, Peter tried to capitalize and make permanent this transient glory. To the Savior, it was an anticipation of what was reflected from the other side of the Cross; to Peter, it was a manifestation of an earthly Messianic glory that ought to be housed. The Lord Who called Peter "Satan" because he would have a crown without a Cross now ignored his noncrucial humanism, for He knew that "he spoke at random." But after the Resurrection, Peter would know. Then he would recall the scene, saying:

> It was not on tales artfully spun that we relied when we told you of the power of our Lord Jesus Christ and his coming; we saw him with our own eyes in majesty, when at the hands of God the Father he was invested with honour and glory, and there came to him from the sublime Presence a voice which said: This is my Son, my Beloved, on whom my favour rests. This voice from heaven we ourselves heard; when it came, we were with him on the sacred mountain.
>
> All this only confirms for us the message of the prophets, to which you will do well to attend, because it is like a lamp shining in a murky place, until the day breaks and the morning star rises to illuminate your minds. *II Peter* 1:16–20

19. *The Three Quarrelings*

A suffering God-man is a scandal. Men do not like to hear about their sins and the need for expiating them. Hence, whenever Jesus dragged in His Cross and paraded its necessity before His Apostles, they began fighting either Him or themselves. They were still obsessed with the idea that His Kingdom would be political, not spiritual. If He was going to Calvary, then it was best for them to "cash in" as quickly as possible on rewards, or posts, and privileges which were immediately available. The more explicit His prediction of His Cross, the more their ambitions, envies, and animosities were aroused.

Nothing is more beautiful in Our Lord's character than the way He prepared His Apostles for that unpalatable lesson of seeming defeat as the condition of victory. How slow they were to understand the story of why He *must* suffer! It is no wonder Our Lord spoke openly but rarely of His Cross and Resurrection. For it was something few could understand until after it came to pass and the Spirit of Christ came into His followers. Many were the times He spoke of His death in a veiled manner; but three times He was explicit about the purpose of His coming:

1 After Peter's affirmation of His Divinity and the conferring of the power of keys.
2 After His Transfiguration en route to Capharnaum.
3 On His last journey to Jerusalem.

But what strange reactions on the part of His Apostles! It was as if they would salvage for themselves, from the wreck of His Kingdom, some vestige of power and authority. That the Cross was the condition by which His Kingdom would be ushered in was farthest from their minds.

THE FIRST QUARRELING: CAESAREA PHILIPPI

When Our Blessed Lord came into this most northerly city of the Holy Land, a city that was half Jewish and half pagan, He spoke of the Church He would found. But before doing so, He had to make clear the form of government which would govern it. These forms could be threefold: democratic, aristocratic, and theocratic. The democratic is one in which authority and truth is decided by a vote or an arithmetical majority; the aristocratic is one in which authority is derived from a select few; the theocratic is one in which God Himself supplies and guides the revelation and the truth.

First appealing to the democratic, He asked His Apostles what was the general popular opinion concerning Him. If there had been a poll or a vote taken basing itself on the fallible judgments of men, what would be their answer to this question?

Who do men say that the Son of Man is? *Matthew* 16:13

The inability of men to agree among themselves concerning His Divinity was revealed in their answer:

They answered, Some say John the Baptist, others Elijah, others Jeremiah, or one of the prophets. *Matthew* 16:14

Human opinion can give only conflicting, contrary, and contradictory answers. The four popular opinions show that Our Blessed Lord enjoyed a high reputation among His fellow men, but that none of them had recognized Him for what He was. Herod Antipas fancied that Our Lord was One animated by the spirit of John the Baptist; others thought He was Elijah, because he had been taken up into heaven; and others, Jeremiah, because some believed that Jeremiah was to come as the percursor of the Messiah.

Since no Church could ever be founded on a confusion of this kind, Our Blessed Lord now turned to the aristocratic form of government by asking His chosen ones, His little parliament, His apostolic band, their view.

And you, he asked, who do you say I am? *Matthew* 16:15

The appeal here was to all of them who had heard His teachings, had seen His miracles, and had been blessed even with the power of working miracles on others. This higher parliament had no answer—partly because they could not agree among themselves; in five minutes they would be quarreling. Judas certainly doubted His financial sagacity; Philip doubted His relations with His heavenly Father; and all of them were more or less expecting some secular liberator, who would put an end to the screaming eagles of Rome in their land.

Then, without solicitation or consent of the others, Peter stepped forward and gave the right and final answer:

You are the Messiah, the Son of the living God. *Matthew* 16:16

Peter confessed Christ was the true Messiah, commissioned by God to reveal His will to men and fulfilling all prophecies and the Law; He was the Son of God, begotten from all Eternity, but also the Son of Man begotten in time—true God and true man.

Our Blessed Lord revealed to Peter that he did not know this of and by himself; that no natural study or discernment could ever reveal this great truth.

> Simon son of Jonah, you are favoured indeed! You did not learn that from mortal man; it was revealed to you by my heavenly Father.
>
> *Matthew* 16:17

Our Blessed Lord called him first by the name that he had before he was summoned to be an Apostle. Then He called him by the new name He gave him, namely, the Rock, indicating that it was on him, the Rock, that He would found His Church. Peter was addressed by His Lord in the second person singular to indicate that it was not Peter's confession of Divinity, but Peter himself who would hold primacy in the Church.

> I say this to you: You are Peter, the Rock; and on this rock I will build my church, and the powers of death shall never conquer it. I will give you the keys of the kingdom of Heaven; what you forbid on earth shall be forbidden in heaven, and what you allow on earth shall be allowed in heaven. *Matthew* 16:18–20

After promising that the gates of hell, or error, or evil would never conquer His Church, Our Lord made the first of the most open confessions of His coming death. He had already given many veiled hints concerning it; but the Apostles had been slow to recognize that the Messiah would suffer as Isaiah had foretold. They missed the full implication of what He said when He cleansed the temple, that He was the Temple of God, and that the Temple would be destroyed. They had missed His teaching about the serpent lifted up as a prophecy of how the Son of Man would be lifted up on the Cross. But now that the man whom He had chosen as the chief of His apostolic body had confessed His Divinity, He openly showed them that the way to glory both for Him and for them led to suffering and death.

> From that time Jesus began to make it clear to his disciples that he had to go to Jerusalem, and there to suffer much from the elders, chief priests, and doctors of the law; to be put to death and to be raised again on the third day. *Matthew* 16:21

Our Lord said nothing openly of His death while His Apostles believed Him only to be man; but once He was acknowledged to be God, He spoke openly of His death. This was in order that His death might be viewed in its proper light as a sacrifice for sins.

Once more the mysterious "must" which ruled His life appeared. It was a strong cable that bound Him and was made up of a warp and a woof; obedience to the Father on the one hand, and love of men on the other. Because He would save, He must die. The "must" was not merely a death; for He immediately mentioned His Resurrection on the third day.

An intrinsic connection existed between the affirmation of Christ's Divinity and His death and Resurrection. At the very moment that Christ received the loftiest of all titles, and the confession was made of His exalted dignity, He prophesied His greatest humiliation. Both the human and the Divine natures of Christ were involved in this prediction, namely, that the Son of Man Who appeared before them and the Son of the Living God Who had just been confessed.

Peter puffed up with the authority that had been given him, took Our Lord aside and began rebuking Him saying:

No, Lord, this shall never happen to you. *Matthew* 16:22

The Divinity of Christ, he would accept; the suffering Christ, he would not. The rock had become a stumbling stone; Peter would have a half Christ for the moment, the Divine Christ, but not the Redeemer Christ. But a half Christ was no Christ. He would have the Christ Whose glory was announced at Bethlehem, but not the full-orbed Christ, Who would be a sacrifice for sins on the Cross.

Peter thought, if He was the Son of God, why should He suffer? Satan on the Mount of Temptation tempted Him from His Cross by promising popularity through giving Bread, working scientific marvels, or becoming a Dictator. Satan did not confess the Divinity of Christ, since he prefaced each temptation with an "if"—"If Thou art the Son of God." To the credit of Peter, he did confess Divinity. But along with this difference, there was this likeness: both Peter and Satan tempted Christ from His Cross and therefore from Redemption. Not to redeem was Satan's mind; to have the crown without the Cross was Satan's spirit. But, it was also Peter's. Therefore, Our Lord called him Satan:

Away with you, Satan; you are a stumbling-block to me. You think as men think, not as God thinks. *Matthew* 16:23

In an unguarded moment Peter had let Satan in his heart, thus becoming a stumbling stone on the road to Calvary. Peter thought it was unworthy of Christ to suffer; but to Our Lord such thoughts were human, carnal, and even Satanic. Only by Divine illumination did Peter or anyone else know Him to be the Son of God; but it took another Divine illumination for Peter or anyone else to know Him for the Redeemer. Peter would have kept Him a Teacher of humanitarian ethics—but so would Satan.

Peter never forgot this rebuke. Years later, with the idea of a stumbling block still in his mind, he wrote about those who refused to accept the suffering Christ as he had at Caesarea Philippi:

> The great worth of which it speaks is for you who have faith. For those who have no faith, the stone which the builders rejected has become not only the corner-stone, but also a stone to trip over, a rock to stumble against. *I Peter 2:7*

That the Apostles had their eloquent spokesman in Peter, and that they were all equally shocked at their Master's suffering, is evident from the fact that after personally rebuking Peter, He spoke to all of His disciples and bade even the multitude to heed His remarks. To all who would ever profess to be His followers He enumerated three conditions:

> Anyone who wishes to be a follower of mine must leave self behind; he must take up his cross, and come with me. *Mark 8:34*

The Cross was the reason of His coming; now He made it the earmark of His followers. He did not make Christianity easy; for He implied not only must there be a voluntary renouncement of everything that hindered likeness with Him, but also there must be the suffering, shame, and death of the Cross. They did not have to blaze a trail of sacrifice themselves, but merely to follow His tracks zealously as the Man of Sorrow. No disciple is called to the task that is untried. He had taken the Cross first. Only those who were willing to be crucified with Him could be saved by the merits of His death and only those who bore a Cross could ever really understand Him.

There was no question of whether or not men would have sacrifice in their lives; it was only a question of which they would sacrifice, the higher or the lower life!

> Whoever cares for his own safety is lost; but if a man will let himself be lost for my sake, that man is safe. *Luke 9:24*

If the physical, natural, and biological life was saved for pleasure, then the higher life of the spirit would be lost, but if the higher life of the spirit was chosen for salvation, then the lower or physical life had to be submitted to the Cross and self-discipline. There might be some natural virtues without a Cross, but there would never be a growth in virtue without it.

Cross-bearing, He then explained, was based on exchange. Exchange implies something that one can get along without, and something one cannot get along without. A man can get along without a dime, but he cannot get along without the bread which the dime will buy; so he exchanges one for the other. Sacrifice does not mean "giving-up" something, as if there were a loss; rather it is an exchange: an exchange of lower values for higher joys. But nothing in all the world is worth a soul.

> What does a man gain by winning the whole world at the cost of his true self? What can he give to buy that self back? *Mark 8:39*

At the very moment the Apostles were ashamed of Him because He spoke of His defeat and death, He warned against anyone being ashamed of Him or His words, or denying Him in times of persecution. If He had been only a Teacher, it would have been absurd for Him to claim that all men must openly and unashamedly confess Him as their Lord and Savior; it would have sufficed if they merely mouthed one or the other of His teachings. But here He makes it a condition of being saved that men boldly confess that He Who is the Son of God was crucified.

> If anyone is ashamed of me and mine in this wicked and godless age, the Son of Man will be ashamed of him, when he comes in the glory of his Father and of the holy angels. *Mark 8:38*

THE SECOND QUARRELING: CAPHARNAUM

The second overt announcement of His Passion was after the Transfiguration and the driving out of the demon from the young boy. The Master and His Apostles had turned toward Capharnaum. The many miracles that Our Blessed Lord had worked between Caesarea Philippi and Capharnaum put the Apostles in a high state of excitement.

> Amid the general wonder and admiration at all he was doing . . .
> *Luke 9:44*

The Apostles began translating this power into the hope of an earthly royalty and human sovereignty, despite the severe lessons they were given about the Cross. This kind of religious excitement, which would leave humanity unredeemed, Our Lord frowned upon.

> What I now say is for you: ponder my words. The Son of Man is to be given up into the power of men. But they did not understand . . .
> *Luke 9:44*

> The Son of Man is now to be given up into the power of men, and they will kill him, and three days after being killed, he will rise again.
> *Mark 9:30*

Our Lord repeated clearly the prediction of Calvary so that when it did take place, His disciples would not be weak in their faith or abandon Him. The repeated declarations also assured them that He was not going to the Cross by constraint, but as a willing sacrifice. The prospect which Our Lord put before them about His death they regarded with aversion; they not only refused to pay any attention, but even disdained to ask Our Lord any questions about it.

> But they did not understand this saying; it had been hidden from them, so that they should not grasp its meaning, and they were afraid to ask him about it. *Luke 9:45*

The second announcement of His death and glory provoked the second quarrel. As they walked back to Capharnaum, they disputed among themselves, but not within the hearing of Our Blessed Lord.

> A dispute arose among them: which of them was the greatest?
> *Luke 9:46*

How superficial must have been the impression that Our Lord made upon them about His death, as they still inquired among themselves about priority in what they imagined to be a political and economic setup called the Kingdom of God! From the lips of the Divine Master, they had heard something of His sufferings, but now they wrangled about rank. Possibly the high position given to Peter at Caesarea Philippi intensified the dispute; perhaps also the fact that Peter, James, and John were chosen as witnesses to the Transfiguration aroused some resentment. In any case, they quarreled as they always did whenever He unveiled the Cross.

Knowing that the crisis was at hand when He would establish the Kingdom, they were stirred by ambition. But Our Blessed Lord knew what was in their hearts; and when they came into the house at Capharnaum where they usually enjoyed hospitality, probably Peter's:

> He asked them, What were you arguing about on the way? They were silent, because on the way they had been discussing who was the greatest. *Mark 9:32*

Tongues that were loud on the roadway where they disputed were now silent when the Master read their thoughts and when their own consciences accused them. The little attention they paid to His words about the Cross might be the reason for their not grasping why One full of the power they had seen in His miracles and in the resurrection of the dead should ever be so seemingly powerless. Why should He submit Himself to a death from which at any moment He could extricate Himself? It was a mystery that could not be understood until it was accomplished; and even after its accomplishment, it still remained a scandal to unbelievers among the Jews and the Greeks. As St. Paul wrote to the Corinthians:

> Jews call for miracles, Greeks look for wisdom; but we proclaim Christ —yes, Christ nailed to the cross; and though this is a stumbling-block to Jews and folly to Greeks, yet to those who have heard his call, Jews and Greeks alike, he is the power of God and the wisdom of God. *I Corinthians* 1:23,24

Evidently, the natural or carnal man was geared to receive Him as One Who came to give a moral code such as could be posted on church lawns; but to take Him for One coming into the world as a "ransom" for mankind required a higher wisdom. As St. Paul suggested:

> A man who is unspiritual refuses what belongs to the Spirit of God; it is folly to him; he cannot grasp it, because it needs to be judged in the light of the Spirit. *I Corinthians* 2:14

This time, in order to correct their false ideas of superiority, with great solemnity He called a child to Himself:

> Set him in front of them, and put his arm round him. *Mark* 9:35

Since the Apostles had disputed as to who was highest in the Kingdom, Our Lord now gave the answer to their ambitious minds:

> I tell you this: unless you turn round and become like children, you will never enter the kingdom of Heaven. *Matthew* 18:3–4

The greatest of all His disciples would be those who would be like little children; for a child stands as a representative of God and His Divine Son upon the earth. There was a nobility in His Kingdom, but it was opposite to the rank of the world. In His Kingdom one rose by sinking; one increased by decreasing. He said that He came not to be ministered to, but to minister. In His own Person, He was exemplifying humiliation as ascending to the depths of defeat of the Cross. Since they understood not the Cross, He bade them to learn of a child whom He embraced to His heart. The greatest are the least, and the least are the greatest. Honor and prestige are not to him who sits at the head of the table, but to him who girds himself with a towel and washes the feet of those who are his servants. He who is God became man; He who is Lord of heaven and earth humbled Himself to the Cross; this was the incomparable act of humility which they were to learn. If for the moment they could not learn it from Him, they were to learn it from a child.

THE THIRD QUARRELING:
ON THE ROAD TO JERUSALEM

The third clear prophecy of Our Lord concerning the Cross which resulted in a dispute among the Apostles took place a little more than a week before He was crucified. He was on His way with His Apostles to Jerusalem for the last time. There was haste in His stride; resolution and fixed purpose were so stamped on His face that the Apostles could not miss them.

> They were on the road, going up to Jerusalem, Jesus leading the way; and the disciples were filled with awe, while those who followed behind were afraid. *Mark 10:32*

The Master was walking well in advance of His Apostles up the steep mountain path. While they lagged behind, shrinking in uncomprehending terror as He hastened to His Cross, there was one thought uppermost in His mind: His voluntary submission to sacrifice. According to the Father's plan, the Cross was necessary for Him as a means of imparting life to others. The Apostles, on the other hand, until the very last moment, were looking for some manifestation of His power which would release their nation from political bondage and lift them personally to some glory and dominion. They were amazed at His readiness to enter Jerusalem, which meant suffering. They were dreaming of thrones, and He was thinking of a Cross. Knowing their thoughts, He took the Apostles aside:

> We are now going to Jerusalem, he said; and the Son of Man will be given up to the chief priests and the doctors of the law; they will condemn him to death and hand him over to the foreign power. He will be mocked and spat upon, flogged and killed; and three days afterwards, he will rise again. *Mark 10:32–34*

Once again He wrapped up the gall of His Passion in the honey of the Resurrection. Calvary was not something before Him that He could not avoid, and therefore had to accept as a martyr's role. There was the human shrinking from the suffering which evil would visit upon Him; but that shrinking never became a purpose. As the ship might be tossed on the waves, while maintaining its equilibrium, so too His physical nature might toss from side to side, while underlying it was the Father's purpose, fixed and unalterable. But the Apostles could not understand a death that was vicarious, because offered for others, and at the same time a propitiation for sin.

> But they understood nothing of all this; they did not grasp what he was talking about; its meaning was concealed from them. *Luke 18:34*

How could He, Who had power over death, the winds, and the seas, and Whose mind could silence the tongues of the Pharisees, leave them comfortless and throw them back again into the world because He could not resist His enemies? That was their worry.

As on the other two occasions, now that He had spoken again of His death, a new quarrel broke out among the Apostles. James and John, who already had made themselves prominent by resenting the rudeness of the Samaritan villagers and asking Our Lord to destroy them, now made a request. The two brothers, who once had asked that fire descend upon their enemies, now asked that a great advantage be given to them. In irreverent presumptuousness, they asked Our Blessed Lord, immediately after He had spoken of His death, to become the tool of their own vanity.

> Grant us the right to sit in state with you, one at your right and the other at your left. *Mark* 10:37

There was some recognition of Christ's authority, for they implied that He was a King Who could grant requests; but the conception of His Kingdom was worldly. Family influence and personal preferment gave high places in a secular kingdom; James and John, assuming that the kingdom of God was worldly, thought that their promotion could be on that basis. But Our Blessed Lord answered them:

> You do not understand what you are asking. Can you drink the cup that I drink, or be baptized with the baptism I am baptized with?
> *Mark* 10:38

The bestowal of honors in His Kingdom was not a matter of favoritism, but of incorporation to the Cross. If He had to die in order to rise to glory, they would have to die to discover glory. If He had to drink the bitter cup to overcome evil, they must drink of the cup. The "cup" was here used as a symbol of the defeat which would be poured out to Him by faithless men. In the baptism of blood, He would be totally immersed in it; but the imagery also implied Purification or Resurrection.

In answer to the question about drinking the chalice James and John answered, "We can." Though they did not understand precisely what they were accepting, Our Lord prophesied the fulfillment of their faith. James was the first to share in Christ's baptism of blood, being murdered by Herod. John, indeed, did suffer; he lived a long life of persecution and banishment. After being put into a cauldron of boiling oil, he was miraculously preserved and died at an old age in Patmos. James became the patron of all the Red martyrs, who shed their blood because they drink of His cup. John became the symbol of

what might be called the White martyrs, who endure physical sufferings and yet die a natural death.

Now begins the quarrel.

> When the other ten heard this, they were indignant with James and
> John. *Mark 10:41*

They were indignant because they all shared the same desire. Our
Lord called the ten others to Him. James and John had been given
their lesson; now it was time for the other ten to receive theirs. The
first lesson He gave them was a repetition of what He had suggested
in Capharnaum when He placed a little child in the midst of them,
namely, the lesson of humility. What they were now to be taught was
not what would make them pre-eminent in His Kingdom, but rather
the meaning of that pre-eminence. He suggested a contrast between
the despotism of worldly potentates and the dominion of love in His
Own Kingdom. In the earthly kingdoms those who rule, such as kings,
and nobles, and princes, and presidents, are ministered unto; in His
Kingdom, the mark of nobility would be the privilege of ministry or
serving.

> You know that in the world the recognized rulers lord it over their
> subjects, and their great men make them feel the weight of authority.
> That is not the way with you; among you, whoever wants to be great
> must be your servant, and whoever wants to be first must be the will-
> ing slave of all. *Mark 10:42–45*

In His Kingdom those who are the lowliest and the most humble will
be the greatest and the most exalted. Though He regarded His Apostles as kings, they were, nevertheless, to establish their rights by being
the least of men.

But the Savior would not merely give them a moral injunction without pointing to His Own Life, as an example of the humility He
wished them to have. The whole truth was that He came not to be
ministered unto, but to minister. In effect, He was saying that He
was a King and He would have a Kingdom; but this Kingdom would
be obtained in a way other than the one by which secular princes
secured theirs. He introduced the direct relationship between His laying-down His life and the spiritual sovereignty which that death would
purchase.

> For even the Son of Man did not come to be served but to serve, and
> to give up his life as a ransom for many. *Mark 10:45*

Here, as elsewhere, He spoke of Himself as "coming" into the world
in order to indicate that a human birth was not the beginning of His

personal existence. He began His service long before men saw Him serve in compassion and mercy. His service began when He stripped Himself of heavenly glory and girded Himself with flesh woven in the looms of Mary.

The purpose of His coming into this world was to supply ransom and redemption. If He were merely the son of a carpenter, it would have been folly for Him to say that He came to minister. A servile position would have been routine and accepted; but for the King to become a servant, for God to become a man, was not presumption but humility. There was a ransom to be paid and that was death; for the "wages of sin is death." Ransom would be meaningless if human nature was not in debt. Suppose a man were sitting alongside a pier on a bright summer day fishing contentedly; suddenly another man jumps off the pier in front of him into the river, as he goes down under the water for the third time to drown, he shouts to the man on the pier:

> There is no greater love than this, that a man should lay down his life for his friends. *John* 15:31

The whole proceeding would have been quite unintelligible because the man on the pier was in no danger and, therefore, not in need of rescue. If, however, he had fallen into the water and was drowning, then the individual who offered his life to save him would have significance in his death. If human nature had not fallen into sin, the death of Christ would be meaningless; if there had been no slavery, there would be no talk of ransom.

Many individuals disclaim responsibilities for the faults and failings of a collectivity. For example, when there is corruption in government, individuals often deny that they are involved. The more sinful people are, the greater they disclaim all relationship to those that are sinners. They almost assume that their responsibility varies in direct ratio with their sinfulness. Their argument is that since they are not responsible for the mistakes of society, they are not involved.

Actually, the contrary is true in those who are *most* sinless. The greater the sinlessness, the greater the sense of the responsibility and awareness of corporate guilt. The truly good man feels the world is the way it is because in some way he has not been better. The keener the moral sensitiveness, the greater is the compassion for those languishing under a burden. This can become so deep that the other person's agony is directly felt as one's own. The only person in the world who had eyes to see would want to be a staff to the blind; the only person in the world who was healthy would want to minister to the sick.

What is true of physical suffering is also true of moral evil. Hence the sinless Christ would take on the ills of the world. As the more healthy are better able to minister to the sick, so too the more innocent can better atone for the guilt of others. A lover would, if possible, take on the sufferings of the beloved. Divinity takes on the moral ills of the world as if they were His own. Being man, He would share in them; being God He could redeem for them.

Calvary, He was telling His quarreling Apostles, would be no interruption of His life activities, no tragic and premature spoiling of His plan, no evil end which hostile forces would impose upon Him. The giving of His life would take Him out of the pattern of martyrs for righteousness, and of patriots for glorious causes. The purpose of His life, He said, was to pay a ransom for the liberation of the slaves of sin; this was a Divine "must" that was laid upon Him when He came into the world. His death would be offered in payment for evil. If men were only in error, He might have been a Teacher fenced in by all the comforts of life; and after having taught the theory of pain, He would die on a soft bed. But then He would have left no other message than a code to obey. But if men were in sin, He would be a Redeemer and His message would be "Follow Me," to share in the fruit of that Redemption.

20. *The Attempted Arrest at the Feast of Tabernacles*

The centrality of the Cross in His life now became clearer. He had made implicit references to it, under the figure of a temple and a serpent; and more explicitly when He promised in His glory after His Resurrection to allow men to live by His Body and Blood.

Here at the most popular feast of the year, the Feast of Tabernacles, two things happened: first, He directed attention to the fullness of the Divine Presence, Truth, and Soul Refreshment dwelling in Himself. There was no moral, no belief, no slaking of thirst, apart from Him. He smashed every illusion of His auditors that He was giving a morality apart from Himself, a doctrine distinct from His Person, or that a higher ethic could be reconciled with a lowered sense of the living God. He let them know that He would not be a pious "extra," an addendum, or a spiritual luxury to those who would quote His words. Buddha might be left out of Buddhism; but He could no more be left out of what He taught or wrought than a ray of sunshine could exist without the sun. To the vast multitudes present at this eight-day ceremony, He explained the meaning of the ceremony: the tabernacle, the water, the lights. He made each center in His Person, as He affirmed Himself one with God, one with all illumination of mind, and one with all peace of thirsty souls. The identification was complete: there was no God but the God He revealed, no Truth but His Person, no contentment but in Him.

The second effect of His Words was violence, resentment, and a resolve to put Him to death. If He had spoken words, and had not claimed to be the Word; if He had given truths separable from His Person and solace of soul distinct from His Divine Presence, He might have been less propelled to His Cross. Hatred against Him on the part of the temple authorities made them twice try to arrest Him: the first time was at this Feast of Tabernacles; the second was in the Garden of Gethsemane. In neither instance did the police have the power to seize Him; not at this Feast, because Our Lord "arrested" them by His Presence. Not even in the Garden was the power to seize given until after they had been made powerless. At this Feast, as He said, "His Hour was not yet come"; in the Garden, He would say: "This is your hour." Here He said that He was the Light of the World; then He would tell them that it was the "Hour of Darkness."

In both instances, He could not be taken until He voluntarily surrendered; in both instances, the intent of men in the face of Divine
Goodness was to crucify, for deeds of darkness cannot stand the light.
The second arrest led directly to the Cross, so this first arrest was the
rehearsal for it. The Shadow of the Cross was falling everywhere—
over the tents, over the fountains, the candelabra, and even over the
people at the Feast of Tabernacles.

This greatest of all Feasts was a commemoration of the Flight from
Egypt, when God guided the people of Israel through the desert by
means of a cloud during the day and a pillar of fire by night. As pilgrims during that forty years of wandering, the Jews lived in tents or
booths which could be easily pitched and silently rolled away. In the
midst of the tents was the Tabernacle symbolizing the presence of
God.

This Feast, mentioned in both Leviticus and Exodus, was celebrated at the time of the ingathering of the harvest. Though there
was thanksgiving for the harvest, this Feast looked to the future, and
for that reason was sometimes called the "Hour of Outpouring,"
symbolic of the Spirit of God which would be poured out on the people.

When this eight-day feast began, Our Lord was in Galilee where
He had retired for six months because of the opposition of the temple
leaders after the cleansing of the temple and the miracle at Bethsaida.
His enemies were

> This made the Jews still more determined to kill him, because he was
> not only breaking the Sabbath, but, by calling God his own Father, he
> claimed equality with God. *John 5:18*

As the time of the Feast drew near, He began to be heckled by His
relatives and associates because He was not publicity-minded. Why
work miracles in Galilee for its fishing villages and ignorant coun-
tryfolk, when the big city, Jerusalem, would give Him so much
renown? Furthermore, great crowds would be gathering at the feast,
and He could be known by everyone, if He would only do something
spectacular. Retirement is compromising.

> Surely no one can hope to be in the public eye if he works in seclu-
> sion. If you really are doing such things as these, show yourself to the
> world. *John 7:4*

Our Lord answered them:

> The right time for me has not yet come, but any time is right for you.
> The world cannot hate you; but it hates me to exposing the wicked-
> ness of its ways. *John 7:5,6*

His time, or His Hour for full revelation, had not yet come. Intensify-
ing the contrast between Himself and the world, He told them with a
certain irony that their words, attitudes, and judgments were not
sufficiently out of harmony with the world to provoke the world's
hatred. But it was different with Him: His words and His life had already provoked the hatred of the world. If He were to go up to
Jerusalem, it would be as the Messiah and Son of God, and would
therefore provoke enmity; but if they went up as pious pilgrims, it
would be only to partake in a national celebration. When Our Lord
talked of the world, He meant it as made up of unregenerate men
who would not accept His grace. Those brethren of His who would
have loved the limelight and the notoriety were part of that un-
Crossed world, violating none of the precepts nor its spirit.

He was conscious of His Cross, while they were not conscious of it.
Not until there was a command from the Heavenly Father would He
go up to the city. Satan before had already offered Him all the kingdoms of the world and He had refused them. Jerusalem would not be
enough to tempt Him to display His miracles to those who would not
believe in His Person. Those who suggested the glare of popularity
could go up and they would find plenty of unbelievers like themselves;
they were floating with the stream, like dead logs. Note that Our
Blessed Lord did not say that He would not go up to the Feast of the
Tabernacles. What He said was that He would not go up at that moment. The worldly-minded therefore left Him for the feast.

He later decided to go up, not as a public Person, but in secret or
incognito. How great the contrast between His first visit, when He
had appeared suddenly in the temple and cast out the money-
changers, and His going up now as an anonymous pilgrim! But everyone was curious about Him. He immediately became the source of
division. Those who were attracted kept quiet for fear of the temple
authorities, who had already plotted His death.

> The Jews were looking for him at the festival and asking, Where is
> he? and there was much whispering about him in the crowds. He is
> a good man, said some. No, said others, he is leading the people
> astray. However, no one talked about him openly, for fear of the
> Jews. *John 7:11–13*

The Feast of Tabernacles, as it was said, commemorated the place
where the Divine Presence dwelt among the Jews during their long
pilgrimage from Egypt. And now here in the midst of the crowds
stood the Divine Presence in Person.

> So the Word became flesh; he came to dwell among us. *John 1:14*

The Greek word "to dwell" in the Gospel could equally be translated "to be tabernacled" and is thus suggestive of the Tabernacle placed in the center of the tents of the Israelites. Christ was the Tabernacle of God among men.

The Jewish Targums often substituted for the phrase "glory of the Lord," the word *Sheekinah* or "dwelling," thus indicating God's intimate sojourn with His people. Those at the feast remembered that Our Lord had called Himself the "Temple of God," and prophesied that it would be destroyed but on the third day would rise again. That they intended to destroy this Temple of the Tabernacled God among them was evident, as some of the people of the city asked:

> Is not this the man they want to put to death? *John 7:26*

The procession celebrating the feast started from the temple. When it reached the pool of Siloe, the priest filled his golden pitcher from its waters and returned to the temple, where the water was poured out with a burst of trumpets amidst the "alleluias" of the people. It was so much associated with joy that a common saying declared that "He who has not seen the rejoicing at the pouring of the water from the pool of Siloe has never seen rejoicing in his life." The ceremony was not only an acknowledgment of the mercy of God in watering their fields, but also a commemoration of the miraculous supply of water in the desert, which came from the rock. At the moment the water was offered by the priest in the temple the words of Isaiah were quoted:

> And so you shall draw water with joy from the springs of deliverance. *Isaiah 12:3*

Our Lord, Who said that He had come not to destroy the Law or the Prophets but to fulfill them, now spoke out to affirm that He was the substance of which these rites were but dim shadows. His voice rang out above the pouring of the waters as He said:

> If anyone is thirsty let him come to me; whoever believes in me, let him drink. As Scripture says, Streams of living water shall flow out from within him. *John 7:37,38*

He was bidding them recall their Scriptures. In Exodus God commanded Moses to smite the rock, promising that out of it water would come from which the people would drink. All through the Old Testament, water was the symbol of spiritual blessing, particularly in Ezekiel, where a mighty fountain is described as flowing from the Tabernacle or temple, healing all nations. The Fountain of Life for thirsty souls, He now declared, is His own Person. He did not say, "Come to waters," but "Come to Me." The Talmud asked about this ceremony, "Why is the name of it called the drawing of the water?" Because of the pouring-out of the Holy Spirit, according to what is said, "With joy shall you draw water out of the wells of salvation." St. John explained in the same way the words of Our Lord:

> He was speaking of the Spirit which believers in him would receive later; for the Spirit had not yet been given, because Jesus had not yet been glorified. *John* 7:39

The satisfaction of the thirst of the human heart was joined up with the work of the Spirit. Our Lord was looking forward to the production of a blessing conditioned by what had not yet happened, namely, His triumph over death and His Ascension into heaven. This gift of the Spirit would come to men not as a magical outpouring, but as something intrinsic to His Redemptive Act and their faith in Him. The physical presence of Christ on earth in His yet unfulfilled mandate of the Father to be a ransom for sin excluded the realization of His Presence in souls until after His glory and the sending of His Spirit.

Another ritual connected with the Feast of the Tabernacles was in reference to the pillar of fire which had guided the Israelites by night. To celebrate the light which God was to them, two immense candelabra were lighted in the Court of the Women; and according to some Rabbinic testimony, they illumined all Jerusalem. The people had looked forward also to Messianic times when God would kindle for them a great light among the nations. The light also signified the glory of God which was present in the temple.

When Our Blessed Lord was a Babe held by Simeon, the old man had pronounced over Him these words:

> A light that will be a revelation to the heathen, and glory to thy people Israel. *Luke* 2:32

Now as a grown man walking in the full glare of these lights, He proclaimed:

> I am the light of the world. No follower of mine shall wander in the dark; he shall have the light of life. *John* 8:12

Here He made a universal claim such as had been prophesied by Isaiah that He would be the Light of all peoples and all nations. Not everyone would follow the Light; some would prefer to walk in darkness and would therefore hate the light. He Who was standing in the temple in which the lights were gradually dimming proclaimed Himself the Light of the World. Previously, He had called Himself the Temple; now He affirmed that He is the Glory and the Light of that

Temple. He was declaring Himself more necessary for the life of souls than the light of the sun is for the life of our body. It was not His doctrine, nor His law, nor His commandments, nor His teaching, that constituted this light; it was His Person.

In the midst of Our Lord's affirmation that He was the Messiah, there began some of the judicial and civil measures which were later to culminate in the Crucifixion. The Pharisees sent police officers to arrest Our Lord. Before they arrived, Our Lord made another reference to His death:

> For a little longer I shall be with you; then I am going away to him who sent me. You will look for me, but you will not find me. Where I am, you cannot come. *John 7:33–34*

He foresaw all that would happen. Six months remained until the Passover; there was only a little time left before He would fulfill the reason of His coming. They were already planning His death, but their plans would be unsuccessful until He delivered Himself voluntarily into their hands. Then the door would be shut and the time of their visitation would have passed. The separation between them and Him would not be distance but unlikeness in mind and heart, which is the greatest of all distance.

The police who were ordered to arrest Him returned to the chief priests and Pharisees empty-handed. The officials asked them:

> Why have you not brought him? No man, they answered, ever spoke as this man speaks. The Pharisees retorted, Have you too been misled? Is there a single one of our rulers who has believed in him, or of the Pharisees? As for this rabble, which cares nothing for the Law, a curse is on them. *John 7:46–49*

The temple officials had contempt for the people; their assumption was that no vulgar person is pious. The very fact that the policemen had an overwhelming impression made upon them and yielded themselves to His fountains of benediction was an indication of the power He had over men of good will. The vocation of a policeman was sanctified that day when these officers refused to arrest the Savior.

Plutarch, speaking of the extraordinary eloquence of Mark Antony, says that when soldiers were sent to kill the orator, he pleaded for his life with such eloquent language that he disarmed them and melted them to tears. But these officers were vanquished not by the force of arguments from a man pleading for his life, but on hearing one of His ordinary discourses which was not directed to them at all. The police were fully armed; the Preacher had no weapons, and yet they could not arrest Him. Civil authorities do not always employ the most intellectual or spiritual men to carry out such duties, and yet those sent were affected by His eloquence and proved to be the more intelligent. The Pharisees in their anger told the police that the intellectual people did not believe in Him. Since none of the Pharisees believed in Him, nor had been impressed with His message, the police could have had, therefore, no reason for being so affected.

There would be another moment in the Garden of Gethsemane when officers would be so impressed with Our Blessed Lord that they would cast themselves prone on the ground, when He said that He was Jesus of Nazareth. On that night, they would have their way because His Hour had come. But for the present they were powerless.

The story of the Feast of Tabernacles ends with the words, "His Hour has not yet come." A particular hour existed for everything He had to do; even His birth is described as the "fullness of time." So His Cross had its appointed hour. Every orb that rolls through the immensity of space is bound to reach a certain point at its own hour. Man's decrees and proposals often fail, but it is otherwise with the designs of the Almighty. The unity of His life was not in His scattered deeds and parables and utterances, but in Its consummation. Bethlehem was the foundation of Calvary and His glory. The stairs mount upward from the stable, for even then "there was no room" for Him; the "contradiction" prophesied by Simeon was another step; the Feast of the Tabernacles, another. He knew every step of the way, for He was not merely a man doing his best before God, but God doing His best for man, through the Love revealed in the sacrifice of Himself.

21. *Only the Innocent May Condemn*

The day after the attempted arrest, a scene took place in which Innocence refused to condemn a sinner. The dilemma of justice and mercy was involved—a dilemma that lay at the heart of the Incarnation. If God is merciful, shall He not forgive sinners? If God is just, shall He not punish them or force them to make amends for their crimes? Being all holy, He must hate sin, otherwise He would not be Goodness. But being all merciful, should He not, like a kind of grandfather, be indifferent to the children smashing the commandments? Somehow or other, His death on the Cross and Resurrection were involved in the answer to this dilemma.

The night before this scene took place, Sacred Scripture reveals one of the most vivid contrasts in all literature; and it is done in two sentences. Our Lord had been teaching all day in the temple; when night came, the Gospel speaks first of Our Lord's enemies who had been tantalizing and haranguing Him:

> And they went each to his home. *John 7:53*

But of Our Lord it is simply said:

> . . . and Jesus to the Mount of Olives. *John 8:1*

Among all those who were in the temple—friends or foes—there was not one without a house, except Our Lord. Truly He said of Himself:

> Foxes have their holes, the birds their roosts; but the Son of Man has nowhere to lay his head. *Luke 9:58*

In all Jerusalem, He probably was the only homeless and houseless man. While men went to their houses to take counsel with their fellow men, He went to the Mount of Olives to consult not with flesh and blood, but with His Father. He knew that in a short time this Garden would be a sacred retreat where He would sweat large drops of blood in His terrible conflict with the powers of evil. During the night, He slept Eastern-fashion on the green turf under ancient olive trees so twisted and gnarled in their passion of growth as to foreshadow the tortuous Passion that would be His own.

The season was the Feast of Tabernacles, which brought not only a vast concourse of people from all over the world but also produced general excitement, much prayer, and some relaxation. It was only natural that it should degenerate into an occasional case, here and there, of license and immorality. Such had evidently happened. For early the next morning, as Our Lord appeared at the temple and began to teach, the Scribes and Pharisees brought to Him a woman who had been found committing adultery. So set were they on their barren controversy with the Messiah that they did not scruple to use a woman's shame to score a point. Apparently, there was no question about her guilt. The indelicate, almost indecent way in which the men told the story, reveals that the facts could not be challenged. They said:

> Master, this woman was caught in the very act of adultery. *John 8:4*

Caught in the act! What sneaking, spying, and rottenness are hidden in their words! The accusers brought her into the midst of the crowd while Our Blessed Lord was teaching. The "holier than thou" men who had caught her in the act were very anxious that she should be publicly paraded, even to the point of interrupting the discourse of Our Blessed Lord. Human nature is base when it headlines and parades crimes of others before their fellow men. The pot thinks it is clean if it calls the kettle black. Some faces are never so gay as when regaling a scandal, which the generous heart would cover and the devout heart pray over. The more base and corrupt a man, the more ready is he to charge crimes to others. Those who want credit for good character foolishly believe that the best way to get it is to denounce others. Vicious people like a monopoly on their vices, and when they find others with the same vices, they condemn them with an intensity that the good never feel. All one has to do to learn the faults of men is to listen to their favorite charges against others. In those days there were no scandal columns, but there were scandalmongers. Dragging her into full view of the crowd was their way of dragging her into publicity. The hooting throng pushed her forward, the woman hid her face in her hands and pulled her veil over her head to shield her shame. As they dragged their trembling prisoner, exposed before the curious eyes of men to the bitterest degradation that any Eastern woman could suffer, they said to Our Blessed Lord with feigned humility:

> Master, this woman was caught in the very act of adultery. In the Law Moses has laid down that such women are to be stoned. What do you say about it? *John 8:4,5*

They were right in saying that the Law of Moses ordered stoning for adultery. Our Lord instinctively discerned their mock respect in calling Him "Master"; He knew that it was merely a cloak for their own sinister designs. On the one hand, His soul shrank from the spectacle before Him; for He had taught the sanctity of marriage, and this woman had violated it. On the other hand, He knew that the Scribes and Pharisees saw in the incident nothing but a chance of tripping Him in His speech. He knew they were ready to use her as the passive instrument of their own hatred against Him—not because they were morally indignant at a sin, nor vigilant of the rights of God, but only to provoke the people against Him.

A double trick was hidden in presenting her to Our Blessed Lord. First of all, because of the conflict between the Jews and the Romans. The Romans, who were the conquerors of the country, had reserved to themselves the right to put anyone to death. But there was another side; the Law of Moses was that a woman who had been taken in adultery should be stoned. Here was the dilemma in which they put Him: If Our Blessed Lord let the woman off without the death penalty, He would be disobeying the Law of Moses; but if He respected the Law of Moses, and said that she should be stoned because of adultery, then He would be encouraging the breaking of the Roman law. In either case He would be caught. The people would oppose Him for violating the Mosaic Law, while the Roman courts would charge Him with violating their law. He was either a heretic to Moses or a traitor to the Romans.

There was still another trick in their question. Either He would have to condemn the woman, or release her. If He condemned her, they would say He was not merciful; but He called Himself merciful. He had taken dinner with publicans and sinners, He allowed a common woman to wash His feet at dinner; should He condemn her, He could no longer say that He was a "friend of sinners." Did He not say:

> The Son of Man has come to seek and save what is lost. *Luke 19:10*

On the other hand, if He released her, then He would be acting in contradiction to the Sacred Law of Moses, which He had come to fulfill. Did He not say:

> Do not suppose that I have come to abolish the Law and the prophets; I did not come to abolish, but to complete. *Matthew 5:17*

Since He said He was God, the Law of Moses must have come from Him. If He disobeyed that Law, He was negating His own Divinity. Hence their questions, "Moses in his Law prescribed that such persons should be stoned to death; what of Thee? What is Thy sentence?"

It would be a hard question for a mere man to solve, but He was God as well as man. He Who had already reconciled justice and mercy in His Incarnation now applied it further as He leaned over and wrote something on the ground—it is the only time in the life of Our Blessed Lord that He ever wrote. What He wrote, no man knows. The Gospel simply says:

> Jesus bent down and wrote with his finger on the ground. *John 8:6*

They had invoked the Law of Moses. So would He! Whence did the Law of Moses come? Who wrote it? Whose finger? The Book of Exodus answers:

> Moses turned and went down the mountain with the two tablets of the Tokens in his hands, inscribed on both sides; on the front and on the back they were inscribed. The tablets were the handiwork of God, and the writing was God's writing, engraved on the tablets.
> *Exodus 32:15–17*

They reminded Him of the Law! He in turn reminded them that He had written the Law! The same finger, in a symbolical sense, that was now writing in the tablets of stone of the temple floor, also wrote on the tablets of stone on Sinai! Had they eyes to see the Giver of the Law of Moses standing before them? But they were so bent on ensnaring Him in His speech that they ignored the writing and kept on hurling questions; so sure were they that they had trapped Him.

> When they continued to press their question he sat up straight and said, That one of you who is faultless shall throw the first stone. Then once again he bent down and wrote on the ground. *John 8:7,8*

Moses had written on stone his Law of death against unchastity. Our Lord would not destroy the Mosaic Law, but perfect it by enunciating a higher Law: none but the pure may judge! He was summoning a new jury; only the innocent may condemn! He looked from the Law to conscience, and from the judgment of men to the judgment of God. Those who have guilt on their souls must withhold judgment.

A rusty old shield one day prayed, "O sun, illumine me"; and the sun answered, "First, polish yourself." Should, therefore, this woman be judged by men who were guilty? It was a solemn affirmation that only the sinless have a right to judge. If on this earth there is anybody really innocent, it will be found that his mercy is stronger than his justice. True it is that a judge on the bench may very often condemn a criminal for a crime of which he himself is guilty; but in his official capacity he acts in God's name, not in his own. These self-constituted accusers were no fit subjects to defend or execute the Mosaic Law.

Our Blessed Lord was putting in one sentence what He had already said in the Sermon on the Mount.

> Pass no judgement, and you will not be judged. For as you judge others, so you will yourselves be judged, and whatever measure you deal out to others will be dealt back to you. Why do you look at the speck of sawdust in your brother's eye, with never a thought for the great plank in your own? Or how can you say to your brother, Let me take the speck out of your eye, when all the time there is that plank in your own? You hypocrite! First take the plank out of your own eye, and then you will see clearly to take the speck out of your brother's. *Matthew 7:1–5*

As He wrote on the ground, the Scribes and the Pharisees had stones in their hands ready to execute judgment. One would reach to his neighbor's hand, take out his stone, weigh both in his own hand to see which was the heavier, and give the lighter one back, that he might cast the heavier one at the woman. Some of these men had kept themselves from her vice, because they had other vices. Some are exempt from certain vices simply because of the presence of other vices. Just as one disease is cured by another disease, so one vice often excludes another vice; the alcoholic may not be the thief, though he is often a liar; and the thief, like Judas Iscariot, may not necessarily be the adulterer, though the movies always paint Judas that way. There are many people who sin by pride, by avarice, by the craving for power, and think that they are virtuous simply because these sins in modern society bear the note of respectability. The respectable sins are the more odious, for Our Lord said that they make men like "whitened sepulchres, outside clean, inside full of dead men's bones." The baser sins of the poor create public burdens, such as social service and prisons, and are frowned upon; but the respectable sins, such as corruption in high public office, disloyalty to country, teaching of evil in universities, are excused, ignored or even praised as virtues.

Our Lord here implied that He even regarded the respectable sins as more odious than those which society reproved. He never condemned those whom society condemned, for they had already been condemned. But He did condemn those who sinned and who denied that they were sinners.

He now looked up at each in turn, beginning with the eldest; it was one of those calm penetrating looks which anticipate the last judgment.

> When they heard what he said, one by one they went away, the eldest first. *John 8:9*

Perhaps the older they were, the more they had sinned. He did not condemn them; rather he made them condemn themselves. Perhaps

He looked up at one old man, and his conscience glowed with the word "thief"—and he dropped his stone and fled. A still younger one saw his conscience charge him as murderer, and he left; one by one they left until only one young man was left. As the Savior gazed at this last survivor, it could have been "adulterer" that his conscience charged him; he dropped his stone and fled. No one was left!

But why did He stoop over and write again? Since they appealed to the Mosaic Law; so would He reappeal. Moses broke the first tablets on which the finger of God had written, when he found his people adoring the golden calf. So God wrote a second tablet of stone, and this was brought into the Ark of the Covenant, where it was put on the mercy seat and sprinkled with innocent blood. Such would be the way the Law of Moses would be brought to perfection by the sprinkling with Blood—the Blood of the Lamb.

By defending the woman, Christ proved Himself a friend of sinners, but only of those who admitted that they were sinners. He had to go to the social outcasts to find bigness of heart and unmeasured generosity which, according to Him, constituted the very essence of love. Though they were sinners, their love lifted them above the self-wise and the self-sufficient, who never bent their knees in prayer for pardon. He came to put a harlot above a Pharisee, a penitent robber above a High Priest, and a prodigal son above his exemplary brother. To all the phonies and fakers who would say that they could not join the Church because His Church was not holy enough, He would ask, "How holy must the Church be before you will enter into it?" If the Church were as holy as they wanted it to be, they would never be allowed into it! In every other religion under the sun, in every Eastern religion from Buddhism to Confucianism, there must always be some purification before one can commune with God. But Our Blessed Lord brought a religion where the admission of sin is the condition of coming to Him. "Those who are well have no need of a physician, but those who are ill."

He looked up to the woman, who was standing alone, and asked her:

Where are they? Has no one condemned you? *John 8:11*

The Mosaic Law required two witnesses to a crime before sentence could be carried out; they were even to assist in executing sentence. But these so-called defenders of the Mosaic Law were no longer present to bear witness. Notice, Our Blessed Lord called her "woman." There were many other names that He might have given her; but He made her stand for all the women of the world who had aspirations for cleanliness and holiness in union with Him. There was a touch of playful irony in His first question. "Woman, where are they?" He was drawing attention to the fact that she was alone! He had excluded her accusers. In that solitariness He asked:

Has no one condemned you?

She answered:

No one, sir.

If there was no one to cast the stone, neither would He. She who came to Him as a Judge, found Him a Savior. The accusers called Him "Master"; she called Him, not "Sir," but "Lord," as if to recognize that she was standing here in the presence of Someone Who was infinitely superior to herself. And her faith in Him was justified, for He turned to her and said:

Nor do I condemn you. You may go; do not sin again. *John 8:11*

But why would He not condemn her? *Because He would be condemned for her.* Innocence would not condemn, because innocence would suffer for the guilty. Justice would be saved, for He would pay the debt of her sins; mercy would be saved, for the merits of His death would apply to her soul. Justice is first, then mercy; first the satisfaction, then the pardon. Our Lord really was the only One in that crowd who had the right to take up the stone to execute judgment against her, because He was without sin. On the other hand, He did not make light of sin, for He assumed its burden. Forgiveness cost something and the full price would be paid on the hill of the three Crosses where justice would be satisfied and mercy extended. It was this release from the slavery of sin that He called the beautiful name of freedom.

If then the Son sets you free, you will indeed be free. *John 8:36*

22. *The Good Shepherd*

Philosophers, scientists, and sages often lay claim to the superiority of their respective systems. Not surprising is it, therefore, that since both Our Lord and the Pharisees were teachers, there should be a dispute between them concerning their doctrines. But Jesus, as always, refused to put Himself on the level with human teachers; He claimed uniqueness as a Divine Teacher. But he went even further. He came to sacrifice Himself for His sheep, not to be a Master over pupils. The Pharisees and He argued about their doctrines. On the one hand, He called Himself the Door affording the sole admission to the Father; the Porter or Keeper of the Sheepfold; He called Himself also the Shepherd or Guardian of the sheep, and finally He was the Sheep who would become a victim. On the other hand, He compared the Pharisees to those who entered not by the door, and therefore sought to prey on the flock; and to mercenaries who would run when the wolves came; and finally to wolves who would devour the sheep.

The dispute arose after Our Blessed Lord had restored sight to a man blind from birth. The Pharisees began making an investigation of the miracle. There was no denying the fact that the blind man could now see; but the Pharisees were so determined that this should not be accounted a miracle that they went to his parents, who testified that the boy had been born blind. They made up their minds that no amount of evidence would ever change their opinion, for they had now

> For the Jewish authorities had already agreed that anyone who acknowledged Jesus as Messiah should be banned from the synagogue.
>
> *John 9:22*

The man born blind thus was the first of a long line of confessors who Our Lord said would be driven out of synagogues. The Pharisees, finding the blind man, said that Christ could not possibly have done it because they said, "He is a sinner." When he who was blind became impatient with the questions of the Pharisees and their refusal to accept the evidence of their senses, he argued against them:

> If that man had not come from God he could have done nothing.
>
> *John 9:33*

The beggar was far wiser in his understanding of the miracle than the Pharisees, as Joseph was wiser than the so-called wise men of Egypt in the interpretation of the dream of Pharaoh. The progress in the blind man's thinking and faith was like that of the woman at the well. First, the blind man said of Him:

The man called Jesus. *John* 9:11

Later on, after further questioning, he said, as did the woman at the well:

He is a prophet. *John* 9:17

Finally, he declared that He must come from God. Such is often the progress of those who finally come to the truth about Christ. When the cured man confessed Christ to be the Son of God, the Pharisees excommunicated him from the synagogue. This was serious; for it cut off the beggar from the outward privileges of the commonwealth of the people and made him an object of derision. Hearing of the ban, Our Lord, restless until He found the lost sheep, sought out the condemned man. Meeting him face to face, He asked:

Have you faith in the Son of Man? *John* 9:35

And the beggar said:

Tell me who he is, sir, that I should put my faith in him. *John* 9:36

Our Lord answered as He did to the woman at the well:

You have seen him . . . indeed it is he who is speaking to you.
John 9:37

The man who was blind then prostrated himself before the Lord in adoration. His was not the faith that confessed with the lips, but which worshiped Truth Incarnate. His reasoning was so simple and yet so sublime. He Who could perform such a miracle must be of God. Then if He was of God, His testimony must be true.

The Pharisees had made a complete investigation of the miracle; there was no doubt among the witnesses; the parents and the man himself admitted that a great miracle had been done: a miracle of the eyes to restore his vision; and of the soul, giving him faith in Christ. Because the Pharisees rejected the evidence, Our Lord told them that they were the blind leaders, and because they had rejected Him, judgment would fall upon them. He told them they had a chance to be illumined by Himself, the Light of the World. Without that illumination, their blindness could be a calamity; but now, it was a crime.

They had closed the door of the synagogue on the man born blind.

The Pharisees imagined that they had thus cut him off from all communication with the Divine. But Our Lord told the crowd that though the door of the synagogue was shut, another door opened:

> I am the door; anyone who comes into the fold through me shall be safe. He shall go in and out and shall find pasturage. *John 10:9*

He did not say that there are many doors, nor that it made little difference through which other door one sought the higher life; He did not say that He was a door, but The Door. There was only one door in the ark through which Noah and his family entered to be saved from the flood; there was only one door in the Tabernacle or Holy of Holies. He claimed for Himself the sole right of admission or rejection with respect to the true fold of God. He did not say His teaching or His example was the door, but that He personally was the unique entrance to the fulness of the Godlife. He stands alone and shares no honors with His colleagues, not even with Moses, and much less with Zoroaster, Confucius, Mohammed, or anyone else.

> No one comes to the Father except by me. *John 14:6*

After telling the Pharisees that they were really not teachers, but blind leaders, strangers, and hirelings, He set Himself in contrast to them not only as the Unique Teacher but as something infinitely more. He was not merely giving ideas or laws, He was giving life.

> I have come that men may have life, and may have it in all its fullness. *John 10:10*

Men have existence, but He would give them life, not biological or physical life, but Divine life. Nature suggests but cannot give this more abundant life. Animals have life more abundantly than plants; man has life more abundantly than animals. He said that He came to give a life beyond the human. As the oxygen could not live the more abundant life of the plant, unless the plant came down to it, so neither could man share Divine Life unless Our Lord *came* down to give it.

Next, He proceeded to demonstrate that He gave this life not by His teaching, but by His dying. He was not uniquely a Teacher, but primarily a Savior. To illustrate again the purpose of His coming, He reached back into the Old Testament. No figure is more often employed in the Exodus to describe God leading His people from slavery to freedom than that of a shepherd. The prophets also often spoke of the shepherds who preserved a flock in good pastures as distinct from false shepherds. God is depicted by Isaiah as carrying His sheep in His arms, and by Ezekiel as a shepherd looking for His lost sheep.

Zechariah gave the saddest picture of all in prophesying that the Messiah-shepherd would be struck, and the sheep dispersed. Best known is Psalm 23 where the Lord is pictured as leading His sheep into green pastures.

The Lord revealed at what cost these green pastures are purchased. He was not the Good Shepherd because He provided economic plenty, but because He would lay down His life for His sheep. Once again the Cross appears under the symbol of the shepherd. The shepherd-patriarch Jacob and the shepherd-king David now pass into the Shepherd-Savior, as the staff becomes a crook, the crook a sceptre, and the sceptre a Cross.

> The Father loves me because I lay down my life, to receive it back again. No one has robbed me of it; I am laying it down of my own free will. I have the right to lay it down, and I have the right to receive it back again. *John 10:11,17,18*

His death is neither accidental nor unforeseen; nor does He speak of His death apart from His glory; nor of the laying-down of His life without taking it up again. No mere man could have said this. The invisible aid of heaven was at His call. Here Our Lord established that His Father's love had sent Him on the mission that He was to accomplish on earth. It did not mean the beginning of the Father's love, as it might be the beginning of a love of a parent for one who rescued his child from drowning. He was already the Eternal Object of an Eternal Love. But now in His human nature, He gives an additional reason for that love, namely, the proving of His love by dying. Since He was sinless, death had no power over Him. The taking-up of His life was just as much a part of the Divine plan as was the laying-down of it. The sacrificial lambs offered through the centuries were sin-bearers by imputation, but they were also dumb sufferers led in ignorance to an altar. The priest of the Old Law would lay his hand over the sheep in order to indicate that he was imputing sins to the one to be sacrificed. But He willingly took on sin for the sake of the new life He would bestow after the Resurrection. When He said that He laid down His life for His sheep He meant not only in behalf of them, but also in the stead of them. After the Resurrection, when He gave Peter the triple injunction to feed His lambs and sheep, He prophesied that Peter would have to die for His flock, as He had done.

The Father loved Him, He said, not merely because He laid down His life, for men can become victims of superior forces. If He died without resuming His life, His function would have ceased after His sacrifice; He would have been only a beautiful memory. But the Father's love contemplated more than this. He also was to take up His life and to continue to exercise the royal rights. In retaking life, He would be able to continue sovereignty on different terms.

This double action was the mandate of His Father.

> This charge I have received from my Father. *John 10:18*

Thus, while the surrender of His life and the taking-up of His life was spontaneous, it was also a consequence of an appointment and an ordinance which He received from the Heavenly Father when He became man. The Father did not will that His Son should perish, but rather that He should triumph in the greatest possible act of love. Later on, during the Agony in the Garden, He would confirm this blending of His own freedom with the Divine order. Previously, His hearers had heard Him say:

> I have come down from heaven, not to do my own will, but the will of him who sent me. *John 6:38*

Thus, the dispute that began on the subject of leadership through teaching ended on the subject of an increase of life through Redemption. The miracle of giving sight to the man born blind was like all of His miracles—they pointed to His work of giving His life as a ransom for mankind. Every moment of His life had the Cross in it; His teaching had value only because of the Cross. His active exposure to the Cross for the sake of love was quite different from a stoic acceptance of it when it came. But He entered voluntarily the gate of Calvary for the sake of righteousness. Paul would tell the Romans later on the wonders of this love of the Shepherd for His black sheep.

> For at the very time when we were still powerless, then Christ died for the wicked. Even for a just man one of us would hardly die, though perhaps for a good man one might actually brave death; but Christ died for us while we were yet sinners, and that is God's own proof of his love towards us. And so, since we have now been justified by Christ's sacrificial death, we shall all the more certainly be saved through him from final retribution. *Romans 5:6–8*

23. *The Son of Man*

No title did Our Lord use more often to describe Himself than "the Son of Man." No one else ever called Him by that title, but He used it of Himself at least eighty times. Nor is it "a Son of Man," that He called Himself, but "the Son of Man." His existence, both eternal and temporal, is in it. In His conversation with Nicodemus He indicated that He was God in the form of man.

> No one ever went up into heaven except the one who came down from heaven, the Son of Man whose home is in heaven. God loved the world so much that he gave his only son . . . *John 3:13,16*

That "the Son of Man" referred to His human nature, which was in Personal union with His Divine nature, is evidenced from the fact that the first time Our Lord ever referred to Himself as "the Son of Man" was when He was recognized by His disciples as the Son of God.

Christ entered into human existence under a form which was not natural to Him as the Son of God. This assuming of a human nature was a humiliation, an emptying, a stripping and a *kenosis* of His glory. The fundamental renouncement of His Divine glory created a physical condition of life which made Him appear like a man; His suffering and death were the logical consequences of this humiliation. As God He could not suffer; as man He could.

This distinction between the Son of Man and Son of God, He often made. On one occasion, when His enemies sought to kill Him, He said:

> You belong to this world below, I to the world above. *John 8:23*

Sometimes the title "the Son of Man" is used with reference to His coming on the last day to judge all men; at other times, it referred to His Messianic mission to establish the Kingdom of God on earth and to bring forgiveness of sinners; but more often it refers to His Passion, death and Resurrection. Hidden in it was His mission as Savior and His humiliation as God in the weakness of human flesh. As a king might take another name while traveling incognito, so the Son of God took another name, "the Son of Man," not to deny His Divinity but better to affirm the new condition He had taken. Since He was humbling Himself and making Himself obedient, even to the death on the Cross, the title "Son of Man" stood for the shame, abasement, and grief which is the human lot. It was descriptive of what He *became*, rather than of what He *is* from all eternity. "The Son of Man" or the "Man of Sorrows" was, He said, also the object of prophecy:

> How is it that the scriptures say of the Son of Man that he is to endure great sufferings and to be treated with contempt? *Mark 9:11*

Because the name implied not only humiliation but identification with sinful mankind, *He never used the term after He had redeemed humanity and risen from the dead.* The glorified lips of the "Resurrection and the Life" never again pronounce "the Son of Man." He had left behind Him the oneness with unredeemed humanity.

That the lowliness of His present condition was what He wished to emphasize became evident from His oneness with the woes and miseries of men. If men were homeless, He would be homeless:

> Foxes have their holes, the birds their roosts; but the Son of Man has nowhere to lay his head. *Matthew 8:20*

Since the truth He came to bring to this earth was reserved for those who accepted His Divinity, and was not something to tickle ears, He never used "The Son of Man" as the source of that truth. The truth He brought was Divine truth, final and absolute. Hence He avoided using the term "Son of Man" in relation to His Divine nature, which was one with the Father.

> In truth I know him and obey his word. *John 8:55*
>
> I am the truth. *John 14:16*
>
> I tell you this: the truth is . . . *John 6:32*

But when it came to judging the world, at the end of time, separating the sheep and the goats, holding the scales of virtue and vice in each soul, that privilege and authority was His because He suffered and redeemed mankind as "the Son of Man." Because He was obedient unto death, His Father exalted Him as Judge. Knowing what was in man, as "the Son of Man," He could best judge man.

> As the Father has life-giving power in himself, so has the Son, by the Father's gift.
>
> As Son of Man, he has also been given the right to pass judgement.
> *John 5:27*

Though "the Son of Man" expressed His federation with humanity, He was very careful to note that He was like man in all things save

sin. He challenged His hearers to convict Him of sin. But the consequences of sin were all His as "the Son of Man." Hence the prayer to
let the chalice pass; His endurance of hunger and thirst; His agony
and bloody sweat; perhaps even His seeming older than He actually
was; His condescension to wash the feet of His disciples; His absence
of resentment as the swine-owning capitalists ordered Him from their
shores; His endurance of false charges of being a winebibber, a glutton; His gentleness, which expressed itself in hiding when His enemies would have stoned Him; above all, His endurance of worry, anxiety, fear, pain, mental anguish, fever, hunger, thirst, and agony during
the hours of His Passion—all these things were to inspire men to imitate "the Son of Man." Nothing that was human was foreign to Him.

The human family has its trials; so He sanctified them by living in a
family. Labor and work done by the sweat of the brow were humanity's lot; therefore He, "the Son of Man," became a carpenter. No single human affliction which befalls man as the result of sin escaped His
oneness with it.

> He took away our illnesses and lifted our diseases from us.
> *Matthew 8:17*

Isaiah had prophesied this incorporation with human frailty. Though
there is no evidence in the Gospels that Our Lord was ever ill, there
are many instances where He felt sickness as if it were His own, as He
felt sin as if it were His own. Hence in the performance of a cure, He
sometimes "sighed" or "groaned" after looking up to heaven, the
Source of His power. Human infirmity touched Him so deeply, because deafness, dumbness, leprosy, insanity were the effects of sin, not
in the person afflicted but in humanity. Because His death would
remove sin which was the cause (though the final release from
sickness and error would not come until the resurrection of the just),
He said that it was just as easy for Him to heal one as the other.

> Is it easier to say, Your sins are forgiven, or to say, Stand up and walk?
> *Matthew 9:5*

He sighed because He was a High Priest Who was touched by all the
"ills that flesh is heir to." Tears! He wept three times, because humanity weeps. When He saw others weep, such as Mary in grief at
her brother's death, He felt the sorrow as His own.

> When Jesus saw her weeping and the Jews her companions weeping,
> he sighed heavily and was deeply moved. *John 11:33*

In the death and burial of Lazarus He saw the long procession of
mourners from the first to the last, and the reason of it all: how death

came into the world with the sin of Adam. Within a few days, He knew that He as the second Adam or "the Son of Man," would take on "the sins of the world," and thereby give death its death. The restoring of physical health to humanity cost Him something, as the restoring of spiritual health cost His life. In the first instance, as the Son of Man, He felt as if an energy that was lost to Him went into humanity. When the woman touched the hem of His garment, the Gospel records that He was:

Jesus, aware that power had gone out of him . . . *Mark 5:30*

Though, therefore, no disease or sin touched Him by a contagion, He bore them as a loving mother bears the agony of her child and would, if possible, take it upon herself. But a mother does not have that representative character over her family that Christ had over the human race. He was the new Adam and could bring forgiveness and life to all men, as the first Adam brought to all men sin and death.

Finally, the title "the Son of Man" meant that He was representative not of the Jews alone, nor of the Samaritans alone, but of all mankind. His relation to mankind was similar to that of Adam. The human race has two heads: Adam and the new Adam, Christ. "The Son of Man" was not a particular man, a personal man, but rather a Pattern Man, a Universal Man. It was into the human family that God chose to enter, the perfect phrase to describe it being, *Homo factus est.* He was made man and qualified Himself for copartnership with human nature. He entered into the reality of common humanity. He assumed a human nature into His Sacred Person. Aristotle said that if the gods take interest in human affairs, they may be expected to look with most satisfaction on what is most akin to their own nature. This would imply a certain amount of disdain for the human; hence the Greeks said that manifestations of deity "were too fair to worship, too divine to love." But in the person of Christ it is the reverse that was true: "He came unto His own." A sanctifier must be one with those whom He sanctifies. The very separateness in character between the two parties makes it necessary that in some way they should be one. There must be a point of contact, one with the other. He who is like his brethren will have more power over them than one who is not like them. Hence, in order to be a sanctifier, Our Blessed Lord had to be a man like His unholy brethren. He would make them holy by reproducing in His life the lost ideal of human character and bringing that ideal to bear on their minds and hearts.

The Ideal had to be an ideal *man*, "bone of our bone, flesh of our flesh"—"the Son of Man." He had to be in humanity, stripped of all social advantages, down to the level of the common mass, and presenting there the ideal of excellence among menial surroundings. Thus would He be a compassionate High Priest Who could feel for man and be his true representative before God. The closer He was to His constituents, the better fitted He was for His office. By having compassion on the ignorant and erring, He acquired through His own experience and consciousness of infirmity a likeness to men who suffer.

He could not be a High Priest for man and intercede for man, and pay his debts to the Father, unless He was taken *from* among men. The title "Son of Man" proclaimed this brotherhood with men. But men cannot be brothers unless they have a common father, and God is not a Father unless He has a Son. To believe in the brotherhood of man without the Fatherhood of God would make men a race of bastards.

But sympathy alone is not the full explanation of this title "Son of Man." He was not only willing, but eager—even under a necessity— to come to their lot. Sympathetic love brought Him down from heaven to earth, and fellowship in suffering followed as a matter of course. Love is a vicarious principle. A mother suffers for and with her sick child, as a patriot suffers for his country. No wonder that the Son of Man visited this dark, sinful, wretched earth by becoming Man— Christ's unity with the sinful was due to His love! Love burdens itself with the wants and woes and losses and even the wrongs of others.

He suffered because He loved. But something more is to be added. It was not just enough for a man to love another man; if this suffering was ever to have any value, He must have something to offer to God for us, and His offering must possess that quality needful to efficacy. It must be perfect and eternally valid; He, therefore, had to be God as well as man, otherwise the reparation and Redemption of sinful man would not have value in the sight of God. Sympathy alone would not suffice to form unity between God and the unholy. There must be a divine appointment to the office. In virtue of the Divine "must," He was not only a Priest but a *Victim*. He put away sin by the sacrifice of Himself. As a Priest, He was humanity's representative; as a Victim, He was humanity's substitute. He offered Himself as an acceptable sacrifice to God. It is a perfect example of self-surrender and devotion to the Divine will, and God accepted the sacrifice not by a man, but by "the Son of Man," or the human race represented by this Archetypal or Pattern Man. Acting as sin-bearer did not in any way alter His relationship to His Heavenly Father; though Christ was actually the sin-bearer only while on earth, He was the sin-bearer by destiny before He came into the world. Hence, Scripture calls Him the "Lamb slain before the foundation of the world."

No one—not the demons, not His enemies, not even the Apostles —ever called Him "the Son of Man." As "Son of God" applied to Himself had a unique meaning, namely, the only begotten Son of the Eternal Father, so had this title, coined by Himself and applied to Himself alone. No one else ever stood as a representative of the human race. "The Son of God" is a stranger to the human race, because He is its Creator; but the "Son of Man" was one with the human race except for its sin. As man He could die. To die is a humiliation; but to die for others is glorification. His Father, therefore, manifested a singular love to His Divine Son by allowing Him as the Son of Man to taste death for others. The family tree of earthly ancestors was really not important; what was important was the family tree of the children of God He planted on Calvary.

24. *Caesar or God*

Men talk most about health when they are unhealthy. So too they talk most about freedom when they are in danger of losing it or when they are enslaved. At times freedom has been identified with license at one extreme, or with tyranny at the other. Since Our Lord came into a country that was enslaved and subjugated, it was to be expected that some would have a desire for no other kind of freedom than the political, or release from a conqueror's yoke. If He was an ethical reformer that is precisely the freedom He should have given; but if He was a Savior, as indeed He was, then spiritual freedom was more important than political freedom.

On the mountaintop, Satan tried to make Him concentrate on a political career but failed. It was the political that was to serve the Divine, not the Divine the political. Later on, when the masses attempted to make Him king, He fled into the mountains. But the idea of political liberation was rampant and foremost in the popular mind. All Israel had been in the hands of the Romans ever since Pompey entered the Holy City defended by Aristobulus and carried him and thousands more off into captivity. The country, then, was a tributary of Rome. When the word "freedom" was used, it was almost always understood in the political sense of overthrowing the slavery of Caesar.

Our Lord, therefore, constantly had to deal with this problem— either because some hoped He would be a political liberator, or because whenever He spoke of freedom it was misunderstood as liberation from Rome. In three separate incidents He cleared up His position on this subject, leaving no doubts as to what He regarded as the True Freedom:

1 Political freedom from Caesar was not primary.
2 True Freedom was spiritual and meant liberation from sin.
3 To acquire this Freedom for everyone, Jew and Gentile alike, He would submit Himself voluntarily as a ransom for sin.

Two groups held contrary views concerning Caesar: the Herodians and the Pharisees. The Herodians were not a sect or a religious school, but a political party. Outwardly they were friends of Caesar and of the Roman authority; though they were not Romans, they favored the House of Herod as the occupant of the Jewish throne; this made them friends of pagan Rome and Caesar, Herod himself being the vassal of Caesar. Wishing to see Judea eventually brought under the sceptre of a prince of the Herodian line, they in the meantime submitted as fellow travelers to the pagan Roman authority.

Another party was the Pharisees, who were now at the height of their power. Being Puritans concerning the Law and Jewish traditions, they refused to acknowledge any authority to Rome; they had even attempted, according to Josephus, to put Herod to death. As nationalists, they refused to acknowledge Roman dominion and hoped that one day the Jews under their Messiah-King would rule the world.

Both of these groups were enemies, not only because the Herodians sided with Caesar and were willing to pay tribute to the conqueror, while the Pharisees despised Caesar and paid tribute under protest, but also because the Herodians were not particularly interested in religion, while the Pharisees professed to be its most exemplary models.

One day after Our Lord had cured a man on the Sabbath, the Pharisees began plotting with those of Herod's party to make away with Him. That the Pharisees should have tolerated even such a temporary alliance with the Herodians, shows the virulence of the hatred directed against Our Blessed Lord. The Gospel suggests that this new conspiracy was directed to handing Him over to the authority of the Roman Governor, or else to the people.

> So they watched their opportunity and sent secret agents in the guise of honest men, to seize upon some word of his as a pretext for handing him over to the authority and jurisdiction of the Governor.
>
> Luke 20:20

The Herodians could not have come before Our Blessed Lord without arousing some suspicion of their base motives, nor did the Pharisees, always astute, come to Him in person. They sent some of their young scholars, as though in their guileless simplicity they were merely seeking information. The Pharisees gave Our Blessed Lord the impression that a dispute had arisen between them and the Herodians, as indeed would have been very natural. They desired to settle it by referring it to Him as the great scholar. They began by praising Him, thinking foolishly that He might be won over by a little flattery.

> Master, you are an honest man, we know; you teach in all honesty the way of life that God requires, truckling to no man, whoever he may be. *Matthew 22:16*

Then came the question, and a real trick question it was:

> Give us your ruling on this: are we or are we not permitted to pay
> taxes to the Roman Emperor?   *Matthew* 22:18

"This tax which we Pharisees so much detest, but the legality of
which these Herodians support, ought we or ought we not to pay?
Which of us is right—we the Pharisees who loathe and resent it, or
the Herodians who justify it?"

They expected Our Blessed Lord to answer either "Herodians" or
"Pharisees." If He answered, "No, it is not lawful to render tribute to
Caesar," then the Herodians would have delivered Him over to the
Roman authorities, who in turn would order His death for conspiring
to revolution. If He said, "Yes, it is lawful," then He would displease
the Pharisees, who would go before the people and say that He was
not a Messiah, for no Messiah, or deliverer, or Savior would ever consent that the people should put their necks under the yoke of an invader. If He refused to pay the tax He was a rebel; if He agreed to pay
it, He was an enemy of the people. To say "No" would make Him a
traitor to Caesar; to say "Yes" would make Him antinational, antipatriotic. In either case it would seem that He was caught in a trap. The
fellow travelers would condemn Him for being an enemy of the great
leader, Caesar; the semireligious would damn Him for being an enemy
of His country. The snare in the question was heightened by the fu-
sion of the religious and the political elements in the ancient history
of Israel; but now the two were separated. How could an absolute
standard be applied to both God and Caesar?

To this trick question so maliciously proposed, Our Divine Lord
replied:

> You hypocrites! Why are you trying to catch me out?
> 						*Matthew* 22:19

Despite the fact that they began with a compliment, Our Blessed
Lord could hear the hiss of the serpent. Though they boasted that He
was fearless and impartial, He blinded them with the flash of the one
indignant word "hyprocrites." He then said to them:

> Show me the money in which the tax is paid.   *Matthew* 22:19

Our Lord had none. So they produced a coin and put it into His
hand. On one side was stamped the features of the Emperor,
Tiberius Caesar, and on the other side of the coin was stamped his
title *Pontifex Maximus*. A great hush must have come over the crowd
at that moment as they saw the coin laying there in the hand of Our
Blessed Lord. Not many days hence, He Who was the King of kings

would have those very hands pierced by the nails under the orders of the representative of the man at whose portrait He looked. Our Lord asked them:

Whose head is this, and whose inscription?

They answered:

Caesar's.

Then came His answer:

Then pay Caesar what is due to Caesar, and pay God what is due to God. *Matthew* 22:21,22

Our Lord took no sides, because the basic question was not God or Caesar, but God and Caesar. That coin used in their daily marketings showed they were no longer independent from a political point of view. In that lower sphere of life, the debt to the government should be discharged. He fostered no aspirations for independence; He promised no aid in liberation. It was even their duty to acknowledge the present dominion of Caesar, *imperante Tiberio*. The Greek word in the Gospel for "give back" or "render" implied a moral duty such as St. Paul later on told the Romans, *imperante Nerone*:

Every person must submit to the supreme authorities. There is no authority but by act of God. *Romans* 13:1

But in order to remove the objection that service to the government exempted from service to God, He added:

And pay God what is due to God.

Once again He was saying that His Kingdom was not of this world; that submission to Him is not inconsistent with submission to secular powers; that political freedom is not the only freedom. To the Pharisees who hated Caesar came the command: "Give unto Caesar"; to the Herodians who had forgotten God in their love of Caesar came the basic principle: "Give unto God." Had the people rendered to God His due, they would not now be in their present state of having to render too much to Caesar. He had come primarily to restore the rights of God. As He told them before, if they first sought first the Kingdom of God and His Justice, all these things such as political freedom would be added unto them.

That coin bore the image of Caesar, but whose image did the questioners bear? Was it not the image of God Himself? It was this image He was interested in restoring. The political could remain as it was for the time being, for He would not lift a finger to change their coinage.

But He would give His life to have them render unto God the things that are God's.

THE TRUE FREEDOM

This question of freedom arose during Our Lord's second visit to Jerusalem. He had just discoursed on truth as the condition of freedom, saying:

> The truth will set you free.   *John* 8:32

As in the order of mechanics, a man is most free to run a machine when he knows the truth about it, so spiritually a man is most free whose mind is illumined by Him Who said, "I am the Truth."

His listeners resented what seemed to them to be an implication that they were enslaved.

> We are Abraham's descendants; we have never been in slavery to any man. What do you mean by saying, You will become free men?
>
> *John* 8:33

This proud boast was utterly unfounded. Even at that very moment Romans were collecting taxes from them as a conquered people. Seven times, according to the Book of Judges, they were enslaved to the Canaanites. Besides, had they forgotten the seventy years in Babylon? They had been in bondage to the Philistines, to the Assyrians, and to the Chaldeans; and now within the poorest vision was the Roman garrison, and in their pockets Roman money, and in Jerusalem, Pilate the Roman.

But Our Lord ignored the political background; such bondage could be suffered. But the slavery of which He spoke was the slavery of sin. The human will cannot be assaulted from without; it can only be betrayed from within, by a free decision which, multiplied, forges the chain of habit:

> In very truth I tell you that everyone who commits sin is a slave. The slave has no permanent standing in the household.   *John* 8:34

The very freedom which the sinner supposedly exercises in his self-indulgence is only another proof that he is ruled by the tyrant. Our Lord now contrasted a slave and a son, after He had accused His listeners of being slaves of sin. The slave does not live in the house forever. The Jubilee year was a provision against such perpetuity; a time comes when the slave must leave. But it is not so with a son; he is bound to the home with ties which time cannot destroy. Our Lord compared the slave, who did not belong perpetually to the master, to the slave-sinner, who likewise did not belong to the house of the

Heavenly Father. No sinner is in his true home as long as he is in bondage to Satan. But He Who stood in the midst of them was the Son of that Heavenly Father.

> The son belongs to it for ever. *John 8:35*

He, the Son, came among them who were slaves of sin to set them, not politically but spiritually, free. This deliverance would restore the slaves of sin to the Father's house. No slave need abide forever under the tyranny of sin, because there is One Who will ransom him from evil. There will be deliverance from one house to another. That they might know Who it was Who would effect this redemption, He said:

> If then the Son sets you free, you will indeed be free. *John 8:36*

The Son is no other than the speaker, Christ Himself, and He can free men from sin, precisely because He is from the Father. The deliverer Himself must be free; if He were in any way enslaved by sin, He could not liberate. The doors of the prison of evil can be unlocked only from the outside and by One Who Himself is not a prisoner.

There was nothing new in this proclamation that He came to emancipate from sin and give to His followers the "glorious liberty of the children of God." His first public utterance in His native town was the message of salvation.

> The spirit of the Lord is upon me because he has anointed me; he has sent me . . . to proclaim release for prisoners . . . and to let the broken victims go free. *Luke 4:18*

When He said this, they attempted to kill Him by throwing Him over a cliff; this audience was no more receptive than the audience of Nazareth. The contrast He made between the slaves of sin and the Son of God was too much for them. They knew very well that His words about freedom could not possibly apply to their emancipation from Roman power. There was no mistaking either that for Him the only true freedom was freedom from sin. But still they would not accept Him, and He gave them the reason.

> But I speak the truth and therefore you do not believe me. Which of you can prove me in the wrong? If what I say is true, why do you not believe me? He who has God for his father listens to the words of God. You are not God's children; that is why you do not listen.
> *John 8:45–47*

Generally a man is believed when he speaks the truth; now it is the truth which causes disbelief. Truth can be hated when it reveals falsity within. Though they rejected Him, He challenged them to point to one blot on His sinless Character. Even Judas after the betrayal would call Him "innocent." He taught His disciples to pray "forgive us our trespasses," but He never prayed thus; rather did He forgive the trespasses of others. If sin be slavery, then sinlessness is perfect freedom. Freedom is not in its essence release from a foreign yoke; it is really a release from the captivity of sin. He was not a Teacher discoursing about liberty; He was a liberator—and from a greater thraldom than Rome. "The Son makes you free men." But it will cost something, as He explained in His next discussion about freedom.

THE PRICE OF TRUE FREEDOM

The time of the visitation to Galilee was about over; Our Blessed Lord avoided public attention as much as possible, and gave Himself up to impressing upon His disciples the lesson of the Cross, which they did not understand until after Pentecost. Immediately upon arriving in Capharnaum, the collectors of the temple tax approached Peter, either out of hostile curiosity about the tax, or else in order to have an accusation against Peter's Master, saying to him:

> Does your master not pay temple-tax? *Matthew 17:25*

The temple tax was originally levied against each person as a ransom for his soul, in the sense of an acknowledgment that his life had been forfeited by sin. Exodus levied it against every male twenty years of age in order to pay for the temple service. The tax was a half shekel and amounted to about thirty cents in American money.

The question about Our Lord paying the temple tax was not a simple one. He had said that He was the Temple of God, and had exercised His Divine rights over the material temple by purging it of buyers and sellers. Would He Who said that He was a Temple of God because Divinity was dwelling in His human nature now pay the temple tribute? To pay the temple tax after His clear affirmation at the Feast of the Tabernacles that He was the Son of God would have given rise to some serious misunderstandings. The point at issue was not the poverty of the Master; it was whether or not He Who is the living Temple of God would subordinate Himself to the symbol and sign of Himself.

In answer to the question of the temple tax collector, Peter replied that Our Lord did pay the tax. Peter had not consulted with Our Lord as to whether or not He had paid the tax. After answering, he went into the house. Before Peter had a chance to speak, Our Lord addressed him, showing that He was well acquainted with the conver-

sation which took place outside. All things were naked and open to
His eyes; concealment was impossible.

> What do you think about this, Simon? From whom do earthly mon-
> archs collect tax or toll? From their own people, or from aliens?
>
> *Matthew* 17:24

He knew that Peter gave an affirmative answer to the tax collectors.
The question implied that Peter had lost sight, for the moment, of
the dignity of his Master, Who was the Son in His own house, the
Temple, and not a servant in another's house. It was somewhat the
same idea that Our Blessed Lord had emphasized when talking to the
Pharisees. He told them that they were servants, not just of a political
power but servants of sin, and He was interested only in relieving
them from that slavery of sin. When Peter answered:

> From aliens . . . Why then, said Jesus, their own people are exempt!
>
> *Matthew* 17:25

A king does not impose a tax on his own family to maintain the palace in which he lives. Then, since He is God, should He pay the ransom tax—*He Who is giving His life as ransom?* Since He is the Temple of God, then should He pay a tax for a sacrifice, since He is both
the Temple and the Sacrifice? He thus put Himself outside the circle
of sinful men. The freedom He gives is spiritual, not political.

After having affirmed that as the King of Heaven He was immune
from earthly tributes, He turned to Peter and said:

> As we do not want to cause offence, go and cast a line in the lake;
> take the first fish that comes to the hook, open its mouth, and you
> will find a silver coin; take that and pay it in; it will meet the tax for
> us both. *Matthew* 17:25

The king's son is free. But He Who is the Son of God became the
Son of Man sharing the poverty, trials, the labors, and the homelessness of men. Later on, He would subject Himself to arrest, the
crown of thorns, and to the Cross. Presently, as the Son of Man, He
would not stand on His dignity as the Son of God, nor claim immunity from servile obligations, but would voluntarily concede to a tax in
order to avoid scandal. It is not a mark of greatness always to affirm
one's right, but often to suffer an indignity. There might be scandal if
He showed contempt for the temple. As He submitted Himself to
John's baptism to fulfill all righteousness; as His mother offered doves,
though she needed no purification from His birth; so He would submit Himself to the tax to sanctify the human bonds He wore.

In His answer He closely associated Peter with Himself. Never once in speaking of His Heavenly Father did He ever say of mankind and Himself "Our Father." It might seem at first sight that He did so in the prayer "Our Father," thus implying that man and He were the same kind of sons of the Heavenly Father. But actually the Apostles asked Him how to pray, and He told them to pray "Our Father." Our Lord always made the distinction between "Our Father" and "My Father." He is the natural Son of God; men were the adopted sons of God. In like manner, He never associated any human being with Himself except Peter, as He does here when He says, "We will not hurt their consciences." He who had been called the rock, he who would be called the shepherd, and he who was given the keys of the Kingdom of Heaven was here associated more closely with Christ than any other human being.

Although He was free from the tax, He prepared to pay it; though free from sin too, He took on its penalties; though free from the necessity of death, He accepted it; though free from the Cross, He embraced it. As the tax collectors did not force money from Him, so neither would the Roman soldiers nor the Sanhedrin fasten Him to the Cross without His own will. There would no longer be a plague, for He would pay the ransom price.

Peter paid the tax, but Our Lord paid it with him. Both shared in the submission. Hence, Our Lord said, "Make payment to them for Me and for thyself." He does not say "for us," because there was the infinite difference between the Person of God and the person of Peter. Our Lord would pay the debt for ransom from sin, though exempt. Peter would pay it, because he was liable. Our Lord would pay it because of humility; Peter would pay it because of duty.

The manner in which the tax was paid might have been a lesson to Peter that, even while submitting Himself to the temple authorities, He was nevertheless showing Himself the Lord of all creation. The Apostles were once before astounded that the winds and the seas obeyed Him; now what was in the sea obeyed. Just as death and glory were always connected in every statement of His, so now the humiliation of paying the tax was associated with His kingly supremacy over nature and the fish of the sea. The tax money was supplied by a miracle of both omniscience and lordship over creation, in which the fish Peter caught was found to contain a stater, or the exact tax necessary for Himself and for Peter. The two strands of humiliation and majesty are thus woven together as they were in every word of His concerning His Cross and His glory. Never one without the other. At the very beginning, the helplessness of a Babe in a stable was compensated for by the song of the angels and the movement of a star guiding Wise Men to His feet. So now, as the Son of God He was exempt from ecclesiastical law, yet He paid the tax; later on, though exempt from political law, He would tell Pilate that his authority as a judge came from Him, yet He would accept a false judgment.

For centuries, ever since those forty years in the desert, every son of Abraham had been paying ransom for his soul which needed redemption. No more ransom money will be needed, for the Sinless One will take on sin. He told His listeners, "Give back to Caesar what is Caesar's." So now, He gave back to the earthly temple the things that are the earthly temple's. Exemptions from these duties do not necessarily make men free. The first freedom, which is immunity from evil, will be purchased by One Who made Himself a slave. As St. Paul put it:

> For the divine nature was his from the first; yet he did not think to snatch at equality with God, but made himself nothing, assuming the nature of a slave. Bearing the human likeness, revealed in human shape, he humbled himself, and in obedience accepted even death— death on a cross. Therefore God raised him to the heights and bestowed on him the name above all names, that at the name of Jesus every knee should bow—in heaven, on earth, and in the depths— and every tongue confess, Jesus Christ is Lord, to the glory of God the Father. *Philippians 2:6–11*

25. *His Hour Had Not Yet Come*

When Our Lord declared Himself to be the Son of God and One with His Heavenly Father, His enemies made attempts on His life. When He told His Apostles that He must be crucified and be a suffering Son of Man, they quarreled either with Him or among themselves for the first place in His Kingdom.

Divinity and a suffering Savior were both repugnant to unregenerated men; Divinity, because man secretly wants to be his own god; suffering, because the ego cannot understand why a seed must die before it springs forth unto new life. The Son of God became a stumbling block when He humiliated Himself to the human level, taking on the form and habit of man. It is hard on the intelligentsia to believe that Greatness can be so little. On the other hand, the Son of Man became a scandal when He took upon Himself the weakness and even the guilt of man and did not use His Divine power to escape the Cross.

Several attempts were made on His life; most of them during one of the great feasts, but always after He had proclaimed His Divinity. The first attempt was in Nazareth. Every man has his own country, his own home, and his own kindred. It is among these that he would be loved and remembered. But as Our Lord hastened to His Cross, His speed was quickened by the rejection of His Own home town.

NAZARETH

As the lengthening shadows of Friday's sun were closing about the little village that nestled in the cup of hills, a blast from the trumpet of the master of the synagogue proclaimed the beginning of the Sabbath. The following morning Our Blessed Lord went to the synagogue, where He had often been as a child and as a young man. Very likely when He entered the synagogue this time, the news of the miracles at Cana and at the Jordan where the heavens proclaimed His Divinity had already brought the people to a high pitch of expectancy.

> Then Jesus, armed with the power of the Spirit, returned to Galilee; and reports about him spread through the whole country-side.
>
> *Luke 4:14*

In the synagogue, He was given the Book of Isaiah. The particular prophecy which He read dealt with the Suffering Servant of God.

The spirit of the Lord is upon me because he has anointed me; he has sent me to announce good news to the poor, to proclaim release for prisoners and recovery of sight for the blind; to let the broken victims go free, to proclaim the year of the Lord's favour.   *Luke 4:18,19*

This passage was familiar to the Jews. It was an Old Testament prophecy concerning the release of the Jews from the Babylonian captivity. But He did something unusual; He took this text woven out of the Exile, and wrapped it around Himself. He changed the meaning of the "poor," the "enslaved," and the "blind." The "poor" were those who had no grace and lacked union with God; the "blind" were those who had not yet seen the Light; the "enslaved" were those who had not yet purchased true freedom from sin. He then proclaimed that all these centered in Himself.

But above all, He declared the Jubilee. The Mosaic code made provision for every fiftieth year to be one of special grace and restoration. All debts were remitted; family inheritances which had, by the pressure of time, been alienated, were restored to their original owners; those who had mortgaged their liberty were restored to freedom. It was a Divine safeguard against monopolies; and it kept family life intact. The Jubilee year was to Him a symbol of His Messianic appearance which He proclaimed because He had been anointed with the Spirit to do so. There were to be new spiritual riches, a new spiritual light, a new spiritual liberty, all centering in Him—the Evangelist, the Healer, the Emancipator. All who were in the synagogue had their eyes fixed on Him. Then came the startling, explosive words:

Today in your very hearing this text has come true.   *Luke 4:21*

He knew they were expecting a political king who would throw off Roman domination. But He proclaimed redemption from sin, not from military dictatorship. In this way alone they must expect the prophecy of Isaiah to be fulfilled.

It was understandable that the people of Nazareth, who had seen Jesus grow up among them, were surprised to hear Him proclaim Himself the anointed of God, of whom Isaiah spoke. They now had a double alternative before them: either they could accept Him as the fulfillment of the prophecy; or they could rebel. The privilege of being the home town of the long-awaited Messiah and the One Whom the Heavenly Father in the Jordan proclaimed His Divine Son was too much for them, because of their familiarity with Him. They asked:

Is not this the carpenter, the son of Mary?   *Mark 6:3*

They believed in God in a kind of way, but not the God Who touched their neighborhood, entered into close dealings with them, and lifted hammers in the same trade shop. The same kind of snobbery that was found in the exclamation of Nathanael: "Can anything good come out of Nazareth?" now became the prejudice against Him in His Own city, and among His Own people. He was indeed the Son of a carpenter, but also of the Carpenter Who made heaven and earth. Because God had taken upon Himself a human nature, and had been seen in the lowliness of a village artisan, He failed to win the respect of men.

Our Blessed Lord "was astonished at their unbelief." Twice in the Gospels, He is said to have "marveled" and to have been "astonished": once because of a Gentile's faith; a second time because of His townsmen's lack of faith. From His own people He might have reckoned on some touch of sympathy; some predisposition to welcome Him. His wonder was the measure of His pain, as well as of their sin, as He told them:

> A prophet will always be held in honour except in his home town, and among his kinsmen and family. *Mark 6:4*

In order to bring home to their souls that their self-esteem was wounded, and that if His own received Him not, He would take His salvation elsewhere, He placed Himself in the category of Old Testament prophets, who themselves received no better treatment. He quoted two examples from the Old Testament. Both were a foreshadowing of the direction that His Gospel was to take, namely, to *embrace the Gentiles*. He told them that there had been many widows among the people of Israel in the days of Elijah when the great famine came over the land, and when the heavens were shut up for over three years. But Elijah was not sent to any one of these; he was sent to a widow of Sarepta in the land of the Gentiles. Taking another example, He said that there had been many lepers in the time of Elijah, but none of them except Naaman, the Syrian, was made clean. The mention of Naaman was particularly humiliating, because he at first had been unbelieving, but later he believed. Since both were Gentiles, He implied that the benefits and blessings of the Divine Kingdom were coming in answer to *faith*, not in answer to *race*.

God, He told them, was no man's debtor; His mercies would flow to other people if His own rejected them. His townsmen were reminded that it was their earthly-minded expectation of a political kingdom that withheld them from the realization of the great truth that heaven had visited them in Himself. His own home town became the stage on which was trumpeted the salvation not of a blood, or a nation, but of the whole world. The people were filled with indignation, first of all because He had claimed to bring deliverance from sin in His capacity as the Holy Anointed of God; secondly because of the warning that salvation which was first of the Jews would, on rejection, pass into a mission to the Gentiles. Saints are not always recognized by those who live with them. They would cast Him out, for He had rejected them, and made Himself the Christ. Their violence was a preparation for His Cross.

Nazareth lies in a cup of hills. A short distance from it to the southeast was a wall of rock about eighty feet high which drops about three hundred feet to the Plains of Esdraelon. It is there that tradition places the scene where they attempted to cast Him off.

But he walked straight through them all, and went away. *Luke 4:30*

The hour of His Crucifixion had not yet come, but the minutes were ticking off in a succession of violence whenever He proclaimed that He was sent by God, and that He was God.

BETHSAIDA

Another assault on His life came after the curing of the disabled man at Bethsaida. At this pool in Jerusalem, a number of sick, sorrowful, emaciated, and helpless gathered in the hope of healing. One poor man had been disabled for thirty-eight years. When Our Lord saw him there, He asked:

Do you want to recover? *John 5:6*

When the powerless man expressed confidence in His power, Our Lord said to him:

Rise to your feet, take up your bed and walk. *John 5:8*

With the commandment came the bestowal of power. Whenever man attempts to do what he knows to be the Master's will, a power will be given to him equal to the duty. As St. Augustine said, "Give what thou commandest, and command what thou wilt." As soon as the man was cured, he went to the temple. Later the same day, Our Lord found him there, as the cured man had been telling everyone that it was Jesus Who had made him whole. Trouble started brewing, because this was the Sabbath day. When the leaders of the people had found the man who was cured they said to him:

It is the Sabbath. You are not allowed to carry your bed on the Sabbath. *John 5:11*

Then they began to arouse ill will against Jesus "for doing such things on the Sabbath." Our Lord had healed men on all days, but Sabbaths were high days of grace on which six miracles have been recorded: He cast out an evil spirit; He restored the withered hand of a man; the woman who was crippled He made straight; He cured the man with the dropsy; and He opened the eyes of the blind man.

Many answers were made to the leaders of the people about healing on the Sabbath. He recalled the teaching of the prophets that holy things were of secondary importance compared with the benefit of God's people; afterward, He appealed to the Law, to show that the Sabbath was secondary to the work of the sanctuary. The implication was that there stood among them One greater than the sanctuary. Again He said that the Sabbath was made for man and not man for the Sabbath. On another occasion, He asked:

> What hypocrites you are! Is there a single one of you who does not loose his ox or his donkey from the manger and take it out to water on the Sabbath? *Luke 13:15*

But instead of rendering thanks to God because a sick man had been cured, or rejoicing like the prophetess Anna because they had looked upon the Redemption of Israel, they protested because the man was carrying his bed on the Sabbath. When they sought to kill Him because He had done this on the Sabbath, He answered them:

> My Father has never yet ceased his work, and I am working too.
> *John 5:17*

It is true that God rested on the seventh day from His creative work, though the seventh day was not necessary for His recuperation. But it was necessary for man to rest and sanctify the seventh day, because work tires; and under the present dispensation work is also a penalty. But the Savior here said that though God had rested from His creative work, He did not rest from His Providential work of supplying the needs of His creatures. As St. Chrysostom said:

> How doth the Father work, Who ceased on the seventh day from all His works? Let him learn the manner in which He worketh, what is it? He careth for, He holdeth together all that hath been made. When thou beholdest the sun rising, the moon running in her path, the lakes, the fountains, the rivers, the rains, the course of nature in seeds, and in our own bodies and those of irrational beings, and all the rest, by means of which the universe is made up, then learn the ceaseless working of the Father.

To think of God as not operative in the universe is to imply that He has no interest in it. Evolution and the natural unfolding of things are neither self-explained nor self-operative. They are neither apart from God, nor opposed to Him. After the first creation God did not enter upon an inaction. Since there was evil in the world, the Spirit that moved on formless matter must now begin to move among men.

But the Master was saying more than this, and those who heard Him knew that He was. He was affirming a unique affiliation and oneness with the Father. If the Father was working now in a spiritual realm, so was He; if all things were created "by the power of the Word," now "the Word became flesh"; if the Father ministered to the needs of His creatures on a Sabbath, then it must also be the right of His Son to engage in works of mercy on the Sabbath. Thus did He unequivocally claim absolute equality with the Father. The Father's work and His were the same. The deep sense of His Divine Sonship thrilled through His human nature. The leaders of the people accepted His words as affirming His own Divine Sonship, and the Gospel says that the leaders became

> Still more determined to kill him, because he was not only breaking the Sabbath, but, by calling God his own Father, he claimed equality with God. *John 5:18*

Hostility increased in direct ratio to the affirmation of His Divine authority. They passed over the miracle, and made resolute plots against His life. He was on His way to the Cross, not because He had faults but because of His Divinity and the high purpose of His coming. His Cross would be a witness against their folly, as the Resurrection would be a witness to His Divinity. The Cross was at the end of His life from the point of view of time; but it was at the beginning of His life from the point of view of His intent to offer Himself as a ransom for man.

JERUSALEM

Another attempt on His life was made at Jerusalem during the Feast of the Tabernacles. He had been questioned about how He knew so much.

> How is it that this untrained man has such learning? *John 7:15*

There was no human accounting for His knowledge. The secret fountain of it was His unique relation to the Godhead, which He explained thus:

> The teaching that I give is not my own; it is the teaching of him who sent me. *John 7:16*

There was no mistaking His meaning. He was claiming to be God in the form of man. Their reaction was physical—another attempt on His life; and He quietly asked:

> Why are you trying to kill me? *John 7:20*

Later on, there was another attempt. The immediate occasion of their resentment was His remarks concerning Abraham. The Pharisees, because Our Blessed Lord had spoken of His Father, told Him that Abraham was their father: thus did they distinguish themselves from the heathen, by affirming their lineage with the founder of the Jewish people. They were, indeed, children of Abraham, and their bond with him was witnessed in their flesh, through circumcision. Our Lord did not deny their affiliation with Abraham, but He affirmed another affiliation in the spiritual realm: there can be no true paternal relationship where there is opposition in conduct.

On the part of the Savior there was no desire to minimize Abraham. The memory of Abraham was held in such high honor among the Jews that to be reckoned among his children here below was to them an assurance of being carried into Abraham's bosom. He was not only the father of their race, he was the fountainhead and channel through which the promise of the Messiah flowed to his people. The great promise was also made to Abraham that he would be the instrument of blessing to all the world. It seemed impossible of fulfillment when he was an old man; yet he was led out of his tent under the starry heavens and told that as was the number of the stars, so his seed would be.

It was he who was commanded later on to take his son Isaac, his only son, with whom the promise was bound up, and offer him in sacrifice on Mount Moria. The command was clear: he was about to carry it into effect when his son was spared by God, and a lamb was provided. It might have been on that day that Abraham caught the first true glimpse of another Son, a willing Victim, Who would be offered by the Heavenly Father for the world's sin and salvation. As Chrysostom said, "He saw the Cross of Christ when he laid the wood on his son and in will offered up Isaac."

When the leaders claimed that their spiritual descent had to be from God, since their descent from Abraham was legitimate, the Lord answered that if their spiritual descent was from God, they would not be rejecting His message and seeking to kill Him, but would recognize and love Him.

> If God were your father, you would love me, for God is the source of my being, and from him I come. I have not come of my own accord; he sent me. *John 8:42*

They then asked Him:

> Are you greater than our father Abraham, who is dead? *John 8:53*

> You are not yet fifty years old. How can you have seen Abraham? *John 8:57*

Our Lord answered:

> Your father Abraham was overjoyed to see my day; he saw it and was
> glad . . . In very truth I tell you, before Abraham was born, I am.
>
> *John 8:56-59*

He intimated that Abraham had looked forward with joy to seeing
what Our Lord called "the day of My coming." Notice that he did
not say "My birth." When they challenged Him that He was not yet
fifty years old, it was to indicate not so much His age as the physical
impossibility of His ever having seen Abraham. Their assumption here
was that He was just a man. Our Lord now used the same word that
was used by God on Sinai: "I am Who am." He did not say, "before
Abraham was, I was," but "before Abraham came to be, I am." He
was attributing to Himself not a simple priority over Abraham, but an
existence from all eternity. A moment before, He had said that His
Incarnate Life engaged Abraham's most rapturous attention as he
looked over the shoulders of the ages to catch a glimpse of the
fulfillment of the promises. Long before Abraham's age, He possessed
priority of Being, not created being but uncreated, eternal and self-
existent Being, not moving to greater perfection because already possessed of it. There was a time when Abraham was not, but there was
never a time when the Son of God was not. Christ was not claiming
that He had come into existence before Abraham; but that He had
never come into being at all. He is the "I am" of ancient Israel, the
"I am" without past or future; the "I am" without beginning and
without end, the great eternal "now."

Because they understood that He was saying that He was God:

> They picked up stones to throw at him, but Jesus was not to be seen;
> and he left the temple. *John 8:59*

The alternatives were worship or stoning, and they chose the latter.
The stones were probably those that were lying about in a courtyard,
for the temple was not yet completed. They had sought to kill Him
before when He identified Himself with the Father; now they sought
to stone Him because He said that He antedated Abraham, and
Abraham in prophecy looked forward to Him Who possesses the eternal existence of God.

It is not likely that the hiding to which St. John refers was in any
way interposing anything between Himself and them. The hiding was
rather from those who would not hear His truth, merely by making
Himself invisible to those who sought Him. Once before He had done
the same thing to the same people. His "Hour" was not yet come.
Since no one could take away His life until He would lay it down of
Himself, He retired from the way of His enemies. It was in the tem-

ple they attempted to stone Him. For the stoning of the Divine Temple, there would come a day when there would not be left a stone upon a stone in the temple made by human hands.

JERUSALEM AGAIN

Later on, He visited the last remnant of the old temple, which was known as Solomon's Porch. The feast was that of the Dedication, the last great feast prior to the Passover. It was instituted by Judas Machabeus to celebrate the purification of the temple after it had been profaned by the Syrians. The feast lasted eight days. John in his Gospel noted that it was winter, which would indicate not only a climate but also a disposition of soul. His enemies, as always, gathered around Him asking:

> How long must you keep us in suspense? If you are the Messiah say so plainly. *John 10:24*

Our Lord had openly proclaimed His Messiahship, and confirmed it by works and miracles. But their ideas of a Messiah did not correspond with God's idea of a Messiah. They were looking for someone who would break the Roman yoke, liberate the people and give them material prosperity. Therefore, they were anxious to know if He was going to purify the city of Jerusalem and its courts of Roman soldiers, Roman authority, Roman coins, and Roman magistrates such as Pilate. Had not Judas Machabeus done this, for which they were now celebrating the feast? If the temple had been purged of Syrian profanations, why could not the city be purged of Roman desecrations? If, therefore, He was to be the political Messiah, let Him openly proclaim Himself.

He went on to tell them that there were moral conditions necessary for understanding the Messiahship. He had worked miracles, but miracles would not coerce the will, nor destroy freedom of adhesion. But now He would let them know openly and clearly who the Messiah was:

> My Father and I are one. *John 10:30*

> I am God's son. *John 10:36*

In the Greek, the word "one" is neuter, which means not one person but one substance, one nature. His Father, He the Son, and the Holy Spirit were one in the nature of God. The leaders of the people had been looking for a Messiah sent to establish His Kingdom; but in the last few centuries, with the decline of prophecy, their hopes degenerated into a search for a political liberator. They were not looking for a real indwelling of a Divine Person among them. It was becoming clear to them that the Christ, or the Messiah, was the Son of God Who shared the nature of the Father, though in His human nature, or as the Son of Man, the Father was greater than He. He was now reaffirming that He had been in Being before His human nature was formed; that He had come forth from the Father to assume a human nature; clad in it, He as a Divine Person was conscious of no change in His Divine nature; what had a beginning was His human nature appearing as "the Suffering Servant." When He now affirmed His Divinity, they

> Once again the Jews picked up stones to stone him. *John 10:31*

He said to them:

> I have set before you many good deeds, done by my Father's power; for which of these would you stone me? *John 10:32*

Their answer was that they could not conceive of the humiliation of God in the form of man. The world can understand a man divinizing himself, but it cannot understand a God becoming a man: hence they said the reason they stoned Him was

> We are not going to stone you for any good deed, but for your blasphemy. You, a mere man, claim to be a god. *John 10:33*

His answer was that though a mere man could not be God, God could become man, while still remaining God.

> This provoked them to one more attempt to seize him. But he escaped from their clutches. *John 10:39*

Blasphemy was punishable by stoning. But the little cordon of men around Him, with stones in their hands, could not lay hands on Him: for "His Hour had not yet come." It appeared so easy to take Him, and yet so difficult. When the moment would come, when He would deliver Himself over to them, the first thing that would happen to them was that they would all fall backward upon the ground.

26. The Mightiest Arrow in the Divine Quiver

Our Blessed Lord worked miracles never for Himself, but as credentials for His Person. They were manifest signs that He had a special mission for the realization of God's work among men. Even in the Old Testament there were miracles demanded as a sign to confirm a prophet's word. It was a mark of unbelief in Achaz that he would not ask God for a sign in confirmation of the prophet's word. But the prophet, nevertheless, gave him a sign of the Messiah, namely, the Virgin Birth.

The miracles of Our Blessed Lord moved within a sphere of redemption. They were not merely manifestations of power but an index of man's deliverance from something, namely sin. Hence in the moral order there were miracles of redemption from the tyranny of demons; in the physical order, redemption from other manifestations of sin, such as fever, palsy, leprosy, blindness, and death; redemption of nature in the quelling of the sea and making the winds His servants.

Not including summaries of miracles, which are numerous, there are twenty miracles mentioned in Matthew, twenty in Luke, eighteen in Mark and seven in John. No one can say how many miracles the Savior worked, for many of them are referred to collectively, such as "He cured the sick, the blind, and the lame." The last words of the Gospel of John are:

> There is much else that Jesus did. If it were all to be recorded in detail, I suppose the whole world could not hold the books that would be written. *John 21:25*

He worked miracles to provoke faith in His claim as the Messiah and the Son of God.

> There is enough to testify that the Father has sent me, in the works my Father gave me to do and to finish—the very works I have in hand. *John 5:36*

The refusal of men to accept the indisputable evidence of the senses made their unbelief inexcusable.

> If I had not come and spoken to them, they would not be guilty of sin; but now they have no excuse for their sin: he who hates me, hates my Father. *John 15:22*

Miracles are no cure for unbelief. Some would not believe though one were to rise daily from the dead. No sign could be wrought which would bring complete conviction, for the will can refuse assent to what the intellect knows to be true. The Pharisees admitted:

> This man is performing many signs. *John* 11:48

But though miracles were admitted, the Person Who worked them was denied. Toward the very close of His public life, the survey is completed.

> In spite of the many signs which Jesus had performed in their presence they would not believe in him. *John* 12:37

The incredulity was foreseen centuries before by Isaiah. The prophecy is introduced into the Gospel story at this point, as another proof that Jesus was the Christ. The text of Isaiah is mentioned six times throughout the New Testament and always in connection with lack of faith. It was not that the people did not believe in order that the prophecy might be fulfilled, but rather their unbelief was the fulfillment of the prophecy. The quotation which John took from Isaiah was:

> Lord, who has believed what we reported, and to whom has the Lord's power been revealed? *John* 12:38

This is the first verse in chapter fifty-three of Isaiah, which contains the prophecies concerning Our Lord's sufferings. God's foreknowledge of what will happen does not in any way deprive sinners of their responsibility; yet when the guilt appears and the unbelief is manifested, the causes can be analyzed. Those who refuse to see lose the power to see. God was ratifying an attitude to which men had come by their own choice. Foretelling judgment on unbelief, He warned:

> There is a judge for the man who rejects me and does not accept my words; the word that I spoke will be his judge on the last day. I do not speak on my own authority, but the Father who sent me has himself commanded me what to say and how to speak. *John* 21:48,49

There would be nothing arbitrary in the judgment which He will administer to men on the Last Day; the glorious words of mercy would be invested with judicial authority. This foretelling of how all men would be judged by their attitude toward Him was because He was sent by God. His humanity began to be in time, and was of a lower order and rank than His Divinity, which He shared with the Father; hence, the rejection of Him in His human nature was the rejection of the Father Who sent Him. But for the present, He came not to judge but to save the world.

But though they did not believe in Him, as Isaiah foretold, He had one arrow left in His quiver, which would convince men that He was their Savior.

> And I shall draw all men to myself, when I am lifted up from the earth. *John* 12:32

The Cross would have such attractiveness that it would draw all men, not merely those to whom He was speaking, for His Kingdom was to be the world itself. His death would accomplish what His life could not, for there was more in it than human heroism or devotion. What would draw would not be the surrender to death but the laying bare of the heart of God's love. The love of God was made visible in sacrifice. On Calvary, He would prove Himself man by dying as every other man dies; but He would prove Himself Divine by dying as no other man died. Twenty years later St. Paul would repeat, "We preach Christ and Him crucified." The Divine alone can capture man, and the sublimest manifestation of Divine love is to die for our guilt that we might live. "God so loved the world . . ." The drawing to Himself would be through the allurements of love.

The Cross which was the focal point of His coming, now became a judgment of the evil of the world.

> Now is the hour of judgement for this world; now shall the Prince of this world be driven out. *John* 12:31

A judge passes judgment on the criminal; His Cross passes judgment on the world. Seeing in His mind far beyond the narrow confines of a land extending from Dan to Bersabee, He declared again that all men will be judged by their attitude to the Cross—not only because their sins hung Him there, but because of the love which made Him embrace it. The final judgment would be merely a ratification of the judgment each man passes on Good Friday.

The Cross ended the tolerance extended to the "prince of this world," or Satan, who exercised dominion over man. The Cross would finally convince men of sin, as law or ethics could never do. It would show what sin really is: the Crucifixion of Divine Goodness in the flesh; but it would show them also Who forgives sin, namely, the One they lifted up, even to heaven, to make intercession for men. The Throne erected for Our Lord by men would show the hostility and the reign of evil in their hearts; but it would also show that He was not of the earth. His regnancy would be from a higher sphere of heaven where He would draw His subjects to Him and become the

"Lord of all." What Our Lord said that day—that evil would be finally overcome in Him, through the Cross—St. Paul reiterated:

> For he has forgiven us all our sins; he has cancelled the bond which pledged us to the decrees of the law. It stood against us, but he has set it aside, nailing it to the cross. On that cross he discarded the cosmic powers and authorities like a garment; he made a public spectacle of them and led them as captives in his triumphal procession.
>
> *Colossians 2:14,15*

Though men could not believe in His miracles, He still had the mightiest arrow left in His quiver. It was being lifted up from the earth. The lifting-up was Calvary, but the attracting of all men to Himself looked to the Resurrection and the Ascension, for certainly a dead Savior could draw no one. The Cross which lifted Him above the earth, and the Ascension which lifted Him to heaven, would free Him from all earthly, carnal, and national ties, and enable Him to exercise universal sovereignty over man. Once crucified, He promised to become a magnet of attraction, drawing all nations and tongues and peoples to Himself. Never did He say that His moral precepts would draw all men to Himself. Rather it would be by being violently lifted up from the earth, as if the earth He made and those who were on it would have no part with Him.

Since the same word "lifted up," is used for His Ascension, He implied that, once exalted to heaven, it would be not only Jew but Gentile, or "all men" that He would draw to Himself.

The attraction of the Cross would not be its ignominy which alone is seen on Good Friday, but its love and victory which are seen on Easter and the Ascension. Some religions draw by force of arms; He would draw by force of love. The attraction would not be His words, but Himself. It was His Person around which His teaching centered; not His teaching around which He would be remembered. "Greater love than this no man hath"—that was the secret of His magnetism. As Blake put it:

> Wouldst thou love One Who did not die for thee?
> And wouldst thou die for One Who did not die for thee?

If He had come for some other purpose than Redemption from sin, it would not be the crucifix but a picture of Christ on the Mount as the Teacher that would be held in honor. If the Cross was not eventually to be a glory and a triumph, men would have drawn a veil over that ignominious hour to which He was pointing. If He had died in a bed, He might have been honored, but never as a Savior. The Cross

alone could show that God is all holy, and therefore hates sin; the
Cross also showed that God is all love and therefore dies for sinners,
as if He were guilty.

At this point the crowd asked Him a queer question:

> Our Law teaches us that the Messiah continues forever. What do you
> mean by saying that the Son of Man must be lifted up? What Son of
> Man is this? *John* 12:34

It was strange that they who were acquainted with the Old Testament should have been scandalized by the fact that their Messiah
must die, for certainly they had read that in Isaiah; they had also read
in Daniel that the Son of Man was to be violently cut off. Their objection was that Christ, when He came, would be One Who would
endure eternally; how therefore could He die? It was very clear to
them that being lifted up meant dying on the Cross; it was also clear
that He claimed to be the Christ or the Messiah. But that on which
they stumbled was His death. They could not reconcile a glorious
Messiah with a suffering One, as Peter could not reconcile a Divine
Christ with a crucified Christ. They were right in saying that the Messiah would be eternal, for Gabriel announced to the Blessed Mother
that He would reign over the House of Jacob "forever." But on the
other hand, throughout the Old Testament ran the idea that He was
to be a sacrifice for sin and a Lamb led to the slaughter.

Our Lord met their taunt by drawing aside the veil of His Divinity
and reminding them to avail themselves of His ransom. Some teachers
might kindle lights in souls; others might be flickering candles; but everyone has caught illumination from Him, as He called Himself again
the Light of the World. This Light would not be among them much
longer. There is only one sun to light a world; if they put out the
unique Light of the World, then darkness would overwhelm them.
Spiritual blindness is worse than physical blindness. As the light of
reason is the perfection of the light of the senses, so He called Himself the Light by which reason itself is illumined and perfected. Those
who would walk in faith with Him, He called children of light.

> The light is among you still, but not for long. Go on your way while
> you have the light, so that darkness may not overtake you. He who
> journeys in the dark does not know where he is going. While you have
> the light, trust to the light, so that you may become men of light.
> *John* 12:35,36

The reason Our Lord did not spend more time in correcting their
stumbling at His sacrifice was because they had already stumbled at
the prophecies of the Old Testament, at His miracles, and their obedience to His Word. For the moment, He took their eyes off Calvary

and bade them look into their own consciences. With pity and tenderness, He invited them to avail themselves of His Light while He walked among them. This was His last and farewell utterance to the public, namely, the warning about going into darkness and the invitation to accept not a truth but the Truth.

> After these words Jesus went away from them into hiding.
> *John 12:36*

On that Tuesday evening of Holy Week He left the temple. The following day:

> In the early morning the people flocked to listen to him in the temple.
> *Luke 21:38*

But He did not appear. The sun was going into eclipse; it was as night. The Hour was nigh.

27. More than a Teacher

Great teachers give instructions to their disciples, but has any teacher ever made his death the pattern of theirs? This is impossible, because no earthly teacher could foresee the manner of his death nor was death ever the reason why he came to teach. Socrates, in all his wisdom, never told the young philosophers of Athens to drink hemlock juice, because he would die by it. But Our Lord did make His Cross the basis of His first instruction to His Apostles. It is because this fact is so often missed, and for the moment was missed by the Apostles themselves, that the true vision of the Christ is beclouded. Even when He acted as a Teacher, He made the Cross to cast its shadow over His Apostles. The sufferings they would endure would be identical to what He would endure. He had been called the Lamb of God Who would be sacrificed for the sins of the world; and since they were identified with Him, He warned them of their fate:

> Look, I send you out like sheep among wolves; *Matthew* 10:16

They were to beware of the fickleness of men. When He multiplied bread the crowds immediately sought to make Him their economic King, instead of taking the miracle as a sign of His Divinity. At the beginning of His public life, when He wrought miracles, the attachment of the Apostles was equally shallow. And John wrote:

> But Jesus for his part would not trust himself to them. He knew men so well, all of them, that he needed no evidence from others about a man, for he himself could tell what was in a man. *John* 2:24,25

They would accept Him as a wonder-worker for their eyes, but not as the Light of their souls. He would not give Himself to any credulity based simply on the spectacular. Knowing that popularity toward Him would turn into popularity against Him within five days' time, He said to His Apostles:

> Be on your guard, for men will hand you over to their courts . . .
> *Matthew* 10:17

As He had no illusions about what the world would do to Him, so He had no illusions about those who would be linked closest to Him as branches to the vine. No sage or mystic, no Buddha or Confucius has ever believed that his teaching would so awaken the antagonism of men as to bring about his violent death; but more important still, no human teacher has ever believed that his disciples would suffer a similar fate, just because they were his disciples. Mediocrity never arouses such hatred; animals generally do not destroy their own species; neither does man in ordinary relations. But man, being the golden mean between matter and spirit, has the power, however, to destroy both; he uproots the plants and slaughters the animals which are beneath him in dignity. But he can also hate and even kill whatever is above him in dignity. If, in his pride, he considers God as a challenge, he will deny Him; and if God becomes man and therefore makes Himself vulnerable, he will crucify Him. But Our Lord did not shrink from painting a microcosmic Crucifixion for His followers, as He paints a macrocosmic Crucifixion for Himself.

What is of the world, the world never opposes. What is of God, the spirit of the world opposes, maligns, persecutes, and crucifies. The ransom He would pay for mankind would lead Him to two distinct courts of justice; in the interval between trials, He would be scourged. So too, the Apostles and all their successors through the centuries must expect nothing better:

> For men will hand you over to their courts, they will flog you in the synagogues, and you will be brought before governors and kings, for my sake, to testify before them and the heathen. *Matthew 10:17,18*

The Apostles were not yet persecuted, nor were they annoyed very much before the Crucifixion and Pentecost. But He told them the kind of treatment they were to expect of men later on. Hardly prepared for what would happen to Him, how could they even faintly imagine what would happen to themselves? This hatred of the world, He warned, would be disguised; they would be accused on judicial grounds, that is, hauled before courts in mock trials, charged with "imperialism" or "perverting the nation." The instinct of justice in the human heart is so deep that, even in great deeds of injustice, the villains wear the mantle of justice. It was not so much that isolated bigots would persecute; rather, it is that men would organize juridically against them, His disciples, as they did against Him. Though the mask and disguise of the courts would be justice, the real reason for the hate would be the evil in their hearts.

> Here lies the test: the light has come into the world, but men preferred darkness to light because their deeds were evil. Bad men all hate the light and avoid it, for fear their practices should be shown up. The honest man comes to the light so that it may be clearly seen that God is in all he does. *John 3:19–21*

Men of the world did not begin with a conscious hatred of the Light, because Truth is as native to the mind as light to the eye. But when that Light shone on their souls and revealed their sins, they hated it just as the bank robber hates the searchlight the policeman has turned on him. The truth which He brought, men recognized as claim on their allegiance, because they were made for it; but since they had perverted their natures by evil behavior, His truth stirred their consciences and they despised it. All their habits of life, their dishonesties, and baser passions roused them in violent opposition to that Light. Many a sick man will not undergo a medical examination, for fear the doctor may tell him something he does not like. He told them therefore that He was not a Teacher asking for a disciple who would parrot His sayings; He was a Savior Who first disturbed a conscience and then purified it. But many would never get beyond hating the disturber. The Light is no boon, except to those who are men of good will; their lives may be evil, but at least they want to be good. His Presence, He said, was a threat to sensuality, avarice, and lust. When a man has lived in a dark cave for years, his eyes cannot stand the light of the sun; so the man who refuses to repent turns against mercy. No one can prevent the sun from shining, but every man can pull down the blinds and shut it out.

Our Lord next told them that in the continuing persecution against Him, they were not to be concerned as to how to answer their persecutors. No written-out statements, no prepared manuscripts will be necessary. He promised to speak to them through His Spirit.

> When you are arrested, do not worry about what you are to say; when the time comes, the words you need will be given you; for it is not you who will be speaking: it will be the Spirit of your Father speaking in you. *Matthew 10:19–21*

Foretelling, without telling how, that He would be betrayed by one who was so close to Him, He gave them a better view of the Cross by telling them that betrayers will be of their own household, that brothers will betray brothers.

> All will hate you for your allegiance to me. *Matthew 10:22*

The heifers which brought home the ark out of the land of the Philistines were offered up to God as a sacrifice. Such would seem to be the reward for being identified with Him. As St. Paul put it:

> You have been granted the privilege not only of believing in Christ but also of suffering for him. *I Philippians 1:29*

But as in His life there was never the "Hour" of Calvary without the "Day" of Victory, so neither would their defeat be permanent:

> The man who holds out to the end will be saved. *Matthew 10:22*

> By standing firm you will win true life for yourselves. *Luke 21:18*

The possession of a soul means the undisturbed mastery of oneself which is the secret of inner peace, as distinguished from a thousand agitations which make it fearful, unhappy, and disappointed. Only when the soul is possessed can anything else be enjoyed. Our Lord here meant patience in adversity, trial, and persecution. At the end of three hours on the Cross, He would so possess His soul that He would render it back to the Heavenly Father.

At this point in His discourse to the Apostles, He made clear that since He came to die and not live, so they must be prepared to die and not live. If the world gave Him a Cross, then they must expect one; if the world would say He had a devil, they could expect to be called "devils."

> A pupil does not rank above his teacher, or a servant above his master. The pupil should be content to share his teacher's lot, the servant to share his master's. If the master has been called Beelzebub, how much more his household! *Matthew 10:24,25*

But the power to do harm would never affect the souls of the Apostles. As His own Resurrection would be a proof of that, He now gave them anticipated assurance. The body can be injured without the consent of the soul, but the soul cannot be injured without its own consent. The only thing to be feared is losing, not human life, but the Divine life which is God.

> Do not fear those who kill the body, but cannot kill the soul. Fear him rather who is able to destroy both soul and body in hell.
>
> *Matthew 10:28*

There would be a vindication for the wrong done them; and all the hidden things would be revealed. The mercy of God that watches over the sparrows and counts the hairs of our heads had them under a watchful eye and Providence. He warned them not to be "secret disciples," nor compromising, nor too "liberal" in confessing His Divinity. Becoming bolder as He paraded the Cross before them, He turned to the analogy of the sword. He would be no peacemaker from the outside; neither would they. When they preached Him, they would evoke opposition and thus cause all the enemies of Goodness to unsheath their swords:

> Whoever then will acknowledge me before men, I will acknowledge him before my Father in heaven; and whoever disowns me before men, I will disown him before my Father in heaven. *Matthew 10:32*

> You must not think that I have come to bring peace to the earth; I have not come to bring peace, but a sword. *Matthew 10:34*

There are two kinds of swords: the swords that pierce outwardly and destroy, and the swords that pierce inwardly and mortify. What He

meant was that His very coming would provoke swords on the part of
His enemies. James heard these very words about a sword and later on
would have them verified, when Herod would slay him with his sword,
as he became the first Apostle to be martyred. Simone Weil para-
phrased the words of Our Lord that He who takes the sword will perish by the sword, by saying that "he who takes a Cross will perish by
the sword," because the Cross will create opposition.

Next, the Apostles were forewarned that those who accepted Him
would be hated by the members of their own families. The Gospel
would stir up strife between those who would accept Him and those
who would reject Him. The unconverted mother would hate her converted daughter, and the unconverted father would hate the converted
son, so that a man's bitterest foes would be those of his own household. But they were not to think that all this was a loss. There is a
double life; the physical and the spiritual. Tertullian noted that when
the Romans put the early Christians to death, the pagan appeal always was: "Save your life; do not throw your life away." But as He
would lay down His life and take it up again, so too what they would
lose biologically, they would save spiritually. What was sacrificed to
Him was never lost. They did not understand what He was saying,
but He was summarizing for them again His Cross and Resurrection:

> By gaining his life a man will lose it; by losing his life for my sake, he
> will gain it.   *Matthew* 10:39

The Apostles had often seen the Romans, who possessed their land,
crucify many of their own people. Our Lord's words referred to the
custom of criminals carrying a cross before they were crucified upon it.
That the Cross was the crowning incident in His life, the primary
reason for His coming, is evident once again as He invited them to
Crucifixion. It is unthinkable that He would urge them to a ransoming death unless He Himself had willed it for Himself as the Lamb
slain from the beginning of the world. Later on, Peter and Andrew
would understand what He meant that day, when they too would be
crucified.

Immediately after Pentecost, when Christ sent His Spirit upon the
Apostles, the full meaning of the Crucifixion dawned on Peter, and he
summarized what he heard in the pre-Calvary instructions of Our
Lord:

> You used heathen men to crucify and kill him. But God raised him to
> life again, setting him free from the pangs of death, because it could
> not be that death should keep him in its grip.   *Acts* 2:23,24

The Cross was no accident in His life; it would be none in theirs or
His followers' either.

28. *The Pagans and the Cross*

Christ, the Son of God, came into the world to save all men, all nations, and all peoples. Though this was His ultimate goal, His plan was to limit His Gospel at first to the Jews. Later His mission was rendered universal, so as to embrace the whole pagan world as well.

> These twelve Jesus sent out with the following instructions: Do not take the road to gentile lands, and do not enter any Samaritan town; but go rather to the lost sheep of the house of Israel.
>
> *Matthew 10:5,6*

The first explicit direction to the Apostles was to avoid the pagans. Today the pagans would be known as the "foreign missions." Even the Samaritans were to be excluded for the time being, for they were a hybrid people of both Jewish and Assyrian origin. This explicit instruction to the people to confine themselves at first to the House of Israel was underlined by the fact that He chose twelve of them, who roughly corresponded to the twelve tribes of Israel. The lingering remembrance of this order made Peter hesitate when the time came to baptize Cornelius, the Roman centurion. For that act, he required an explicit declaration on the part of God Himself.

Despite this first mandate to the Apostles, Our Blessed Lord had several contacts with pagans; He even worked miracles on their behalf. Though these miracles do not give a complete answer to the question as to when Our Lord began to make His mission universal, nevertheless they do give a clue.

The first of the three contacts which Our Lord had with pagans, and therefore with the foreign missions, was with the Roman centurion; the second, with the daughter of the Syro-Phoenician woman; and the third, with the young man possessed of a devil in the land of the Gerasenes. There were many elements common to all three miracles.

The first two miracles were performed at a distance. Probably the centurion was a member of the Roman garrison stationed at Capharnaum. By birth, therefore, he must have been a heathen. It is very likely that he, like the centurion Cornelius, whom Peter baptized and like the eunuch in the court of the Queen of Ethiopia, had become at least sentimentally attached to the worship of Jahve. This Roman official had been in the country long enough to know that there was a strong wall of partition between Jew and Gentile. This explains the fact that when his servant lay sick, even to the point of death, he did not directly approach Our Blessed Lord, but

> sent some Jewish elders with the request that he would come and save his servant's life. *Luke* 7:3

Our Blessed Lord must have shown some reluctance to work this miracle, because Luke says that those who interceded

> pressed their petition earnestly. *Luke* 7:4

While Our Lord was on His way to the servant, the centurion sent word to Him through messengers not to trouble Himself:

> It is not for me to have you under my roof. *Luke* 7:7

St. Augustine was later to say of this: "Counting himself unworthy that Christ should enter into his doors, he was counted worthy that Christ should enter into his heart."

The pagan centurion compared Our Blessed Lord's power to his own authority over his soldiers. He himself was a sergeant with a hundred men under him, who did his bidding; but the Lord was the true Caesar, or King, the supreme commander of the highest hierarchy, with angels to obey His orders. Surely, then he would not have to enter the house to perform the miracle; the pagan suggested that He should give an order from where He was. The miracle was performed, as the centurion requested, at a distance. Reflecting on the faith of this pagan and anticipating the faith that would come from foreign missions, which He contrasted with the present home mission, Our Blessed Lord said:

> I tell you, nowhere, even in Israel, have I found faith like this.
>
> *Luke* 7:10

This first pagan who received such praise from Our Divine Lord for his faith was one of "those children of God" scattered abroad in the world who were eventually to be brought into unity through the Redemption.

The second miracle performed by Our Lord on a pagan was the healing of the daughter of the Syro-Phoenician woman. This reluctance to work a miracle for the centurion had only been implied, but here He refused explicitly, perhaps to draw out the woman's faith. The miracle took place in the neighborhood of Tyre and Sidon. St. Chrysostom and other commentators have actually thought that Our Lord left the borders of what was later on to be known as foreign mission territory. The woman is described as coming from Canaan and being of Syro-Phoenician descent. She was, therefore, completely set apart from the Jews. When she asked a boon for her daughter, whom she described as "truly cruelly troubled by an evil spirit," Our Lord:

> said not a word in reply. His disciples came and urged him: Send her away; see how she comes shouting after us. *Matthew 15:23*

The Apostles were not asking for a miracle to be worked for the woman's sake; they only wanted to be left alone, undisturbed, in selfish ease. As she continued to plead and to worship Him, Our Blessed Lord proceeded to test her faith with a seemingly hard remark:

> It is not right to take the children's bread and throw it to the dogs.
> *Matthew 15:26*

The children He was referring to were, of course, the Jews. The term "dogs" signified contempt, and it was not beyond the Jews to apply it often to the Gentiles.

As the Roman centurion endured a seeming delay, so this woman suffered a stunning rebuff. She, however, responded with a perfect act of faith:

> True, sir, and yet the dogs eat the scraps that fall from their masters'
> table. *Matthew 15:27*

This woman was saying to Our Lord: "I accept this title and the dignity that goes with it: for even the dogs are fed by the Master; they may not be given the full feast which has been spread for the children of Israel, but the dogs will get a portion; and it will still come from the Master's table." She pleaded that she belonged to the Master's household, even though her place in it was lower. According to the very name which the Lord had given her, she was not an alien. And by accepting this name, she could claim all that it included.

She had conquered by faith, and the Master said to her:

> Woman, what faith you have! Be it as you wish! *Matthew 15:28*

Like Joseph of old, who showed severity to his brethren for but a brief time, the Savior did not maintain His apparent disdain for long; and He granted the healing of the daughter, again at a distance.

The third early contact of Our Blessed Lord with the pagans occurred when He entered the country of the Gerasenes. A man possessed of an unclean spirit came out of the tombs to meet Him. The actual scene was Decapolis, a predominantly Gentile region. Josephus strongly implied that Gerasa was a Greek city. The very fact that the people there were swineherds would seem to indicate further that they were not Jews. It is conceivable that they were Jews defying the Mosaic Law.

Considerable symbolism may be attached to the fact that in this pagan land, Our Blessed Lord came face to face with discords and forces far worse than those which disturb the winds and waves and the bodies of men. Here there was something wilder, and more fearful, than the natural elements, which could bring confusion, anarchy, and ruin to the inner man. There had been a wholesome faith in the centurion and in the Syro-Phoenician woman. But there was nothing in this young man but the dominion of the devil. The other two pagans had spoken from their own hearts in tribute to Our Savior. Here, however, it was an alien's spirit, a fallen spirit, that made the young man affirm the Divinity:

> What do you want with me, Jesus, son of the Most High God? I implore you, do not torment me. *Luke 8:28*

When the Savior released the young man from the evil spirit and permitted it to enter into the swine instead, the townspeople ordered Our Lord to depart from their coast. The spirit of capitalism, in its most evil form, made them feel that the restoring of a soul to the friendship of God, was nothing compared to the loss of a few pigs. While the respectable Gerasenes bade Him depart, the Samaritans, who were sinners, wanted Our Lord to stay with them.

These three incidents involving foreign missions were exceptions to the Divine plan that salvation must first come to the Jews, and that He must limit His teaching, for the time being, only to the lost sheep of Israel.

These sporadic contacts with pagans did not suffice to establish a principle of world-wide evangelization. On the other hand, it cannot be supposed that Our Blessed Lord turned to the Gentiles simply because His own people refused Him, as if the rest of humanity were only an afterthought in His life. He always knew that there would come a point when He would lose both the leaders and the masses of His own people. In fact, this came to pass after the miracle of the multiplication of the loaves. After that, Our Blessed Lord could count on neither an aristocratic nor a popular following among the Jews. Even so, He continued for the time being to concentrate on teaching His own people, to the exclusion of the foreign missions.

Our Savior did not use any of His three contacts with the pagans to tell His Apostles to take the Gospel beyond the confines of Israel. Nevertheless, there was clear and intrinsic connection between the Gentiles and the reason of His coming. Noteworthy is the fact that in those moments where there was a very strong hint and suggestion of

His death and Redemption, there was also some involvement of the Gentiles. Quite apart from the three miraculous contacts, there were three other moments when pagans were closely associated with Him. Each of these moments had some reference to His Passion and to His death and glorification.

The first of these was at His birth. The shepherds represented the home mission; the Magi stood for the foreign missions. Jew and Gentile were both next to the crib; but the coming of the Gentiles coincided with the first attempt upon His life. Hardly was the Divine Ship launched than King Herod sought to sink it, by ordering the massacre of all male children under the age of two. And it was the Gentiles whom Herod questioned concerning the prophecy about the star from Bethlehem. Already, the shadow of death had fallen across the Infant Jesus.

The second moment of the close association with Gentiles in His life was when the Greeks came seeking, through the intercession of Philip and Andrew, to see Him. On this occasion, Our Blessed Lord did not refer to a prophecy from the Jewish script (for that would have been unavailing to the Gentile); He appealed instead to a law of the natural order, the law of the seed.

> A grain of wheat remains a solitary grain unless it falls into the ground and dies; but if it dies, it bears a rich harvest. *John 12:24*

As the Wise Men from among the Gentiles discovered Wisdom at the crib, so the wise men from Gentile ranks now learned the law of sacrifice: that through death, a new life would spring forth. The closer Our Lord came to His Cross (and here He was only a week away from it), the closer the pagans were to Him. They now began to appear for the first time in His entourage. On the occasion of this visit of the heirs of Socrates, Aristotle, and Plato, Our Blessed Lord began to speak of His glory:

> The hour has come for the Son of Man to be glorified. *John 12:23*

The third moment when the Gentiles were closely associated with Him was during His Crucifixion. He was tried in a Roman court, and the wife of a Roman governor interceded for Him, because she had been troubled in a dream. Simon of Cyrene, who was interested in watching this man going to His death, was forced to help Him to carry the cross. It is known that at least a hundred Roman soldiers were present at the scene of His Crucifixion, for a centurion commanded at least that number. Never before were there so many Gentiles and pagans around Our Lord, as at the moment of His death. Looking forward to that moment, after His miracles had failed to convince men of His Divinity, He had given the Cross as the final argument. Now that the Son of Man was being lifted up, He began to draw all men to Himself. He made it clear that it was "all men" that He would draw, and not merely the people of Judea and Galilee. At the very moment when He spoke of giving His own life, He added:

> There are other sheep of mine, not belonging to this fold, whom I must bring in; and they too will listen to my voice. *John 10:16*

The death of Christ was the realization of the Kingdom of God for the entire world. Up to the point of Calvary, men had been taught by preaching. After Calvary, they would be taught by His Resurrection and Ascension. The principle of universality became effective. It was the death of Christ that broke down the wall of partition between Jew and Gentile to reveal the universal mission of the Messiah, which had been dimly hinted at in the Old Testament. It took Golgotha to universalize the mission of Christ. The foreign missions were the fruit of the Passion and the death of Our Blessed Lord. What greater proof is there than this, that it was not until after His Resurrection and the moment of His Ascension that the missionary mandate was given:

> Go forth therefore and make all nations my disciples. *Matthew 28:19*

Now the pagans would come into their own, not only those who had lived before His coming, but those who would live until His final glory. And there will come a day when:

> At the Judgement, when this generation is on trial, the men of Nineveh will appear against it. *Matthew 12:41*

The Gentiles who lived in the days of Solomon, and in particular the Queen of Sheba, would point an accusing finger at Israel for not having been as responsive as the Gentiles to the death of Christ.

The coast of Tyre and Sidon that produced a woman of faith would receive a more tolerant judgment than Capharnaum, which had once cradled the Body of the Divine Fisherman:

> It will be more bearable, I tell you, for Tyre and Sidon on the day of judgement than for you. And as for you, Capernaum, will you be exalted to the skies? No, brought down to the depths! *Matthew 11:22*

Even Sodom, which had been synonymous with everything that was evil, would have more merciful judgment than Israel, to whom the revelation was first restricted:

> For if the miracles had been performed in Sodom which were performed in you, Sodom would be standing to this day. But it will be

more bearable, I tell you, for the land of Sodom on the day of judge-
ment than for you. *Matthew* 11:23

As for the future, all the Gentiles would profit by His death and
Resurrection:

> They will see the Son of Man coming on the clouds of heaven with
> great power and glory. With a trumpet blast he will send out his
> angels, and they will gather his chosen from the four winds, from the
> farthest bounds of heaven on every side. *Matthew* 25:31,32

Had Our Lord been only a preacher or a teacher, there would never
have been any foreign missions. The Faith would never have been
propagated all over the world. The Gospel, which the missionaries
bring, is not an epic that belongs to a particular people, but a Redemption as wide as humanity itself. From the moment of Calvary,
the missionary belonged to Christ and not to the prince of this world.
Another King entered into rightful possession of the Gentiles. The
principal distinction between the Old and the New Testament was in
regard to scope. The former had been restricted almost exclusively to
a single nation, but the blood of the New Covenant shed on Calvary
broke down that wall of partition between the Jews and other nations.

The sacrifice of Christ was universal in three ways: time, place, and
power. As regards time, its efficacy was not limited to one generation
or dispensation:

> Predestined before the foundation of the world, he was made manifest
> in this last period of time for your sake. *I Peter* 1:20

There was universality too in space, for the effectiveness of Christ's
death was not confined to any single nation:

> Thou art worthy to take the scroll and to break its seals, for thou wast
> slain and by thy blood didst purchase for God men of every tribe and
> language, people and nation; thou hast made of them a royal house,
> to serve our God . . . *Apocalypse* 5:9

Finally, there was universality in power, for there is no sin whatever
that His Redemption cannot blot out:

> We are being cleansed from every sin by the blood of Jesus his Son.
> *John* 1:7

It was on the Cross that Christ made His mission world-wide. The
closer missionaries live to their cross, the more quickly will they fulfill
His mission to all nations.

29. *The Growing Opposition*

The opposition and hatred of the Pharisees, Scribes, and temple leaders against Our Lord grew from the inside out, as it does in most human hearts. First, they hated Him in their own hearts; second, they expressed their hatred to His disciples; then, they manifested their hatred openly to the people; and finally, the hatred centered on Christ Himself.

The evil dispositions of their own hearts were manifested when a man sick of the palsy was brought to Our Lord at Capharnaum. Instead of immediately working the miracle, Our Lord forgave his sins. Since sickness, death, and evil were the effects of sin, though not necessarily personal sin in any individual, He went first to the root of the disease, namely sin, and pardoned it:

> My son, your sins are forgiven. *Mark 2:6*

Instead of considering the miracle as evidence of the One Who worked it, His enemies:

> Why does the fellow talk like that? This is blasphemy! Who but God alone can forgive sins? *Mark 2:7*

They did not mistake the implications that Christ was acting as God. The Old Testament did say that such power belonged to God. True, only God could forgive sins, but God could do it and was doing it now through His human nature. Later on, He would give that power to His Apostles and their successors:

> If you forgive any man's sins, they stand forgiven; if you pronounce them unforgiven, unforgiven they remain. *John 20:23*

But men who exercised this authority would still be only human instruments of His Divinity, as in a greater way His human nature was the instrument of His Divinity. Though the thoughts of the Pharisees remained in their own minds, no thought of man is unknown to God.

> Jesus knew in his own mind that this was what they were thinking, and said to them: Why do you harbour thoughts like these? Is it easier to say to this paralysed man, Your sins are forgiven, or to say, Stand up, take your bed, and walk? But to convince you that the Son of Man has the right on earth to forgive sins—he turned to the paralysed

man—I say to you, stand up, take your bed, and go home. And he got up, and at once took his stretcher and went out in full view of them all, so that they were astounded and praised God. Never before, they said, have we seen the like.   *Mark 2:8–12*

In their minds, He was guilty of blasphemy because He claimed the power of God. Concerning His authority to forgive sins, He gave them sensible evidence that His claim was not fictitious. Though they could not deny what they had seen, they did not acknowledge His power. Faith in Christ was increasing among the people but decreasing among these Pharisees, Scribes, and Doctors of the Law and of every village of Galilee and Judea and in Jerusalem. Miracles are not necessarily a cure for unbelief. If the will is perverse, all the evidence in the world would not convince, not even a Resurrection from the dead.

Up to this moment, the Scribes and others merely thought evil. The hatred now found utterance on their lips against the disciples of the Lord. The occasion was when He called Matthew, the publican, as an Apostle. A publican was a Jew who betrayed his own people by becoming a tax collector for the Romans who occupied their country. The publican would promise to collect a certain sum in taxes from a community; but all he took over and above that amount, he retained. Naturally, this gave rise to many dishonesties; as a result the publican was one of the most despised of citizens.

When Our Lord saw the publican at his table receiving taxes, He gave no promise to Matthew, but merely said, "Follow Me." Matthew followed immediately. He who was so antipatriotic later on wrote the first Gospel and became the most patriotic of citizens, recounting a hundred times from prophecies the glory of Israel in having begotten the Savior.

Our Lord accepted an invitation to eat in the house of Matthew. This was a great scandal to the Pharisees and their strait-laced righteousness. But when they saw:

> When Jesus was at table in the house, many bad characters—tax-gatherers and others—were seated with him and his disciples.

they asked the disciples:

> Why is it that your master eats with tax-gatherers and sinners?
> *Matthew 9:11*

He was being recognized as a Master and a Teacher, but now He was hazarding His reputation by associating with the outcasts of society. If lepers herded together, was there not in His companionship with sinners a proof that He was a sinner, too?

Before He read their thoughts; this time the disciples probably told Him the charge of the Pharisees, to which He answered that it was precisely because He was unlike sinners that He came into their midst. Their rigid formalism which expressed itself in external sacrifices ignored the real sacrifice of self which would save sinners. They boasted of their knowledge of Scripture, so He gave the Pharisees a reference to Hosea that God delighted more in mercy than in formalisms.

> It is not the healthy that need a doctor, but the sick. Go and learn what that text means, I require mercy, not sacrifice. I did not come to invite virtuous people, but sinners. *Matthew 9:12,13*

Once more, He said that He "has come" into the world, not that He was born. Always, there is the affirmation that He did not begin to be in time, but only that He as God became something He was not, namely, a man. And the reason of His coming was not to write a new code of morals; He came to do something for sinners. Those who, like the Pharisees, refused to admit that they were sick with sin, did not need Him as the Physician of their souls. The blind who refused to admit the existence of light could never be healed. Not for a mere literal adherence to ceremonial law, understood as "sacrifice," but to lift up the fallen, had He come. As a Physician, He could do no good to those who were curious, or who denied guilt, or called it an Oedipus complex; He came only to be a sin-bearer, and hence only the sinners and not the self-righteous would profit by His coming.

Love of the sinners was a new thing on the earth. If He came uniquely to be a teacher, He would have written His law as did Laotze, and He would have told men to "Learn and practice." But since He came to be a Savior and to give His life "as a ransom," He summoned men to a purging of evil:

> I have not come to invite virtuous people, but to call sinners to repentance. *Luke 5:32*

Opposition now came more into the open when Our Lord cured the dumb demoniac. It now left the closed circle of their own dark hearts and was directed to the people to stir them up against Him. The multitudes who saw the miracle were filled with amazement, saying that nothing like this was ever seen in Israel. This drove the Pharisees to open blasphemy:

> He casts out devils by the prince of devils. *Matthew 9:34*

Our Lord answered the charge by showing that He drove out Satan through the power of His Godhead, using the analogy of a besieged house occupied by a strong man. But someone stronger than he enters and seizes all the weapons, defenses, and possessions of the house. Our Lord said that if He entered the domain of evil, and took possession of the house, such as the body of the one possessed, then there was manifested some great anti-satanic power which was nothing less than that of God Himself. But because they had said He had an unclean spirit, they were guilty of the unpardonable sin; they were putting themselves beyond forgiveness. If they poisoned the fountain of living water, from which alone they could slake their thirst, then they must die of the poison. If they blasphemed the One from Whom forgiveness flowed, then where was the hope of forgiveness? The deaf who deny they are deaf will never hear; the sinners who deny there is sin deny thereby the remedy of sin, and thus cut themselves off forever from Him Who came to redeem.

The final stage of their attack was directed against Our Lord Himself.

> Once about that time Jesus went through the cornfields on the Sabbath; and his disciples, feeling hungry, began to pluck some ears of corn and eat them. The Pharisees noticed this, and said to him, Look, your disciples are doing something which is forbidden on the Sabbath.
>
> *Matthew 12:1–3*

The Old Testament did not forbid the plucking of the corn from a field; but doing so on the Sabbath, according to the Pharisees, involved a double sin. As the Talmud put it:

> In case a woman rolls wheat to remove the husks, it is considered as sifting; if she rubs the heads of wheat, it is regarded as threshing; if she cleans off the side-adherences, it is sifting out fruit; if she bruises the ears, it is grinding; if she throws them up in her hand, it is winnowing.

What scandalized the Pharisees was not the breach of Biblical law, but the breach of rabbinic law. Having seen what they thought was a desecration of the Sabbath day, they now openly attacked Our Blessed Lord for something the disciples did.

The answer of Our Lord was threefold: first, He appealed to the Prophets, then to the Law, then to One Who was greater than either, namely, Himself. Both instances which He quoted were those in which ceremonial niceties gave way to a higher law. Our Lord appealed to their great national hero, David, who ate the shewbread which was forbidden to all save the priests. If they allowed David to break a Divine prohibition of a mere ceremonial affair in favor of bod-

ily necessity, why should they not allow it to His disciples? When
David was flying away from Saul and was hungry, Our Lord said that
he and his followers:

> Went into the House of God and ate the sacred bread, though neither
> he nor his men had a right to eat it, but only the priests.
>
> *Matthew* 12:4

The Pharisees certainly would have admitted that the danger to life
superseded the ceremonial law; but more than that, David was allowed to eat of this bread not just because he was hungry but because
he pleaded that he was in the service of the king. The Apostles, who
were following Our Lord, were also in the service of someone greater;
and ministering to Him was more important than David ministering
to an earthly master.

Our Lord then answered more directly the charge of violating the
Sabbath law. The ones who accused Him labored in the temple on
the Sabbath; they prepared sacrifices, they lighted lamps; and yet because these were part of the temple service, they were not considered
as violating the Sabbath law. But here, on this Sabbath, in the midst
of this field of corn, and with no apparent trappings of glory stands
One Who is greater than the temple.

> I tell you, there is something greater than the temple here.
>
> *Matthew* 12:6

These profound words were blasphemy to the Pharisees, but they were
another affirmation of what He said when He cleansed for the first
time the temple in Jerusalem, saying that His Body was a Temple because the Godhead dwelt therein. In Him the Godhead dwelt corporally; nowhere else on earth was God to be found except veiled in
His humanity. His Apostles, therefore, if they had broken a ceremonial regulation, were guiltless because they were in the service of the
Temple, aye, even of God Himself.

Seven times in all, they accused Him of breaking the Sabbath. He
confounded them once in the synagogue of Capharnaum, after
healing the man with the withered hand, by saying:

> Suppose you had one sheep, which fell into a ditch on the Sabbath;
> is there one of you who would not catch hold of it and lift it out? And
> surely a man is worth far more than a sheep! It is therefore permitted
> to do good on the Sabbath.   *Matthew* 12:12,13

Now the opposition closes. From hateful hearts, it passed to disputa-
tious words to disciples, then to blasphemous charges in the hearing

of the people, and finally to the Lord Himself. Not being able to answer Him, after the miracle in Capharnaum:

> But the Pharisees, on leaving the synagogue, laid a plot to do away with him. *Matthew 12:14*

Our Lord withdrew from their strife. It was not the time for judging them. Matthew, at this point, quoted a passage from Isaiah in which was foretold the meek character of Christ:

> He will not snap off the broken reed, nor snuff out the smouldering wick, until he leads justice on to victory, In him the nations shall place their hope. *Matthew 12:20,21*

There was nothing more feeble than a cracked reed which sometimes was used by shepherds with which to pipe tunes; nor was there anything more weak than a flickering wick of a candle; yet neither of these would He crush, so gentle would be His character. He would not quench the slightest aspiration toward Him nor regard any soul as beyond use. A smoking wick could no longer illumine a room, but no soul would ever be regarded as such an offensive object. The bruised reed could not entertain with sweet music, but no soul is to be discarded as useless and beyond hope of responding to heavenly harmonies. The bruised reed could be mended, and the smoking flax could be re-enkindled by a power and a grace outside of either.

The Gospel could not have chosen, in the midst of such conflict and hatred and bitterness, a better moment to have pictured His patience, gentleness, and forbearance than in the midst of the assaults of the Scribes and Pharisees. They were distinct parties, but because they had found a greater enemy, they united and came to Him this time in a semipolite manner and they asked:

> Master, we should like you to show us a sign. *Matthew 12:39*

The miracles of healing and the like were not enough, they said. They desired some extraordinary sign from heaven. He answered:

> It is a wicked, godless generation that asks for a sign. *Matthew 12:39*

Some versions have it an "adulterous" generation, because the sin of adultery was used in the metaphorical sense of spiritual unfaithfulness to God. Once again He affirmed the importance of moral conduct as an essential for seeing truth. He contrasted the practical conduct and faith of the repentance of Nineveh at the preaching of Jonah, and the faith and zeal of the Queen of Sheba when she heard of the wisdom of Solomon, with the unrepentance of the Scribes and Pharisees and the coldness of their hearts. Though the visitor of Solomon was a queen, she journeyed for a great distance for no other reason than the quest of wisdom; she, therefore, would rise up in judgment against the Scribes and Pharisees who spurned truth.

> She came from the ends of the earth to hear the wisdom of Solomon; and what is here is greater than Solomon. *Matthew* 12:42

Our Lord here claimed superiority to the one great prophet of the Jews who was listened to by the Gentile nations, and who drew an enquirer from the ends of the earth. The Gentile believers will judge those very Pharisees who saw Him and yet rejected the Gospel. But not only will the real intellectuals of the world rise up in judgment against those who refuse to accept Him who was greater than Solomon, but also:

> The men of Nineveh will appear against it and ensure its condemnation, for they repented at the preaching of Jonah; and what is here is greater than Jonah. *Matthew* 12:41

The men of Nineveh were heathen and if they did penance at the preaching of Jonah, then should not the Scribes and Pharisees do penance at the preaching of One Who was greater than Jonah? The people of Nineveh had not the privileges of these Scribes and Pharisees of talking to God in the form of man; the rejection of Him was therefore a presage of the coming judgment. In asking for a sign they showed moral perversity, for if He did the kind of miracle that they required they would still not believe. They wanted signs not for conviction, but in order to condemn Him.

This brought Him to the only sign that He would give them: the sign of the prophet Jonah.

> Jonah was in the sea-monster's belly for three days and three nights, and in the same way the Son of Man will be three days and three nights in the bowels of the earth. *Matthew* 12:39–40

Once again the shadow of the Cross falls on the Scribes and the Pharisees. In veiled language He told them that on the third day He would rise again. He would be treated as was Jonah by the sailors, except that Jonah was thrown into the sea, and He would be thrown into a grave. But as Jonah escaped the heart of the sea on the third day to fulfill his mission of preaching penance, so He would rise to fulfill His Mission of sending His Spirit unto the healing of sin and the preaching of repentance. The miracle of Jonah was a sign that he was a Divinely commissioned prophet, and it authenticated his calling of the Ninevites to repentance; so the Resurrection would authenticate His works. Those who will not accept the sign of humiliation and death, and then of Resurrection and glory, would accept no other sign.

What is here is greater than Jonah.   *Matthew 12:41*

If the Ninevites repented at the preaching of Jonah, then why did they not repent unto Him, to Whom Jonah pointed? They asked for a sign to condemn Him; He gave them a sign which condemned them. They wanted a sign from heaven; He gave them one from the depths of the earth; they wanted a sign which would excite wonder; He gave them one which would stir up repentance; they wanted a sign for themselves alone; He gave them one from the land of the Gentiles to which His Gospel would pass after His Resurrection. At Nazareth, when His fellow citizens attempted to kill Him, He gave two examples from the Old Testament drawn from the Gentiles to show that His Gospel would pass to them. In this controversy, He used three more examples from the Gentiles. But since "salvation is of the Jews," as He told them, they must first reject Him before the Gentile world would receive His truth and life. Once more, the Cross and risen glory are placarded before them as the reason of His coming from heaven to earth.

30. *The Fox and the Hen*

The Cross was lifted up again for the Pharisees to view when Our Blessed Lord was in Galilee in the territory of Herod. The Pharisees who had already plotted His death attempted to agitate and disturb the Master, saying:

> You should leave this place and go on your way; Herod is out to kill you. *Luke 13:31*

The Pharisees were certainly not interested in the safety of Our Blessed Lord, but they were anxious to call Him to Judea, where He would fall more directly under the power of themselves and the Sanhedrin. Their story was certainly not an invention, for at the beginning of the public life, the Pharisees with the Herodians had plotted against His life. Furthermore, Herod's conscience was already heavy with the murder of John the Baptist. The presence of the Divine Master, along with His popularity, disturbed Herod the more. The Pharisees were willing to become involved in the plot of Herod to rid his dominions of Christ; at the same time it would have prospered their own design to bring Him into Jerusalem to hasten His death.

Our Blessed Lord saw through the crafty design and sham friendliness of the Pharisees. He quickly dismissed them with the answer:

> Go and tell that fox, Listen: today and tomorrow I shall be casting out devils and working cures; on the third day I reach my goal.
> *Luke 13:32*

Israel, in the Old Testament, was described as the vineyard of the Lord; who better deserved the name of a despoiler of the vineyard than the fox who slew the precursor of the Messiah? Herod, He added, need have no fears that His popularity would lead to political intrigue or revolution. His work of driving evil spirits from men possessed and the lifting-up of palsied limbs would continue. These harmless labors He would not interrupt until the time for His death and glory. "Today and tomorrow" indicated short periods of time, as they did in the prophet Hosea. Then would come His Crucifixion and, at the end of that Crucifixion, He would say that His purpose in coming had been achieved. Only at the end of the third day, and not before it, would He finish His course. He knew the time of His own death, and He knew that the time had not yet come. The Pharisees, the Herodians, and the Sadducees who were entering into unholy alliance would not have their Victim until He would deliver Himself into their hands.

That He was in complete control of His life, He reaffirmed by saying that He would not die in Galilee, where He was then, but in Jerusalem:

> It is unthinkable for a prophet to meet his death anywhere but in Jerusalem. *Luke 13:33*

No matter how much Herod would try to kill Him, He would not alter the "Hour" set by His Father. To Jerusalem belonged the monopoly of killing the prophets. In that city would His Cross be erected. As for the menace to His life, Our Lord despised it. It was in the Holy City under Pontius Pilate He would be killed, and not in the provinces under Herod. The "Today, tomorrow, and the third day" was the exact period of time Our Savior needed to travel from Peraea, where He was, to Jerusalem. Nor did He say that He would "die," but rather that He would "reach His consummation." Once on the Cross in Jerusalem He would say, "It is achieved," thus linking up the Divine Mission from the Father with His own will to preach, cast out devils, and then offer Himself as a propitiation for the sins of man. The same expression Our Lord used about consummating His life is repeated twice in the Epistle to the Hebrews, once as having His sufferings crowned by bringing men to salvation, and once:

> Perfected, became the source of eternal salvation for all who obey him.
> *Hebrews 5:9*

The mention of Jerusalem brought to His mind not only His death, but also His patriotic love of the city:

> O Jerusalem, Jerusalem, the city that murders the prophets and stones the messengers sent to her! How often have I longed to gather your children, as a hen gathers her brood under her wings; but you would not let me. Look, look! there is your temple, forsaken by God. And I tell you, you shall never see me until the time comes when you say, Blessings on him who comes in the name of the Lord! *Luke 13:34,35*

Never was there an apostrophe uttered by a patriarch over a land or a city equal to the love which the Master showed for the city that was the appointed place of the Eternal, where the glory of God was to dwell, and which was to be the vehicle of revelation to all nations. His imagination turned from the fox to the hen as an example of civic love. The figure of the wings stretched out for shelter and warmth was common in the books of the Old Testament and in the prophets, but the tragedy was in His rejection by men. God said: "I would," and men answered: "We will not." The prophecy was fulfilled literally concerning Jerusalem within a generation. When Socrates was sentenced to death by the Athenian judges, the executioner who gave him the hemlock juice to drink wept as he passed it into his hands. Our Blessed Lord, being God, knew in advance that the rulers and judges of Jerusalem would sentence Him to death, and He wept over them. In the case of Socrates, the executioner wept over the executed, but here, it is the One Who is to be executed Who weeps over the executioners. Such is the difference between a philosopher and God.

Tremendous is the power of freedom: man has it always within himself to reject or accept the protecting and saving wings of God. So too, the God-man had it within Himself freely to offer His life for Jerusalem and the world. If He were compelled to suffer, it would be the height of injustice, nor would the Father accept a sacrifice offered reluctantly. Previously, Our Lord had called those who were willing to be shepherded by Him, His sheep; now He calls them His brood. Here as elsewhere the Cross was before Him, but it would be a perfecting, a consummation, a glory. Once again, He associated His Cross and His Resurrection; the two were never separated. He would go to the Cross not as a martyr but as a Victor. Certainly men would crown Him with thorns and fix Him to a Cross, but all this was on the *human level*. It would not happen before the Divinely appointed Hour. St. Peter, who was with Our Lord on this occasion, would later speak of the Divine side of His Crucifixion in his Pentecost sermon:

> A man singled out by God and made known to you through miracles, portents, and signs, which God worked among you through him, as you well know. When he has been given up to you, by the deliberate will and plan of God, you used heathen men to crucify and kill him.
>
> *Acts 2:23*

Jerusalem would reject Him on Good Friday after having accepted Him the preceding Sunday. Perhaps the triumphant entry would be a symbol of how Jerusalem would later on, at the end of the world, receive Him. The Apostle who describes himself as the one whom Jesus loved gave this interpretation of that Second Coming:

> Behold, he is coming with the clouds! Every eye shall see him, and among them those who pierced him. *Apocalypse 1:17*

The fox and the hen had met. The fox might now conspire with the Pharisees, as later on he would conspire with Pilate, to put the hen to death. But the Lord of History judges all by whether they devour like the fox, or gather like the hen. They who would not come under the wings of the hen, He warned, would be caught up by the talons of the devouring eagle of Rome.

31. The Resurrection That Prepared His Death

Many were the attempts on the life of Christ, particularly when He declared Himself to be the Son of God. But His death was formally decided upon when He showed His power over death by the resurrection of Lazarus.

> So from that day on they plotted his death. *John 11:53*

Previously, He often spoke of His death first, and then His Resurrection. This time He spoke of His Resurrection first as His enemies appointed His death. The empty tomb of Lazarus provoked the decision to give Him a Cross; but He in return would give up the Cross for the empty tomb.

It was not the first time He had spoken of His Resurrection. Early in His public life, when He fed the multitudes and promised Himself as the Bread of Life, He said that He would give resurrection to others:

> It is his will that I should not lose even one of all that he has given me, but raise them all up on the last day. For it is my Father's will that everyone who looks upon the Son and puts his faith in him shall possess eternal life; and I will raise him up on the last day . . . No man can come to me unless he is drawn by the Father who sent me; and I will raise him up on the last day . . . Whoever eats my flesh and drinks my blood possesses eternal life, and I will raise him up on the last day.
> *John 6:38–55*

These words went beyond predictions of His Own Resurrection; they were an affirmation that all who believed in Him and lived by His Risen Life would enjoy resurrection through His power.

Previously, He had raised at least two others from the dead. One was the daughter of Jairus, the other was the son of the widow of Naim. The first had just died; the second was already in his coffin; but the most astounding of all was Lazarus.

Our Lord, at this particular time, was preaching east of the Jordan in Peraea. Some distance away was the city of Bethany, which was about two miles outside of Jerusalem. In that city lived two sisters, Martha and Mary, and their brother Lazarus, with whom Our Lord often enjoyed hospitality. When Lazarus fell sick, Martha and Mary sent a messenger to Jesus saying:

> Sir, you should know that your friend lies ill. *John 11:4*

The sisters later called Him "Lord," indicating a recognition of His deity and authority. Nor did they put source of the love in Lazarus; rather its source was put in Christ Himself. The sisters appealed to His love, and left it to His decision to do what was best. (So His Own Mother had done at the marriage feast of Cana, where she merely observed, "They have no wine.") When Our Lord received the message, He said:

> This illness will not end in death; it has come for the glory of God,
> to bring glory to the Son of God. *John 11:4*

There must have been present to His mind at one and the same moment both the death of Lazarus and His own Resurrection; for later on, when He visited Bethany and raised Lazarus from the dead, He said to Martha:

> Did I not tell you that if you have faith you will see the glory of God?
> *John 11:40*

Honor and glory He associates with Himself, not as Messiah, but as the Son of God, the One Who is united with the Father. When Our Lord said that the sickness of Lazarus was not unto death, He did not mean that Lazarus would not die, but rather the end and purpose of His death was His own glorification as the Son of God.

Very likely the sisters felt that as soon as Our Lord received their message, He would hurry to the bedside of Lazarus; but He stayed two days at the place where He was after receiving the news. If the last chapter of the death of Lazarus had not been written, it would have seemed that Our Blessed Lord was lacking in sympathy. It happened that this was one of the rare instances about death and sickness and misfortune where the last chapter was written, and where God's purposes are seen even in His delay.

The distance separating Our Lord from the house where Lazarus lived was about a day's journey. If, therefore, He remained two days more in Peraea and we add another day for the journey, in all it would have been four days since He received the news. God's delays are mysterious; sorrow is sometimes prolonged for the same reason for which it is sent. God may abstain for the moment from healing, not because Love does not love, but because Love never stops loving, and a greater good is to come from the woe. Heaven's clock is different from ours. Human love, impatient of delay, would urge speed. The same delay took place when He was on the way to the house of Jairus, whose daughter He restored to life. Here Our Blessed Lord, instead of speeding along the way, took out some precious moments to heal a woman who was suffering from an issue of blood, as she touched His garments in the crowd. The works of evil are sometimes done in a hurry. Our Lord told Judas to go about his dirty work "quickly."

After two days, Our Lord spoke again about the family He loved. He did not say, "Let us go to Lazarus" or "to Bethany," but rather "Let us go back to Judea"—the capital of which was Jerusalem, where the opposition against Him was centered. When the disciples heard this, immediately realizing the threatenings against His life and the stonings in Jerusalem, they said concerning the Pharisees and the leaders of the people:

> The Jews there were wanting to stone you. Are you going there again?
>
> *John* 11:8

Our Lord was testing them. Just a few weeks before, John recounted of His enemies:

> This provoked them to one more attempt to seize him. But he escaped from their clutches.   *John* 10:39

He was now suggesting to his Apostles that they go back to the center of opposition. His Hour was near. The Apostles could not see the prudence or the common sense of such a step. They were fearing for their own safety as well as that of their Master, though they did not mention themselves as being afraid; rather, they spoke only of the enemies that were threatening to stone Him. The answer the Lord gave them was another indication of the Divine disposition of His life, and that no man could take it away from Him.

> Are there not twelve hours of daylight? Anyone can walk in day-time without stumbling, because he sees the light of this world. But if he walks after nightfall he stumbles, because the light fails him.
>
> *John* 11:9,10

As was His custom, He was stating a simple truth with a double meaning, one literal, the other spiritual. The literal sense was: There is the natural light of the sun; for about twelve hours man works or makes a journey; during these daylight hours the sun shines on his path. If, however, a man journeys or works at night, he stumbles or else fumbles his work. The spiritual sense was that He had called Himself the Light of the World. As no one can stop the sun from shining during its appointed hours of the day, so no one could ever check or stop Him in His mission. Even though He went up to Judea, no harm could befall Him until He permitted it. As long as His light was shining on the Apostles they would have nothing to fear, even in the city of persecutors. It was the same idea that He had given in answer to Herod when He called him a fox. There would come a time when He would permit the light to be put out and that would be when He would say to Judas and His enemies in the garden, "This is your hour and the power of darkness." But until He gave permission, His enemies could do nothing. The day exists until the Passion; the Passion is the night.

> While daylight lasts we must carry on the work of him who sent me; night comes, when no one can work. While I am in the world I am the light of the world. *John 9:4,5*

No one could take from Him one single second of the appointed twelve hours of light with which He was to teach; as no one could hasten one second of the hour of darkness when He would go to His death. When He did finally announce that they should start on their journey, melancholic and pessimistic Thomas said to his fellow disciples:

> Let us also go, that we may die with him. *John 11:16*

Knowing the tremendous opposition there was in Jerusalem, Thomas now suggested that they might all die together in the Holy City. Whatever else may be said of Thomas, it must be admitted that quicker than all the others, he recognized the death that was in store for Our Blessed Lord, though he was the last to recognize the Resurrection. If Our Blessed Lord desired to have Himself killed, Thomas was willing to be killed with Him. Whenever Thomas appears in the Gospel, he is always taking the black side. And yet, if the only way of continuing to be with the Master was to die with Him, Thomas was willing to do that.

When Our Blessed Lord arrived at Bethany, Lazarus had already been buried for four days. Bethany, being less than two hours away from Jerusalem and within sight of the temple, was the scene of a great concourse of people and particularly of enemies when His arrival was announced. Many comforters had also come to console the poor sisters. When the news came of the arrival of Jesus, Martha, the active one, rose up and went out to meet Him, while Mary remained in the house. Martha had some confidence in the power of Christ, but it was still a very limited one, for she told Him:

> If you had been here, sir, my brother would not have died.
> *John 11:22*

When Our Lord said that her brother would rise again, Martha acknowledged that he would, in the general resurrection on the last day. It was strange that Martha had not heard or remembered, what Our Lord had spoken earlier in the temple:

> In truth, in very truth I tell you, a time is coming, indeed it is already here, when the dead shall hear the voice of the Son of God, and all

who hear shall come to life . . . all who are in the grave shall hear
his voice and come out. *John 5:28*

The faith that Martha expressed in the resurrection was that of most
of the Jews, with the exception of the Sadducees. As the woman at
the well knew that the Messiah would come, and yet did not know
that He was already talking to her, so Martha, though believing in the
resurrection, did not know that the Resurrection was standing before
her. As Our Lord told the woman at the well that He was the Messiah, so now He said to Martha:

I am the resurrection and I am life. *John 11:25*

If Christ had said: "I am the Resurrection," without promising to bestow spiritual and eternal life, there would have been only the promise
of reincarnations into successive layers of misery. If He said: "I am
the Life," without saying, "I am the Resurrection," we would have
merely the promise of our continued discontents. But by combining
the two, He affirmed that in Him was a life which, by dying, rises to
perfection; therefore death was not the end, but the prelude to a resurrection in the newness and fullness of life. It was a new way of combining the Cross and glory, which ran like an antiphon through the
Psalm of His life. The moment He said this, He walked deliberately
into His enemies in Judea. Our Blessed Lord was reluctant to use the
word "death," which proved that His whole life was set against it. He
used the same word about the daughter of Jairus as He did about
Lazarus, namely, they were "asleep." It would be the same word the
followers of Christ would use about Stephen, that he "fell asleep."

When Our Lord asked Martha if she believed that whoever
believed in Him would never die, she answered:

I now believe that you are the Messiah, the Son of God who was to
come into the world. *John 11:27*

This full faith in the Incarnation prepared for the miracle to follow.
Mary came weeping upon the scene. When Our Lord saw her tears
and those of her friends:

He sighed heavily and was deeply moved. *John 11:33*

Rather active than passive, He entered into sympathy with death and
sorrow, two of the major effects of sin. He hungered because He
willed it; He was sorrowful because He willed it; He would die because He willed it. The long procession of mourners through the centuries, the ghastly effect of the death which He Himself was about to
take upon Himself, roused Him to sip the cup of the Cross. No
worthy High Priest could He be without having compassion on our
sorrows. As He was weak in our weakness, poor in our poverty, so He

was sorrowful in our sadness. This deliberately willed sharing of the sorrows of those whom He would redeem caused Him to weep. The Greek word that is used implies a calm shedding of tears. Our Blessed Lord is described in the Scriptures as weeping three times; once over a nation, when He wept over Jerusalem; once in the Garden of Gethsemane, when He wept over the sins of the world; and in this instance over Lazarus, when He wept for the effect of sin, which is death. None of these tears were for Himself, but for the human nature which He had assumed. In every instance, His human heart could distinguish the fruit from the root, the evils which affect the world from their cause, which is sin. Truly, He was "the Word made Flesh."

Many around the grave of Lazarus said:

> How dearly he must have loved him!

But others who also wept with sorrow showed their fangs as they asked:

> Could not this man, who opened the blind man's eyes, have done something to keep Lazarus from dying? *John 11:36*

There was evidently here a halfhearted belief that He was the Messiah on account of other wonders that He had done. On the Cross too, they would admit every miracle, except the fact that He apparently could not come down from the Cross. Now they were willing to admit every miracle; but certainly if He were the Messiah and the Son of God, He would have prevented Lazarus from dying. Since He did not, therefore, He was not the Christ. Ignoring their taunts, when He came to the tomb where Lazarus was laid, He suggested that the stone be taken away. Martha confirmed the certain death of Lazarus saying to Him:

> Sir, by now there will be a stench; he has been there four days.
> *John 11:39*

She was warning Our Lord that the condition of the dead man was such as to abandon all hope of his resurrection until the last day. But when in obedience to Our Lord's command the stone was taken away, Our Lord addressed Himself to His Heavenly Father in prayer. The burden of His prayer was that through this miracle everyone who saw it might believe that the Father and He were One, and that the Father had sent Him into the world. Then:

> Then he raised his voice in a great cry: Lazarus, come forth.
> *John 11:44*

Lazarus came from the tomb with the graveclothes wrapped about him; the loving hands of his sisters removed the towel that covered his face; and he who had been captive by death was restored to life. Here in the full glare of a noonday sun, in the presence of hostile witnesses, a man who had been dead for four days was restored to life in a moment.

As the sun shines on mud and hardens it, and shines on wax and softens it, so too this great miracle of Our Blessed Lord hardened some unto unbelief, and softened others unto belief. Some believed: but the general effect was a resolve to put Our Lord to death. Many went off to the Pharisees, and reported all that Christ had done.

> Thereupon the chief priests and the Pharisees convened a meeting of the Council. What action are we taking? they said. This man is performing many signs. If we leave him alone like this the whole populace will believe in him. *John 11:47,48*

There was no question about the fact of the resurrection; the problem was how to prevent Him from becoming popular in virtue of such power. He had clearly demonstrated by His miracles that He was the Christ. But miracles are no cure for unbelief. Some would not believe even though one were to rise daily from the dead. Their reasoning was curious:

> Then the Romans will come and sweep away our temple and our nation. *John 11:48*

They implied that if He continued to work such miracles and manifest such power, the people might accept Him as their King. But this, they thought, would antagonize the Romans who occupied their country. Their aim was to sacrifice Christ in order not to be sacrificed to the Romans. But what they feared came to pass, as Our Lord told them it would happen. The Romans under Titus destroyed their city, burned their temple, and brought the nation into shameful captivity.

Caiphas, the high priest, was present at this council. While the others professed themselves at a loss as to what to do, crafty Caiphas reproached them and offered a solution which contained more truth than he suspected.

> You know nothing whatever; you do not use your judgement; it is more to your interest that one man should die for the people, than that the whole nation should be destroyed. *John 11:51*

"Let Rome, not us, decide on His death," was his argument. "We will be without blame for killing One so loved by the people, and the Romans will be responsible." Our Lord would thus be made a great scapegoat to propitiate the Roman authority. The Crucifixion of This Man would placate Caesar, and remove suspicions that the Jews were in revolt against Rome.

Little did Caiphas realize the significance of his words, that it was expedient that One Man should die for the nation rather than the whole nation perish. Centuries before, the motive of Joseph's brethren was evil when they threw him into a well and sold him into slavery; but they nevertheless fulfilled the purposes of God, for Joseph later on said to his brethren:

> You meant to do me harm; but God meant to bring good out of it by preserving the lives of many people, as we see today. *Genesis 50:20*

Here too, from the human side, there was murder for political ends; from the Divine side, Caiphas unconsciously affirmed that Christ was an offering for the Jewish people, and for all people. His death would be vicarious; His life would be a sacrifice for others. The high priest in ancient times was believed to have the power of prophecy, and the Gospel comments on this knave's statement as being true prophecy.

> He was prophesying that Jesus would die for the nation—would die not for the nation alone but to gather together the scattered children of God. *John 11:51,52*

Toward the evening of His life, a brusque Sadducee who did not believe in the Resurrection thus affirmed what an angel had announced at the Birth of Him Whose name was Jesus, namely, that:

> He will save his people from their sins. *Matthew 1:21*

Caiphas proclaimed a new unity, a new covenant which would be achieved by One Who substituted Himself for others and thus saved them. Our Lord had said that He came to give His life as a ransom for sinful humanity; Caiphas said it, too, without realizing what he said. The Good Shepherd would die in order that there might be "one fold and one Shepherd."

A resurrection sealed His death. Because a stone had been rolled away from a grave and a dead man called back to life, authorities now decreed that a stone should be rolled in front of His grave.

> So from that day on they plotted his death. *John 11:53*

32. The Woman Who Dimly Foresaw His Death

A woman's intuition dimly guessed at more than the Apostles understood, even though to them in explicit language He foretold His Passion and death. The woman was Mary, who had been a sinner. The
time was six days before Good Friday; the place was Simon's house—
the Simon who had been a leper.

Recumbent at table the Master sat among His Apostles and a number of others: John and James who had but recently sought first
places; Peter the Rock who would have a Divine, but not a suffering,
Christ; Nathanael, the new Jacob, without guile, who was promised
that he would see Christ as the Mediator between heaven and earth;
Judas, the treasurer of apostolic funds; and the remaining apostles
who would act as a unit within a few minutes; Lazarus, so recently
risen from the dead by the power of Him Who called Himself "the
Resurrection"; Martha, still serving and bent on hospitable cares; and
Mary, the repentant sinner.

As the meal drew to a close, Mary passed to the back of the Savior's
couch, carrying a vase of pure spikenard ointment. This ointment was
costly; Judas, who put a price on everything, valued it at about a
year's wages. The ointment was costly for Mary, but not too costly for
the Son of God. The vessel in which this extract of myrrh was carried
was likely of alabaster, with a long thin neck. Mary broke the vessel to
permit an unmeasured flowing upon His head and His feet. In a few
days, at the Last Supper, He would break bread as a token of His
Body which would be broken on the Cross. From Mary's "broken and
contrite spirit," which God never despises, came this other broken
thing in dim prefiguration of His death. At His birth, the Wise Men
brought myrrh for His death and burial; now, at the close of His
earthly life, Mary brought the myrrh again for His death. After
anointing first His head, and then His feet, she wiped the latter with
her hair.

Jacob, of old, poured ointment on a stone dedicating it as an altar
of sacrifice to God. Now this woman poured out on the new Israel an
ointment which prepared Him for sacrifice. This is precisely the way
Our Lord interpreted her action; even His name "Christ" meant "the
Anointed of God," or the Messiah.

Judas Iscariot then spoke; but all the Apostles concurred in his judgment:

> Why was this perfume not sold for thirty pounds and given to the poor?
> *John* 12:5

These are the first recorded words of Judas in the Scriptures. Judas would turn away all thoughts from Christ to the poor. Mary had emptied the vessel of perfume, but Judas would have filled his bag with money. The other disciples entertained in their minds similar thoughts about the primacy of the economic. A "bread king" was more important than a "Savior King." In their indignation, they asked:

> Why this waste? *Matthew* 26:8

From what they knew of Our Lord, they thought that He would have preferred giving to the poor rather than showing glory to His Body, which was to be broken for their Redemption. Philanthropy, at least in the case of Judas, was serving as a cloak for covetousness. Counted as wasted was that which was expended on God's honor.

Our Divine Lord immediately came to the defense of the woman:

> Leave her alone. *John* 12:7

Actually, it was He the Apostles were insulting; but in His humility, He censured them only for their attitude to the woman. Then what was confusedly in her mind, namely, His impending death, He now brings out into the clear light of the day:

> She is beforehand with anointing my body for burial. *Mark* 14:8

She was making an offering to Him as the Victim for the sins of the world. The effusion of ointment was an anticipation of the embalming of His Body. It might have been unconscious in Mary's mind, as it was unconscious in the minds of the Magi who also anticipated His death, but He made the unconscious conscious. Six days before His death, she anointed Him for His burial. The Apostles could not bring themselves to see His death, so often foretold; but this woman saw, at last, the reason of His coming—not to live, but to die and live again. And she must have looked beyond His death, for was she not seated with Lazarus who was brought back to life through Him Who called Himself "the Resurrection and the Life"?

Then, answering the objection about the poor, Our Lord said:

> You have the poor among you always, but you will not always have me.
> *John* 12:8

The words, "Let her alone," were in the singular, and hence addressed to Judas alone; the remaining words were in the plural, and therefore an admonition to all the Apostles. To the Son of God in His role as the suffering Son of Man, only six days more remained. The economically poor would always exist on earth, and the opportunity to serve them would always be present. Service to them in His name, He would account as done to Himself. But within a week, God in the form and habit of man would end a brief sojourn before passing to His eternal glory at the right hand of the Father. Gone then would be all occasions to console, to hear, to touch, and to see Him. Suffer then this poor woman to unite herself with My death, for I shall never die again. To be one with the "length and breadth, height and depth" of My Passion is to surpass in value all almsgiving. Furthermore, those who give out of love of the death of Christ and His glory, are those who always give to the poor. But those who would ignore the Savior Christ as Judas did, are those who hustle off after a defense of the poor to sell the Master for thirty pieces of silver.

Enduring honor was put upon the woman's deed by the Savior Who foretold that Mary's deed would be enshrined for all time. Though she did it for His burial, He used the incident to inform His Apostles that His Gospel would be world-wide and Mary's renown trumpeted everywhere.

> I tell you this: wherever in all the world this gospel is proclaimed, what she has done will be told as her memorial.   *Matthew 26:13*

As Chrysostom wrote:

> While countless kings and generals and the noble exploits of those whose memorials remain, have sunk into silence; while those who have overthrown cities and encompassed them with walls, and set up trophies, and enslaved many nations, are not known so much as by hearsay, nor by name, though they have both set up statutes and established laws; yet this woman, who was a harlot and who poured out oil in the house of some leper in the presence of a dozen men—this all men celebrate through the world.

33. Entrance into Jerusalem

It was the month of Nisan. The Book of Exodus ordered that in this month the Paschal Lamb was to be selected, and four days later was to be taken to the place where it was to be sacrificed. On Palm Sunday, the Lamb was chosen by popular acclaim in Jerusalem; on Good Friday He was sacrificed.

His last Sabbath Our Lord spent in Bethany with Lazarus and his sisters. News was now circulated that Our Lord was coming into Jerusalem. In preparation for His entrance, He sent two of His disciples into the village, where they were told they would find a colt tethered, on which no man had ridden. They were to untie it and bring it to Him.

> If anyone asks why you are untying it, say, Our Master needs it.
> *Luke 19:31*

Perhaps no greater paradox was ever written than this—on the one hand the sovereignty of the Lord, and on the other His "need." This combination of Divinity and dependence, of possession and poverty was the consequence of the Word becoming flesh. Truly, He who was rich became poor for our sakes, that we might be rich. He borrowed a boat from a fisherman from which to preach; He borrowed barley loaves and fishes from a boy to feed the multitude; He borrowed a grave from which He would rise; and now He borrowed an ass on which to enter Jerusalem. Sometimes God pre-empts and requisitions the things of man, as if to remind him that everything is a gift from Him. It is sufficient for those who know Him to hear: "The Lord hath need of it."

As He approached the city, a "great multitude" came to meet Him; among them were not only the citizens but also those who had come up for the feast and, of course, the Pharisees. The Roman authorities also were on the alert during great feasts lest there be an insurrection. On all previous occasions, Our Lord rejected the false enthusiasm of the people, fled the spotlight of publicity, and avoided anything that savored of display. At one time:

> He then gave his disciples strict orders not to tell anyone that he was
> the Messiah. *Matthew 16:20*

When He raised the daughter of Jairus from the dead:

> He gave them strict orders to let no one hear about it. *Mark 5:43*

After revealing the glory of His Divinity in the Transfiguration:

> He enjoined them not to tell anyone what they had seen until the Son of Man had risen from the dead. *Mark 9:8*

When the multitudes, after the miracle of the loaves, sought to make Him King:

> Aware that they meant to come and seize him. *John 6:15*

When His relatives asked Him to go to Jerusalem and publicly astound the festival with miracles, He said:

> The right time for me has not yet come. *John 7:6*

But the entrance into Jerusalem was so public, that even the Pharisees said:

> All the world has gone after him. *John 12:19*

All this was in opposition to His usual manner. Before He dampened all their enthusiasms; now He kindled them. Why?

Because His "Hour" had come. It was time now for Him to make the last public affirmation of His claims. He knew it would lead to Calvary, and His Ascension and the establishment of His Kingdom on earth. Once He acknowledged their praise, then there were only two courses open to the city: confess Him as did Peter, or else crucify. Either He was their King, or else they would have no king but Caesar. No Galilean seacoast or mountaintop, but the royal city on the Passover was the best time to make His last proclamation.

He drew attention to His Kingship in two ways, first by the fulfillment of a prophecy familiar to the people, and second by the tributes of Divinity which He accepted as His own.

Matthew explicitly states that the solemn procession was to fulfill the prophecy made by Zechariah years before:

> Tell the daughter of Zion, Here is your king, who comes to you in gentleness, riding on an ass. *Matthew 21:5*

The prophecy came from God through a prophet, and now God Himself was bringing it to fulfillment. The prophecy of Zechariah was meant to contrast the majesty and the humility of the Savior. As one looks at the ancient sculptured slabs of Assyria and Babylon, the murals of Egypt, the tombs of the Persians, and the scrolls of the Roman columns, one is struck by the majesty of kings riding in triumph on horses or in chariots, and sometimes over the prostrate bodies of their foes. In contrast to this, here is One Who comes triumphant upon an ass. How Pilate, if he was looking out of his fortress that Sunday, must have been amused by the ridiculous spectacle of a man being proclaimed as a King, and yet seated on the beast that was the symbol of the outcast—a fitting vehicle for one riding into the jaws of death! If He had entered into the city with regal pomp in the manner of conquerors, He would have given occasion to believe that He was a political Messiah. But the circumstance He chose validated His claim that His Kingdom was not of this world. There is no suggestion that this pauper King was a rival of Caesar.

The acclaim of the people was another acknowledgement of His Divinity. Many took off their garments and spread them before Him; others cut down boughs from the olive trees and palm branches and strewed them on the way. The Apocalypse speaks of a great multitude standing before the Throne of the Lamb with palms of victory in their hands. Here the palms, so often used throughout their history to signify victory, as when Simon Maccabeus entered Jerusalem, witnessed to His victory—even before He was momentarily vanquished.

Then taking verses from the great Hillel which referred to the Messiah, the multitudes followed Him, shouting:

> Blessings on him who comes as king in the name of the Lord.
> *Luke 19:38*

Admitting now that He was the One sent by God, they practically repeated the song of the angels of Bethlehem, for the peace He brought was the reconciliation of earth and heaven. Repeated too is the salutation the Wise Men gave Him at the crib: "the King of Israel."

A new chant was taken up as they cried out:

> Hosanna to the Son of David! Hosanna in the heavens!
> *Matthew 21:9*

> King of Israel. *John 12:13*

He was the promised Prince of David's line; the One Who came with a Divine Mission. Hosanna, which was originally a prayer, was now a triumphant welcome to a Savior King. Not wholly understanding why He was sent, nor the kind of peace He would bring, they nevertheless confessed that He was Divine. The only ones who did not share in their acclaim were the Pharisees:

> Some Pharisees who were in the crowd said to him, Master, reprimand your disciples. *Luke 19:39*

It was unusual that they should have appealed to Our Lord, since they were disgusted with Him for having accepted homage from the crowds. With awful majesty, Our Lord retorted:

> I tell you, if my disciples keep silence the stones will shout aloud.
>
> *Luke 19:40*

If men were silent, nature itself would cry out and proclaim His Divinity. Stones are hard, but if they would cry out, then how much harder must be the hearts of men who would not recognize God's mercy before them. If the disciples were silent, enemies would have nothing to gain, for mountains and seas would become vocal.

The entry has been called triumphant; but well He knew that "Hosannas" would change to "Crucify," and palms would be turned into spears. Amid the shouts of the multitude He could hear the whispers of a Judas and the angry voices before Pilate's palace. The throne to which He was hailed was a Cross, and His real coronation would be a Crucifixion. Garments aplenty beneath His feet today, but on Friday He would be denied even His own. From the very beginning He knew what was in the heart of man, and never once did He suggest that the Redemption of men's souls could be accomplished by vocal fireworks. Though He was a King, and though they now admitted Him as their King and Lord, He knew the King's welcome which awaited Him was to be Calvary.

Tears were in His eyes, not because of the Cross which awaited Him, but because of the woes impending over those whom He came to save and would have none of Him. Looking over the city:

> He wept over it and said, If only you had known, on this great day, the way that leads to peace! But no; it is hidden from your sight.
>
> *Luke 19:41,42*

He saw with historical accuracy the descent of the forces of Titus, and yet the eyes that saw the future so clearly were almost blinded with tears. He spoke of Himself as willing and able to have averted that doom by gathering the guilty ones under His wing as the hen doth gather chickens, but they would not. As the great patriot of all ages, He looked beyond His own suffering and fixed His eye on the city that rejected Love. To see evil, and to be unable to remedy it because of human perversity, is the greatest anguish of all. To see the wickedness and be baffled by the waywardness of the evildoer is enough to break a heart. The father is cast down with anguish when he sees the wrongdoing of his son. What prompted His tears were the eyes that would not see and the ears that would not hear.

In the life of every individual and in the life of every nation, there are three moments: a time of visitation or privilege in the form of a blessing from God; a time of rejection in which the Divine is forgotten; and a time of doom or disaster. Judgment (or disaster) is the consequence of human decisions and proves that the world is guided by God's presence. His tears over the city showed Him as the Lord of History, giving men grace, and yet never destroying their freedom to reject it. But in disobeying His will, men destroy themselves; in stabbing Him, it is their own hearts they slay; in denying Him, it is their city and their nation that they bring to ruin. Such was the message of His tears as the King goes to the Cross.

34. The Visit of the Greeks

Not only to the Jews but also to the Gentiles Our Lord revealed the purpose of His coming, namely, to lay down His life for His sheep. To the former, He revealed Himself as fulfilling prophecies of His coming. But the Gentiles had no such revelation as was contained in the Old Testament; hence for them He drew an analogy from nature which they could readily understand.

The time was less than a week before His Crucifixion. He had already shown Himself as the Resurrection by raising Lazarus from the dead; He had fulfilled for His own people an ancient prophecy concerning His humble but triumphant entrance into Jerusalem. Now it was time for the Gentiles to be given a lesson concerning the reason for His coming. The Gentiles were here represented by the Greeks, as later on they were represented by the Ethiopian eunuch who had embraced the religion of the Old Testament and was coming up to Jerusalem for the festivals. Because the Gentiles had not submitted to circumcision, they were forbidden access to the Sanctuary, but were permitted to circulate in the spacious Court of the Gentiles.

The Pharisees had already complained that the "whole world was running after Him." As a proof of it, the Greeks, or the other sheep who were not of the fold, presented themselves to the Good Shepherd. While the enemies were plotting to kill Him, the Greeks wished to see Him. At His birth, the Wise Men of the East came to His cradle; now the Greeks, who were the Wise Men of the West, came to the Cross. Both the Magi of the East and the Magi of the West were to see a humiliation; in the first instance, God in the form of a Babe in Bethlehem, and in the latter, God in the form of a criminal on the Cross. As a sign leading to an understanding of His Divinity, the Magi were given the star; the Greeks, a grain of wheat. There is even some similarity in their questions. The Greeks said to Philip:

Sir, we should like to see Jesus. *John 12:21*

The Wise Men of the East had asked:

Where is the child who is born to be king of the Jews? *Matthew 2:2*

These Greeks had seen the triumphant entry into Jerusalem and must have been edified by the noble bearing of Our Lord. Perhaps what appealed most to them was the fact that Our Blessed Lord had cleansed the temple and said that His Father had made it "a house for all nations." This revolutionary concept must have deeply stirred the spirit of universalism which was a characteristic of the Greeks. When Andrew and Philip brought their request to Our Lord that the Greeks wanted to see Him, He answered:

> The hour has come for the Son of Man to be glorified. *John* 12:23

At Cana, Our Lord had told His mother that His "Hour" had not yet come; during His public ministry no man could lay hand on Him because His "Hour had not yet come"; but here He announced, within a few days of His death, that the time had come when He would be glorified. The glorification referred to the lowest depths of His humiliation on the Cross, but it also referred to His triumph. He did not say the Hour was near for Him to die, but for Him to be glorified. He grouped Calvary and His triumph together as He would do after His resurrection when speaking to the disciples on the way to Emmaus:

> Was the Messiah not bound to suffer thus before entering upon his glory? *Luke* 24:26

To His followers the Cross presently seemed as the depth of humiliation; to Him it was the height of glory. But His words to the Greeks also meant that the Gentiles were to be a feature of His glorification. The wall dividing Jew and Gentile was to be broken down. From the first, He saw the full fruits of the Cross growing in heathen lands.

The answer He gave to the Greeks was most appropriate. Their ideal was not self-renunciation but beauty, strength, and wisdom. They had a disdain for extremes. Apollo was the very opposite of Our Lord whom Isaiah prophesied would have "no comeliness" in Him as He hung on the Cross.

To bring the lesson of Redemption home to the Greeks, He used an example from nature:

> In truth, in very truth I tell you, a grain of wheat remains a solitary grain unless it falls into the ground and dies; but if it dies, it bears a rich harvest. *John* 12:24,25

He had often used many parables about seeds and sowing, and had called Himself a seed: "The Word is the seed." In one parable He likened His Mission to a seed falling on different kinds of ground, explaining the response different souls made to His grace. Now He revealed that His life would have its greatest influence through His death. Nature, He said, was stamped with a Cross; death is the condition of a new life. The disciples would have kept Him as a seed in the granary of their narrow lives. But if He did not die in order to give new life, He would be a Head without a body, a Shepherd without a flock, a King without a kingdom.

One wonders if the Greeks, knowing that His life was in danger, had not suggested that He go to Athens to be immune from the cruel fate awaiting Him. Jerusalem, they may have warned, intended to kill Him; Athens had killed only one of their great teachers, Socrates, and it had regretted it ever since. In any case, He reminded them He was not merely a Teacher; that if He went among them it would not be to play the role of a Plato or a Solon. Thus, He might indeed save His life, but the purpose of His coming was to lay it down.

Human nature, He was telling the Greeks, does not achieve greatness through poetry and art, but by passing through a death. It is likely that He even spoke of the "grain of wheat" to infer that He was the Bread of Life. Nature is a Book of God, as is the Old Testament, though not supernatural, as is the latter. But the finger of God traced the same lesson in both. The seed decomposes to become the plant. Making application of nature's law, He told the Greeks that if He lived on, His life would have been impotent. He came not to be a moralist, but a Savior. He came not to add to the precepts of Socrates but to give new life; but how could the seed give new life without its Calvary? As St. Augustine said: "He Himself was the grain to be mortified and to be multiplied; to be mortified by the unbelief of the Jews; to be multiplied by the belief of all nations."

The second lesson immediately followed: they should apply the example of His death to themselves.

> The man who loves himself is lost, but he who hates himself in this world will be kept safe for eternal life. *John 12:26*

No real good is ever done without some cost and pain to the doer. Like the legal impurities mentioned in the Old Testament, the purging and cleansing is done along with blood. Self-expression or the blind following of instincts received its death blow in this counsel to the Greeks. The Cross put into practice is self-discipline and the mortification of pride, lust, and avarice; only in this fashion, He said, will hard hearts be broken and harsh characters made peaceful.

The Greeks had come to Our Lord saying, "We wish to see Jesus," probably because of the majesty and beauty of appearance which they revered so highly as followers of Apollo. But He pointed to His torn and battered self on a hill, and then added that only through the Cross in their lives will there ever be beauty of soul in the newness of life.

He then paused for a moment as His soul was seized by a frightening apprehension of the Passion and being "made sin," of being be-trayed, crucified, and abandoned. Out from the depths of His Sacred Heart welled these words:

> Now my soul is in turmoil, and what am I to say? Father, save me from this hour. No, it was for this that I came to this hour. *John* 12:27

These are almost the same words that He used later on in the Gar-den of Gethsemane—words that are inexplicable except for the fact that He was bearing the burden of the world's sins. It was only natu-ral for Our Blessed Lord to undergo a struggle inasmuch as He was a perfect man. But it was not the physical sufferings alone which trou-bled Him; He, like Stoics, philosophers, men and women of all ages, could have been calm in the face of great physical trials. But His dis-tress was directed less to the pain, and more to the consciousness of the sins of the world which demanded these sufferings. The more He loved those for whom He was the ransom, the more His anguish would increase, as it is the faults of friends rather than enemies which most disturb hearts!

He certainly was not asking to be saved from the Cross, since He reprimanded His Apostles for trying to dissuade Him. Two opposites were united in Him, separated only in utterance: the *desire* for release, and *submission* to the Father's will. By laying bare His own soul, He told the Greeks self-sacrifice was not easy. They were not to be fanatics about wanting to die, for nature does not want to crucify itself; but on the other hand, they were not to turn their eyes from the Cross in cowardly dread. In His own case, now as always, the most sorrowful moods pass into the most blissful; there is never the Cross without the Resurrection; the "Hour" in which evil has mastery passes quickly into the "Day" where God is Victor.

His words were a kind of soliloquy. To whom could He turn in this Hour? Not to men, for it is they who need salvation! "Only My Fa-ther Who sent Me on this mission of ransom can sustain and deliver Me! I will not ask Him to release Me. This was the Hour for which time was made; to which Abel, Abraham, and Moses pointed. I have only reached this Hour of trial that I might undergo it."

At the very moment when He spoke of coming to this Hour to un-dergo it for the redemption of men:

> A voice sounded from heaven: I have glorified it, and I will glorify it again. *John* 12:28

The voice of the Father had come to Him on two other occasions when His Mission to the Cross was foremost: at His baptism, when He appeared as the Lamb of God to be sacrificed for sin; at His

Transfiguration, when He spoke of his death to Moses and Elijah while bathed in radiant glory. Now the Voice came, not in a river scene, not on a mountaintop, but above the temple, in the full hearing also of the representatives of the Gentiles. "I have made it known," could have referred to the Father's glorification up to the moment of His death; "and I will yet make it known," could have referred to its fruits after the Resurrection and Ascension. Possibly too, since He was talking to the Gentiles in the precinct of the temple of the Jews, the first part could have referred to the revelation made to the Jews; the second, to the Gentiles after Pentecost.

In each of the three manifestations of the Father, Our Lord was in prayer to His Father, and His sufferings were predominantly before Him. On this occasion, it was the effects of His ransoming death that were proclaimed.

> This voice spoke for your sake, not mine. Now is the hour of judgement for this world; now shall the Prince of this world be driven out.
>
> *John 12:30,31*

The Father spoke to convince His hearers of the purpose of His Mission—not just to give the world another code, but to give a new life through death. He spoke as if His Redemption were already accomplished. The sentence or judgment passed on the world was His Cross. All men, He said, are to be judged by it. They will either be *on* it, as He bade the Greeks to mount it, or *under* it, as were those who crucified Him. The Cross would reveal the moral state of the world. On the one hand, it would show the depth of evil by the Crucifixion of the Son of God; on the other hand, it would make evident the mercy of God by offering pardon to all who "take up their cross daily" and follow Him. Not He, but the world, was being judged. Not He, but Satan, was being cast out. The Cross alone mattered; teachings, miracles, fulfillment of prophecies—all these were subordinate to His Mission to earth, to be like a grain of wheat which would pass through the winter of a Calvary and then become the Bread of Life. St. Paul later on picked up the theme of the seed that died to live and described it to the Corinthians.

> His purpose in dying for all was that men, while still in life, should cease to live for themselves, and should live for him who for their sake died and was raised to life. With us therefore worldly standards have ceased to count in our estimate of any man; even if once they counted in our understanding of Christ, they do so now no longer.
>
> *II Corinthians 5:15–17*

35. The King's Son Marked for Death

Tuesday of the week in which He died, Our Lord told one of His last parables which tied up the prophecies of the Old Testament and pointed to what would happen to Him within seventy-two hours. The temple rulers had just been questioning Our Lord concerning His authority. The position that they took was that they were representatives and guardians of the people; therefore, they must prevent the people from being misled. Our Lord answered them in a parable showing them the kind of guardians and guides they were.

> A man planted a vineyard and put a wall round it, hewed out a wine-press, and built a watch-tower. *Mark 12:1*

The One Who planted the vineyard was God Himself, as His listeners already knew from reading the first few verses of the fifth chapter of Isaiah. The wall that He put around it was a wall that separated them from the idolatrous nations of the Gentiles and allowed God to tend His fruitful vine, Israel, with special care. The winepress, which was hollowed out of rock, had some reference to the temple services and sacrifice. The tower whose purpose was the watching and the guarding of the vineyard symbolized the special vigilance God exercised over His people.

> Then he let it out to vine-growers and went abroad. *Mark 12:1*

This meant the commitment of responsibility to His own people who were so guarded from pagan infection. This commitment began with Abraham when he was called out of the land of Ur, and with Moses, who gave his people commandments and the laws of worshiping the true God. As God had said through His prophet Jeremiah:

> I sent my servants the prophets especially. *Jeremiah 35:15*

From that moment on, the vineyard of Israel should have given to God the fruits of fidelity and love proportionate to the blessings they had received. But when the owner of the vineyard sent three of his servants successively to gather fruits, they were maltreated by the vinedressers. What these divine messengers, or prophets, suffered is described in the eleventh chapter of Hebrews. St. Stephen, the first martyr, later on would describe the infidelity of the people to the prophets.

> Was there ever a prophet whom your fathers did not persecute? They killed those who foretold the coming of the Righteous One; and now you have betrayed him and murdered him. *Acts* 7:52

But God's love was not wearied out with the cruelty of the vine-dressers. There were fresh calls to repentance after each new act of violence.

> Again, he sent other servants, this time a larger number; and they did the same to them. *Matthew* 21:36

According to Mark, some were beaten over the head and used outra-geously, and others killed, which signified the climax of iniquity. These statements are general, but they could nevertheless refer to the beating which was given to Jeremiah and the killing of Isaiah.

> Then the owner of the vineyard said, What am I to do? I will send my own dear son; perhaps they will respect him. *Luke* 20:13

God is represented as soliloquizing with Himself as if to throw His love in clearer light. What more could He do for His vineyard than He had done? The "perhaps" was not only a doubt that the Divine Son would be accepted, but also an expectation that He would not. The history of God's relation with a people was told in a few minutes.

Those who listened to Our Blessed Lord fully understood the many references He had made to the way of the prophets who had been set upon by the people and their message repudiated. They had also heard Him declare Himself to be the Son of God. Under the thin veil of the parable, He was answering the question, namely, by what au-thority He did certain things. Our Lord here not only reaffirmed the personal relationship of Himself to His Heavenly Father, but also His infinite superiority over the prophets and servants.

Then revealing to His listeners the death that He would undergo at their hands, He continues:

> But when they saw the son his tenants said to one another, This is the heir; come on, let us kill him, and get his inheritance. And they took him, flung him out of the vineyard, and killed him.
>
> *Matthew* 21:38–40

The vinedressers are here represented as knowing the Son and the Heir of the vineyard. With unmistakable clarity, the Lord revealed the dreadful doom He would suffer at their hands, that He would be cast "out of the vineyard" to the hill of Calvary which was outside

Jerusalem, and that He was the Father's last appeal to a sinful world. There were no illusions about the reverence that He would meet from mankind. Rebuffs and injuries and insults would be the greeting extended to the Son of the Heavenly Father.

Within three days of the telling of the story, it came true. The accredited keepers of the vineyard, such as Annas and Caiphas, cast Him out from the city on to a hill that was a dump and put Him to death. As Augustine said: "They slew Him, that they might possess, and because they slew, they lost."

After Our Lord said that those who killed the Son would lose the inheritance, He then sent the minds of His hearers back to Sacred Scripture.

> He looked straight at them and said, Then what does this text of Scripture mean: The stone which the builders rejected has become the main corner-stone? *Luke 20:17*

This was a quotation from their very familiar one hundred and seventeenth Psalm:

> The stone which the builders rejected has become the chief cornerstone. This is the Lord's doing; it is marvellous in our eyes.

The Old Testament contained many prophecies concerning Our Lord as a stone. Five times Our Blessed Lord had availed Himself of the parable of the vine. Now after using the figure to indicate the cruelty to God's only begotten Son, sent from Heaven to secure His Father's rights, He dropped the figure altogether and took up the figure of the cornerstone. The Son of God would be the despised and rejected stone. But He foretold that He would be the stone Who would unite and bind all together.

Never is there a mention of the tragedy without the glory; so too here the evil treatment the Son received is compensated for by the ultimate victory, in which as the cornerstone He unites Jew and Gentile in one holy house. Thus the builders of His death were overruled by the Great Architect. Even their own unconscious rejection of Him made them unconscious, voluntary instruments of His purpose. Whom they refused, God would raise up as King. Under the figure of the vineyard He foretold His death; under the figure of the cornerstone, His Resurrection. He told His own fate and destiny as if it were already done and accomplished, and pointed out the futility of any opposition to Him even though they killed Him. Remarkable words they were, from a man Who said that in three days He would be crucified. And yet they revealed in clear words what they dimly knew in their own hearts. With dramatic suddenness which caught them unaware, He anticipated the judgment He said He would exercise over all men and nations on the last day. For the moment He ceased to be the Lamb and began to be the Lion of Juda. His last days are now at an end; the rulers must decide now whether they will receive Him or reject Him. He warned them that for taking His life, His Kingdom would pass to the Gentiles:

> Therefore, I tell you, the kingdom of God will be taken away from you, and given to a nation that yields the proper fruit.   *Matthew* 21:43

Continuing the analogy, taken from Daniel, of the stone which grinds to powder the kingdoms of the earth, He thundered:

> Any man who falls on this stone will be dashed to pieces; and if it falls on a man he will be crushed by it.   *Matthew* 21:44

There are two figures: one is of a man dashing himself against the stone that is laid passively on earth. Our Lord here meant rejecting Him during this time of His humiliation. The other figure is of the stone actively considered as when it falls, for example, from a cliff. By this He meant Himself as glorified and crushing all earthly opposition. The first would refer to Israel in the present moment when it rejected Him, and for which Jerusalem, He said, would be desolate. The other would refer to those who rejected Him after His glorious Resurrection, Ascension, and the progress of His Kingdom on earth.

Every man, He claimed, had some contact with Him. He is free to reject His influence, but the rejection is the stone which crushes him. No one can remain indifferent once he has met Him. He remains the perpetual element in the character of every hearer. No teacher in the world ever claimed that rejecting him would harden one's heart and make a man worse. But here is One Who, within three days of going to His death, said that the very rejection of Him would decay the heart. Whether one believes or disbelieves Him, one is never the same afterward. Christ said that He was either the rock on which men would build the foundation of life, or the rock which would crush them. Never did men just simply pass Him by; He is the abiding Presence. Some may think that they allow Him to pass by without receiving Him, but this He called fatal neglect. A fatal crushing would follow not only neglect or indifference, but also when there was formal opposition. No teacher who ever lived told those who heard him that the rejection of his words would mean their damnation. Even those who believe that Christ was only a teacher would scruple at this judgment about receiving His message. But being primarily a Savior, the alternative was understandable. To reject the Savior was to reject Salvation, as Our Lord called Himself in the house of Zacchaeus. The questioners of His authority had no doubt of the spiritual significance of the parable and the reference to themselves. Their motives were discovered, which only exasperated more those whose designs were evil. When evil is revealed in the light, it does not always repent; sometimes it becomes more evil.

> The lawyers and chief priests wanted to lay hands on him there and then, for they saw that this parable was aimed at them. *Luke 20:19*

The good repent on knowing their sin; the evil become angry when discovered. Ignorance is not the cause of evil, as Plato held; neither is education the answer to the removal of evil. These men had an intellect as well as a will; knowledge as well as intention. Truth can be known and hated; Goodness can be known and crucified. The Hour was approaching, and for the moment the fear of the people deterred the Pharisees. Violence could not be triggered against Him until He would say, "This is your Hour."

36. The Last Supper

Some things in life are too beautiful to be forgotten, but there can also be something in death that is too beautiful to be forgotten. Hence a Memorial Day, to recall the sacrifices of soldiers for the preservation of freedom of their country. Freedom is not an heirloom, but a life. Once received, it does not continue to exist without effort, like an old painting. As life must be nourished, defended, and preserved; so freedom must be repurchased in each generation. Soldiers, however, were not born to die; death on a battlefield was an interruption to their summons to live. But unlike all others, Our Blessed Lord came into this world to die. Even at His birth, His Mother was reminded that He came *to die*. Never before did any mother in the world see death wrap its skeletoned arms so quickly about an Infant Birth.

When He was still only an Infant, the old man Simeon looked into the face of Him Who turned back eternity and was made young, and said that He was destined to be a "sign to be contradicted," or a signal that would call out the opposition of the deliberately imperfect. The mother, on hearing that word "contradicted," could almost see Simeon's arms fade and the arms of the Cross take their place to enfold Him in death. Before two years of His life had been lived, King Herod sent out horsemen pounding like thunderbolts, and with swords flashing like lightning, in an attempt to decapitate His Infant Head, not yet strong enough to bear the weight of a crown!

Since Our Divine Lord came to die, it was fitting that there be a Memorial of His death! Since He was God, as well as man, and since He never spoke of His death without speaking of His Resurrection, should He not Himself institute the precise Memorial of His own death and not leave it to the chance recollection of men? And that is exactly what He did the night of the Last Supper. Our Memorial Day was not instituted by soldiers who foresaw their death. But His Memorial was instituted, and this is important, not because He would die like a soldier and be buried, but because He would live again after the Resurrection. His Memorial would be the fulfillment of the Law and the prophets; it would be one in which there would be a Lamb sacrificed, not to commemorate political freedom, but spiritual freedom; above all, it would be a Memorial of a New Covenant.

A Covenant or Testament is an agreement or compact or alliance, and in Scripture it means one between God and man. At the Last Supper, Our Lord would speak of the New Testament or Covenant, which is best understood in relation to the Old. The Covenant that God made with Israel as a nation was done through Moses as the mediator. It was sealed with blood, because blood was considered as a sign of life; those who mixed their blood or plunged their hands into the same blood were thought to have a common spirit. In the Covenants between God and Israel, God promised blessings if Israel remained faithful. Among the principal phases of the Old Covenant were the one with Abraham with a guarantee of progeny, the one with David and the promise of kingship, and the one with Moses in which God showed His power and love to Israel by delivering them from bondage to Egypt and promising that Israel would be for Him a kingdom of priests. When the Hebrews were in bondage in Egypt, Moses received instructions for a new rite.

After the plagues, God struck the Egyptians further to prompt the release of His people by smiting the firstborn in each Egyptian house. The Israelites were to save themselves by offering a lamb, then dipping some hyssop in the blood, and marking their doorways with blood. The angel of God seeing the blood would pass by. The Lamb was therefore the Pesach or the Passover of the destroying angel, that is, a "pass" which secured safety. God then ordered its continuation year after year.

This institution of the slain Paschal Lamb mentioned in Exodus was followed by the implementation of the Covenant with Moses in which God made Israel a nation; it was the birth of the Israelites as the chosen people of God. The Covenant was concluded by various sacrifices. Moses erected an altar with twelve pillars. Taking the blood of the sacrifice, he poured one half of it on the altar, and the other half on the twelve tribes and the people with the words:

> This is the blood of the covenant which the Lord has made with you.
> *Exodus 24:8*

By pouring out blood on the altar, which symbolized God or one party to the Covenant, and by sprinkling blood on the twelve tribes and people, which represented the other party, both were made partakers of the same blood and brought into a kind of sacramental union.

This Covenant or Testament with Israel was meant to be perfected through a more complete revelation on the part of God. The prophets later on said that the exile of the Israelites was a punishment because they had broken the Covenant; but as they were restored to the Old

Covenant, so would there be a New Covenant or Testament which would include all nations. The Lord speaking through Jeremiah told the people:

> This is the covenant which I will make with Israel after those days, says the Lord; I will set my law within them and write it on their hearts. *Jeremiah 31:33*

The Last Supper and the Crucifixion took place during the Passover, when the Eternal Son of the Father mediated a New Testament or Covenant, as the Old Testament or Covenant was mediated through Moses. As Moses ratified the Old Testament with the blood of animals, so Christ now ratified the New Testament with His own Blood, He Who is the true Paschal Lamb.

> This is my blood, the blood of the covenant. *Matthew 26:28*

The Hour of His exaltation having come, for within less than twenty-four hours He would surrender Himself, He gathered His twelve Apostles about Him. In one sublime act He interpreted the meaning of His death. He declared that He was marking the beginning of the New Testament or Covenant ratified by His sacrificial death. The whole Mosaic and pre-Messianic system of sacrifice was thus superseded and fulfilled. No created fire came down to devour the life that was offered to the Father, as it did in the Old Testament, for the fire would be the glory of His Resurrection and the flames of Pentecost.

Since His death was the reason of His coming, He now instituted for His Apostles and posterity a Memorial Action of His Redemption, which He promised when He said that He was the Bread of Life.

> He took bread, gave thanks, and broke it; and he gave it to them, with the words: This is my body which is given for you. *Luke 22:19*

He did not say, "This represents or symbolizes My Body," but He said, "This *is* My Body"—a Body that would be broken in His Passion.

Then taking wine into His Hands, He said:

> Drink from it, all of you. For this is my blood, the blood of the covenant, shed for many for the forgiveness of sins. *Matthew 26:28*

His coming death on the following afternoon was set before them in a symbolic or unbloody manner. On the Cross, He would die by the separation of His Blood from His Body. Hence He did not consecrate the bread and wine together, but separately, to show forth the manner of His death by the separation of Body and Blood. In this act,

Our Lord was what He would be on the Cross the next day: both Priest and Victim. In the Old Testament and among pagans, the victim, such as a goat or a sheep, was apart from the priest who offered it. In this Eucharistic action and on the Cross, He, the Priest, offered Himself; therefore He was also the Victim. Thus would be fulfilled the words of the prophet Malachi:

> From furthest east to furthest west my name is great among the nations. Everywhere fragrant sacrifice and pure gifts are offered in my name; for my name is great among the nations, says the Lord of Hosts.
>
> *Malachi* 1:11

Next came the Divine command to prolong the Memorial of His death:

> Do this as a memorial of me. *Luke* 22:19

Repeat! Renew! Prolong through the centuries the sacrifice offered for the sins of the world!

Why did Our Blessed Lord use bread and wine as the elements of this Memorial? First of all, because no two substances in nature better symbolize unity than bread and wine. As bread is made from a multiplicity of grains of wheat, and wine is made from a multiplicity of grapes, so the many who believe are one in Christ. Second, no two substances in nature have to suffer more to become what they are than bread and wine. Wheat has to pass through the rigors of winter, be ground beneath the Calvary of a mill, and then subjected to purging fire before it can become bread. Grapes in their turn must be subjected to the Gethsemane of a wine press and have their life crushed from them to become wine. Thus do they symbolize the Passion and Sufferings of Christ, and the condition of Salvation, for Our Lord said unless we die to ourselves we cannot live in Him. A third reason is that there are no two substances in nature which have more traditionally nourished man than bread and wine. In bringing these elements to the altar, men are equivalently bringing themselves. When bread and wine are taken or consumed, they are changed into man's body and blood. But when He took bread and wine, He changed them into Himself.

But because Our Lord's Memorial was not instituted by His disciples but by Him, and because He could not be conquered by death, but would rise again in the newness of life, He willed that as He now looked *forward* to His redemptive death on the Cross, so all the Christian ages, until the consummation of the world, should look *back* to the Cross. In order that they would not reenact the Memorial out of whim or fancy, He gave the command to commemorate and announce His redemptive death until He came again! What He asked His Apostles to do was to set forth in the future this Memorial of His Passion, death and Resurrection. What He did looked forward to the Cross; what they did, and which has continued ever since in the Mass, was to look back to His redemptive death. Thus would they, as St. Paul said, "announce the death of the Lord until He came" to judge the world. He broke the bread to set forth the breaking of His own human Body and also to show that He was a Victim by His own free will. He broke it by voluntary surrender, before the executioners would break it by their voluntary cruelty.

When the Apostles and the Church later on would repeat that Memorial, the Christ, who was born of Mary and suffered under Pontius Pilate, would be glorified in heaven. That Holy Thursday Our Lord had given to them not another sacrifice than His unique Redemptive Act on the Cross; but He gave a new manner of Presence. It would not be a new sacrifice, for there is only one; He gave a new presence of that unique sacrifice. In the Last Supper, Our Lord acted independently of His Apostles in presenting His sacrifice under the appearances of bread and wine. After His Resurrection and Ascension and in obedience to the Divine command, Christ would offer His sacrifice to His Heavenly Father through them or depending on them. Whenever that sacrifice of Christ is memorialized in the Church, there is an application to a new moment in time and a new presence in space of the unique sacrifice of Christ Who is now in glory. In obeying His mandate, His followers would be representing in an unbloody manner that which He presented to His Father in the bloody sacrifice of Calvary.

After changing the bread into His Body and the wine into His Blood:

He . . . gave it to them. *Mark 14:22*

By that communion they were made one with Christ, to be offered with Him, in Him, and by Him. All love craves unity. As the highest peak of love in the human order is the unity of husband and wife in the flesh, so the highest unity in the Divine order is the unity of the soul and Christ in communion. When the Apostles, and the Church later on, would obey Our Lord's words to renew the Memorial and to eat and drink of Him, the Body and Blood would not be that of the Physical Christ then before them, but that of the glorified Christ in heaven Who continually makes intercession for sinners. The Salvation of the Cross, being sovereign and eternal, is thus applied and actualized in the course of time by the heavenly Christ.

When Our Lord, after He changed the bread and wine to His Body and Blood, told His Apostles to eat and drink, He was doing for the soul of man what food and drink do for the body. Unless the plants sacrifice themselves to being plucked up from the roots, they cannot nourish or commune with man. The sacrifice of what is lowest must precede communion with what is higher. First His death was mystically represented; then communion followed. The lower is transformed into the higher; chemical into plants; plants into animals; chemicals, plants, and animals into man; and man into Christ by communion. The followers of Buddha derive no strength from his life but only from his writings. The writings of Christianity are not as important as the life of Christ, Who living in glory, now pours forth on His followers the benefits of His sacrifice.

The one note that kept ringing through His life was His death and glory. It was for that that He came primarily. Hence the night before His death, He gave to His Apostles something which on dying no one else could ever give, namely, Himself. Only Divine wisdom could have conceived such a Memorial! Humans, left to themselves, might have spoiled the drama of His Redemption. They might have done two things with His death which would have fallen so short of the Way of Divinity. They might have regarded His redemptive death as a drama presented once in history like the assassination of Lincoln. In that case, it would have been only an incident, not a Redemption—the tragic end of a man, not the Salvation of humanity. Regrettably, this is the way so many look upon the Cross of Christ, forgetting His Resurrection and the pouring-out of the merits of His Cross in the Memorial Action He ordered and commanded. In such a case, His death would be only like a national Memorial Day and nothing more.

Or they might have regarded it as a drama which was played only once, but one which ought often to be recalled only through meditating on its details. In this case, they would go back and read the accounts of the drama critics who lived at the time, namely, Matthew, Mark, Luke, and John. This would be only a literary recall of His death, as Plato records the death of Socrates, and would have made the death of Our Lord no different from the death of any man.

Our Lord never told anyone to write about His Redemption, but He did tell His Apostles to renew it, apply it, commemorate it, prolong it by obeying His orders given at the Last Supper. He wanted the great drama of Calvary to be played not once, but for every age of His own choosing. He wanted men not to be readers about His Redemption, but actors in it, offering up their body and blood with His in the re-enactment of Calvary, saying with Him, "This is my body and this is my blood"; dying to their lower natures to live to grace; saying that they cared not for the appearance or species of their lives such as their family relationships, jobs, duties, physical appearance, or talents, but that their intellects, their wills, their substance—all that they truly were—would be changed into Christ; that the Heavenly Father looking down on them would see them in His Son, see their sacrifices massed in His sacrifice, their mortifications incorporated with His death, so that eventually they might share in His glory.

37. The Servant of the Servants

Within the brief span of five days there took place two of the most famous feet washings in history. On the Saturday before Good Friday, a
penitent Mary anointed the feet of Our Divine Savior; on Thursday
of the following week, He washed the feet of His disciples. No
defilement being in the Savior, His feet were anointed with fragrant
spikenard; but so much of the dust of worldliness still adhered to the
feet of the disciples that they had to be washed.

> It was before the Passover festival. Jesus knew that his hour had come
> and he must leave this world and go to the Father. *John 13:1*

His mind leaped back to the moment when the Father gave all things
into His hands, and He came forth from Him. But now the Hour to
return had come. The first part of His ministry was with those "who
received Him not"; the closing moments would be with those "who
received Him," whom He would assure He loved "unto the end."

The hour of departure is always an hour of quickened affection.
When the husband leaves the wife for a long journey, there are more
tender acts of devotion shown than in the continuing presence in the
home. Often Our Blessed Lord had addressed His Apostles with the
words: "My brethren," "My sheep," "My friends," "Mine," but in
this Hour He called them His "Own," as if to imply the dearest kind
of a relationship. He was about to leave the world, but His Apostles
were to stay in it to preach His Gospel and establish His Church. His
affection for them was such that not all the glories of heaven in the
act of opening to receive Him could for a moment disturb His warm
and compassionate love of them.

But the closer He got to the Cross, the more they quarreled among
themselves.

> Then a jealous dispute broke out: who among them should rank high-
> est? *Luke 22:24*

At the very hour when He would leave them the Memorial of His
love, and when His tender heart would be pierced by the betrayal of
Judas, they showed their contempt of His sacrifice by a vain dispute
about precedence. He looked to the Cross; they disputed as if it did
not mean self-abnegation. Their ambition blinded them to all His les-

sons about dominion, thinking a man was great because he exercised authority. This was the idea of greatness among the Gentiles, for which they must substitute unmeasured service to others:

> But he said, In the world, kings lord it over their subjects; and those in authority are called their country's Benefactors. Not so with you: on the contrary, the highest among you must bear himself like the youngest, the chief of you like a servant. *Luke 22:25–27*

Our Lord admitted it, that in a certain sense, His Apostles were kings; neither did He deny their instinct for aristocracy, but theirs was to be the nobility of humility, the greatest becoming the least. To drive the lesson home, He reminded them of the position He occupied among them, as Master and Lord of the table—and yet one in which every trace of superiority was killed. Many times He told them He came not to be served but to serve. To bear the burden of others and particularly their guilt was the reason He became the "Suffering Servant" foretold by Isaiah. His previous words about making themselves servants, He now reinforced by example.

> During supper, Jesus, well aware that the Father had entrusted everything to him, and that he had come from God and was going back to God, rose from table, laid aside his garments, and taking a towel, tied it round him. Then he poured water into a basin, and began to wash his disciples' feet and to wipe them with a towel. *John 13:4*

The minuteness with which every action of Our Lord is related is striking, for no less than seven distinct actions are mentioned: rising, laying His garments aside, taking a towel, putting it about Him, pouring water, washing the feet, wiping with a towel. One can imagine an earthly king, just before he returns from a distant province, rendering a humble service to one of his subjects, but one would never say that he was doing it because he was returning again to his capital. But Our Blessed Lord is here described as washing the disciples' feet because He is to go back again to the Father. He had taught humility by precept, "He that humbleth himself shall be exalted"; by parable, as in the story of the Pharisee and Publican; by example, as when He took a child in His arms; and now by condescension.

The scene was a summary of His Incarnation. Rising up from the Heavenly Banquet in intimate union of nature with the Father, He laid aside the garments of His glory, wrapped about His Divinity the towel of human nature which He took from Mary; poured the laver of regeneration which is His Blood shed on the Cross to redeem men, and began washing the souls of His disciples and followers through the merits of His death, Resurrection and Ascension. St. Paul expressed it beautifully:

> For the divine nature was his from the first; yet he did not think to snatch at equality with God, but made himself nothing, assuming the nature of a slave. Bearing the human likeness, revealed in human shape, he humbled himself, and in obedience accepted even death—death on a cross. *Philippians 2:6–8*

The disciples are motionless, lost in mute astonishment. When humility comes from the God-man as it does here, it is obvious that it will be through humility that men will go back to God. Each one would have pulled his feet out of the basin were it not for love which pervaded their hearts. This work of condescension proceeded in silence, until the Lord came to Peter who felt keenly this inversion of values.

> Peter said to him, You, Lord, washing my feet? *John 13:6*

Peter had difficulty with the humiliation the Cross demanded. When Our Blessed Lord at Caesarea Philippi told him that He was to go to Jerusalem to be crucified, Peter protested against the repugnance of that humiliation. The same state of mind appears again. Peter combined, on the one hand, a genuine recognition of the mastership of Our Divine Lord and, on the other hand, a determination that glory should be achieved without suffering. The hardest lesson for this self-confident man to learn was that he still had something to learn. Moments there are when man can wash his own cheeks with penitential tears, and Peter's tears will flow within a few hours. But such tears fall only when man has let the Lord wash and clean him from sin. Then Jesus said to Peter:

> You do not understand now what I am doing, but one day you will.
> *John 13:6*

Such love and condescension Peter could not understand until the full humiliation on the Cross was crowned by His Resurrection and the gift of His Spirit. Peter before had rebuked the Cross; now he rebuked the example of humiliation that led to the Cross. Illumination of many mysteries belongs to the future; now we know only in part. A man may do and say many things which are confounding to the mind of a child; how much more is man confounded by the actions of the Infinite God! The humble man will wait, for it is the last act that crowns the play.

The Divine Master did not impart knowledge to Peter, and then ask him to submit. He asked him to submit, with the promise that it would all be made clear later on. The light became clearer as he followed it. If he had turned his back on it, the gloom would have increased. The Master washed clean, though Peter still protested, as the mother washes the face of her infant, though the child complains. The mother waits not for the child to know what she is doing, but completes her work of love. The tree does not understand the pruning, nor the land the plowing, nor can Peter understand the mystery of this great humiliation, as he vehemently says:

> I will never let you wash my feet. If I do not wash you, Jesus replied, you are not in fellowship with me. *John* 13:8

Our Lord reminded Peter that true humility should not object to His humiliation, but, on the contrary, should recognize its necessity for mankind's deliverance from sin. Why object to the Son of God made man washing external dirt from feet, when He Who is God had already humbled Himself in order to wash foulness from souls? Peter was ignoring his own need of inner redemption under the guise of protesting against a humiliation which was trivial when compared to the Incarnation. Was it a greater humiliation for the Word made flesh to gird Himself with a towel than it was for Him to be wrapped in swaddling bands and laid in a manger?

Our Lord went on to tell Peter that the condition of communion, fellowship, and companionship with Him was to be washed in a more effectual manner than the washing of feet. A refusal to accept Divine cleansing is exclusion from intimacy with Him. Not to understand that Divine love means sacrifice was to separate himself from the Master. The idea of having no part with Our Lord humbled him unspeakably, as he committed not his feet, but his whole being, to the Master:

> Then, Lord, not my feet only; wash my hands and head as well!
> *John* 13:9

It was not only his feet that were dirty, but even the deeds of his hands and the thoughts of his mind needed purification. Rather than persuade himself that sin was of no importance, and that a sense of guilt was abnormal, Peter in the presence of Innocence practically cried out: "Unclean! unclean!"

When Our Lord had finished washing their feet, He put on His garments, sat down, and taught them the lesson that if He Who was Lord and Master renounced Himself and even His very life, then they who were His disciples must do the same.

> Do you understand what I have done for you? he asked. You call me Master and Lord, and rightly so, for that is what I am. Then if I, your Lord and Master, have washed your feet, you also ought to wash one

another's feet. I have set you an example: you are to do as I have done for you. In very truth I tell you, a servant is not greater than his master, nor a messenger than the one who sent him. *John 13:12–17*

He had even washed the feet of Judas! But though He fulfilled the office of a menial slave, He was still "Master and Lord." Never once while on earth did the Apostles address Him as Jesus, though that was the name given to Him by the angel, meaning "Savior." When He asked for increased vocations for His missions, He told them to pray to the "Lord of the harvest"; when He called for the donkey on Palm Sunday, He justified the claim saying, "The Lord hath need"; and when He planned on using the upper room, it was the "Lord" who spoke of the need. The Apostles, too, called Him "Lord," as Peter did when drowning, as James and John did when they sought to destroy the Samaritans, as they would do a few minutes later asking, "Lord, is it I?" On Easter, they would say the "Lord is risen." Thomas later would call Him "Lord"; so would John when He recognized Our Lord at the shore.

On the other hand, whenever the Gospels describe Our Lord, they always refer to Him as "Jesus," e.g., "Jesus was tempted by the Devil," and "Jesus taught." The Gospels written under the inspiration of the Holy Spirit used that name which became so glorious when He wrought Salvation and ascended into heaven. From then on, His name was often to be referred to as "the Holy Name of Jesus."

Therefore God raised him to the heights and bestowed on him the name above all names, that at the name of Jesus every knee should bow—in heaven, on earth, and in the depths—and every tongue confess, Jesus Christ is Lord, to the glory of God the Father.

Philippians 2:10

38. Judas

One day a babe was born at Kerioth. His parents, looking forward to the promise of a great manhood, named him "Praise." Friends and relatives brought gifts in tribute to the new life that was born into the world. Not so very far away, another Babe was born in the village of Bethlehem. Shepherds and Wise Men brought gifts to this Child whose name was called "Savior." Many years later, the Babe of Bethlehem met the babe of Kerioth; Our Divine Lord called Judas to be an Apostle.

He was the only Judean in the apostolic band, all of the others being Galileans. Probably because of the talent for administration which was common among the Judeans, Judas was naturally more fitted to be the treasurer of the apostolic band than any Galilean. To use a man for what he is naturally best fitted is to keep him, if one can, from apostasy and dissatisfaction. At the same time, life's temptations come most often from that for which one has the greatest aptitude. There must also be an inward failure before there can be an outward one. The only failure noted in Judas, as far as the records are concerned, was the sin of avarice. In him this was a kind of a root sin, for out of it, as from a dirty fountain, poured the sin, so great that it were:

Alas for that man by whom the Son of Man is betrayed!
Matthew 26:24

A superficial reading of the life of Judas bases the beginning of the betrayal the night of the Last Supper. This is not the fact, for the first record of the betrayal of Judas is when Our Blessed Lord announced Himself as the Bread of Life. The beginning and the end of Judas' act of betrayal were both associated with Christ as the Bread of Life. The first knowledge of the betrayal of Judas is not when Our Lord instituted the Memorial of His death at the Last Supper, but when he promised it at the beginning of His public life. Into this incident of the Divine life becoming the food of men was inserted the first record of the betrayal of Judas.

Jesus knew all along who were without faith and who was to betray him. John 6:65

The hand on the dial already pointed to the hour of His death; from that moment on, Our Blessed Lord endured the presence of the one who would betray Him. The announcement of the Bread of Life was the beginning of the disenchantment of Judas; it was another kind of Kingdom Our Lord was speaking of than the one for which Judas hoped. This dissatisfaction of Judas must have increased enormously the next day, when Judas found that Our Blessed Lord refused to become a king and fled into the mountains alone.

The sixth day before the Crucifixion a great supper was made at Bethany at which Martha served, and Lazarus was one of them that were at table with Him. Mary, realizing the future better than any other guest and how near He was to His death, anointed Him in preparation for the burial. When Judas saw the ointment being poured forth, he immediately set a price upon it. This was the week of price-setting, for in a few days he would value the life of Our Lord at thirty pieces of silver. And now the ointment he valued at about two hundred days' wages, for in those days the average wage of a man was a penny a day. As John describes it:

> At this, Judas Iscariot, a disciple of his—the one who was to betray him—said, Why was this perfume not sold for thirty pounds and given to the poor? *John 12:4,5*

As jealousy has been described as the tribute that mediocrity pays to genius, so critics may be described as men who have failed. Judas was too materialistic to be concerned with the beauty of the deed. He failed to see that some offerings are so sacred that a price cannot be put upon them. Intimate indeed is the relation existing between acquisitiveness and the betrayal of Christ. The latter is often the consequence of the former. Judas knew only that his betrayal of the Master was near; Mary knew that the death of the master was near. Putting on the mask of charity, Judas simulated anger that such precious perfume should be wasted, but John gave the reason for his statement:

> He said this, not out of any care for the poor, but because he was a thief; he used to pilfer the money put into the common purse, which was in his charge. *John 12:6*

While Mary, in her devotion, was unconsciously providing for the honor of the dead, Judas, in his selfishness, was consciously bringing about death itself. What a contrast between the money box of Judas and the alabaster box of Mary; between the thirty pieces of silver, and the two hundred silver pieces; between true liberality and hypocritical interest in the poor. Judas became the spokesman of all those who through the centuries would protest the ornamentation of the Christian cult and would feel that, when the best of gold and jewels were given to the God Who made them, there was some slight made to the poor—not because they were interested in the poor, but because they were envious of that wealth. The chances are that if Judas had the two hundred silver pieces, he would not give them to the poor.

Our Lord was going to His grave. There would be no chance to anoint His physical body again, but there would be a chance to serve the poor. When Our Blessed Lord again spoke openly of His death, saying that Mary was anointing Him for a sacrifice, Judas knew that, if he was to realize anything out of his association with Christ, it must be done quickly. In a cataclysm, something must be salvaged.

> Then one of the Twelve, the Man called Judas Iscariot, went to the chief priests and said, What will you give me to betray him to you? They weighed him out thirty silver pieces. From that moment he began to look out for an opportunity to betray him.
>
> *Matthew 26:14–16*

Eight hundred years before, Zechariah had prophesied:

> If it suits you, give me my wages; otherwise keep them. Then they weighed out my wages, thirty pieces of silver. *Zechariah 11:12*

Symbolic it was that Our Lord was paid for out of the temple money which was destined for the purchase of sacrifices; more symbolic still was it that He Who took the form of a Servant was sold at the price of a slave.

Finally, at the Passover Feast, Our Blessed Lord, after rebuking the disciples' ambitions and teaching humility by washing their feet, announced the betrayal. As the first scene of the drama, when the Bread of Life was promised, marked the beginning of the treason, so now the Upper Room and the giving of the Bread marked its end.

> In the evening he sat down with the twelve disciples; and during supper he said, I tell you this: one of you will betray me. In great distress they exclaimed one after the other, Can you mean me, Lord?

After washing the feet of His Apostles, knowing that the betrayer was already in the midst, He said:

> You are clean, though not every one of you. *John 13:10*

It was one thing to be *selected* as an Apostle; it was another thing to be *elected* to Salvation through conformity to its obligations. But that His Apostles would know that this heresy or schism or fall in His ranks was not unexpected, He cited Psalm 40 to show it was the fulfillment of prophecy:

> He who eats bread with me has turned against me. I tell you this now, before the event, so that when it happens you may believe that I am what I am. *John 13:18,19*

The reference was to what David suffered at the hands of Achitophel, which disloyalty is now revealed as a prefigurement of what the Royal Son of David would suffer. The lowliest part of the body, the heel, in both instances was described as inflicting the wound. In the Book of Genesis, it is the heel of the Seed of the Woman which was prophesied as crushing the head of the serpent or the devil. It now seemed that the devil would for the moment have his revenge, by using the heel to inflict the wound on the seed of the woman—the Lord. On another occasion Our Lord said:

> A man will find his enemies under his own roof.   *Matthew 10:36*

Only one who has suffered such betrayal from within the household can even faintly grasp the sadness of the Savior's soul that night. All the good example, counsel, companionship, and inspiration are fruitless with those who will to do evil or "sell out" to those who are bent on destruction. One of the strongest expressions used of the sorrows of Our Lord was now used to describe His love of Judas and his freely willed doom:

> Jesus exclaimed in deep agitation of spirit, In truth, in very truth I tell you, one of you is going to betray me. *John 13:21*

The "one of you" was one whose feet He had washed, one whom He called to the apostolic office of spreading His Church throughout the world after the coming of His Spirit, one whose presence He suffered so patiently that not one of the other Apostles knew who it was.

> The disciples looked at one another in bewilderment; whom could he be speaking of? *John 13:22*

Judas must have been very clever in hiding his turpitude and greed from the knowledge of the eleven. Our Lord, on the other hand, must have treated Judas with the same loving gentleness as the others, to have kept his sin hidden. Nothing could have disturbed their peace of soul more than to know that one of them failed the Prince of Peace.

> In great distress they exclaimed one after the other, Can you mean me, Lord? *Matthew 26:22*

Probably, the one Apostle who did not ask, "Is it I?" was John, for at that moment he was leaning his head on the Sacred Breast of Our Divine Lord. John was always proud of that fact and described himself always as "one whom Jesus loved." Peter, too, however, shared possibly some doubt that he was a betrayer, for he told John to ask Our Lord, "Who is it?" When Our Lord was asked, He answered:

> It is the man to whom I give this piece of bread when I have dipped it in the dish. Then, after dipping it in the dish, he took it out and gave it to Judas son of Simon Iscariot. *John* 13:26,27

Throughout the first part of the Passover meal, both Our Lord and Judas had been dipping their hands in the same dish of wine and fruit. The very fact that Our Lord chose bread as a symbol of the betrayal might have reminded Judas of the Bread promised at Capharnaum. Humanly speaking, it would seem that Our Lord should have thundered out His denunciation of Judas, but rather in a last attempt to save him He used the bread of fellowship.

> He answered, One who has dipped his hand into this bowl with me will betray me. The Son of Man is going the way appointed for him in the scriptures; but alas for that man by whom the Son of Man is betrayed! It would be better for that man if he had never been born.
> *Matthew* 26:21–25

In the presence of Divinity, no one can be sure of his innocence, and everyone asked, "Is it I?" Every man is a mystery to himself, for he knows that within his heart there lie, coiled and dormant, serpents that at any moment would sting a neighbor with their poison, or even God. One of them could be sure that he was the traitor, and yet no one could be sure that he was not. In the case of Judas, even though Our Lord revealed His knowledge of the treason, there was still his fixed determination to do the evil. Notwithstanding the revelation of the knowledge of the crime and the fact that his evil was stripped naked, he was not ashamed to consummate it in all of its ugliness. Some men turn away from horror at their sins, when the sins are put bluntly before them. They might conceivably shrink from "sowing their wild oats," when such conduct is described as lust and immorality. But here Judas saw his treachery described in all its deformity, and practically said in the language of Nietzsche, "Evil, be thou my good." Our Lord gave a sign to Judas. In answer to the question of the Apostles, "Is it I?" He answered:

> It is the man to whom I give this piece of bread when I have dipped it in the dish. Then, after dipping it in the dish, he took it out and gave it to Judas son of Simon Iscariot. *John* 13:26,27

Judas was free to do evil as is proved from the remorse he showed later on. So too was Christ free to make His betrayal the condition of His Cross. Evil men seem to run counter to the economy of God and to be an errant thread in the tapestry of life, but they all fit some way into the Divine Plan. The wild wind roars from the black heavens, and somewhere there is a sail to catch it and yoke it to the useful service of man.

When Our Lord said:

> It is the man to whom I give this piece of bread when I have dipped it in the dish.

He was actually using a gesture of friendship. The giving of the morsel seems to have been an old Greek custom as well as an Oriental one. Socrates said that, in all instances, the giving of a morsel to a table neighbor was a mark of favor. Our Lord held open to Judas the opportunity for repentance, as He would do later on in the Garden of Gethsemane. But though Our Lord held open the door, Judas would not enter. Rather Satan would enter in.

> As soon as Judas had received it Satan entered him. Jesus said to him, Do quickly what you have to do. *John 13:27*

Satan can possess only willing victims. The mark of mercy and friendship extended by the Victim should have moved Judas to repentance. The bread must have burned his lips, as the thirty pieces of silver later on would burn his hands. A few minutes before the hands of the Son of God had washed the feet of Judas; now the same Divine hands touch the lips of Judas with a morsel; in a few hours, the lips of Judas will kiss the lips of Our Lord in the final act of betrayal. The Divine Mediator, knowing all that would befall Him, gave the order to Judas to open the curtain wider on the tragedy of Calvary. What Judas was to do, let him do quickly. The Lamb of God was ready for sacrifice.

The Divine mercy did not identify the traitor, for Our Lord hid from the Apostles the fact that the betrayer was Judas. The world that loves to spread scandals—even those which are untrue—is here reversed even in the hiding of what is true. When the others saw Judas leave, they assumed it was because he was on a mission of charity.

> No one at the table understood what he meant by this. Some supposed that as Judas was in charge of the common purse, Jesus was telling him to buy what was needed for the festival, or to make some gift to the poor. *John 13:28*

But Judas, instead of going out to buy, had gone out to sell; nor would it be to the poor he would minister, but to the rich in charge of

the temple treasury. Even though Our Blessed Lord knew the evil intention of Judas, He nevertheless acted kindly because He would bear
the ignominy alone. In many instances, He acted as though the effects
of the deeds of others were unknown to Him. He knew that He
would raise Lazarus from the dead, even when He wept. He knew
who believed Him not and who would betray Him, yet this did not
harden His Sacred Heart. Judas rejected the last appeal, and from that
time on there was only despair in his heart.

Judas went out, "and it was night"—a fitting description for a deed
of darkness. It perhaps was a relief to be away from the Light of the
World. Nature is sometimes in sympathy and sometimes in discord
with our joys and sorrows. The sky is gloomy with clouds when there
is melancholy within. Nature was suiting itself to the evil deeds of
Judas, for as he went out he found not the face of God's smiling sun
but the Stygian blackness of night. It would also be night at midday
when the Lord would be crucified.

> When he had gone out Jesus said, Now the Son of Man is glorified,
> and in him God is glorified. *John 13:31*

His death would not be a martyrdom, a disgrace, or an inevitable
consequence of betrayal. When the Father spoke of His Divine Son at
the baptism in the Jordan, Our Lord did not say that He Himself was
glorified; nor on the Mount of Transfiguration when the heavens
opened again did He speak of it, but in this Hour—when His Soul
faced sorrow, His Body a scourging, His mind a travesty of justice, His
will a perversion of goodness—did He thank the Father. The Father
would be glorified by His redemptive death, and He would be glorified
by the Father in His Resurrection and Ascension.

39. *The Divine Lover's Farewell*

The words of the Master flowed more freely once the restraint of the traitor had been removed. Furthermore, the departure of Judas on his mission of betrayal brought the Cross within a measurable distance of Our Lord. He now spoke to His Apostles as if He was feeling the crossbeams. If His death would be glorifying, it must have been because something would be done by it which was not accomplished by His words, miracles, and His healing of the sick. All through His life He had been trying to communicate His love for mankind, but it was not until His Body, like the alabaster box, would be broken, that the perfume of His love would pervade the universe. He said also that, in His Cross, God the Father was glorified. This was because His Father did not spare His own Son, but offered Him to save man. He put a new meaning into His death, namely, from His Cross would beam forth the pity and the pardon of God.

He now addressed His Apostles in two different ways: as a dying parent to His children, and as a dying Lord to His servants.

My children, for a little longer I am with you. *John 13:33*

Here He was speaking in terms of the deepest intimacy to those gathered about Him, answering their childish questions one after another. Because they were as infants in understanding His sacrifice, He used the simple analogy of a road they could not presently travel:

Where I am going you cannot come. *John 13:33*

When they would see the clouds of glory enveloping Him in His Ascension into heaven, then they would know why they could not presently go with Him. Later on, they would follow Him, but first they needed the schooling of Calvary and of Pentecost. How little the Apostles understood His life was revealed by Peter's question:

Lord, where are you going? *John 13:36*

Even in his curiosity, the beautiful character of Peter was revealed, for he could not bear separation from His Master. Our Lord answered him:

Where I am going you cannot follow me now, but one day you will.
John 13:36

Peter was yet unfit for the deeper realization of the Resurrection. The Savior's Hour had come, but Peter's had not. As on the Mount of the Transfiguration, Peter would have had the glory without the death, so now he would have the company of the Divine Master in heaven without the Cross. Peter considered the answer of Our Blessed Lord about following Him afterward as a reflection upon his courage and fidelity. So he made another request, and declared his bravery:

> Lord, why cannot I follow you now? I will lay down my life for you.
>
> *John* 13:37

Peter's emotion at that second was to follow His Master; but when the occasion to follow presented itself, Peter would not be at Calvary. Peering into Peter's heart, Our Lord foretold what would happen when there would be a chance to follow Him.

> Will you indeed lay down your life for me? I tell you in very truth, before the cock crows you will have denied me three times.
>
> *John* 13:38

The Omnipotent Mind of Our Lord pictured the fall of the one whom He had called the Rock. But after the coming of His Spirit, Peter would follow Him. The significance of this is preserved in a beautiful legend, which pictures Peter flying from the persecution of Nero in Rome. Peter met the Lord on the Appian Way and said to Him, "Lord, whither goest Thou?" Our Blessed Lord answered: "I go to Rome to be crucified again." Peter went back to Rome, and was crucified on the site where the Church of St. Peter stands today. The Sacred Heart now looked beyond that dark Hour to the days when He and His Apostles and their successors would be one with Him in Spirit. If there was any moment calculated to take a mind away from the future, it was this awful present moment. But since He had already spoken of the unity between the Apostles and Himself through the Eucharist, He would take up the theme again under the figure of the vine and the branches. This unity of which He spoke was not such as existed at that moment, for within an hour they would all desert Him and flee. Rather it was the unity that would be consummated through His glorification. The figure of the vine He used was a very familiar one in the Old Testament. Israel was called a vine, the vine that was brought out of Egypt; Isaiah spoke of God as having planted that chosen vine. Jeremiah and Hosea bemoaned and complained that it was not bringing forth fruit. As Our Blessed Lord, in contrast to the manna that was given by Moses, called Himself the "True Bread"; as in contrast to the brilliant lights of the Feast of the Tabernacles, He called Himself the "True Light"; as in contrast to the temple built by hands, He called Himself the "Temple of God," so now in contrast to the vine of Israel, He said:

I am the real vine, and my Father is the gardener.   *John* 15:1

This unity between Himself and His followers of the new Israel would be like the unity between the vine and the branches; the same sap or grace that flowed through Him will flow through them:

I am the vine and you the branches. He who dwells in me, as I dwell in him, bears much fruit; for apart from me you can do nothing.

John 15:5

Separated from Him, a man is no better than a branch separated from a vine, dry and dead. The branch may bear clusters, but it does not produce them; He alone produces them. As He went to His death, He said that He lived, and they would live in Him. He saw beyond the Cross and affirmed that their vitality and energy would come from Him, and the relationship between them would be organic, not mechanical. He saw those who professed to be united outwardly to Him, but who nevertheless would be inwardly separated from Him; others He saw who would need a further purification by His Father through a Cross, which He speaks of in terms of a knife pruning and cutting.

Every barren branch of mine he cuts away; and every fruiting branch he cleans, to make it more fruitful still.   *John* 15:2

The ideal of the new community is holiness, the One Who holds the knife is His Heavenly Father. The object of the pruning is not the chastisement, but chastening and perfection—except in the case of those who are useless; these are excommunicated from the vine. When Our Lord first called the Apostles, He reminded them of all they must suffer for His sake. As He went to the Cross, He gave them a new understanding of His previous message that they should take up the Cross daily and follow Him. Unity with Him would come not merely from knowing His teaching, but principally from the cultivation of the Divine within them through the pruning of all that was ungodly:

He who does not dwell in me is thrown away like a withered branch. The withered branches are heaped together, thrown on the fire, and burnt.   *John* 15:6

One of the effects of self-discipline to intensify this union between them and Himself would be joy. Self-denial does not bring sadness, but happiness.

I have spoken thus to you, so that my joy may be in you, and your joy complete.   *John* 15:11

He talked of joy, within a few hours of the kiss of Judas; but the joy He expressed was not in the prospect of suffering, but rather the joy of making an absolute and complete submission in love to His Father for the sake of mankind. Just as there is a kind of joy in giving a precious gift to a friend, so there is a joy in giving one's life for humanity. That joy of self-sacrifice He promised would be theirs, if they kept His commandments as the commandments of His Father. The unhappy Apostles, who saw the dream of a purely earthly kingdom fade away, could not fathom His words of joy; they would understand it later only when the Spirit came upon them. Immediately after Pentecost, as they were before the same council which condemned Christ, their hearts would be so happy, because as branches they were pruned to be made one with the Vine:

> So the apostles went out from the Council rejoicing that they had been found worthy to suffer indignity for the sake of the Name. *Acts 5:41*

In addition to joy, a second effect of union with Him would be love.

> This is my commandment: love one another, as I have loved you. There is no greater love than this, that a man should lay down his life for his friends. *John 15:13*

Love is the normal relation of branches to one another, because all are rooted in the vine. There were to be no limits to His love. Peter once set a limit to love when he asked how many times he should forgive. Was it seven? Our Lord told him seventy times seven, which implied infinity and denied any mathematical calculation. There are to be no limits to their mutual love, for they must all ask themselves, what was the limit of His love? He had no limit, for He came to lay down His life.

Here again He spoke of the purpose of His coming, namely, Redemption. The Cross is foremost. The voluntary character of it is emphasized when He said that He laid down His life; no one takes it away. His love would be like the heat of the sun: those who were nearest to it would be warm and happy; those who were farthest away would still know its light.

Only through death for others could He show love. His death would not be like the death of one man out of love for another, or like a soldier for his country, because the man who saves others must die eventually anyway. However great the sacrifice, it would be a premature payment of a debt that had to be paid. But in the case of Our Savior, He need not have died at all. No one could take away His life from Him. Though He called those for whom He died "friends," the friendship was all on His side and not on ours, for as sinners we were enemies. John later on expressed it well when he said that He died for us while we were yet sinners.

Sinners can show a love for one another by taking the punishment which another deserves. But Our Blessed Lord was not only taking the punishment but also taking the guilt as if it were His own. Furthermore, this death that He was about to die would be quite different from the death of martyrs for His cause, since they have the example of His death and the expectancy of the glory which He promised. But to die upon the Cross without a pitying eye, to be surrounded by a multitude who mocked Him, and to die without being obliged to die —such was the peak of love. The Apostles could not understand such depths of affection, but they would later on. Peter, who then understood nothing about such sacrificial love, later on, seeing his sheep go to death under Roman persecution, would tell them:

> For it is a fine thing if a man endure the pain of undeserved suffering because God is in his thoughts. What credit is there in fortitude when you have done wrong and are beaten for it? But when you have behaved well and suffer for it, your fortitude is a fine thing in the sight of God. To that you were called, because Christ suffered on your behalf, and thereby left you an example; it is for you to follow in his steps. *I Peter 2:19–21*

John, too, would paraphrase what he heard that night, as he leaned against the heart of Christ:

> It is by this that we know what love is: that Christ laid down his life for us. And we in our turn are bound to lay down our lives for our brothers. *I John 3:16*

THE HATRED OF THE WORLD

After having finished His discourse about the unity existing between His Apostles and Himself, Our Lord passed to the next subject which logically followed, namely, their separation from those who did not share His Spirit and His life. He was referring not just to a condition or opposition that would exist between His followers and the world immediately after His leaving the world, but rather to a permanent and an inevitable condition. The contrast was between the great mass of unregenerate and unbelieving who would refuse to accept Him, and those who would be united to Him as branches to vine. The world of which He spoke was not the physical universe or the cosmos but rather a spirit, a *Zeitgeist*, a unity of the forces of evil against the forces of good. The Beatitudes set Him in immediate opposition to the world, and therefore prepared for His Cross. Now He warned them that they too would have a Cross, if they were really His disciples. To have no Cross would make one suspect of lacking the indelible brand of being one of His own.

> If the world hates you, it hated me first, as you know well. If you belonged to the world, the world would love its own; but because you do not belong to the world, because I have chosen you out of the world, for that reason the world hates you. *John 15:18,19*

Seven times during this discourse on the world, He used the word "hate"—a solemn witness to its persistence and enmity. The world loves the worldly; but to preserve its codes, practices, and mental fashions, it must hate the unworldly or the Divine. Let the Apostles or any of His followers join a sun cult or an Oriental sect; will they find themselves hated? No, that is because the world knows its own. Let them be one in Christ following rigorously His commandments; will they be hated? Yes, "Because I have singled you out of the midst of the world." For the moment, the Apostles could not understand this hate; even after His Resurrection they were unmolested and permitted to go back to their nets and boats. But once He ascended into heaven and sent His Spirit, they would experience the full malignity of the world's hate. James, who heard these words at the Last Supper, would later repeat them from knowledge and experience:

> You false, unfaithful creatures? Have you never learned that love of the world is enmity to God? Whoever chooses to be the world's friend makes himself God's enemy. *James 4:4*

John, too, would remind his people that the world is antagonistic to Christ.

> Do not set your hearts on the godless world or anything in it. Anyone who loves the world is a stranger to the Father's love. *I John 2:15*

Our Lord then explained that the world would not hate them as it hated him, but *because* of Him. No servant could be greater than the Master; they would be persecuted because of His name's sake:

> It is on my account that they will treat you thus, because they do not know the one who sent me. *John 15:21*

Our Lord gave no hope of converting everyone in the world; the masses would be more won by the spirit of the world than by Him. To share His life was to share His fate. The world would hate His followers, not because of evil in their lives, but precisely because of the absence of evil or rather their goodness. Goodness does not cause hatred, but it gives occasion for hatred to manifest itself. The holier and purer a life, the more it would attract malignity and hate. Mediocrity alone survives. Perfect Innocence must be crucified in the world where there is still evil. As the diseased eye dreads the light, so an evil conscience dreads goodness which reproves it. The world's hatred is not innocent or guiltless:

> If I had not come and spoken to them, they would not be guilty of sin; but now they have no excuse for their sin; he who hates me, hates my Father . . . However, this text in their Law had to come true: They hated me without reason. *John 15:22–25*

Their hatred for Him revealed their hatred for the Father. Evil has no capital of its own, it is a parasite on goodness. Pure hatred draws its blood from contact with goodness; this makes hell begin on earth, but it does not make it end here. His Gospel, He said, would in one way aggravate men's sin by their willful rejection of it. There had been sin and evil throughout history; there were Cains who killed Abels, the Gentiles who persecuted the Jews, Sauls who sought to kill Davids, but all that evil was a trifling thing compared, the Lord was saying, to the monstrous evil that would be done Him. He had taught that there would be degrees of punishment meted out to those who were lost; now He added that the degree would be determined by the degree of light that they had sinned against. His coming had brought a new standard of measurement into the world. It would be more tolerable for Sodom and Gomorrah on the Day of Judgment than for Capharnaum, because the latter had turned its back upon the King of kings and the Lord of lords.

This spirit of enmity against Him would not be only while He lived, or while the Apostles lived, but as long as time endured. When Alexander died, no one raised clenched fists over his grave; hatred against any tyrant perished with the tyrant. No one hates Buddha; he is dead. But hatred against Him would live on, because He lives— "the same, yesterday, today, and forever." To be forewarned was to be forearmed.

> The time is coming when anyone who kills you will suppose that he is performing a religious duty. *John 16:2*

From uncharitable censures, men would pass even to taking the lives of His followers. And they would do so under the persuasion that they were acting religiously, as the Scribes and Pharisees did, and as Paul too did, before his conversion. What He predicted for His followers came to pass: Matthew suffered martyrdom by the sword in Ethiopia; Mark was dragged through the streets of Alexandria unto his death; Luke was hanged on an olive tree in Greece; Peter was crucified at Rome with his head downward; James was beheaded at Jerusalem; James the Less was thrown from a pinnacle of the temple and beaten to death below; Philip was hanged against a pillar in Phrygia; Bartholomew was flayed alive; Andrew was bound to a cross, and he preached to his persecutors till he died; Thomas had his body pierced; Jude was shot to death with arrows; Mathias was first stoned and then beheaded. It is very likely when these things happened, they recalled the words of Our Lord at the Last Supper:

> I have told you all this so that when the time comes for it to happen you may remember my warning. *John* 16:4

The counsel that He was giving to His Apostles about the expectation of the Cross in their own lives was a proof that the Cross was paramount in His own. To His followers, He promised in this world no immunity from evil, but He promised victory over it:

> I have told you all this so that in me you may find peace. In the world you will have trouble. But courage! The victory is mine; I have conquered the world. *John* 16:33

The enjoyment of peace was not inconsistent with the endurance of tribulation. Peace is in the soul, and comes from union with Him, though the body may feel pain. Trials, tribulation, anguish, anxiety are permitted by the very One Who gives peace.

THE SPIRIT

The next subject which engaged the attention of the Savior the night of His agony, was the Holy Spirit. The prophet Ezekiel had long before foretold that a new Spirit would be given to the world:

> I will give you a new heart and put a new spirit within you; I will take the heart of stone from your body and give you a heart of flesh. I will put my spirit into you and make you conform to my statutes, keep my laws and live by them. *Ezekiel* 36:26,27

Adam's body was made when God breathed the spirit of life into him. Israel's tabernacle and temple had to be built before the *Shekinah* and the glory of God came to take possession of it; so there had to be a renovation within man as the condition of God's own Spirit dwelling there. With the coming of Christ, the fulfillment of the prophecy of Ezekiel began to take place. The Spirit had played a very important role in His life. John the Baptist had foretold two things about Christ: first, that He was the Lamb of God and would take away the sins of the world; and the other, that He would baptize His disciples with the Holy Spirit and with fire. The shedding of the blood was for the sinful; the gift of the Spirit was for His obedient and loving followers. When Our Lord was baptized in the Jordan, the Holy Spirit came upon Him. He was baptized in the Spirit; *but He must suffer*

before giving that Spirit to others. That is why, the night when His
Passion began, He spoke most profoundly of the Spirit. In His conversation with the woman at the well, He said the time was come when
true worshipers would worship:

> God is spirit, and those who worship him must worship in spirit and
> in truth. *John 4:23*

His words "in Spirit" did not mean a contrast between an internal or
sentimental religion as contrasted with external observances, but
rather a contrast between a worship inspired by the Spirit of God as
opposed to a purely natural spirit. "In truth" did not mean "sincere
and honest," but rather in Christ, who is the Word or Truth of God.
Later on, when Our Blessed Lord promised to give His Body and
Blood under the appearance of bread and wine, He implied that He
must first ascend to heaven before the Spirit would be given.

> What if you see the Son of Man ascending to the place where he was
> before? The spirit alone gives life; the flesh is of no avail; the words
> which I have spoken to you are both spirit and life. *John 6:63,64*

He began by telling them that His death would happen on the following day; they would see Him no longer with eyes of the flesh. A little more time must pass, that is to say, the interval between His death
and His Resurrection when they would see Him glorified with their
bodily eyes. His loss, He assured them, would be compensated for by
a greater blessing than His presence in the flesh. The Apostles could
not understand what He was saying about the short interval between
His death and Resurrection during which their eyes were to be
dimmed.

> A little while, and you see me no more; again a little while, and you
> will see me. . . . Because I am going to my Father. *John 16:16*

He was now down to the level of the Apostles' mentality, for their
principal concern was what would happen to Him. But in two hours
they would have a better understanding of these words, for within
that time interval the Apostles would momentarily lose sight of their
Master, after He was arrested. Because Our Lord said that He was
going to the Father, the Apostles were extremely troubled, for that
meant His absence from them; they said:

> We do not know what he means. *John 16:18*

He knew that they were eager to question Him further on this
point. Their sorrow and wonderment was not just because He said
that He was about to leave them, but also because of the disap-

pointment of their hopes, for they had looked to the establishment of
some kind of an earthly Messianic kingdom. He assured them that
while they were presently cast down with grief, the hour would be
very brief, just long enough for Him to prove His power over death
and to go to His Father. When He passed into the Hour, they would
be sad, while His enemies or the world would rejoice. The world
would believe that it had done away with Him forever. The grief of
His chosen ones, however, would be transitory, for the Cross must
come before the crown.

> In very truth I tell you, you will weep and mourn, but the world will
> be glad. But though you will be plunged in grief, your grief will be
> turned to joy. *John 16:20*

Their passage from sorrow into joy is symbolized by the analogy of the
pains and the bliss of motherhood:

> A woman in labour is in pain because her time has come; but when
> the child is born she forgets the anguish in her joy that a man has been
> born into the world. So it is with you: for the moment you are sad at
> heart; but I shall see you again, and then you will be joyful, and no one
> shall rob you of your joy. *John 16:21–22*

Providence had wisely ordered that the pangs of the mother are compensated for by her joy in her child. So too, the Cross-pangs are the
precursors of Resurrection-joys. There must be fellowship with His
sufferings before there can be fellowship with His glory. At present,
they had sadness because they would no longer see Him in the flesh,
but their joy would come through a spiritual quickening, and that joy
would have a permanent character about it which the world could not
take away.

The nature of this ultimate joy that was to be theirs, the Savior explained in terms of the Comforter or Paraclete whom He would send.

> I will ask the Father, and he will give you another to be your Advo-
> cate, who will be with you for ever—the Spirit of truth. The world
> cannot receive him, because the world neither sees nor knows him;
> but you know him, because he dwells with you and is in you . . . In
> a little while the world will see me no longer, but you will see me;
> because I live, you too will live; then you will know that I am in
> the Father, and you in me and I in you. *John 14:16–20*

There would be another Comforter, or "Another to befriend them."
"Another" is not a difference in quality, but rather a distinction of
persons. He had been their Comforter; He was at their side; He had
been One with them and in His Presence they had gained strength
and courage; but their trouble was that He was going. He now prom-

ised them another Comforter or Advocate. As He would be the Advocate with God in heaven, so the Spirit dwelling within them would plead the cause of God on earth and be their Advocate. The Divine secret that He gave was that their loss would now have the greater blessing of the coming of the Spirit. The Father had given a twofold revelation of Himself; the Son was His image walking among men, reminding them of the Divine original and also the Model to which they were to be restored. In the Spirit, the Father and the Son would send forth a Divine Power, Who would dwell within them and make of their bodies a temple.

It was better that He go away, for His return to the Father was the condition of the coming of the Spirit. *If He remained among them, He would have been only an example to be copied; if He left and sent the Spirit, He would be a veritable life to be lived.*

> I tell you the truth: it is for your good that I am leaving you. If I do not go, your Advocate will not come, whereas if I go, I will send him to you. *John 16:7*

The return of His human nature in glory to heaven was a necessary preliminary to the mission of the Spirit. His going would not be a loss but a gain. As the fall of the first man was the fall of his descendants, so the Ascension of the Son of Man would be the ascension of all who were grafted unto Him. His atoning death was the condition of receiving the Spirit of God. If He did not go away, that is to say, unless He died, nothing would be done; the Jews would remain as they were, the heathens would remain in their blindness, and all would be under sin and death. The corporal presence had to be removed in order that the spiritual presence might take its place. His continued presence on earth would have meant a localized presence; the descending of the Spirit would mean that He could be in the midst of all men who would be incorporated unto Him.

The indwelling of the Spirit would mean more than His physical presence among them. So long as Our Lord was with them on earth, His influence was from without inward; but when He would send the Spirit, His influence would radiate from within outward; those who possessed it would have the Spirit of Christ Jesus on earth.

There would be a twofold glorification of Himself: the one by the Father; the other by the Spirit; the one would take place in heaven, and the other on earth. By the one, He is glorified in God Himself, and by the other, He is glorified in all who believe in Him:

> He will glorify me, for everything that he makes known to you he will draw from what is mine. All that the Father has is mine, and that is why I said, Everything that he makes known to you he will draw from what is mine. *John 16:14,15*

He would be glorified when His human nature would be seated at the right hand of the Father. But this heavenly spiritual glory could not be truly apprehended unless He sent the Spirit Who reveals the glory of Christ in them by dwelling and working within. Though they knew Christ by the flesh, they are now reassured that they would know Him so no longer.

Obedience was described as the necessary condition of receiving the Spirit:

> If you love me you will obey my commands; and I will ask the Father and he will give you another to be your Advocate, who will be with you for ever—the Spirit of truth. *John 14:15,16*

The Spirit came to Christ in the Jordan after His thirty years of obedience to His Heavenly Father and to His foster father Joseph and His mother. His second act of obedience was accepting the command of the Father to bear the Cross in response to the Divine "must." It was only after obedience that the Spirit would be given to the Apostles. As He sent His Spirit because of His obedience to His Father, so His believers would receive the Spirit through obedience to Him. God dwelt in the temple of Jerusalem because they obeyed His instruction in building it. In the last two chapters of Exodus, eighteen times the expression had been made that all was done as the Lord had commanded. So now as Our Blessed Lord prepared to make human bodies the temples of His Holy Spirit, He too laid down the same condition that they obey His commandments.

Peter himself would speak of this immediately after Pentecost:

> Exalted thus with God's right hand, he received the Holy Spirit from the Father, as was promised, and all that you now see and hear flows from him. *Acts 2:33*

He next explained that the Spirit would teach them new truths by recalling the old truths, and would recall the old truths in the teaching of the new. Christ had communicated a germinal form of truth, but not its fullness. When He sent His Spirit, there would be an extraordinary refreshment of memory and a conviction of truth which would surpass even the preparatory knowledge.

> Your Advocate, the Holy Spirit whom the Father will send in my name, will teach you everything, and will call to mind all that I have told you. *John 14:26*

As a light shone on the Old Testament through the coming Christ, so a light would shine on the life of Christ through the Spirit. The strengthening office of the Spirit was thus brought into immediate connection with Christ's illumining office of a Teacher. Those who would get back to the pure form of the Gospel forget that the Master of the Gospel, Christ Himself, spoke of the development, the evolution, the unfolding of His Truth through the Apostles. As the Son had made known the Father, so the Spirit would make known the Son; as the Son had glorified the Father, so the Spirit would glorify Christ. It was indeed only after the Resurrection and the Descent of the Holy Spirit that the Apostles remembered the things that He had said to them, and also came into full comprehension of the meaning of the Cross and Redemption.

There were two trees in the Garden of Paradise: the tree of Divine Life, and the tree of the knowledge of good and evil. It was God's plan to have man remain with Him through communion with the tree of life which he should eat and thereby live forever. Satan assured man that the way to peace was through the tree of the knowledge of good and evil. But man forgot that when evil is in him, it begins to take possession of him. By the false path of the knowledge of good and evil, man was led to destruction. Now the tree of life is erected on Calvary and given again to man. The tree of life then became the tree not of the knowledge of good and evil, but the tree of Truth itself through the Spirit.

> When he comes who is the Spirit of truth, he will guide you into all the truth; for he will not speak on his own authority, but will tell only what he hears; and he will make known to you the things that are coming. *John 16:13*

He said that the Spirit of Truth that comes from the Father and Himself would cause truth to enter the soul in such a way as to make it a reality. Natural truth is on the surface of the soul, but Divine truth is in its depths. To know the Father one must know the Son; to know the Son, one must have the Spirit, for the Spirit will reveal the Son who said:

> I am the truth. *John 14:6*

If all mankind needed was a teacher, man would long ago have been holy, for he has had teachers from the Indian sages up to this very hour. But it takes more than the spirit of man to make a man holy, or to know the truth; it requires the Spirit of Truth. Human truths can be known only by living them and Divine truths can be lived only by living in the Spirit.

In His promise of the Spirit, Our Lord affirmed four truths concerning Himself. First, He said that He had "come out from the Father," in other words, He is generated from all eternity as the Word or the Son of God. Next He said, "I am come into the world," which referred to His Incarnation and the revelation of His Godhead to men.

Third, "I am leaving the world," which meant His rejection by the world, His sufferings, His Passion, and His death. Now He told His Apostles, "I go to the Father," which referred to His Resurrection from the dead, His Ascension to the Father and glory, and the Descent of His Spirit. What effect these basic truths would have on the world He now proceeded to elaborate.

THE THREEFOLD MISSION OF THE SPIRIT

> When he comes, he will confute the world, and show where wrong and right and judgement lie. He will convict them of wrong, by their refusal to believe in me; he will convince them that right is on my side, by showing that I go to the Father when I pass from your sight; and he will convince them of divine judgement, by showing that the Prince of this world stands condemned. *John* 16:8

This is the description of the triple victory which the Holy Spirit would gain over the world through the Apostles—a victory not physical, but moral. On the one side, there would be Divine truth, on the other, the false spirit of the world. The mission of the Spirit would be one of convicting and proving the world wrong in three areas: the world's view of sin, the world's view of righteousness, the world's view of judgment.

> He will convict them of wrong, by their refusal to believe in me.
> *John* 16:9

The first conviction of the Spirit or demonstration would be the truth that man is sinful. Sin is never understood fully in terms of a law that is broken; evil is revealed when there is seen what it does to one who is loved. The unbelief which produced the Crucifixion was, therefore, sin in its essence. Sin, in its fullness, is the rejection of Christ. The usual way to win men to truth is by some popular appeal. But the Spirit will win men to truth by convincing them of their sinfulness; in doing this, there would be revealed the fact that Christ was primarily a Redeemer or Savior from sin.

The ministry of the Spirit would convict the world of sin from another point of view, because it refused to believe in Him. By unbelief, or by refusing to accept the deliverance from sin which Christ brought, antagonism to the Divine is affirmed. The very unbelief which men would show toward Him would unveil sin in its hiding place. Nothing but the Spirit could convince man of sin; conscience could not, for it can sometimes be smothered; public opinion cannot, for it sometimes justifies sin; but the gravest sin of all which the Spirit would reveal would not be intemperance, avarice, or lust, but unbelief in Christ. It is this same Spirit of God which renders the sinner not merely conscious of his state, but also contrite and penitent, when he accepts Redemption.

To reject the Redeemer is to prefer evil to good. The crucifix is an autobiography in which man can read the story of his own life, either to his own salvation or his own condemnation. So long as sin was regarded only from a psychological point of view, the Cross of Christ appeared as an exaggeration. The sand of the desert, the blood of a beast, or water could just as well purify man. But once sin was seen under the sight of Infinite Holiness, then the Cross of Christ alone could equal and satisfy for this tragic horror.

The second indictment of the Spirit had to do with righteousness.

> He will convince them that right is on my side, by showing that I go to the Father when I pass from your sight. *John* 16:10

At first it seemed farfetched to see how Christ could say that His Ascension to the Father would have anything to do with uprightness of heart. But He here added to what was said about sin. As the world sometimes sees sin only in acts of transgressions and not in unbelief, so it often sees righteousness in acts of philanthropy but not in the justification which man has at the right hand of the Father through Christ. Once Our Lord ascended into heaven, the Spirit would show how wrong the world was in regarding Him as a criminal and as a malefactor. The Ascension upset all the world's standards of right and wrong. The fact that the Father exalted Him at His right hand would prove that all the charges against Him were false. It was the world that was unrighteous in rejecting Him.

Once man is convinced of his own sinfulness, he cannot be convinced of his own righteousness; once a man is convinced that Christ has saved him from sin, then he is convinced that Christ is his righteousness. But one cannot talk righteousness to one who is not a sinner. The Pharisee in the front of the temple was convinced of his own righteousness; the temple leaders who put Him to death were convinced of their own righteousness. Good Friday seemed to ascribe sin to Christ and righteousness to His judges, but Pentecost and the coming of the Spirit would assign righteousness to the Crucified and sin to His judges. To those who rejected Him, righteousness would one day appear as a terrible justice; to the sinful men who accepted Him and allied themselves to His life, righteousness would show itself as mercy.

> He will convince them of divine judgement, by showing that the Prince of this world stands condemned. *John* 16:11

The last of the three convictions had to do with judgment. When sin and righteousness collide, there will be judgment in which sin will be destroyed. The one who is judged here is the "one who rules the world," or Satan, the prince of the world. The judgment of the prince of the world was effected by the Cross and the Resurrection, for evil could never do anything mightier than slay the Son of God in the flesh. Defeated in that, it could never be victorious again. Adam and Eve, after their sin, were confronted with the righteousness of God, and the judgment was exile from paradise; in the Deluge, the sins of mankind were confronted with the holiness of God, and the flood came as judgment; when Israel came out of Egypt, the Exodus was accomplished by a Divine judgment; so now when the Spirit of Truth is come, He will bring home to the hearts and minds of men the judgment that was inherent in Our Lord's life and death and His ultimate victory over evil. The world would not be convicted in its own eyes, but it would be convicted in the eyes of those whose vision has been purged by the Cross. The Holy Spirit would reveal to men the true nature of the great drama that was consummated on the Cross.

40. Our Lord's "My Father"

An aviator, a submarine commander, or an officer in the field will sometimes send back to his superior officer the laconic message: "Mission accomplished." Our Blessed Lord had said His last word to the world; He had worked His miracles as a sign of His Divinity; He had finished the business His Father had given Him to do. The time had come to address to His heavenly Father the high priestly prayer of "Mission accomplished." In no literature can there be found the simplicity and depth, the grandeur and fervor of this last prayer. He taught men how to pray the "Our Father"; now He would say His "My Father."

His prayer was based on His consciousness as Mediator between the Father and mankind. For the seventh time He spoke of His "Hour," which invariably referred to His death and glory.

> After these words Jesus looked up to heaven and said: Father, the hour has come. Glorify thy Son, that the Son may glorify thee. For thou hast made him sovereign over all mankind, to give eternal life to all whom thou hast given him. This is eternal life: to know thee who alone art truly God, and Jesus Christ whom thou hast sent.
>
> I have glorified thee on earth by completing the work which thou gavest me to do; and now, Father, glorify me in thine own presence with the glory which I had with thee before the world began.
>
> *John 17:1–5*

During the Last Supper Our Blessed Lord used the word "Father" forty-five times. Up until then, the world had only known the Supreme Being as God. He now emphasized that God is a *Father*, because of His intimate and paternal attitude toward men; He also intimated that now He, His Divine Son, had completed His temporal mission on earth, and His humanity was ready to receive celestial glory. When the Word became flesh, there was a descent, an emptying, and an enslavement. What He asked for was not the glory of His Divine nature, for that was never lost, but rather the glorification of something that He had not before He came into this world, namely, the glorification of the human nature which He took from Mary. His human nature had the right to glory because of its union with Himself. He afterward told His disciples on the way to Emmaus:

> Was the Messiah not bound to suffer thus before entering upon his glory? *Luke 24:26*

Eternal life He defined as knowing the Father and His Divine Son, Jesus Christ. It was not enough to know the existence of God as proved by reason; this indeed is the basis of natural religion, but eternal life comes only from knowing Jesus Christ. What was remarkable about His affirmation that He is Eternal Life was that it came within eighteen hours of His death. His Father, He said, was glorified indirectly in His mortal suffering. This was done by fulfilling the Father's mission of redeeming humanity. Throughout history, men's minds were directed to God, but there were only guesses as to what was God's will in detail. Jesus here said He had a blueprint before He came, and He spoke of it as being finished even before He was crucified, so intent was His will in obeying the Father. No young man of thirty-three has ever lived who could say: "I received a mandate from God and I fulfilled it." But here was the affirmation that the last thread had been drawn in the tapestry of Providence. He was the "Lamb slain from the foundation of the world" by Divine intention. Now had come the "Hour" or moment of execution of that intent. With it, He asked the Father to take His human nature into the glory of the pre-existent majesty of the Godhead.

AUTHORITY OF THE APOSTLES

The next part of His prayer spoke of the relation between the Father, Himself, and the Apostles; it had to do with the authority of the Apostles.

> I have made thy name known to the men whom thou didst give me out of the world. They were thine, thou gavest them to me, and they have obeyed thy command. Now they know that all thy gifts have come to me from thee; for I have taught them all that I learned from thee, and they have received it: they know with certainty that I came from thee; they have had faith to believe that thou didst send me.
>
> I pray for them; I am not praying for the world but for those whom thou hast given me, because they belong to thee. *John* 17:6–9

God is not power alone or some vague immobile Mover, such as Aristotle conceived; He is an all-loving Father Who is not thoroughly known and understood except by His Son. He next described the Apostles in whom His Presence has been felt: they were separated from the world which was seated in unbelief, but they were owned by the Father. All who become His followers, He said, are gifts by the Father. He kept them as the Shepherd His sheep, He taught them as a Master His disciples, He healed them as a Physician his patients. Into this sinful mass of humanity, the Father plunged His all-powerful hand and drew out of it men of the world; He then placed them in the arms of His Divine Son, Who in turn gave them power to carry on His work, speak in His Name and apply the merits of His Redemption.

Our Divine Lord here noted the continuity of a mission from the Father to Himself, and from Himself to the Apostles. Any other body of men who might, in fifty, a hundred, or five hundred years, read something that one of His Evangelists wrote after His death, would be lacking that immediacy of contact which was essential for the communication of Divine power. Believing that the Father had sent the Son and that they sat with the Eternal Son made flesh, they could now vouch for the fact that He had sent them. The Cross was to be on their shoulders as it was on His; He was slandered, so would they be vilified. If they shared the spirit of the world, instead of the Spirit that He would give them, they would be loved by the world.

After having asked that the Apostles be kept in love, Our Lord asked His Father that they be kept from evil. He said that He was leaving the world, but they were to stay in it, even though the world would hate them as the world would crucify Him. They, and all who would be united with Him through this apostolic body, were to be *in* the world, but not *of* it. Our Lord did not ask His Father that they be preserved from sickness, mock trials, false charges; He asked only that they be kept from sin. Material assault from without must be met by spiritual resistance from within. Since they were to be ridiculed by the world, He was asking that they bear up under it for His sake. There was to be no escapism. The world would say, "If you embrace Christ, you are an escapist." But Christ said that if we escape Him, we are escapists. He gave the death blow to the charge that His religion was an escape. On the Mount of Beatitude He told His followers to count themselves happy if they were persecuted; now He told them that they must share the hatred of Him. The Cross is no "escape"; it is a burden—a "yoke that is sweet and a burden that is light."

To live in the midst of the infection of the world and at the same time to be immunized from it is something that is impossible without grace. The Father was now asked to keep them holy:

> I pray thee, not to take them out of the world, but to keep them from the evil one. They are strangers in the world, as I am. Consecrate them by the truth; thy word is truth. *John 17:15–17*

In the Old Testament those who served God had to be holy.

> Make a rosette of pure gold and engrave on it as on a seal, Holy to the Lord. Fasten it on a violet braid and set it on the very front of the turban. It shall be on Aaron's forehead. *Exodus 28:36–38*

Holiness had been evidenced by the insignia on the sacerdotal forehead, now it was to be in the heart through the Spirit Who sanctifies.

It was not enough that they be holy; they must be "holy in truth." As the light of the sun purifies the body from diseases, so His truth, He said, sanctified the soul and preserved it from evil.

Holiness must have a philosophical and theological foundation, namely, Divine truth; otherwise it is sentimentality and emotionalism. Many would say later on, "We want religion, but no creeds." This is like saying we want healing, but no science of medicine; music, but no rules of music; history, but no documents. Religion is indeed a life, but it grows out of truth, not away from it. It has been said it makes no difference what you believe; it all depends on how you act. This is psychological nonsense, for a man acts out of his beliefs. Our Lord placed truth or belief in Him first; then came sanctification and good deeds. But here truth was not a vague ideal, but a Person. Truth was now lovable, because only a Person is lovable. Sanctity becomes the response the heart makes to Divine truth and its unlimited mercy to humanity.

Then Our Lord added that as He had been sent on His Father's business, so they, sanctified by the Spirit of holiness, were to go through the earth as His ambassadors.

> As thou hast sent me into the world, I have sent them into the world. *John* 17:18

When the Word was made flesh, the human nature which was united to Him was sanctified and dedicated to God. Now He asked that they who were to act in His name be as dedicated to Him according to their natures as He was dedicated to God according to His nature. On the following day, He would dedicate Himself for their sakes on the Cross that He might purchase for them their own dedication to holiness. More efficacious than the victims of the ancient Law with all of its shadows and figures, the holocaust of Christ would procure for them a veritable sanctification:

> For their sake I now consecrate myself, that they too may be consecrated by the truth. *John* 17:19

He held back nothing; all that He was in Body, Blood, Soul and Divinity He would lay down for them in total surrender. Where His Blood, that of the Lamb of God, would be sprinkled, there would be His Spirit and sanctification. No one would lead Him to slaughter. He would offer Himself "for their sakes" in order to be the fountainhead of their lives. Then both He that sanctified and they who were sanctified would be one. The sins of the world were transferred to Him, and the Cross was the result; His holiness and sanctification were transferred to His Apostles and those who, through them, would believe in Him. St. Paul would paraphrase this idea in his Letter to the Corinthians.

> Christ was innocent of sin, and yet for our sake God made him one with the sinfulness of men, so that we might be made one with the goodness of God himself. *II Corinthians* 5:21

PRAYER FOR THE FAITHFUL

The third part of His prayer was for those who through the centuries would believe in Him because of the Apostles.

> But it is not for these alone that I pray, but for those also who through their words put their faith in me; may they all be one: as thou, Father, art in me, and I in thee, so also may they be in us, that the world may believe that thou didst send me. The glory which thou gavest me I have given to them, that they may be one, as we are one; I in them and thou in me, may they be perfectly one. Then the world will learn that thou didst send me, that thou didst love them as thou didst me.
> *John* 17:20–23

The most profound preoccupations of His Sacred Heart embraced the dimensions of the universe, both of time and of space. He would not only have His Apostles united in love with Him but would have all believing souls, through their ministry, also one with Him. Their oneness with Him would not be global and confused, but personal and intimate, for He said, "I call My sheep by name." Though He was now addressing only eleven men, He had in mind all the millions who later would believe in Him through them and their successors. A bond of unity must exist between believers and Him, built on that higher unity which exist between Him and the Father. Since the Father and He are one in the Spirit, in a few minutes He would tell them that this Spirit must come upon them to make them truly one. That Spirit he called the "Spirit of Truth," i.e., His Spirit. As the body is one because it has one soul, so shall humanity be one when it has the same Spirit which makes the Father and Son one in heaven. The unity which believers were to have with Him was to be through the intermediary of the Apostles. He then concluded this part of His prayer for the holiness and unity of His Mystical Body with these words:

> Father, I desire that these men, who are thy gift to me, may be with me where I am, so that they may look upon my glory, which thou hast given me because thou didst love me before the world began. O righteous Father, although the world does not know thee, I know thee, and these men know that thou didst send me. I made thy name known to

them, and will make it known, so that the love thou hadst for me may
be in them, and I may be in them. *John 17:24–26*

He Who now said that He had completed His earthly work desig-
nated His followers as a community, or a fellowship. At the beginning
of the prayer, He had merely solicited His Father, saying, "It is for
these I pray." Now He becomes more categorical and expresses His
will, "This Father, is my desire." He recognized that this unity is
something that would be completely and perfectly achieved only in
glory and in eternity. This glory all the members of His Mystical Body
would one day see when they are with Him; then would be revealed
the glory that He had before He "the Word became flesh and dwelt
amongst us," the glory that was His "before the foundation of the
world."

In the "Our Father" which He taught men to pray there were seven
petitions. In His "My Father," there were also seven petitions, and
they had reference to His Apostles who were the foundation of His
Kingdom on earth. First, their continual union with Him; second,
their joy as a result of this union; third, their preservation from evil;
fourth, their sanctification in the truth which is Himself; fifth, their
unity with one another; sixth, that eventually they may be with Him;
and seventh, that they may perceive His glory.

41. *The Agony in the Garden*

There is only one recorded time in the history of Our Blessed Lord when He sang, and that was after the Last Supper when He went out to His death in the Garden of Gethsemane.

> After singing the Passover Hymn, they went out to the Mount of Olives. *Mark 14:26*

The captives in Babylon hung their harps upon the willows, for they could not bring a song from their hearts in a strange land. The gentle lamb opens not its mouth when led to the slaughter, but the true Lamb of God sang with joy at the prospect of the Redemption of the world. Then came the great warning that they would all be shaken in their confidence in Him. "The Hour" was rapidly approaching about which He had often spoken; when it would strike Him, they would be scandalized: if He was God, why should He suffer?

> Tonight you will all fall from your faith on my account.
> *Matthew 26:31*

He Who would be the cornerstone of their faith in days to come, now warned that He would also be the stone of their stumbling. He had called Himself their "Good Shepherd," and now it was the hour of laying down His life for His sheep. Reaching back centuries into their prophecies, He now quoted to them what Zechariah had foretold:

> Strike the shepherd, and the sheep will be scattered. *Zechariah 13:7*

For Christ to be a Savior, He must be a sacrifice. This is what would scandalize them. Actually, an hour later, the Apostles all forsook Him and fled. But since He never spoke of His Passion without foretelling His Resurrection, He immediately added words which they did not understand:

> But after I am raised again, I will go on before you into Galilee.
> *Matthew 26:32*

Such a promise was never made before; that a dead man would keep an appointment with His friends after three days in a tomb. Though the sheep would forsake the Shepherd, the Shepherd would find His sheep. As Adam lost the heritage of union with God in a garden, so now Our Blessed Lord ushered in its restoration in a garden. Eden and Gethsemane were the two gardens around which revolved the fate of humanity. In Eden, Adam sinned; in Gethsemane, Christ took humanity's sin upon Himself. In Eden, Adam hid himself from God; in Gethsemane, Christ interceded with His Father; in Eden, God sought out Adam in his sin of rebellion; in Gethsemane, the New Adam sought out the Father and His submission and resignation. In Eden, a sword was drawn to prevent entrance into the garden and thus immortalizing of evil; in Gethsemane, the sword would be sheathed.

The garden was called Gethsemane because of the presence of a press which crushed olives. It was not the first time Our Lord had been in that garden.

> Jesus had often met there with his disciples. *John* 18:2

Furthermore, He had often spent the night there:

> His days were given to teaching in the temple; and then he would leave the city and spend the night on the hill called Olivet.
>
> *Luke* 21:37

Judas had already gone forth on his dirty business of betrayal. Eight of the Apostles were left near the entrance to Gethsemane; the other three, Peter, James, and John, who had been His companions when He raised the daughter of Jairus, and when His face shone as the sun on the Mount of Transfiguration, He took with Him into the garden. It is as if, in that last contest in the valley of the shadow, His human soul craved for the presence of those who loved Him best. For their part, they were strengthened for the scandal of His death, since they had seen the prefigurement of His glory in the Transfiguration. On entering the garden He said to them:

> Sit here while I go over there to pray. *Matthew* 26:36

Beginning to grow "dismayed and distressed," He said to the three Apostles:

> My heart is ready to break with grief. Stop here, and stay awake with me. *Matthew* 26:38

Isaiah had foretold that there would be laid upon Him the iniquity of us all. In fulfillment of that prophecy He tasted death for every man, bearing guilt as if it were His own. Two elements were inseparably bound together—sin-bearing, and sinless obedience. Falling on His face, He now prayed to His Heavenly Father:

> My Father, if it is possible, let this cup pass me by. Yet not as I will, but as thou wilt. *Matthew* 26:39

His two natures, the Divine and the human, were both involved in this prayer. He and the Father were One; it was not "Our Father," but "My Father." Unbroken was the consciousness of His Father's love. But on the other hand, His human nature recoiled from death as a penalty for sin. The natural shrinking of the human soul from the punishment which sin deserves was overborne by Divine submission to the Father's will. The "No" to the cup of the Passion was human; the "Yes" to the Divine will was the overcoming of human reluctance to suffering for the sake of Redemption. To take the bitter cup of human suffering which atones for sin and to sweeten it with little drops of "God wills it" is the sign of One Who suffered in man's name, and yet One Whose suffering had infinite value because He was God as well as Man.

This scene is shrouded with the halo of a mystery which no human mind can adequately penetrate. One can dimly guess the psychological horror of the progressive stages of fear, anxiety, and sorrow which prostrated Him before even a single blow had been struck. It has been said that soldiers fear death much more before the zero hour of attack than in the heat of battle. The active struggle takes away the fear of death which is present when one contemplates it without action. But there was something else besides the quiet anticipation of the coming struggle which added to the mental sufferings of Our Blessed Lord. It is very likely that the Agony in the Garden cost Him far more suffering than even the physical pain of Crucifixion, and perhaps brought His soul into greater regions of darkness than any other moment of the Passion, with the possible exception of the one on the Cross when He cried:

> My God, my God, why hast thou forsaken me?   *Matthew 27:46*

His mental sufferings were quite different from the sufferings of a mere man, because in addition to having human intelligence, He also had a Divine intelligence. Furthermore, He had a physical organism which was as perfect as any human organism could be; therefore it was much more sensitive to pain than our human nature, which has been calloused by crude emotions and evil experiences.

This agony can be faintly portrayed by realizing that there are different degrees of pain felt at the various levels of creations. Humans very often exaggerate the pain of animals, thinking that they suffer as do humans. The reason that they do not suffer as keenly as man is because they do not have an intellect. Each pulsation of animal pain is separate and distinct, and unrelated to every other pulsation. But when a man suffers pain, he can go back into the past with his intellectual memory, add up all his previous aches, and pull them down on himself, saying: "This is the third week of this agony" or "This is the seventh year that I have suffered." By summarizing all the previous blows of the hammer of pain, he makes the one-hundredth stroke almost combine within itself the multiplied intensity of the previous ninety-nine. This an animal cannot do. Hence a man suffers more than a beast.

In addition to that, the human mind not only can bring the past to bear upon the present, it can even look forward and bring the future to bear upon the present. Not only can a man say: "I have suffered this agony for seven years," but also "The prospects are that I will suffer with it for seven more years." The human mind reaches out to the indefinite future, and pulls back upon itself all of this imagined agony that yet lies in store for it, and heaps it upon the present moment of pain. Because of this ability of the mind, not only to throw itself under the heap of the continued sufferings from the past but also under the pile of the imagined tortures of the future, man can suffer far more than any animal. Man loads himself with what has happened and what will happen. That is why, when we bring relief to the sick, we generally try to distract them; by interrupting the continuity of their pain and by relaxing their mind, they are less likely to add up their agony.

But with Our Blessed Lord, two differences from ourselves may be mentioned. First, what was predominant in His mind was not physical pain, but moral evil or sin. There was indeed that natural fear of death which He would have had because of His human nature; but it was no such vulgar fear which dominated His agony. It was something far more deadly than death. It was the burden of the mystery of the world's sin which lay on His heart. Second, in addition to His human intellect, which had grown by experience, He had the infinite intellect of God which knows all things and sees the past and the future as present.

Poor humans become so used to sin that they do not realize its horror. The innocent understand the horror of sin much better than the sinful. The one thing from which man never learns anything by experience is sinning. A sinner becomes infected with sin. It becomes so much a part of him, that he may even think himself virtuous, as the feverish think themselves well. It is only the virtuous, who stand outside the current of sin, who can look upon evil as a doctor looks upon disease, who understand the full horror of evil.

What Our Blessed Lord contemplated in this agony was not just the buffeting of soldiers, and the pinioning of His hands and feet to a bar of contradiction, but rather the awful burden of the world's sin, and the fact that the world was about to spurn His Father by rejecting Him, His Divine Son. What is evil but the exaltation of self-will against the loving will of God, the desire to be a god unto oneself, to accuse His wisdom as foolishness and His love as want of tenderness? He shrank not from the hard bed of the Cross, but from the world's share in making it. He wanted the world to be saved from committing the blackest deed of sin ever perpetrated by the sons of men—the killing of Supreme Goodness, Truth, and Love.

Great characters and great souls are like mountains—they attract the storms. Upon their heads break the thunders; around their bare tops flash the lightnings and the seeming wrath of God. Here for the moment was the loneliest, saddest soul the world has ever had living in it, the Lord Himself. Higher than all men, around His head seemed to beat the very storms of iniquity. Here was the whole history of the world summed up in one cameo, the conflict of God's will and man's will.

It is beyond human power to realize how God felt the opposition of human wills. Perhaps the closest that one can ever come to it is when a parent feels the strangeness of the power of the obstinate will of his children to resist and spurn persuasion, love, hope, or fear of punishment. A power so strong resides in a body so slight and a mind so childish; yet it is the faint picture of men when they have sinned willfully. What is sin for the soul but a separate principle of wisdom and source of happiness working out its own ends, as if there were no God? Anti-Christ is nothing else but the full unhindered growth of self-will.

This was the moment when Our Blessed Lord, in obedience to His Father's will, took upon Himself the iniquities of all the world and became the sin-bearer. He felt all the agony and torture of those who deny guilt, or sin with impunity and do no penance. It was the prelude of the dreadful desertion which He had to endure and would pay to His Father's justice, the debt which was due from us: to be treated as a sinner. He was smitten as a sinner while there was no sin in Him —it was this which caused the agony, the greatest the world has ever known.

As sufferers look to the past and to the future, so the Redeemer looked to the past and to all the sins that had ever been committed; He looked also to the future, to every sin that would be committed until the crack of doom. It was not the past beatings of pain that He drew up to the present, but rather every open act of evil and every hidden thought of shame. The sin of Adam was there, when as the head of humanity he lost for all men the heritage of God's grace; Cain was there, purple in the sheet of his brother's blood; the abominations of Sodom and Gomorrah were there; the forgetfulness of His own people who fell down before false gods was there; the coarseness of the pagans who had rebelled even against the natural law was there; all sins were there: sins committed in the country that made all nature blush; sins committed in the city, in the city's fetid atmosphere of sin; sins of the young for whom the tender heart of Christ was pierced; sins of the old who should have passed the age of sinning; sins committed in the darkness, where it was thought the eyes of God could not pierce; sins committed in the light that made even the wicked shudder; sins too awful to be mentioned, sins too terrible to name: Sin! Sin! Sin!

Once this pure, sinless mind of Our Savior had brought all of this iniquity of the past upon His soul as if it were His own, He now reached into the future. He saw that His coming into the world with the intent to save men would intensify the hatred of some against God; He saw the betrayals of future Judases, the sins of heresy that would rend Christ's Mystical Body; the sins of the Communists who could not drive God from the heavens but would drive His ambassadors from the earth; He saw the broken marriage vows, lies, slanders, adulteries, murders, apostasies—all these crimes were thrust into His own hands, as if He had committed them. Evil desires lay upon His heart, as if He Himself had given them birth. Lies and schisms rested on His mind, as if He Himself had conceived them. Blasphemies seemed to be on His lips, as if He had spoken them. From the North, South, East, and West, the foul miasma of the world's sins rushed upon Him like a flood; Samson-like, He reached up and pulled the whole guilt of the world upon Himself as if He were guilty, paying for the debt in our name, so that we might once more have access to the Father. He was, so to speak, mentally preparing Himself for the great sacrifice, laying upon His sinless soul the sins of a guilty world. To most men, the burden of sin is as natural as the clothes they wear, but to Him the touch of that which men take so easily was the veriest agony.

In between the sins of the past which He pulled upon His soul as if they were His own, and the sins of the future which made Him wonder about the usefulness of His death—*Quae utilitas in sanguine meo*—was the horror of the present.

He found the Apostles asleep three times. Men who were worried about the struggle against the powers of darkness could not sleep— but these men slept. No wonder, then, with the accumulated guilt of all the ages clinging to Him as a pestilence, His bodily nature gave way. As a father in agony will pay the debt of a wayward son, He now sensed guilt to such an extent that it forced Blood from His Body, Blood which fell like crimson beads upon the olive roots of Gethsemane, making the first Rosary of Redemption. It was not bodily pain that was causing a soul's agony; but full sorrow for rebellion against God that was creating bodily pain. It has been observed of old that the gum which exudes from the tree without cutting is always the best. Here the best spices flowed when there was no whip, no nail, and no wound. Without a lance, but through the sheer voluntariness of Christ's suffering, the Blood flowed freely.

Sin is in the blood. Every doctor knows this; even passers-by can see it. Drunkenness is in the eyes, the bloated cheek. Avarice is written in the hands and on the mouth. Lust is written in the eyes. There is not a libertine, a criminal, a bigot, a pervert who does not have his hate or his envy written in every inch of his body, every hidden gateway and alley of his blood, and every cell of his brain.

Since sin is in the blood, it must be poured out. As Our Lord willed that the shedding of the blood of goats and animals should prefigure His own atonement, so He willed further that sinful men should never again shed any blood in war or hate, but would invoke only His Precious Blood now poured out in Redemption. Since all sin needs expiation, modern man, instead of calling on the Blood of Christ in pardon, sheds his own brother's blood in the dirty business of war. All this crimsoning of the earth will not be stopped until man in the full consciousness of sin begins to invoke upon himself in peace and pardon the Redemptive Blood of Christ, the Son of the Living God.

Every soul can at least dimly understand the nature of the struggle that took place on the moonlit night in the Garden of Gethsemane. Every heart knows something about it. No one has ever come to the twenties—let alone to the forties, or the fifties, or the sixties, or the seventies of life—without reflecting with some degree of seriousness on himself and the world round about him, and without knowing the terrible tension that has been caused in his soul by sin. Faults and follies do not efface themselves from the record of memory; sleeping tablets do not silence them; phychoanalysts cannot explain them away. The brightness of youth may make them fade into some dim outline, but there are times of silence—on a sick bed, sleepless nights, the open seas, a moment of quiet, the innocence in the face of a child—when these sins, like spectres or phantoms, blaze their unrelenting characters of fire upon our consciences. Their force might not have been realized in a moment of passion, but conscience is biding its time and will bear its stern uncompromising witness sometime, somewhere, and force a dread upon the soul that ought to make it cast itself back again to God. Terrible though the agonies and tortures of a single soul be, they were only a drop in the ocean of humanity's guilt which the Savior felt as His own in the Garden.

Finding the Apostles asleep the third time, the Savior did not ask again if they could watch one hour with Him; more awful than any reprimand was the significant permission to sleep:

> Still sleeping? Still taking your ease? The hour has come! The Son of Man is betrayed to sinful men. *Matthew 26:45*

The fatigued followers were allowed to sleep on until the last moment. Their sympathy was needed no longer; while His friends slept, His enemies plotted. It is conceivable that there may have been an interval of time between His finding them asleep and the approach of Judas and the soldiers. That time they could continue to pass in sleep. The Hour which He had ardently yearned for was now at hand. In the distance was the regular tramp of Roman soldiers, the uneven and hurried treading of the mob and the temple authorities with a traitor in the front.

> Up, let us go forward; the traitor is upon us. *Matthew 26:46*

42. The Kiss That Blistered

He who had freed Lazarus from the bonds of death now submitted Himself to death. Judas led a band of officers from the chief priests and Pharisees, carrying lanterns, torches, and weapons. Both Jew and Gentile united in the arrest of Christ. Though the moon was full, Judas had to give to the Roman soldiers a sign by which they would know Our Lord; the sign He gave was the kiss. But before the torches could search out the Light of the World, the Good Shepherd went forth to meet them.

Judas had often been with Our Lord in that garden where He took His disciples to pray; he therefore knew where to find Him. The greatest betrayers are those who have been cradled in the sacred associations of Christ and His Church. They alone know where to find Christ after dark.

St. John, who was in the garden that night and witnessed the whole scene, said that nothing that happened took Our Lord by surprise:

> Jesus, knowing all that was coming upon him, went out to them.
> *John* 18:4

Adam hid from God in the Garden of Eden; God now searched out the sons of Adam in the Garden of Gethsemane. In the full consciousness of all the Old Testament prophecies concerning Himself as the Lamb of God and of His self-willed offering for sin, He went forth in self-surrender. Addressing with overpowering majesty the multitude which had gathered armed with swords and stones, He challenged them to name the One they sought:

> Who is it you want? Jesus of Nazareth, they answered. *John* 18:5

They did not say "Thee," or "Thou art the One." It was evident that even under the full moon they did not recognize Him. That was why, too, they had prearranged a sign with Judas by which they would know Him—the kiss. Strangely enough, those who are bent on evil cannot recognize Divinity even when it stands before them. The Light can shine in darkness, but the darkness does not comprehend it. It takes more than lanterns and a full moon to perceive the Light of the World. As St. Paul explained it:

> If indeed our gospel be found veiled, the only people who find it so are those on the way to perdition. Their unbelieving minds are so

blinded by the god of this passing age, that the gospel of the glory of Christ, who is the very image of God, cannot dawn upon them and bring them light. *II Corinthians 4:3,4*

So He told them, "I am Jesus of Nazareth." A paralyzing awe came over all of them, and they fell backward on the ground. His humanity was never separate from His Divinity, as never the Cross without the Resurrection. A moment before He had been undergoing the agony; now the majesty of His Divinity shone forth. Once before, the officers who came to arrest Him were arrested by His words; the would-be captors reeled backward, for no one, as He said, was taking His life away; He would lay it down of Himself. A thousand years before, the Psalmist had foretold this incident, which happened figuratively to David:

> When evildoers close in on me to devour me, it is my enemies, my assailants, who stumble and fall. *Psalm 26:2*

When Isaiah caught a gleam of God he said that he was "undone"; and Moses could not look upon His face. So now the Godhead, dwelling within that human body which was about to be put to death, flashed forth to throw the soldiers and the rabble into a huddled mass. Never is there any humiliation without a hint of glory. When He humbled Himself to ask a woman of the streets for a drink of water, He promised to give the water of life; when He slept from exhaustion in a boat, He arose to command the winds and the seas. Now as He delivered Himself up into the hands of men, there flashed forth His glory. He could have walked away free, with the soldiers and His enemies prone upon the ground, but it was the "Hour" when Love fettered Himself to unfetter man.

Self-sacrifice seeks no vengeance. Judas and the others had no power to capture Him unless He freely delivered Himself into their hands. Giving His enemies power to stand, He, as the Good Shepherd, had only one concern, that of His own sheep:

> If I am the man you want, let these others go. *John 18:8*

He must go to sacrifice alone. The Old Testament ordered that the high priest must be alone when he offered sacrifice:

> No other man shall be within the Tent of the Presence from the time when he enters the sanctuary to make expiation until he comes out, and he shall make expiation for himself, his household, and the whole assembly of Israel. *Leviticus 16:17*

This was His Hour, but not the hour of the Apostles. Later on, they would suffer and die in His name, but presently they could not understand Redemption until the Spirit had enlightened them. He would tread the wine press alone. They were not yet in a spiritual condition to die with Him; in a few moments they would all desert Him. Furthermore, they could not suffer for Christ until He had first suffered for them. The whole purpose of His redemptive death, in a certain sense, was to say to all men, "Let these others go free."

On entering the garden, the Savior had told Peter, James, and John "to watch and pray." Peter now decided to substitute action for prayer. Taking one of the two swords which he carried, he struck Malchus, the servant of the high priest. As a swordsman, Peter was a good fisherman, for the best that he could do, in his wild intent, was to cut off the ear of Malchus. Though Peter's zeal was honest, well-meaning and impulsive, yet it was mistaken in the choice of means. Our Blessed Lord first touched the ear of the wounded man and restored it; then, turning to Peter, He said:

> Sheathe your sword. This is the cup my Father has given me; shall I not drink it? *John 18:11*

Here in contrast were set the sword and the cup; the sword wins by slaying, the cup by submission. Not the impatience of the violent, but the patience of saints was to be His way of winning souls. Often He had referred to His Passion and death under the analogy of a "cup," as when He asked James and John if they could drink the cup of His Passion. Now He speaks of the cup as not coming from Judas, nor from the Sanhedrin, nor from the Jews, nor from Pilate or Herod, but from His own Heavenly Father. It was a cup which contained the Father's will that, in love for men, He should offer His life that they might be restored again to Divine sonship. Nor did He say that a sentence was laid upon Him to undergo His Passion, but rather that He Himself out of love could not do otherwise. "Am I not to drink that cup?" Furthermore, those who arbitrarily and presumptuously resorted to violence, Our Lord told Peter, would feel that violence itself. Revenge brings its own punishment. Bodies can be conquered with unsheathed swords but those same swords often turn against those who wield them:

> All who take the sword die by the sword. *Matthew 26:52*

That was only a human lesson verified by history. Peter had yet to learn that He who seemed so weak was truly Divine; that if He wished, He could summon to His aid an army greater than any of the earth:

> Do you suppose that I cannot appeal to my Father, who would at once send to my aid more than twelve legions of angels? *Matthew 26:53*

He used the Roman term "legion." He had been arrested by what was called a cohort, or the tenth part of a legion (which numbered about six thousand men). He could have, if He had chosen, called to His aid twelve times six thousand to deliver Him from His enemies. If there was to be an appeal to force, Peter's little sword would shrink into insignificance compared to the heavenly hosts under the great Commander. But His refusal to summon the angels was not an involuntary bowing to a fate, or a submitting to pain that He might be purified. It was rather a quiet surrender of some of His own rights; a voluntary abstinence from the use of superior force for the sake of others, a standing unchained with perfect power to go away, and yet submitting for love of mankind—such is sacrifice at white heat.

Turning to the bloodthirsty crowd round about He says:

> Do you take me for a bandit, that you have come out with swords and cudgels to arrest me? Day after day I sat teaching in the temple, and you did not lay hands on me. But this has all happened to fulfil what the prophets wrote. *Matthew 26:55*

But what had the prophets foretold? To quote but one, Isaiah foretold how He would be counted as a wrongdoer by His enemies.

> Therefore I will allot him a portion with the great,
>   and he shall share the spoil with the mighty,
> because he exposed himself to face death
>   and was reckoned among transgressors,
> because he bore the sin of many
>   and interceded for their transgressions.
>   *Isaiah 53:12*

> He was afflicted, he submitted to be struck down and did not open his mouth; he was led like a sheep to the slaughter, like a ewe that is dumb before the shearers. *Isaiah 53:7*

Looking beyond all secondary causes, such as Pilate and Annas, the Romans and the Jews, Our Lord saw not enemies to be defeated by a sword, but a cup offered by His Father. Love was the motive and spring of His sacrifice as He said:

> God loved the world so much that he gave his only Son, that everyone who has faith in him may not die but have eternal life. *John 3:16*

Sin required atonement or reparation. Being man, He could act in man's name; being God, His Redemption for sin would have infinite value. His human nature made Him susceptible to pain and death, and therefore capable of offering Himself as a sacrifice; yet He had to be sinless, otherwise He Himself would need Redemption. The Lamb used in sacrifice had to be "without blemish." The love of the Lamb had to be free; to compel the Lamb of God to suffer would be the height of injustice. Hence the affirmation of power at the moment He delivered Himself into their hands. What God permitted was as equally His will as what He appointed. Here Our Lord refused to see the hand of His enemies in His death, but passed immediately to the idea of the cup His Father gave Him. In that love He reposed even though the cup for the moment was bitter, for good was to come from it.

Delivering Himself into their hands, what Our Lord foretold about His Apostles now came to pass:

> Then the disciples all deserted him and ran away. *Matthew 26:56*

Peter, who had drawn the sword in defense against the cup, fled from sight. Later he secretly followed at a safe distance. John also crept on safely behind the mob, to appear later in the house of the high priest. But Judas remained to hear the word "Hour" the Master had uttered first at Cana:

> This is your moment—the hour when darkness reigns. *Luke 22:53*

Many times He told His enemies and Herod that they could do nothing to Him until His "Hour" had come. Now He announced it; it was the hour when evil could turn out the Light of the World. Evil has its hour; God has His day. He Who, when He took on Himself a human nature at Bethlehem, was bound with swaddling bands and laid in a manger is now to be bound with ropes and laid on a Cross. Once before, when His enemies attempted to arrest Him, He arrested them with the force of His words; now He submitted to arrest because the Hour had come. The Apostles, hearing the clinking of chains and seeing the glistening swords, forgot all the glory of the Messiah, deserted Him, and fled. The High Priest must offer the sacrifice alone.

43. *The Religious Trial*

Our Blessed Lord had two natures: Divine and human. Both were on trial and on totally different charges. Thus was fulfilled the prophecy of Simeon that He was a "sign to be contradicted." The judges could not agree as to why He should die; they could only agree that He must. The religious judges, Annas and Caiphas, found Him guilty of being too Divine; the political judges, Pilate and Herod, found Him guilty of being too human. Before the one, He was too unworldly; before the other, He was too worldly; before the one, He was too heavenly; before the other, too earthly. From that day on, His Church too would be condemned on contradictory charges, either for claiming to be too divine by some, or else for being too human by others. Condemned on contradictory charges, He was sentenced to the symbol of contradiction, which is the Cross.

If Our Lord had been taken in the temple or stoned on the many occasions when His enemies prepared to do so, the many prophecies concerning His appointed sacrifice as the Lamb of God would not have been fulfilled. When earlier the Pharisees had told Him that Herod had a mind to kill Him, Our Lord said that He would not deliver Himself to death in Galilee, but in Jerusalem. Furthermore, He told them no man could take His life away from Him; He would lay it down of Himself.

But in the garden, when:

> Then the disciples all deserted him and ran away.   *Matthew* 26:56

He said to the chief priests:

> This is your moment—the hour when darkness reigns.   *Luke* 22:53

He meant that, when He had taught publicly, voyaging through Judea and Galilee, none of them ever laid hands on Him or did they succeed in throwing Him over the precipice at Nazareth. But evil had its Hour, the Hour of which He had so often spoken. In that Hour, God gave to evil the power to affect a momentary triumph in which the spiritually blind would think they had gained a victory. The hands of the wicked are bound until God allows them to work, nor can they master a stroke one moment after God commands them to stop. The powers of darkness could not touch Job's property or person until God allowed them; nor could they prevent Job's prosperity returning when God willed it. So too, in this Hour, darkness would have a power that would be powerless at the Resurrection.

The soldiers bound Him and led Him away. Perhaps one of the reasons for doing so was because Judas had given orders to hold Him fast. Furthermore, the type of Christ's sufferings was foretold in Isaac when Abraham, preparing to offer his son to God as a sacrifice, implied such forced holding:

> He bound his son Isaac. *Genesis* 22:9

Then they led Him off; He was not driven nor dragged because of His willing submission. As Isaiah foretold, He would be *led* like a lamb to the slaughter. As the new Jeremiah, the Man of Sorrows, He was put in chains for His testimony to the truth.

The route taken was across the brook of the Cedron, then through the "Sheep Gate" which was near the temple and through which the sacrificial animals passed. He was first led away to Annas, who was the father-in-law of Caiphas, the high priest of that year. Inasmuch as the Romans were in authority in the country, it is likely that a high priest was elected every year; Annas, however, was actually the prominent figure of the day, even though Caiphas was the presiding officer of the Sanhedrin at the moment.

Inasmuch as both were representatives of religious power, the first trial was on the grounds of religion. Annas had five sons, and we learn from another source that they had booths in the temple and were among the buyers and sellers cast out by Our Lord when He purged the temple. From Annas, Christ was led to Caiphas. The Old Law ordained that each animal sacrificed for the sins of the people be led before the priest. So Christ, the representative of the priesthood of the Spirit, is led before Caiphas, the representative of the priesthood of the flesh. It was this same Caiphas who had said:

> It would be to their interest if one man died for the whole people.
> *John* 18:14

It was thus evident that he and the Sanhedrin had resolved upon the death of Christ before the trial took place. A night trial of the Sanhedrin was illegal, but in the mad desire to do away with Christ, it was held nevertheless. Though it had no right to proceed to a capital execution, it did retain, however, the power to institute trials. As the trial began:

> The High Priest questioned Jesus about his disciples and about what he taught. *John* 18:19

Since Caiphas had already determined that Our Lord should die, he had no intention of learning anything; rather he sought to find some excuse for the planned injustice. The first questions were about Christ's organization and followers, whom the Sanhedrin feared as a threat to themselves; for earlier the Pharisees had reported:

> You see you are doing no good at all; why, all the world has gone after him! *John 12:19*

The judge was not so much concerned with the names of Christ's followers as with their number; the purpose of this inquiry was to draw from Him an answer suited to their condemnation. The query about His doctrine was to discover if He was the head of a secret society or if He was preaching some novelty or heresy.

Our Lord saw the trickery behind the questions, and with absolute fearlessness, born of innocence, answered that His doctrine was known to the people and those who heard Him could give testimony thereof. He had no underground, no Fifth Column, no doctrine that was for the few. There was nothing secret about His doctrine; everyone heard it, for He preached in public.

> I have spoken openly to all the world; I have always taught in synagogue and in the temple, where all Jews congregate; I have said nothing in secret. Why question me? Ask my hearers what I told them; they know what I said. *John 18:20,21*

Christ spoke to the *world*, as well as to the Jews. He would not testify in His own behalf; everyone knew what He taught. Caiphas was only pretending to be ignorant of that which was common knowledge. Had not the Sanhedrin already excommunicated anyone who believed in Christ? In His humility, He did not ask that the dumb, the halt, the blind, and the lepers be summoned, but rather only those who had heard Him. The temple authorities had long been turning their backs upon the people; now He bade them summon those whom they despised. Against this aristocratic isolation between office and people, Christ placed His doctrine and His followers. It was the first Christian approval put upon the opinion of the man in the street. Thus in reply to the double enquiry, He answered the first by an appeal to the common folk; and the second by affirming that the book of His teaching was never closed; it was open to all.

When Our Lord answered thus, one of the officers who stood nearby struck Him with the palm of his hand saying:

> Is that the way to answer the High Priest? *John 18:22*

Was it the hand of Malchus, he whose ear was cured by the Savior an hour or so before? In any case, it was the first blow struck against the

Body of the Savior—a blow unreprimanded by the judges. Thus Caiphas and the court really put Christ outside the sphere of the law. To escape the content of the message, the soldier criticized its form— a common reaction to religion. Those who have not the capacity to criticize Christ resort to violence. They made Him an outlaw. In all meekness, Our Blessed Lord answered him:

> If I spoke amiss, state it in evidence; if I spoke well, why strike me?
> *John 18:23*

With one breath, Our Lord might have hurled the offender into eternity, but since He was to be stricken for the transgressions of men and to be bruised for their iniquities, He would accept that first blow in patience. But at the same time, He bade the man to testify, if possible, against Him so that there might be a reason for the violence. Our Lord once said that when struck we should turn the other cheek. Did He? Yes! He turned His whole Body to be crucified.

Failing to convict Him out of His own mouth on either His doctrine or His disciples, they now hoped to do so by the testimony of false witnesses:

> The chief priests and the whole Council tried to find some allegation against Jesus on which a death-sentence could be based; but they failed to find one, though many came forward with false evidence.
> *Matthew 26:59*

Now anxious to put Him to death rather than to judge justly, they summoned false witnesses who contradicted one another. Finally two witnesses came forward with conflicting testimony. One of them quoted Him as saying:

> I will pull down this temple, made with human hands, and in three days I will build another, not made with hands.   *Mark 14:58*

These words were a perversion of those which Our Blessed Lord spoke at the beginning of His public ministry when He referred to what was now beginning to take place. After driving the buyers and sellers out of the temple, the Pharisees asked Him for a sign of His authority. Our Lord, referring to the temple of His Body said:

> Destroy this temple and in three days I will raise it again. *John 2:19*

Now the false witnesses claimed that Jesus had said that He would destroy the temple; but what He actually had said was that they would destroy it and the temple would be His Body, which had just received a violent blow. Their earthly temple would have its blow too from the hands of the Romans under Titus. He did not say, "I will destroy," but rather, "You will destroy." Nor did He say, "I will build another," but He said, "I will raise it up," referring to His Resurrection. The distortion of His saying was nevertheless a witnessing to the purpose of His coming and a fixing in their minds of His Cross and glory. As the concave and convex of a circle are made by the same line, so their voluntary wickedness and His voluntary suffering are united. Divine purposes will be attained now as they were in Joseph, His prefigurement, who told his brethren who sold him that they intended evil, but that God would make good come from it. In his delivery into the hands of evil, Judas delivered Our Lord to the Jews, the Jews delivered Him to the Gentiles, and the Gentiles crucified Him. But, on the other side of the picture, Our Lord said that the Father had delivered His Son as a ransom for many. Thus the evil but free actions of men are overruled by God, Who can make a fall a *felix culpa*, or a "happy fault."

The Incarnate Word was wordless during the false testimony: Caiphas, annoyed because thwarted by the contradictions, exclaimed:

> By the living God I charge you to tell us: Are you the Messiah, the Son of God? *Matthew 26:63*

Caiphas here addressed Our Lord in his capacity as high priest or minister of God, and put Christ under an oath to make an answer. Caiphas raised no question about the destruction of the temple or His disciples. The question was: Was He the Christ or the Messiah; was He the Son of God; was He clad with Divine power; was He the Word made flesh? Was it true that God, Who has at sundry times and in diverse manners spoken to us through the prophets, in these last days has spoken to us through His Son? Art Thou the Son of God? Jesus opened His mouth and said two words:

> I am. *Mark 14:62*

With sublime consciousness and majestic dignity, He answered that He was the Messiah and the Son of the Living God. There was a hidden allusion to the name by which God revealed Himself to Moses. Then, passing from His Divine nature to His human nature, He added:

> I tell you this: from now on, you will see the Son of Man seated at the right hand of God and coming on the clouds of heaven.
>
> *Matthew 26:64*

First He affirmed His Divinity, then His humanity; but both under the personal pronoun "I." In the hour when the greatest indignities were heaped upon Him, He gave testimony of being at the right hand of God, whence He will come on the last day. But if He would sit at the right hand of the Father He would ascend into heaven; if He was

to have a Second Coming, it would be to weigh on the scales the reception souls gave to His First Coming, "His humbled existence on
earth." Our Lord was also referring to Psalm 109, which predicted the
exaltation of the Son of God after His humiliation, when He will
make His enemies His footstool. Despite the certain condemnation
facing Him, He permitted His glory to shine forth amidst the civil injustice as He proclaimed His triumph, His reign, and the fact that He
would judge the world. The Psalmist had already prophesied what He
had spoken and Daniel more clearly had foretold:

> I was still watching in visions of the night and I saw one like a man
> coming with the clouds of heaven; he approached the Ancient in Years
> and was presented to him. Sovereignty and glory and kingly power
> were given to him, so that all people and nations of every language
> should serve him; his sovereignty was to be an everlasting sovereignty
> which should not pass away, and his kingly power such as should never
> be impaired. *Daniel 7:13,14*

A few years after this trial, as Stephen was being martyred and as he
fell crushed beneath the weight of stones, He saw what Christ now
said to Caiphas:

> Look, there is a rift in the sky; I can see the Son of Man standing at
> God's right hand. *Acts 7:55*

A storm broke over His head as the Sanhedrin heard Him admit
His Divinity. The clock was about to strike twelve; the first trial
ended as the high priest rendered his decision that He was guilty of
blasphemy:

> At these words the High Priest tore his robes and exclaimed, Blas-
> phemy! *Matthew 26:65*

It was customary with the Hebrews to rend their garments as a manifestation of great grief and pain, as Jacob rent his garments when he
received news of the death of his son Joseph, and as David rent his
clothes at hearing of the death of Saul. In tearing off his garments,
Caiphas was actually stripping off his priesthood, putting an end to
the priesthood of Aaron and opening the way to the priesthood of
Melchisedech. The robes of priesthood were rent and destroyed by the
hands of the high priest himself, but the veil of the temple would be
rent by the hand of God. Caiphas rent from bottom to top as was the
custom; God rent the veil from top to bottom, for no man had a
share in it. Caiphas now asked the Sanhedrin:

> Need we call further witnesses? You have heard the blasphemy. What
> is your opinion? Their judgement was unanimous; that he was guilty
> and should be put to death. *Mark 14:63,64*

The conclusion was quickly reached; the Prisoner had blasphemed God. Life itself must taste death. But His death was determined precisely because He had proclaimed His Eternal Divinity. Caiphas before had said that it was useful that one man should die rather than that the Romans should, more than ever, take over the nation. Now he and the Sanhedrin took a different position; shifting from the utilitarian and the legal, they argued that His death was necessary to preserve the spiritual unity existing between God and His people. The Sanhedrin divested itself of the responsibility for the charge by invoking God against God.

Now that He was condemned as a blasphemer, all things were allowable, for He had no rights.

> Then they spat in his face and struck him with their fists; and others said, as they beat him, Now, Messiah, if you are a prophet, tell us who hit you. *Matthew 26:67,68*

They covered His face and thus shut out the light of heaven; and yet in covering His eyes, it was their own they blinded. The veil was really on their hearts, not on His eyes. They who were so proud of their earthly temple now buffeted the Heavenly Temple, for in Him dwelt the fullness of the Godhead. They used the title "Christ" sarcastically; but they were more right than they knew, for He was the Messiah, the Anointed of God.

Caiphas had obtained what he wanted, namely, to convict Christ by His own words of blasphemy, for He had claimed to be the Son of God by nature. The inquiry was whether or not He was both the Messiah and the Son of God, who had been foretold by the prophets. It was Christ the Prophet, therefore, Who was on trial before Caiphas; it would be Christ the King Who would be on trial before Pilate; and it would be Christ the Priest who would be disowned on the Cross as He offered His life in sacrifice. In each instance, there would be mockery of His office. Here the mockery was directed to Christ the Prophet in fulfillment of the prophecy of Isaiah:

> I offered my back to the lash,
>   and let my beard be plucked from my chin,
> I did not hide my face from spitting and insult.
>   *Isaiah 50:6*

The religious trial was over. The Son of God was found guilty of blasphemy; the Resurrection and the Life was sentenced to the grave; the eternal High Priest was condemned "by the high priest for a year." It is now the Sanhedrin that mocked Him; next it will be the Roman Empire, and then at the Cross it will be both combined. But now that the Sanhedrin had found Him guilty, it proceeded to deliver Him over to Pilate, thinking that he who alone had authority to put Christ to death would do so without hesitation. The prophecy that He would be delivered up to the Gentiles was now fulfilled. But as Judas brought on himself the death he had prepared for Christ, so Caiphas in deciding to put Christ to death out of fear of the Romans, merely prepared for the ultimate destruction of the city of Jerusalem and the temple. As the people gave up Christ to the Romans, so were they later given up to the Roman power.

44. The Denials of Peter

When Our Lord was arrested, Peter followed Him afar off; with him was John. They both went to the house of Annas and Caiphas where Our Lord was tried. The house of the high priest, where the trial was held, was like many Oriental houses built around a quadrangular court, the entrance to which was gained by a passage from the front part of the house. This passage or archway was a porch closed to the street by a heavy gate. The gate, on this occasion, was kept by a maid of the high priest. The interior court to which the passage led was covered with flagstones and open to the sky. The night was cold, for it was early in April. Peter had already failed the Lord in the garden by sleeping; now he had a chance to undo his failure. But danger lurked for Peter, first of all because of his exaggerated self-confidence in his own loyalty. Though an ancient prophet had told that the sheep would be dispersed, Peter felt that, because he was given the keys of the Kingdom of Heaven, he might be dispensed from such a collapse. A second danger was his previous failure when he was bidden to "watch and to pray." He did not watch, for he fell asleep; he did not pray, for he substituted activism for spirituality by swinging a sword. A third danger was that the physical distance he kept from Christ might have been a symbol of the spiritual distance that separated the two. Any distance from the sun of righteousness is darkness.

When Peter entered the courtyard, he began to warm himself by the fire. In the light of the flame, the maiden who had let him in the gate was better able to see his face. If the challenge to Peter's loyalty had come from a sword or from a man, he possibly might have been stronger; but hampered by his pride, a young woman proved too strong for the presumptuous Peter. Christ's plan was to conquer by suffering; Peter's plan was to conquer by resisting. But here there was little obvious opposition. Thrown off guard by the maid, he made his first denial. The maidservant said to him:

You were there too with Jesus the Galilean. *Matthew 26:69*

To everyone round about the fire, Peter answered:

I do not know what you mean. *Matthew 26:70*

Peter began to feel uncomfortable in what seemed to him like the searchlight of a flame that was examining his soul as well as exploring his face; so he moved a little distance toward the porch. Anxious to escape from enquiring faces and busy tongues, he felt safer in the retirement of the darkness of the porch. The same or possibly another maid came to him affirming that he had been with Jesus of Nazareth, and he denied it again this time by invoking an oath saying:

I do not know the man. *Matthew* 26:72

He who had drawn the sword in defense of the Master a few hours before now denied the One Whom he had sought to defend. He who had called his Master "the Son of the living God," now calls Him the "man."

More time passed, and his Savior was accused of blasphemy and delivered over to the brutality of the attendants; but Peter was still surrounded. Though it was midnight or thereafter, the crowds probably swelled at the news of the trial of Our Blessed Lord. Among those that were standing by was a kinsman of Malchus, who distinctly remembered that Peter had cut off the ear of his relative in the garden and that the Lord had restored it. Peter, all the while anxious to cover up his nervousness and to pretend more than ever that he knew not the man, became evidently very garrulous; and this gave him away. His provincial accent showed that he was a Galilean; it was generally known that most of the adherents of Our Lord had come from that area, which lacked the polished dialect of Judea and Jerusalem. There were certain guttural letters which the Galileans could not pronounce, and immediately one of the bystanders said:

Surely you are another of them; your accent gives you away! *Matthew* 26:73

Peter invoked an oath, and now:

At this he broke into curses and declared with an oath: I do not know the man. *Matthew* 26:74

By this time Peter was enraged, so he invoked the Omnipotent God to witness his reiterated untruth. One wonders if there was not a kind of throwback to his fisherman days; perhaps when his net became tangled in the Sea of Galilee, his temper had often got the better of him and he had resorted to blasphemy. In any case, he now swore in order to force belief on the incredulous.

Memories of the past rushed in on him. The Lord had called him "blessed" as He gave him the keys of the Kingdom of Heaven, and permitted him to see His glory in the Transfiguration. Now in the chilly morn as the consciousness of guilt mounted in his soul, he heard an unexpected sound:

At that moment the cock crew. *Matthew* 26:74

Even nature itself protested the denial of Christ. Then there flashed across his mind the words which Jesus had said:

> Before the cock crows you will disown me three times.
> *Matthew 26:75*

At this moment, Our Blessed Lord was led from the scourging, His face covered with spittle:

> The Lord turned and looked at Peter. *Luke 22:61*

Though bound shamefully, the Master's eye sought out Peter with boundless pity. He said nothing; He just looked. The look probably was a refreshment of memory and an awakening of love. Peter might deny the "man," but God would still love the man Peter. The very fact that the Lord had to turn to look on Peter, meant that Peter's back had been turned on the Lord. The wounded stag was seeking the thicket to bleed alone, but the Lord came to Peter's wounded heart to draw out the arrow.

> (Peter) went outside, and wept bitterly. *Luke 22:62*

Peter was now filled with repentance, as Judas in a few hours would be filled with remorse. Peter's sorrow was caused by the thought of sin itself or the wounding of the Person of God. Repentance is not concerned with consequences; but remorse is inspired principally by fear of consequences. The same mercy extended to the one who denied Him would be extended to those who would nail Him to the Cross and to the penitent thief who would ask for forgiveness. Peter really did not deny that Christ was the Son of God. He denied that he knew "the man," or that he was one of His disciples. But he failed the Master. And yet, knowing all, the Son of God made Peter, who knew sin, and not John, the Rock upon which He built His Church that sinners and the weak might never despair.

45. Trial Before Pilate

The trial of Christ the Prophet was over; now began the trial of
Christ the King. The religious judges had found Our Lord too Divine
because He had called Himself God; now the civil judges will condemn Him for being too human. When a higher court hears a case
presented to it by a lower court, there is a continuity of charges. The
religious judges did not have the power of life and death, since the
Romans had conquered their land. It was to be expected, therefore,
that when Our Blessed Lord was led before the superior court of
Pilate, exactly the same charge would be filed against Him, namely,
blasphemy. The approval and sentence of death required, however,
the seal of Pilate. There were two ways in which the Sanhedrin could
have done this: either by Pilate accepting the judgment of the religious court, or by opening a new trial in the civil court of their
conquerors. The second was the method chosen, and shrewdly
enough. The Sanhedrin knew very well that Pilate would laugh at
them, if they told him that Christ was guilty of blasphemy. They had
their God; he had his gods. Furthermore, since this was a purely
religious charge, Pilate might have referred it back to their own court
without sentencing Christ to death.

In order to understand the relationship between the conquered and
the conqueror, a word must be said about Pilate and the Jewish
hatred of him. Pilate, the sixth Roman procurator of Judea since the
conquest, had held his office for some ten years during the reign of
the Emperor Tiberius. His arbitrary and sometimes cruel conduct had
led to repeated uprisings by the Jews which he had suppressed with violent measures. The people of Jerusalem despised him not only because he was the representative of the Roman Emperor and was not
of their own race but also because he once caused painted portraits of
the Emperor to be brought by night into Jerusalem and set up in the
temple. Pilate threatened to slay the Jews with swords if they
protested this act; but the Jews offered their necks to Pilate and complained to Tiberius. The result was that the emblems were removed.
It was Herod Antipas who brought the petition of the Jews to
Tiberius. This might have been the reason for the friction which
existed between Pilate and Herod.

Another reason why Pilate was hated was that he had confiscated
some treasury funds, which he used for building an aqueduct. Some

Jews from Galilee were murdered in a disturbance during its building, and it could have been during some such riot as this that Barabbas was arrested as a leader of the rioters and a robber besides. Pilate had to be very careful about his position in Rome, since Rome had on one occasion failed to sustain him in his action against the Jews.

Very early in the morning, all the members of the Sanhedrin—including the priests, elders, and Scribes—decided to bring Christ to Pilate and ask for the death sentence. The priests were indignant when He had spoken of Himself as the Lamb of God; the elders were offended because, as opposed to their fixed traditionalism, He affirmed that He was the Word of God; the Scribes hated Him because He opposed the letter of the word and promised the Spirit that would illumine it. After completing plans for putting Him to death:

> They then put him in chains and led him off, to hand him over to Pilate, the Roman Governor. *Matthew 27:2*

Several times Our Lord had been bound, when they first seized Him and when He was led into the courts of Annas and Caiphas. Putting Him in fetters for Pilate to see would create the impression that He had committed some fearful crime. Leading Him away to Pilate was one of the turning points in the Passion, for it fulfilled the prophecy that Our Blessed Lord had uttered:

> He will be handed over to the foreign power. He will be mocked, maltreated, and spat upon. They will flog him and kill him. And on the third day he will rise again. *Luke 18:32,33*

The Sanhedrin led Him away because they had rejected the promise of Salvation that came from the Messiah; now it remained for the Gentiles to decide what they would do, whether they would reject the King as the Sanhedrin had rejected the Prophet. The great wall between the Jew and the Gentile was eventually broken down, since both condemned Him to death. As St. Paul wrote:

> Gentiles and Jews, he has made the two one, and in his own body of flesh and blood has broken down the enmity which stood like a dividing wall between them. *Ephesians 2:14*

Thus the responsibility for His death cannot be put upon any one people, but upon all mankind:

> The whole world may be exposed to the judgement of God.
> *Romans 3:19*

The Sanhedrin—which had scruples about using the Judas money that purchased blood—also had scruples about entering the house of a Gentile, in this case, that of Pilate. In bringing the Divine Prisoner to

Pilate, there was one thing the sensitive consciences of the Sanhedrin members feared—defilement. Pilate was a Gentile; to enter his praetorium would defile them so that they could not celebrate the Passover. They had to keep themselves pure in order to shed the innocent blood of the Passover Lamb. On this account they preferred to shed the innocent Blood of the Lamb of God rather than step over a Gentile's threshold. Our Lord had once called the Pharisees "whitened sepulchres," because, like whitewashed tombs, they were clean on the outside, but on the inside were filled with dead men's bones. The judgment was now fulfilled in their dread of contamination with uncircumcised flesh while living with uncircumcised hearts. There were other scruples too; if they entered a house from which all leaven had not been removed, they could not partake of the Passover.

When the officials of the Sanhedrin arrived at the praetorium (or the house of the Governor), Pilate went out to meet them, for he knew that they would consider themselves unclean if forced to come in. Carrying on the Roman tradition of respect for law, he declared that he would not pass sentence unless the evidence showed the accused to be guilty. So he asked the Sanhedrin:

> What charge do you bring against this man? *John* 18:29

In order to capture Pilate's good will, they invited him to trust the judgment that they had already pronounced. Furthermore, they assured Pilate that they would certainly never do anything wrong to an innocent man:

> If he were not a criminal, we should not have brought him before you.
> *John* 18:30

Nothing was said about blasphemy. They knew that charge would be useless before a Gentile, a conqueror, and one whom they despised; so they used the general term "malefactor." And here they were more right than they knew, for Christ was indeed a malefactor or one "bearing the sins of many."

Pilate, knowing their status under Rome was not such as to protect his authority and not wishing to handle the case, told them to judge Him according to their own law. But they answered that they had no power to put any man to death—which indeed was true, since that belonged to Rome. Furthermore, they did not dare put anyone to death on the feast day when they sacrificed the Paschal Lamb.

They now brought three charges against Our Lord in order to force Pilate to hear the case:

> We found this man subverting our nation, opposing the payment of taxes to Caesar, and claiming to be Messiah, a king. *Luke* 23:2

Still no mention of blasphemy; the charge now was sedition; Christ was unpatriotic, He was too worldly, He was too political, He was anti-Caesar, anti-Rome. In short, He was a deceiver who was inducing people to follow another direction than that dictated by Rome. Secondly, He was urging the people not to pay taxes to the king or to Caesar. And thirdly, He was setting Himself up as a rival king to Pilate; this was an abuse of majesty. The Romans, they said, must be on their guard against this political upstart. They even spoke of "the loyalty of our people" to Rome, whereas in their hearts they really despised Pilate and Rome.

Every word was a lie. If Christ had been a ringleader of sedition or if there had been any signs of insurrection connected with His name, Pilate would have heard of it. So would have suspicious Herod; but never had the slightest complaint been brought against Him previously. As for the charge that He had failed to give tribute to Caesar, only a short time before when an attempt was made to entrap Him in the temple, He had told the people "to render to Caesar the things that are Caesar's." The third charge—that He was king—was not that He had made Himself King of the Jews, but rather that He was a king that challenged Caesar. This too was a lie, because when the people sought to make Him that kind of king, He fled into the mountains alone.

Pilate suspected their sincerity because He knew how much the Jews hated him and Caesar. But one charge worried him slightly. Was this Prisoner before him a king? Pilate summoned Our Lord inside the house. Once in the judgment hall, Pilate asked:

Are you king of the Jews? *John 18:33*

The charge was only that He was a king. Pilate knew that if Christ was setting Himself up as a rival king to the Romans, the Gentiles would be there to testify against Him. So he asked if He were King of the Jews. Our Lord in answer to the question penetrated the conscience of Pilate; He asked him if he was saying that because his suspicions had been aroused by the false charge of His enemies. Pilate had expected a direct answer. Our Lord now made clear that a distinction had to be made between a political and religious kingship; political kingship, which was the only interest Pilate had in the case, the Master rejected; religious Kingship which meant that He was the Messiah, Our Lord admitted. To the skeptical Pilate, Our Blessed Lord had to make clear that His Kingship was not that of an earthly kingdom obtained by military power; it was rather a spiritual Kingdom to be established in truth. He would have only moral subjects, not political ones; He would reign in hearts, not in armies.

> My kingdom does not belong to this world. If it did, my followers
> would be fighting to save me from arrest by the Jews. My kingly au-
> thority comes from elsewhere. *John 18:36*

Pilate's worry about a challenge to Roman power was, for the moment, put at ease. Christ's Kingdom was not of this world; therefore
He was not like Judas the Galilean, the son of Ezechias, who had led
a rebellion against Rome a few decades before by inciting the people
not to pay taxes. Pilate may have heard that the night before, when
Peter had argued with the sword, Our Lord had reprimanded the
wielder of the weapon and had healed the injured man. If His Kingdom were of the world, Our Lord argued, He would need the help of
armies of men; but a Heavenly Kingdom was sufficient unto itself, for
its power came from above. His Kingdom was in the world, but not of
it.

The quiet and dignified bearing of the One before him so helplessly
bound with ropes—His face marred with the beatings after the first
trial, His assertion that His Kingdom was not of this world, that He
had servants who would not use the sword, and that He was to establish a Kingdom without fighting—all this puzzled Pilate, who changed
his question. The first time Pilate had asked, "Art Thou King of the
Jews?" Now he asked:

> You are a king, then? *John 18:37*

The religious trial centered on Christ the Prophet, the Messiah, the
Son of God. The civil trial revolved about His Kingship. Strange how
the Gentiles were associated with Christ under this royal title! The
Magi at His birth asked where the King was born; it was the imperial
edict of Caesar that fulfilled the prophecy of Micheas that He would
be born in Bethlehem.

Pilate, satisfied that Christ was not a political rival, in wonderment
prodded a little deeper into the mystery of His Kingly claim. Our
Lord, having already avowed His Kingly state, acknowledged the infer-
ence which Pilate had somewhat scornfully drawn and answered:

> King is your word. My task is to bear witness to the truth. For this was
> I born; for this I came into the world, and all who are not deaf to
> truth listen to my voice. *John 18:37*

All during Our Lord's life He had spoken of Himself as coming into
this world; this was the only time that He ever spoke of being born.
Being born of a woman is one fact, coming into the world is another.
But He immediately followed up this reference to His human birth
with the reaffirmation that He had come into the world. When He
said that He was born, He was acknowledging His human temporal
origin as the Son of Man; when He said He came into the world, He

affirmed His Divinity. Furthermore, He Who came from heaven, came to bear witness, which meant to die for the truth. He laid down the moral condition of discovering truth and affirmed that it was not only an intellectual quest; what one discovered depended in part on one's moral behavior. It was in this sense, Our Lord said once, that His sheep heard His voice. Pilate evidently caught the idea that moral conduct had something to do with the discovery of truth, so he resorted to pragmatism and utilitarianism, and sneered the question:

What is truth? *John 18:38*

Then he turned his back on truth—better not on it, but on Him Who is Truth. It remained to be seen that tolerance of truth and error in a stroke of broadmindedness leads to intolerance and persecution; "What is truth?" when sneered, is followed up with the second sneer, "What is justice?" Broadmindedness, when it means indifference to right and wrong, eventually ends in a hatred of what is right. He who was so tolerant of error as to deny an Absolute Truth was the one who would crucify Truth. It was the religious judge who challenged Him, "I adjure thee"; but the secular judge asked, "What is truth?" He who was in the robe of the high priest called upon God to repudiate the things that are God's; he who was in the Roman toga just professed a skepticism and doubt.

When Our Lord said that everyone that is of the truth would hear His voice, He enunciated the law that truth assimilates all that is congenial to itself. The same idea He had told Nicodemus:

Bad men all hate light and avoid it, for fear their practices should be shown up. The honest man comes to the light so that it may be clearly seen that God is in all he does. *John 3:20,21*

If therefore, the impulse toward truth was in Pilate, he would know that Truth Itself stood before him; if it was not in him, he would sentence Christ to death.

Pilate was one of those who believed that truth was not objective but subjective, that each man determined for himself what was to be true. It is often the fault of practical men, such as Pilate, to regard the search for objective truth as useless theorizing. Skepticism is not an intellectual position; it is a moral position, in the sense that it is determined not so much by reason as by the way one acts and behaves. Pilate's desire to save Jesus was due to a kind of liberalism which combined disbelief in Absolute Truth with a half-benevolent unwillingness to disturb such dreamers and their superstitions. Pilate asked the question, "What is truth?" of the only Person in the world Who could answer it in all its fullness.

Pilate now began the first of several attempts to rescue Christ, such as a declaration of His innocence, a choice between prisoners, a scourging, an appeal to sympathy, a change of judges. Pilate, not understanding how anyone could die for truth, naturally could not understand how Truth Itself could die for those who erred. After turning his back upon the *Logos Incarnate*, he carried to the people outside his conviction that the Prisoner before him was innocent.

> I find no case against him.   *John 18:38*

If there was no fault in Him, Pilate should have released Him. On hearing the Roman Governor's declaration that the Prisoner was innocent, the members of the Sanhedrin became more violent in their accusation that He was an insurrectionist and revolutionist:

> His teaching is causing disaffection among the people all through Judea. It started from Galilee and has spread as far as this city.
>
> *Luke 23:5*

Pilate's supreme interest was the peace of the state; hence the supreme interest of the Sanhedrin was to prove that Christ was a disturber of the peace. As soon as Pilate heard the word "Galilee," he saw an escape from judging Christ. . . . As the Sanhedrin had changed the charge from blasphemy to sedition, so Pilate would turn over jurisdiction of the trial to one who had power in Galilee.

Herod, by reason of the Passover, was now in Jerusalem. Though he and Herod were enemies, Pilate nevertheless was anxious to shift the responsibility of acquitting or condemning Christ to Herod.

TRIAL BEFORE HEROD

This Herod was Herod Antipas, the son of Herod the Great, who had caused all the male children under two years of age to be murdered at Bethlehem. Herod's family was Idumaean, that is to say, descendants from Esau, the father of Edom. It was the seed of Esau which seemed to carry on enmity against the seed of Jacob. Herod Antipas was the uncle of Herod Agrippa who later on slew James the Apostle, and would have slain Peter, if Peter had not been miraculously delivered from prison. Herod was a sensual, worldly man; he had murdered John the Baptist because John condemned him for divorcing his wife and living with his brother's wife. Herod had an uneasy conscience, not only because he had slain the announcer of Christ but also because his superstitions made him believe that John the Baptist had risen and was haunting his soul.

When Our Lord was brought to Herod:

> When Herod saw Jesus he was greatly pleased; having heard about him. He had long been wanting to see him, and had been hoping to see some miracle performed by him.   *Luke 23:8*

The Savior Who had never worked a miracle on His own behalf would certainly not work one now to release Himself. But the frivolous tetrarch, who regarded the Prisoner in the way an audience might regard a juggler, looked for the thrill of some brief moment of magic. As a Sadducee, he did not believe in a future life; and as a man entirely devoted to licentiousness, he identified religion and magic. Herod was the type of man who was curious about religion, studying, reading and sometimes knowing it well, but he also kept his vices. That is why he asked Our Lord many questions. Although the Scribes and the chief priests joined Herod in goading Our Lord, He refused to speak to Herod. If He had spoken, He would only have added to the guilt of the moral trifler. The temptation to accept all the kingdoms of the world by compromising the Cross was once more presented to the Savior. Pilate He could have won—and Herod too with a word— but He refused to speak. He had warned about preaching to those who were insincere in the Sermon on the Mount:

> Do not give dogs what is holy; do not throw your pearls to the pigs:
> they will only trample on them, and turn and tear you to pieces.
>
> *Matthew 7:6*

Religion is not to be given to everyone, but only to those who are "of the truth." Though Herod was glad to see Our Lord, his gladness did not arise from noble motives of repentance. Hence, the Christ, Who spoke to a penitent thief and to Magdalen and Judas, would not speak to the Galilean king, for Herod's conscience was dead. He was too familiar with religion. He wanted miracles, not as motives of credibility, but as delights to his curiosity. His soul was so blinded by appeals, including even the Baptist's, that one more appeal would have only deepened his guilt. It was not his soul for salvation that Herod offered the Lord, but only his nerves for titillation. So the Lord of the world spoke not a word to the worldling. The Book of Proverbs expressed well the Divine attitude to Herod:

> When they call upon me, I will not answer them; when they search
> for me, they shall not find me. Because they hate knowledge and have
> not chosen to fear the LORD. *Proverbs 1:28*

The silence of Our Lord so irritated Herod that his insulted pride turned to scoffing and mockery:

> Then Herod and his troops treated him with contempt and ridicule,
> and sent him back to Pilate dressed in a gorgeous robe. *Luke 23:11*

The voice that commanded that the head of John the Baptist be given to the daughter of Herodias now commanded that the white garment of humiliation be draped about the shoulders of the Prisoner.

The robe that was put upon Him was probably a white robe as a mockery of His claim to be a King. All candidates for public office in Rome wore a *toga candida* or white robe, from which comes the word "candidate." Thus Herod intimated that the pretended King was worthy of contempt, but the white robe was unwittingly also a declaration of innocence.

It is the way of the world for those who have small hates to bury them for the sake of a higher hate. Nazism and Communism united because of a common hatred of God; so did Pilate and Herod:

> That same day Herod and Pilate became friends; till then there had been a standing feud between them. *Luke 23:12*

Pharisaism and Sadduceeism, which were enemies, united in the Crucifixion. The Cross of Christ unites His friends—that is obvious; but the Cross also unites His enemies. The worldly always drop their lesser hates in the face of the hatred of the Divine. It was a good joke, this Prisoner covered with His own Blood, hated by His own people, claiming to be a King. Herod could trust Pilate to see the humor of it. When Pilate and he would laugh over it together, they would no longer be enemies—even when the butt of the humor was God. The only time laughter is wicked is when it is turned against Him Who gave it. One wonders if, as Herod sent the Divine Prisoner back to Pilate to be condemned, he remembered that the Lord had said that He would die in Jerusalem, not Galilee. After the Ascension and the Descent of the Holy Spirit, when Peter and John would be led before judges for preaching Christ and Him Crucified, those who were in their company sent up the first prayer of the Christian Church. In that prayer these two judges would be mentioned together; so would the Jews and Gentiles, for the whole world that shared in His condemnation shared or would share in His Redemption.

> They did indeed make common cause in this very city against thy holy servant Jesus whom thou didst anoint as Messiah. Herod and Pontius Pilate conspired with the Gentiles and peoples of Israel to do all the things which, under thy hand and by thy decree, were foreordained. And now, O Lord, mark their threats, and enable thy servants to speak thy word with all boldness. *Acts 4:27–29*

46. At the Bottom of the List

In the meantime, what happened to Judas? Only Judas knew where to find Our Lord after dark. The soldiers did not know, and therefore they had to be given a sign. Christ was delivered into the hands of His enemies from within. The greatest harm that is done is not always from the enemies, but from those who have been cradled in His sacred associations. It is the failure of those within that provides opportunities for enemies who are still without. The enemies will do the bloody work of Crucifixion, but those who have had the faith and lost it and who are anxious to salve their consciences by destroying the root of moralities commit the greater evil.

The hatred of Judas against Our Blessed Lord was due to the contrast between his sin and the virtue of the Divine Master. Iago says of Cassio: "He hath a daily beauty in his life that makes me ugly." Judas' disgust with himself was vented on One Who made him uncomfortable by His Goodness. The hatred against Divinity is not the result always of unbelief, but very often the effect of antibelief. Conscience, Christ, and the gift of faith make evil men uneasy in their sin. They feel that if they could drive Christ from the earth, they would be free from "moral inhibitions." They forget that it is their own nature and conscience which make them feel that way. Being unable to drive God from the heavens, they would drive His ambassadors from the earth. In a lesser sphere, that is why many men sneer at virtue—because it makes vice uncomfortable. A chaste face is a judgment. Judas was more zealous in the cause of his enemies than he ever was in the cause of Our Lord. When men leave Christ, they seek to redeem their reputation by going to extremes.

The betrayal took place with a kiss. When wickedness would destroy virtue and when man would crucify the Son of God, there is felt a necessity to preface the evil deed by some mark of affection. Judas would compliment and deny Divinity with the same lips. Only one word came back in answer to the kiss: "Friend." It was the last time Our Lord spoke to Judas. For the moment, he was not the traitor but a friend. He had had the right to the fatted calf, but he had rejected it.

When Judas the traitor saw that Jesus had been condemned, he was seized with remorse, and returned the thirty silver pieces to the chief priests and elders. I have sinned, he said; I have brought an innocent man to his death.   *Matthew* 27:3

Though in English we have both Peter and Judas "repenting," the Greek words used in the original are different for Judas and for Peter. The word used in connection with Judas signifies only a change of feeling, a regret of the consequences, a desire of undoing what had been done. This kind of repentance did not ask for pardon, for even the devils in hell repented the consequences of their sin of pride. The reason for his betrayal of Christ now seemed utterly evil and base; the political Messiah whom he expected now seemed unworthy of thought. Before a sin, the devil makes light of it; after the sin, the devil becomes an accuser inciting despair and worse crimes in the guilty. Evidently the devil "left him for a time," which gave Judas time to regret his action and to return the money. But later the devil returned to drive him to despair.

The condemnation of Our Lord produced a double effect: one on Judas, the other on the chief priests of the Sanhedrin. On Judas, it produced the bondage of guilt through the agony of his conscience. The thirty pieces of silver within his purse were weighing him down; he ran to the temple, took the shekels from the money bag and threw them mockingly across the pavement floor of the Holy Place. To get rid of the very advantage of his betrayal was a sign that he was none the richer for the thing that he had gained, and infinitely poorer because of the way he had gained it.

No one has ever denied Christ or sold Him for any fleeting pleasure or temporary recompense, without realizing that he has bartered Him away out of all proportion to His due worth. Judas seemed to be getting so much when the bargain was struck. Afterward, he took the money back to the temple and threw the silver coins jingling and rolling across the floor, because he no longer wanted what he had bargained for. He had cheated himself. The fruits of sin never compensate for the loss of grace. The money was good for nothing now except to buy a field of blood.

Those who were associated with him in the crime now attempted to shake off the responsibility for the common act. One of the punishments in concerted sin is mutual recrimination; whenever men band together to do evil against a good man, they always end by falling out with one another. However, in the case of Judas, we find the reversal of the usual conduct of evil characters. The greater the wrong, the more reluctant one is to admit that it had no justification. Evil men, in order to appear innocent, load accusations of guilt on those whom they have wronged. If there was anything that would have justified the sin of Judas, he certainly would have seized on it and exaggerated it in order to cover up his perfidy and his shame. But Judas himself pronounced Our Lord innocent. He who had once complained about the waste of Mary's precious ointment now wasted his thirty pieces of silver by throwing them away. Could not the money have been given to the poor? Judas no longer thought of them. The shekels lay in the temple where Judas had thrown them. The chief priests hated both them and Judas, their miserable tool. He tried to throw responsibility on the Sanhedrin; they tossed it back in his face. Without in any way confessing to the Divinity of His Master, he, nevertheless, condemned himself. As Cain asked, "Am I my brother's keeper?" so they disdained sympathy for their own accomplice.

But the money must not be left on the temple floor, and so the chief priests gathered it up, saying:

> Taking up the money, the chief priests argued: This cannot be put into the temple fund; it is blood-money. So after conferring they used it to buy the Potter's Field, as a burial-place for foreigners. This explains the name Blood Acre, by which that field has been known ever since.
>
> *Matthew 27:6–8*

Judas' fellow conspirators were willing to consult about the money, but not about the innocent man. They should have rejoiced in the confession of Judas, but they discarded him as a useless tool. He was no longer wanted; neither was the money, so it was used to buy a field of blood.

Judas was repentant unto himself, but not unto the Lord. He was disgusted with the effects of his sin, but not with the sin. Everything can be pardoned except the refusal to seek pardon, as life can forgive everything except the acceptance of death. His remorse was only a self-hatred, and self-hatred is suicidal. To hate self is the beginning of slaughter. It is salutary only when associated with the love of God. Repenting to oneself is not enough. Conscience speaks lowest when it ought to speak loudest. It is a lamp which sometimes goes out in darkness.

When a man hates himself for what he has done and is without repentance to God, he will sometimes pound his breast as if to blot out a sin. There is a world of difference between pounding a breast in self-disgust and pounding it with the *mea culpa* in which one asks for pardon. Sometimes this self-hatred can become so intense as even to pound the life out of a man, and thus it leads to suicide. Though death is one of the penalties of original sin and though it is something to be universally dreaded, nevertheless there are some who rush into its arms. A warning conscience came to Judas before the sin, but the gnawing conscience followed after, and it was so great that he could not bear it. Down the valley of Cedron he went—that valley with all of its ghostly associations. Amidst jagged rocks and between gnarled and stunted trees, he was so disgusted with himself that he would empty himself of self. Everything around him seemed to tell of his destiny and his end. Nothing seemed more hideous to his eyes than the gilded roof of the temple, which reminded him of the Temple of God he had sold; every tree seemed the gibbet to which he had sentenced innocent blood; every branch was an accusing finger; the very hill on which he stood overlooked Calvary whereon the One Whom he had sentenced to death would unite heaven and earth; but he would now separate them as much as it was in his power. Throwing a rope over the limb of a tree, he hanged himself as his bowels burst asunder. God can be sold, but He cannot be bought. Judas sold Him, but his evil collaborators could not buy Him, for He was present again in risen glory on Easter.

An interesting parallel can be drawn between Peter and Judas. There are some similarities, and yet such tremendous differences. First, Our Lord called them both "devils." He called Peter "Satan" when he rebuked Him for saying He would be crucified; He called Judas a devil when He promised the Bread of Life. Second, He warned both that they would fall. Peter said that even though others would deny the Master, he would not. Whereupon, he was told that during that very night, before the cock crowed, Peter would deny Him thrice. Judas, in his turn, was warned when offered the dipped bread; and he was also told, in answer to his question, that he was the betrayer. Third, both denied Our Lord: Peter to the maidservants during the night trial; Judas in the garden when he delivered Our Lord to the soldiers. Fourth, Our Lord tried to save both: Peter through a look, and Judas by addressing him as "Friend." Fifth, both repented: Peter went out and wept bitterly; Judas repented by taking back the thirty pieces of silver and affirming the innocence of Our Lord.

Why, then, is one at the head of the list, the other at the bottom? Because Peter repented unto the Lord and Judas unto himself. The difference was as vast as Divine-reference and self-reference; as vast as the difference between a Cross and a psychoanalytic couch. Judas said he had "betrayed innocent blood," but he never wished to be bathed in it. Peter knew he had sinned and sought redemption; Judas knew he had made a mistake and sought escape—the first of the long army of escapists from the Cross. Divine pardon presupposes but never destroys human freedom. One wonders if Judas, as he stood beneath the tree that would bring him death, ever looked around the valley to the tree that would have brought him life. On this difference between repenting unto the Lord and repenting unto self as did Peter and Judas respectively, St. Paul would later comment in these words:

> For the wound which is borne in God's way brings a change of heart too salutary to regret; but the hurt which is borne in the world's way brings death. *II Corinthians* 7:10

The tragedy of the life of Judas is that he might have been St. Judas.

47. Second Trial Before Pilate

Pilate saw the mob, with Our Lord in the midst of them, returning from Herod and approaching his palace. It is so difficult to wash one's hands of Christ. Obliged to sum up the case before the people, Pilate returned to the primary charge that He had been perverting the people, and proclaimed:

> I have myself examined him in your presence and found nothing in him to support your charges. No more did Herod, for he has referred him back to us. Clearly he has done nothing to deserve death.
>
> *Luke 23:14,15*

Apparently both judges were convinced that, regardless of the report that had been circulated, the Prisoner was guiltless. For a second time, He was declared innocent. Pilate, knowing that the Jews had delivered Christ out of envy, sought another escape from condemning Him. The Sanhedrin actually supplied the excuse by reminding him that it was the custom at the Passover to release a prisoner. There was languishing in jail at the time a "notable" prisoner, Barabbas. This man was a leader of the Jewish underground against the Romans. For both sedition and a murder committed while leading a revolution against Rome, he was put in jail.

Pilate was very clever; he sought to confuse the issue by choosing a prisoner who was guilty of exactly the same charge they brought against Christ, namely, sedition against Caesar. In a few minutes, two figures stood before the multitude on the white marble floor of the praetorium. Pilate sat on a raised platform, surrounded by the imperial guard. Barabbas, on one side, blinked in the sunlight. He had not seen it in months. On the other side stood Christ. Here were two men accused of revolution. Barabbas appealed to national grievances; Christ to conscience. The trumpets sounded. Order was restored. Pilate stepped forward and addressed the mob:

> Which would you like me to release to you—Jesus Bar-Abbas, or Jesus called Messiah? *Matthew 27:17*

The question of Pilate had all the air of democracy and free elections, but it was only its cheap facsimile. Ponder his question. Consider first the people to whom it was addressed, then the question itself. The people themselves were not inclined to put Our Lord to death. For that reason some demagogues:

> Meanwhile the chief priests and elders had persuaded the crowd to ask for the release of Bar-Abbas. *Matthew 27:20*

There is always a ragtag, bobtail group, careless and thoughtless, who are ready to be at the mercy of that kind of oratory which has been called "the harlot of the arts." The people can be misled by false leaders; the very ones who shout "Hosanna" on Sunday can shout "Crucify" on Friday.

What happened on that Good Friday morning was that through propagandists the people became the masses. A democracy with a conscience became a mobocracy with power. When a democracy loses its moral sense, it can vote itself right out of democracy. When Pilate asked:

> Which would you like me to release to you? *Matthew 27:17*

he was holding a fair democratic election. He was assuming that a vote means the right to choose between innocence and guilt, goodness and evil, right and wrong.

In answer to Pilate's question the masses thundered back:

> Bar-Abbas. *Matthew 27:22*

Pilate could hardly believe his ears. Barabbas could hardly believe his ears either! Was he about to be a free man? For the first time, he became aware that he might now carry on his revolt. He turned his swollen burning face toward the Nazarene. He meant to measure his rival from head to foot, but his glance no longer dared to rise. There was something about His eyes which read his soul, as if that Nazarene was really sorry for him because he was free.

> But there was a general outcry, Away with him! Give us Barabbas.
> *Luke 23:18*

> Pilate spoke to them again: Then what shall I do with the man you call the king of the Jews? *Mark 15:12*

> Pilate addressed them again, in his desire to release Jesus, but they shouted back, Crucify him, crucify him! *Luke 23:20,21*

> For the third time he spoke to them: Why, what wrong has he done? I have not found him guilty of any capital offence. I will therefore let him off with a flogging. But they insisted on their demand, shouting that Jesus should be crucified. Their shouts prevailed and Pilate decided that they should have their way. He released the man they asked

for, the man who had been put in prison for insurrection and murder, and gave Jesus up to their will. *Luke 23:22-25*

The majority is not always right. Majority is right in the field of the relative, but not in the absolute. Majority is a legitimate test so long as voting is based on conscience and not on propaganda. Truth does not win when numbers alone become decisive. Numbers alone can decide a beauty queen, but not justice. Beauty is a matter of taste, but justice is tasteless. Right is still right if nobody is right, and wrong is still wrong if everybody is wrong. The first poll in the history of Christianity was wrong!

Barabbas was freed because of Christ, political freedom though it was. But it was a symbol that through His death men were to be made free. It happened at Passover time when a lamb was substituted for the people and went to death in atonement for their sins. The Savior should suffer and the sinner go free. The Book of Exodus had proclaimed that the sinner was to be redeemed with a lamb, but the Lamb could not be redeemed. The Savior could not be released, but the sinner could.

Pilate, still anxious not to condemn Christ, with a most peculiar turn of mind said:

I therefore propose to let him off with a flogging. *Luke 23:16*

Scourging was always inflicted by the Romans before crucifixion, but this scourging was not such a punishment. As Lysias later on had no hesitation to scourge Paul without an offense being proved, so Pilate inflicted a punishment in the hope of moving the crowd to pity. Naturally it was no surprise to Our Lord, Who had foretold that He would be scourged and crucified. Pilate had made three attempts thus far to free Our Lord; one by declaring Him innocent, another by releasing a prisoner at the Passover, and the final one by scourging.

THE SCOURGING

Pilate tried to strike a balance between satisfying the Sanhedrin and his own conscience. But Pilate was wrong in thinking that the drawing of blood would calm their passions and melt them to pity. Such compromises in the face of justice rarely achieve their ends. If guilty, Pilate should have condemned Him to death; if innocent, he should have released Him.

Our Lord looked forward to giving His life as a ransom for sin; He had described Himself as having a baptism wherewith He was to be baptized. John gave Him the baptism of water, but the Roman soldiers now gave Him His baptism of blood. After opening His sacred flesh with violent stripes, they now put on Him a purple robe which adhered to His bleeding body. Then they plaited a crown of thorns which they placed on His head. How the soldiers cursed when one thorn plucked their fingers, but how they sneered when the crown of thorns crowned His brow! They then mocked Him and put a reed in His hand after beating Him on the head. Then they knelt down before Him in feigned adoration. As Isaiah had foretold:

> Yet on himself he bore our sufferings,
>   our torments he endured,
> while we counted him smitten by God,
>   struck down by disease and misery;
> but he was pierced for our transgressions,
>   tortured for our iniquities;
> the chastisement he bore is health for us
>   and by his scourging we are healed.   *Isaiah 53:4,5*

After the scourging, Pilate brought the bleeding Christ before the mob saying:

> Here he is; I am bringing him out to let you know that I find no case against him. Behold the Man!   *John 19:4,6*

You see the kind of man that you are accusing. Behold Him not decorated with ermine, with no other crown but thorns, with no other mark of Kingship than red blood and with no other sign of authority than a reed. Be assured that He will never again assume the title of a King which has cost Him so dearly. I had hoped to find some spark of humanity in you, and that is why I yielded to your wishes.

But when the leaders of the people saw Him, they cried out:

> Crucify! crucify!

Pilate said:

> Take him and crucify him yourselves.

The people answered:

> We have a law; and by that law he ought to die, because he has claimed to be Son of God.   *John 19:6,7*

Pilate said that He was a "man"; they said, "the Son of God." Pilate had declared that He was innocent before the Roman law. They answered that He was guilty before their law. When Pilate heard them calling Him "the Son of God":

> He was more afraid than ever.   *John 19:8*

Superstition goes hand in hand with skepticism. Herod did not believe in the Resurrection; nevertheless, when he heard of Our Lord preaching in his territory, he thought that Christ was John the Baptist who was risen from the dead. Pilate did not believe that He was the Son of God; nevertheless, he wondered at this strange Being before him, Who spoke no words in His own defense. Deeply shaken and fearful that probably Christ was some messenger from the gods, Pilate called Him inside to his judgment chamber and said to Him:

Where have you come from?   *John* 19:9

Pilate did not ask, "Who art Thou?" or "Art Thou the Son of God?" but "Whence art Thou?" The Lord's Galilean origin did not interest him, for he had already sent Christ as the Galilean to Herod. He perceived Christ to be something more than a man. If He was really from heaven he would not crucify Him; therefore, he asked privately for His real origin. Pilate had already asked six questions. There remained only one more which he would ask.

But Jesus refused to answer the question. Pilate had already turned his back on truth. Five times during the trial Our Lord had kept a mysterious silence, before the high priest, the Sanhedrin, Herod, and twice before Pilate. The silence might have meant that bearing the sins of the world He had nothing to say in His own defense. When He spoke it was as a shepherd; when He was silent it was as a "sheep," as Isaiah had foretold:

He was afflicted, he submitted to be struck down and did not open his mouth; he was led like a sheep to the slaughter, like a ewe that is dumb before the shearers.   *Isaiah* 53:7

Pilate had treated Christ as a subject of speculation for he availed himself not of the truth before him. To such men, there is no response from the heavens. In the depths of his own mind, Pilate had reached the conviction of innocence, but he did not act upon it. Therefore Pilate deserved no answer and received none. He had forfeited his title to any further revelation from the Prisoner. Every soul has its day of visitation, and Pilate had his.

CLAUDIA

It may have been at this moment that Claudia, the wife of Pilate, sent her message to her husband.

Claudia was the youngest daughter of Julia, the daughter of Caesar Augustus. Julia had been married three times, the last time to Tiberius. Because of her dissolute life, Julia was exiled when she bore Claudia to a Roman knight. When Claudia was thirteen, Julia sent her to be brought up by Tiberius. When she was sixteen, Pontius Pilate, himself of low origin, met Claudia and asked Tiberius for permission to marry her. Thus Pilate married into the Emperor's family, which assured his political future. On the strength of his marriage, Pilate was made the Procurator of Judea.

Roman governors were forbidden to take their wives with them to the provinces. Most politicians were very happy about this, but not Pilate. Love broke a stern Roman law. After Pilate had been in Jerusalem six years, he sent for Claudia who was more than eager to face the loneliness of life away from the capital of the world amidst an unknown and alien people.

We may reasonably conclude that Claudia must have heard of Jesus, perhaps from the Jewish maid who prepared her bath, or the stewards who brought news about Him. She might actually have seen Him, for the Fortress of Antonia where she lived, was near the temple of Jerusalem and Jesus was often there.

She might even have heard His message, and since "No man ever spoke as this man," her own soul was stirred. The very contrast between Him and His ideas of the world she knew and the thoughts she thought, deepened His appeal. How little did the women of Jerusalem who saw Claudia looking out through the lattice, who tried to catch the flash of gems on her white hands, or mark the pride of her patrician face, ever guess how deep were her thoughts, how intense her sorrow, how profound her yearning?

There was almost a Prussian submission to law among the Romans. No woman was allowed to interfere in the processes of law, nor even to offer a suggestion concerning legal procedure. What made Claudia's entrance onto the scene all the more remarkable is that she sent a message to her husband Pontius Pilate the very day he was deciding the most important case of his career, and the only one for which he ever would be remembered—the trial of Our Blessed Lord.

To send a message to a judge while he was in court was a punishable offense, and only the awfulness of the deed she saw about to be done could have moved Claudia to it.

> While Pilate was sitting in court a message came to him from his wife:
> Have nothing to do with that innocent man; I was much troubled on
> his account in my dreams last night.   *Matthew 27:19*

While the women of Israel were silent, this heathen woman bore witness to the innocence of Jesus, and asked her husband to deal with Him in a righteous way.

The message of Claudia was an epitome of all that Christianity would do for pagan womanhood. She is the only Roman woman in the Gospels and she is a woman of the very highest rank. This dream was an epitome of the dreams and longings of a pagan world, its age-long hope for a righteous man—a Savior.

What the dream was we know not, but a modern writer, Gertrud von Le Fort, has guessed at it. Good Friday morning, as Claudia awoke, she seemed to hear voices in the catacombs saying: "He suffered under Pontius Pilate"; then later on in Roman temples turned into churches: "He suffered under Pontius Pilate"; then gathering like the roar of the sea, the voices multiplied and chanted in churches that rose up like pinnacles in the sky: "He suffered under Pontius Pilate." But whatever was the dream, the intuitive woman was right, the practical man, wrong. Pilate, finding the Prisoner still silent, was full of wrath, for he was accustomed to seeing the accused crawling in dread before him.

> Do you refuse to speak to me? Surely you know that I have authority to release you, and I have authority to crucify you? *John 19:10*

Pilate spoke of his power to release or to condemn. But if the Prisoner before him were innocent, Pilate had no power to crucify; if he were guilty, he had not power to release. The judge is judged, Our Blessed Lord spoke at once, reminding Pilate that any judicial authority which he had came not from Caesar but from God. Pilate had boasted of the arbitrariness of his power, but Christ referred him to a power that is delegated to men.

> You would have no authority at all over me, if it had not been granted you from above. *John 19:11*

The power that Pilate boasted was "given." Whether a governor, king or ruler knows it or not, all earthly authority is derived from on high. "By Me kings reign," said the Book of Proverbs. But Our Lord immediately ascribed a greater sin to both Judas and the high priest.

> Therefore the deeper guilt lies with the man who handed me over to you. *John 19:11*

Pilate, the Gentile, did not know that his power came from God, but Caiphas did; so did Judas. This superior knowledge made each more guilty than the Roman. Pilate sinned through ignorance; Caiphas sinned against knowledge; so did Judas.

CONDEMNATION

This bold rebuke of Pilate, reminding him of his dependence upon God and charging him with the lesser, but nonetheless real, sin, stirred his efforts more than ever toward "releasing Him." Pilate went outside to meet the mob and reaffirm the innocence of the Prisoner. But the mob had their clever answer ready:

> If you let this man go, you are no friend to Caesar; any man who claims to be a king is defying Caesar. *John 19:12*

Pilate was frightened! If he released the Prisoner, complaint would be made to the already suspicious Emperor that he was guilty of conspiracy and treason. If so, he might lose both his governorship and his head. It was very strange that the mob who despised Caesar for his massacres, for all the harm that he had done them, and for his prostitution of the temple, now proclaimed that they had no king but Caesar. By proclaiming Caesar as their king, they renounced the idea of a Messiah and made themselves vassals of the Empire, thus preparing for the Roman armies that swallowed up Jerusalem within a generation. The terrors of Tiberius seemed more real to Pilate than the denying of justice to Christ. But in the end, those who fear men rather than God lose that which they hoped men would preserve for them. Pilate later was deposed by the Roman Emperor on a complaint by the Jews—another instance of men being punished by the very instruments in which they confided. When Pilate heard the threat to inform Caesar of his partiality to a man whom they accused of being an enemy of Caesar, Pilate sat down in his judgment seat. Pointing to the Prisoner robed in dried blood, crowned with thorns and a scarlet cloak, he said to the people:

> Here is your king. They shouted, Away with him! Crucify him!
> *John* 19:14,15

Pilate asked:

> Crucify your king?

The chief priests answered:

> We have no king but Caesar. *John* 19:15

And the king took them at their word! As once before, in the days of Samuel, they rejected the government of God in order to have a king which God gave them in anger, so now, as they rejected the Kingship of Christ they would be ground to the earth under the kingship of Caesar. It was a Roman custom when a criminal was condemned to death to take a long stick, break it in two, and throw it at the prisoner's feet. Pilate followed this custom, and the broken pieces on the marble floor formed the figure of a cross.

Ibis ad crucem ("Thou shalt suffer the Cross") was the Latin edict, followed by the order: *I, Lector, expedi crucem* ("Go, Lector, prepare the Cross").

> Then at last, to satisfy them, (Pilate) handed Jesus over to be crucified. *John* 19:16

Pilate in the delivery of the Prisoner to Crucifixion could never have pleaded that he was powerless; a moment before he had boasted of his power to condemn and to release. Nor could he excuse himself on the ground that he lacked courage to oppose those who willed Christ's death, for a short time later, when they asked that the superscription over the Cross be changed, he proved how stubborn he could be. Pilate was playing a double role. He did not wish to offend those whom he was governing lest he be reported to Caesar, nor did he wish to condemn innocent blood.

The guilt for the Crucifixion is not to be fixed upon any one nation, race, people, or individual. Sin was the cause of the Crucifixion, and all mankind had inherited the infection of sin. Jew and Gentile shared in the guilt, but what is more important is that the Heavenly Father also delivered Him to death, and both Jew and Gentile share in the fruits of Redemption:

> He did not spare his own Son, but gave him up for us all.
> *Romans* 8:32

Pilate then:

> Could see that nothing was being gained, and a riot was starting; so he took water and washed his hands in full view of the people, saying, My hands are clean of this man's blood; see to that yourselves.
> *Matthew* 27:24

Pilate was certainly unconscious of a mysterious rite ordered by Moses, but the people who saw Pilate declaring himself innocent must have thought of it. Moses had commanded:

> Then all the elders of the town nearest to the dead body shall wash their hands over the heifer whose neck has been broken in the ravine. They shall solemnly declare: Our hands did not shed this blood, nor did we witness the bloodshed. Accept expiation, O Lord, for thy people Israel whom thou hast redeemed, and do not let the guilt of innocent blood rest upon thy people Israel. *Deuteronomy* 21:6-9

Now the role was reversed. It was Pilate who declared himself innocent; it was the followers of Moses who did the opposite. The ceremony of Moses prefigured being made innocent by blood, which was the manner of Christ's death. Pilate, however, sought his innocence in water as Mohammed sought his in sand. Spenser in his *Faery Queene* described Pilate all the rest of his life as continually washing his hands. Lady Macbeth did this, but as water could not wash Pilate's heart, so Lady Macbeth complained:

> Will all great Neptune's ocean wash this blood
> Clean from my hand? No. . . .

Though the cowardly Governor washed away symbolically the responsibility for his perversion of justice, history has rung with the cry: "Suffered under Pontius Pilate."

Judas confessed that he had betrayed "innocent blood"; Pilate repeatedly "found no fault" in Him; Herod neither; Claudia Procula regarded Him as a "just man"; the thief on the cross later would say that He had done no wrong; and the centurion would finally proclaim:

Truly this man was a son of God. *Matthew 27:54*

But now when Pilate declared himself innocent of His Blood, the people cried out:

His blood be on us, and on our children. *Matthew 27:26*

That Blood could be upon them for destruction, but it was still redeeming Blood. Though they attached a curse to themselves, the One Whom they crucified had not ratified their sentence. In the end they will repent. Before the end, there is always the remnant that will be saved. Even now, there was not a single woman mentioned among them as desiring His death. Then, too, among them in this hour were noble souls like Joseph of Arimathea, Nicodemus, the steward of Herod's house, and in a few years Paul. But at that moment when He was given over by earth, after He had been given over by heaven, to be crucified, there followed another mocking:

They stripped him of the purple and dressed him in his own clothes.
Mark 15:20

There was nothing said about taking off Him the crown of thorns, though they did take off the robe in which He had been mocked and derided as a false King. His own raiment is put on, which would probably include His outer and inner garments, as well as the seamless tunic, for which the soldiers later on would cast lots. He would go forth in His own garments and be identified as the One Who had preached to His people and walked among them as the Messiah.

Then they took him out to crucify him. *Mark 15:21*

He was led out of the city, which was the custom in all executions. Leviticus had ordered that blasphemers be put to death outside the city. Stephen, when he was stoned later on as the first martyr, was led beforehand outside the city. The law also ordained that the scapegoat, on whom the hands of the priest had been laid as if to impute the sins of the people, should be led outside the city to signify that the sins of the people might be carried away. The Epistle to the Hebrews described this symbolism:

> Those animals whose blood is brought as a sin-offering by the high priest into the sanctuary, have their bodies burnt outside the camp, and therefore Jesus also suffered outside the camp, bearing the stigma that he bore. *Hebrews 13:11,12*

They willed now that He should die, but what He was and what they hated could never die.

> Jesus was now taken in charge and, carrying his own cross, went out to the Place of the Skull, as it is called (or, in the Jews' language, Golgotha). *John 19:17*

48. The Crucifixion

The procession of the cross was usually preceded by a trumpeter to clear the road; then followed a herald announcing the name of the criminal who was being led to execution. Sometimes the name of the criminal and the reason for his condemnation was written on a board and hung about his neck. Two witnesses of the council which sentenced the one condemned to death were also to accompany the procession. A centurion mounted on horseback, along with a considerable detachment of soldiers, formed part of the procession. There were also the two thieves who were to be crucified with Our Lord. He bore the full weight of the Cross on His back and shoulders which were already raw from the scourging.

The Sunday previous He was hailed as "King"; that morning the people shouted: "No King but Caesar." The Jerusalem that saluted Him was now the Jerusalem that disowned Him. Since the temple priests had found Him accursed, they exiled Him from Jerusalem. This was the Law of Leviticus that the sin offering should be driven outside the city gates or the camp.

> The two sin-offerings, the bull and the goat, the blood of which was brought within the Veil to make expiation in the sanctuary, shall be taken outside the camp and destroyed by fire—skin, flesh, and offal.
>
> *Leviticus 16:27*

Christ, the ultimate in sin offering, is driven like the scapegoat outside the city. St. Paul suggests that from that moment the city forfeited its claim to greatness and was replaced by the heavenly Jerusalem.

> Therefore Jesus also suffered outside the gate, to consecrate the people by his own blood. Let us then go to him outside the camp, bearing the stigma that he bore. For here we have no permanent home, but we are seekers after the city which is to come. *Hebrews 13:12–14*

Isaiah had foretold that "His government would be on His shoulder"; it now became clear that the Cross was His government or law of life. He had said that anyone who was to be His disciple must take up his Cross and follow Him.

Fearful that the long scourgings, the loss of blood, the crowning with thorns would bring His end before the Crucifixion, His enemies compelled a stranger, Simon of Cyrene, to help Him carry His Cross.

Cyrene was a town on the northern coast of Africa. But Simon's nationality is uncertain. He could have been Jewish, judging by his name, or a Gentile; it may be that he was even a black African, judging by his native locality and the fact that he was "forced" to help Our Lord carry the Cross. It was the first time the Savior laid His Cross on anyone; to Simon belongs the privilege of first sharing the Cross of Christ.

> A man called Simon, from Cyrene, the Father of Alexander and Rufus, was passing by on his way in from the country, and they pressed him into service to carry his cross. *Mark 15:21*

Simon did not undertake this task willingly, for the Greek word used in the Gospel was adopted from a Persian word which signified the compulsory employment of beasts for the delivery of mail in the Persian Empire. Simon was probably one of the curious thousands who were interested in seeing a man go to death, and who stood on the roadway until the long arm of the Roman law forced him to share the ignominy of a Cross. Though at first reluctant because compelled, he nevertheless must have found, as Our Lord said His followers would, "the yoke sweet and burden light." Otherwise his two sons would not later have been mentioned by Paul as pillars of the Church.

Our Lord during His public life taught gentleness in return for injury:

> If a man in authority makes you go one mile, go with him two.
> *Matthew 5:41*

Simon may never have heard the words; but words were not needed when he followed the Word.

Along the procession route, too, were many women. There are numerous instances of men failing in the Crucifixion, such as the Apostles who slept in the garden, Judas who betrayed, the Jewish and the Gentile courts who condemned, but there is not a record of a single woman ever asking for His death. A heathen woman had interceded for His life with Pilate. At the Cross there would be four women but only one Apostle. During His last week the children shouted "Hosanna," the men cried "Crucify," but the women "wept." To the weeping women He said:

> Daughters of Jerusalem, do not weep for me; no, weep for yourselves and your children. For the days are surely coming when they will say, Happy are the barren, the wombs that never bore a child, the breasts that never fed one. Then they will start saying to the mountains, Fall on us, and to the hills, Cover us. For if these things are done when the wood is green, what will happen when it is dry? *Luke 23:28–31*

Our Lord here referred to words that He had already spoken concerning the approaching doom of Jerusalem:

> For a time will come upon you, when your enemies will set up siege-works against you; they will encircle you and hem you in at every point; they will bring you to the ground, you and your children within your walls, and not leave you one stone standing on another, because you did not recognize God's moment when it came. *Luke 19:43,44*

As in the garden He had told the soldiers to take Him and let the Apostles go their way, so too He told the women not to mourn over Him, for He was innocent, but to mourn over the destruction of Jerusalem, which was a symbol of the destruction of the world at the end of time. Actually, when the destruction of Jerusalem did come, Josephus recorded that the people of Jerusalem hid themselves in dens and rocks of mountains.

This was the first time since His interrogation before Pilate that Our Lord broke His silence. It was the Passion sermon of the Savior, or rather the first part of it; the second part consisted of His Seven Last Words from the Cross.

If there was any one moment when Our Lord might have been pre-occupied with His own sorrows and have taken the tears of others as a solace for His grief, it was this moment on the way to Calvary, and yet He bade the women to shed no tears for Him. He Who wept at Bethany and Whose Blood now wept on the road of Jerusalem, bade them not to weep for Him, for His death was a willed necessity—willed freely by Him, but a necessity for men. Furthermore, since He had promised to wipe away all tears, tears for Him were needless.

The green tree was Himself; the dry tree the world. He was the green tree of life transplanted from Eden; the dry tree was Jerusalem first, and then the unconverted world. His warning meant that if the Romans so treated Him Who was innocent, how would they treat Jerusalem that had condemned Him to death? If He was so bruised because of the transgression of others, how in the final judgment would the guilty be punished for their own iniquities? When there is fire in the forest, the green trees with sap and moisture darken, but how the old dry trees which are rotten to the core will burn! If He Who had no sin suffered, how will they suffer who are rotten with sin!

Peter, who was not mentioned in this scene but who lived so intimately with the Savior, later picked up this same theme, and wrote:

> It is hard enough for the righteous to be saved; what then will become of the impious and sinful? So even those who suffer, if it be according to God's will, should commit their souls to him—by doing good; their Maker will not fail them. *I Peter 4:18-19*

No tears of Dalila would keep this Samson from his work today; no superficial wailings of the women of Jerusalem would weaken Him in His determined purpose of sacrifice; their dowry of tears could not make them the brides of His heart. If He were just a good man going to His death, then let them open the fountain of tears; but because He was a Priest going to sacrifice, then let them weep only if they availed themselves not of its fruits. As He would purge death of death by rising from the grave, so He now purged tears of lamentation, by showing that sin alone was worth tears. They were weeping for Him as a good man, but no such tears would He have at His deathbed. By rejecting their grief, He showed that He was not a good man sent to death, but a God-man saving sinners.

Hidden in His words was a plea for faithfulness to avert the doom of Jerusalem; its destiny was in the hands of women, did they but repent. On this as on many other occasions, He bade His hearers look to the state of their own souls. He diverted attention from Himself Who was sinless, to those who needed Redemption. When the young man told Our Lord he wanted to be His disciple, Our Lord told him He had nowhere to lay His head. Was the condition of the youth's soul fit for such poverty? When Peter said he would die for Him, Our Lord told the Apostle how weak his soul was; so now the women were told not to have misplaced sorrow; let them look to their souls, their children, their city. He needed no tears; they did.

The place assigned for the Crucifixion was Golgotha, or the "Place of the Skull." Legend has it that it was the burial place of Adam. Representations of the Crucifixion often show a skull at the foot of the Cross to indicate that the new Adam was dying for the old Adam. But certainly, it was a place where dead bones were thrown after execution. Once on the hill, the executioners stripped Him of His garments, opening new wounds in His Sacred Body. In all, there were seven distinct bloodsheddings; the Circumcision, the Agony in the Garden, the Scourging, the Crowning with thorns, the Way of the Cross, and now the two that are to follow: the Crucifixion and the Piercing of the Sacred Heart.

The Cross was prepared and over it was placed an inscription written by Pilate in Hebrew, Latin and Greek, reading:

Jesus of Nazareth King of the Jews. *John 19:19*

His death and also His Kingship were proclaimed in the name of the three cities of the world: Jerusalem, Rome, and Athens; in the language of the Good, the True and the Beautiful; in the tongues of Sion, the Forum and the Acropolis. Pilate would be asked to change what he had written, but he would refuse: "What I have written, I have written." His Kingship remained proclaimed, though, for the moment, a Cross would be His throne; His Blood, the royal purple; the nails, His sceptre; the crown of thorns, His diadem. Truth was made to speak when men ridiculed.

Being stripped of His garments meant that He was no longer localized by dress. In His nakedness He became the Universal Man. Exiled outside the city, He now gave up country as well as life. The Sacred Heart was confined by no frontiers. The rough nail was applied to that hand from which the world's graces flow, and the first dull knock of the hammer was heard in silence. Blow followed blow and was quickly re-echoed from the city walls beneath. Mary and John held their ears; the echo sounded as another stroke. Feet too were pinioned, the feet which sought the lost sheep among the thorns. Every detail of prophecy was being fulfilled. A thousand years before, David looked forward to the role hammer and nails would play in greeting the Messiah, as carpenters would put to death Him Who carpentered the universe:

> A herd of bulls surrounds me,
>   great bulls of Bashan beset me.
> Ravening and roaring lions
> open their mouths wide against me.
>   My strength drains away like water
>   and all my bones are loose.
> My heart has turned to wax and melts within me.
>   My mouth is dry as a potsherd,
>   and my tongue sticks to my jaw;
>   I am laid low in the dust of death.
>   The huntsmen are all about me;
>   a band of ruffians rings me round,
> and they have hacked off my hands and my feet.
>   I tell my tale of misery,
>   while they look on and gloat.
> They share out my garments among them
> and cast lots for my clothes.   *Psalm* 21:13–19

Isaiah had foretold that in His death the Messiah would be linked up with criminals and wrongdoers. Being a vicarious victim for sinners, He was accounted no better than the scum of the earth. As Isaiah prophesied:

> He was afflicted, he submitted to be struck down
>   and did not open his mouth;
> he was led like a sheep to the slaughter,
>   like a ewe that is dumb before the shearers.
> Without protection, without justice, he was taken away;

and who gave a thought to his fate,
  how he was cut off from the world of living men,
stricken to the death for my people's transgression?
He was assigned a grave with the wicked,
a burial-place among the refuse of mankind,
though he had done no violence
  and spoken no word of treachery.
Yet the Lord took thought for his tortured servant
and healed him who had made himself a sacrifice for sin;
so shall he enjoy long life and see his children's children,
  and in his hand the Lord's cause shall prosper.
After all his pains he shall be bathed in light,
after his disgrace he shall be fully vindicated;
so shall he, my servant, vindicate many,
himself bearing the penalty of their guilt.
Therefore I will allot him a portion with the great,
  and he shall share the spoil with the mighty,
because he exposed himself to face death
  and was reckoned among transgressors,
because he bore the sin of many
  and interceded for their transgressions. *Isaiah 53:7–12*

Because crucifixion was the most excruciating of all torments, it was customary to offer the condemned a drink to deaden sensitivity to the pain. Probably the women of Jerusalem had brought such a potion with them. In any case, the soldiers:

He was offered drugged wine, but he would not take it. *Mark 15:23*

Our Lord, when it was brought to His lips, knowing it to be a sedative, refused to sip. Though His Body, already exhausted, cried out for water, He would not drink that which would dull His role as mediator. At His birth, His mother was given the gift of myrrh and accepted it as a sign of His ransoming death. At His death, He would refuse the myrrh which would deaden the reason of His coming. He told Peter the night before that He would drink the cup His Father had given Him. But to drink that cup of Redemption He must not drink of the cup that would drive a wedge between His Body and His Spirit.

Our Lord used many pulpits during His public life, such as Peter's bark pushed into the sea, the mountaintop, the streets of Tyre and Sidon, the temple, the country road near a cemetery, and a banquet hall. But all faded into insignificance compared to the pulpit which He mounted now—the pulpit of the Cross. It was lifted slowly off the ground, wavered in midair for a moment, tearing and lacerating His Sacred Flesh; then suddenly with a deep thud that seemed to shake even hell itself, it sank into the pit prepared for it. Our Lord had mounted His pulpit for the last time.

Like all orators, He overlooked His audience. Far off, in Jerusalem, He could see the gilded roof of the temple, reflecting its rays against the sun which was soon to hide its face in shame. Here and there on temple walls He could catch a glimpse of those who were straining their eyes to see Him Whom the darkness knew not. At the edge of the crowd were timid followers, ready to flee in case of danger; there, too, were the executioners getting their dice ready to shake for His garments. Close to the Cross was the only Apostle present, John, whose face was like a cast moulded out of love; Magdalen was there too, like a broken flower, a wounded thing. But foremost among all— God pity her!—was His own mother. Mary, Magdalen, John; innocence, penitence, and priesthood; the three types of souls forever to be found beneath the Cross of Christ.

49. *The Seven Words from the Cross*

Our Lord spoke seven times from the Cross; these are called His Seven Last Words. In the Scriptures the dying words of only three others were recorded: Israel, Moses, and Stephen. The reason perhaps is that no others are found so significant and representative as these three. Israel was the first of the Israelites; Moses, the first of the legal dispensation; Stephen, the first Christian martyr. The dying words of each began something sublime in the history of God's dealings with men. Not even the last words of Peter or Paul or John have been human legacy, for no spirit ever guided a pen to reveal the secrets of their dying lips. And yet the human heart is always anxious to hear of the state of mind of anyone at that very common, and yet very mysterious, moment called death.

In His goodness, Our Blessed Lord left His thoughts on dying, for He—more than Israel, more than Moses, more than Stephen—was representative of all humanity. In this sublime hour He called all His children to the pulpit of the Cross, and every word He said to them was set down for the purpose of an eternal publication and an undying consolation. There was never a preacher like the dying Christ; there was never a congregation like that which gathered about the pulpit of the Cross; there was never a sermon like the Seven Last Words.

THE FIRST WORD

The executioners expected Him to cry, for everyone pinned to the gibbet of the Cross had done it before Him. Seneca wrote that those who were crucified cursed the day of their birth, the executioners, their mothers, and even spat on those who looked upon them. Cicero recorded that at times it was necessary to cut out the tongues of those who were crucified to stop their terrible blasphemies. Hence the executioners expected a word, but not the kind of word that they heard. The Scribes and Pharisees awaited His reaction, and they were quite sure that He Who had preached "Love your enemies," and "Do good to them that hate you," would now forget that Gospel with the piercing of His feet and hands. They felt that the excruciating and agonizing pains would scatter to the winds any resolution He might have taken to keep up appearances. Every one expected a cry, but no one, with the exception of the three at the foot of the Cross, expected the cry they did hear. Like some fragrant trees which bathe in perfume the very axe which gashes them, the great Heart on the Tree of Love poured out from its depths something less a cry than a prayer—the soft, sweet, low prayer of pardon and forgiveness:

Father, forgive them; they do not know what they are doing.
Luke 23:24

Forgive whom? Forgive enemies? The soldier in the courtroom of Caiphas who struck Him with a mailed fist? Pilate, the politician, who condemned a God to retain the friendship of Caesar? Herod who robed Wisdom in the garment of a fool? The soldiers who swung the King of Kings on a tree between heaven and earth? Forgive them? Forgive them, why? Because they know what they do? No, because they know not what they are doing. If they knew what they were doing and still went on doing it; if they knew what a terrible crime they were committing by sentencing Life to death; if they knew what a perversion of justice it was to prefer Barabbas to Christ; if they knew what cruelty it was to take the feet that trod everlasting hills and pinion them to the limb of a tree; if they knew what they were doing and still went on doing it, unmindful of the fact that the very Blood which they shed was capable of redeeming them, they would never be saved! Rather they would be damned! It was only the ignorance of their great sin that brought them within the pale of the hearing of that cry from the Cross. It is not wisdom that saves: it is ignorance!

Men on dying either proclaim their own innocence, or condemn the judges who sentenced them to death, or else ask pardon for sins. But Perfect Innocence asked no pardon; as Mediator between God and man He extended pardon. As High Priest Who offered Himself in sacrifice He pleaded for sinners. In a certain sense, the words of forgiveness were spoken twice: once in Eden, as God promised Redemption through the "seed of the woman" who would crush the serpent of evil; now as God in the form of the Suffering Servant fulfilled the promise. So great was the Divine Love manifested in this First Word from the Cross that echoes were caught of it through history, such as Stephen asking that the Lord lay not to their charge the sin of those who stoned him; and Paul who wrote:

No one came into court to support me; they all left me in the lurch;
I pray that it may not be held against them.   *II Timothy 4:16*

But the prayers of Stephen and Paul were not like His, in which forgiveness was identified with His sacrifice. Being Himself both Priest and Victim, He was upright as a Priest, prostrate as a Victim. Thus

He interceded and offered Himself for the guilty. Abel's blood clamored for the wrath of God to avenge the murder of Cain; the new Abel's Blood spilled by jealous brethren of the race of Cain was raised to lift the wrath and to plead for pardon.

THE SECOND WORD

The Last Judgment was prefigured on Calvary: the Judge was in the center, and the two divisions of humanity on either side: the saved and the lost, the sheep and the goats. When He would come in glory to judge all men, the Cross would be with Him then too, but as a badge of honor, not shame.

Two thieves crucified on either side of Him at first blasphemed and cursed. Suffering does not necessarily make men better; it can sear and burn the soul, unless men are purified by seeing its redemptive value. Unspiritualized suffering may cause men to degenerate. The thief at the left was certainly no better because of pain. The thief on the left asked to be taken down. But the thief on the right, evidently moved by Our Savior's priestly prayer of intercession, asked to be taken up. Reprimanding his brother thief for his blasphemy, he said:

> Have you no fear of God? You are under the same sentence as he. For us it is plain justice; we are paying the price for our misdeeds; but this man has done nothing wrong. *Luke 23:40,41*

Then throwing himself upon Divine mercy, he asked for forgiveness.

> Jesus, remember me when you come to your throne. *Luke 23:42*

A dying man asked a dying man for eternal life; a man without possessions asked a poor man for a Kingdom; a thief at the door of death asked to die like a thief and steal Paradise. One would have thought a saint would have been the first soul purchased over the counter of Calvary by the red coins of Redemption, but in the Divine plan it was a thief who was the escort of the King of kings into Paradise. If Our Lord had come merely as a teacher, the thief would never have asked for forgiveness. But since the thief's request touched the reason of His coming to earth, namely, to save souls, the thief heard the immediate answer:

> I tell you this: today you shall be with me in Paradise. *Luke 23:43*

It was the thief's last prayer, perhaps even his first. He knocked once, sought once, asked once, dared everything, and found everything. When even the disciples were doubting and only one was present at the Cross, the thief owned and acknowledged Him as Savior. If

Barabbas came to the execution, how he must have wished that he never had been released, and that he could have heard the words of the compassionate High Priest. Practically everything about the Body of Christ was fastened by nails, or tortured by whips and thorns, except His Heart and His tongue—and these declared forgiveness that very day. But who can forgive sins, but God? And who can promise Paradise except Him Who by nature is eternal to Paradise?

THE THIRD WORD

The third message of Our Lord from the Cross contained exactly the same word that was used in addressing His mother at the marriage feast of Cana. When she, for the sake of the embarrassed host, made the simple prayer that the guests had no wine, He answered: "Woman, what is that to Me when My Hour is not yet come?" Our Lord always used the word "Hour" in relation to His Passion and His death.

In our own language, Our Lord was saying to His Blessed Mother at Cana: "My dear mother, do you realize that you are asking Me to proclaim My Divinity—to appear before the world as the Son of God, and to prove My Divinity by My works and My miracles? The moment that I do this, I begin the royal road to the Cross. When I am no longer known among men as the son of the carpenter, but as the Son of God, that will be My first step toward Calvary. My Hour is not yet come; but would you have Me anticipate it? Is it your will that I go to the Cross? If I do, your relationship to Me changes. You are now My mother. You are known everywhere in our little village as the mother of Jesus. But if I appear now as the Savior of men, and begin the work of Redemption, your role will change too. Once I undertake the salvation of mankind, you will not only be My mother, but you will also be the mother of everyone whom I redeem. I am the Head of humanity; as soon as I save the body of humanity, you who are the mother of the Head will become also the mother of My Mystical Body or the Church. You will then be the universal mother, the new Eve, as I am the new Adam.

"To indicate the role that you will play in Redemption, I now bestow upon you that title of universal motherhood; I call you— *Woman.* It was to you that I referred when I said to Satan that I would put enmity between him and the woman, between his brood of evil and your seed, Which I am. That great title of woman I dignify you with now. And I shall dignify you with it again when My Hour comes and when I am unfurled upon the Cross like a wounded eagle. We are in this work of Redemption together. What is yours is mine. From this Hour on, we are not just Mary and Jesus, we are the new

Adam and the new Eve, beginning a new humanity, changing the water of sin into the wine of life. Knowing all this, My dear mother, is it your will that I anticipate the Cross and that I go to Calvary?"

Our Blessed Lord was presenting to Mary not merely the choice of asking for a miracle or not rather He was asking if she would send Him to His death. He had made it quite plain that the world would not tolerate His Divinity, that if He turned water into wine, some day wine would be changed into blood.

Three years had passed. Our Blessed Lord now looked down from His Cross to the two most beloved creatures that He had on earth—John and His Blessed Mother. He picked up the refrain of Cana, and addressed Our Blessed Mother with the same title He gave Her at the marriage feast. He called her, "Woman." It was the second Annunciation. With a gesture of His dust-filled eyes and His thorn-crowned head, He looked longingly at Her, who had sent Him willingly to the Cross and who is now standing beneath it as a cooperator in His Redemption; and He said: "Woman, this is thy son." He did not call him John; to do that would have been to address him as the son of Zebedee and no one else. But, in his anonymity, John stood for all mankind. To His beloved disciple He said: "This is thy mother."

Here is the answer, after all these years, to the mysterious words in the Gospel of the Incarnation which stated that Our Blessed Mother laid her "firstborn" in the manger. Did that mean that Our Blessed Mother was to have other children? It certainly did, but not according to the flesh. Our Divine Lord and Savior Jesus Christ was the unique Son of Our Blessed Mother by the flesh. But Our Lady was to have other children, not according to the flesh, but according to the spirit!

There were two great periods in the relations of Jesus and Mary, the first extending from the Crib to Cana, and the second, from Cana to the Cross. In the first, she was the mother of Jesus; in the second, she began to be the mother of all whom Jesus redeemed—in other words, she became the mother of men. From Bethlehem to Cana, Mary had Jesus, as a mother has a son; she even called Him familiarly "Son," at the age of twelve, as if that were her usual mode of address. He was with her during those thirty years, fleeing in her arms to Egypt, living at Nazareth, and being subject to her. He was hers, and she was His, and even at the very moment when they walked into the wedding feast, her name was mentioned first: "Mary, the mother of Jesus, was there."

But from Cana on, there is a growing detachment, which Mary helped to bring on herself. A year after Cana, as a devoted mother, she followed Him in His preaching. It was announced to Our Lord that His mother was seeking Him. Our Lord with seeming unconcern, turned to the crowd and asked:

Who is my mother? *Matthew* 12:48

Then revealing the great Christian mystery that relationship is not dependent on flesh and blood, but on union with Divine nature through grace, He added:

Here are my mother and my brothers. Whoever does the will of my heavenly Father is my brother, my sister, my mother. *Matthew* 12:50

The mystery came to an end on Calvary. There she became our mother the moment she lost her Divine Son. What seemed an alienation of affection was in reality a deepening of affection. No love ever mounts to a higher level without death to a lower one. Mary died to the love of Jesus at Cana, and recovered Jesus again at Calvary with His Mystical Body which He redeemed. It was, for the moment, a poor exchange, giving up her Divine Son to win mankind, but in reality, she did not win mankind apart from Him. On that day when she came to Him preaching, He began to merge the Divine maternity into the new motherhood of all men; at Calvary He caused her to love men as He loved them.

It was a new love, or perhaps the same love expanded over the wider area of humanity. But it was not without its sorrow. It cost Mary something to have men as sons. She could give birth to Jesus in joy in a stable, but she could give birth to Christians only on Calvary, and in labors great enough to make Her Queen of Martyrs. The *Fiat* she pronounced when she became the Mother of God now became another *Fiat*, like unto Creation in the immensity of what she brought forth. It was also a *Fiat* which so enlarged her affections as to increase her pains. The bitterness of Eve's curse—that woman would bring forth children in sorrow—was now fulfilled, and not by the opening of a womb but by the piercing of a heart, as Simeon had foretold. It was the greatest of all honors to be the mother of Christ; but it was also a great honor to be the mother of Christians. There was no room in the inn for that first birth; but Mary had the whole world for her second. Recall that when Our Lord spoke to John, He did not refer to him as John for then he would have been only the son of Zebedee. Rather, in him all humanity was commended to Mary, who became the mother of men, not by metaphor, or figure of speech, but by pangs of birth. Nor was it a mere sentimental solicitude that made Our Lord give John to His mother, for John's mother was present at the Cross. He needed no mother from a human point of view. The import of the words were spiritual and became fulfilled on the day of Pentecost when Christ's Mystical Body became visible and operative. Mary as the mother of redeemed and regenerated humanity was in the midst of the Apostles.

THE FOURTH WORD

From twelve o'clock until three o'clock there was an unearthly darkness that fell over the land, for nature, in sympathy with its Creator, refused to shed its light upon the crime of deicide. Mankind, having condemned the Light of the World, now lost the cosmic symbol of that Light, the sun. At Bethlehem, where He was born at midnight, the heavens were suddenly filled with light; at Calvary, when He entered into the ignominy of His Crucifixion at midday, the heavens were bereaved of light. Centuries before, the prophet Amos had said:

> On that day, says the Lord God, I will make the sun go down at noon and darken the earth in broad daylight. I will turn your pilgrim-feasts into mourning and all your songs into lamentation. *Amos 8:9*

Our Blessed Lord entered into the second phase of His suffering. The catastrophe of being fixed to the Cross was followed by the passion of being crucified. His Blood congealed where it could not flow freely; fever consumed the body; the thorns which were the curse of the earth now are covered with blood poured out as a curse of sin. An unearthly stillness, which was rather normal in darkness, now became frightening in the abnormal darkness of high noon. When Judas came with the band to arrest Him in the garden, Our Lord told him that it was His Hour and "the power of darkness." But this darkness not only signified that men were putting out the Light Who illumined every man coming into this world, but also that He was denying Himself, for the moment, the light and consolation of His Divinity. Suffering now passed from the body into the mind and soul, as He spoke with a loud voice:

> My God, my God, why hast thou forsaken me? *Matthew 27:46*

During this part of the Crucifixion, Our Blessed Lord was repeating the Psalm of David which prophetically referred to Him, though written a thousand years before.

> My God, my God, why hast thou forsaken me . . . All who see me jeer at me, make mouths at me and wag their heads: He threw himself on the Lord for rescue; let the Lord deliver him, for he holds him dear! But thou are he who drew me from the womb, who laid me at my mother's breast . . . Ravening and roaring lions open their mouths wide against me. My strength drains away like water and all my bones are loose. My heart has turned to wax and melts within me. My

mouth is dry as a potsherd, and my tongue sticks to my jaw; I am laid low in the dust of death. The huntsmen are all about me; a band of ruffians rings me round, and they have hacked off my hands and my feet. I tell my tale of misery, while they look on and gloat. They share out my garments among them and cast lots for my clothes.

Psalm 21:13–19

The signal feature in the sufferings of Our Lord revealed in this Psalm was His desolation and solitude. The Divine Son called His Father "My God"—in contrast to the prayer which taught men to say "Our Father Who art in heaven." It was not that His human nature was separated from His Divine nature; that was impossible. It was rather that just as the sun's light and heat can be hidden at the base of a mountain by intervening clouds, though the peak is bathed in sunlight, so too, in taking upon Himself the sins of the world He willed a kind of withdrawal of His Father's face and all Divine consolation. Sin has physical effects, and these He bore by having His hands and feet pierced; sin has mental effects which He poured forth in the Garden of Gethsemane; sin also has spiritual effects such as a sense of abandonment, separation from God, loneliness. This particular moment He willed to take upon Himself that principal effect of sin which was abandonment.

Man rejected God; so now He willed to feel that rejection. Man turned away from God; now He, Who was God united personally with a human nature, willed to feel in that human nature that awful wrench as if He Himself were guilty. Earth had already abandoned Him by lifting His Cross above it; heaven had already abandoned Him by veiling itself in darkness; and yet suspended between both, He united both. In that cry were all the sentiments in human hearts expressive of a Divine nostalgia: the loneliness of the atheist, the skeptic, the pessimist, the sinners who hate themselves for hating virtue, and of all those who have no love above the flesh; for to be without love is hell. It was, therefore, the moment when leaning on nails He stood at the brink of hell in the name of all sinners. As He entered upon the extreme penalty of sin, which is separation from God, it was fitting that His eyes be filled with darkness and His soul with loneliness.

In each of the other words, He acted as the Divine mediator; in the first word, He pleaded for the forgiveness of sinners in general; in the second word, He anticipated His final role at the end of the world when He would separate the good from the bad; in the third word, He was the mediator assigning a spiritual motherhood for redeemed humanity. Now in the fourth word, He acted as mediator for sinful humanity. God and He stand over against each other for the moment. The Old Testament had prophesied that He Who hangs upon a tree is cursed; the darkness gave expression to that burning curse which He would remove by bearing it and triumphing in the Resurrection. One of God's first great gifts to man was the gift of light which He Himself said He caused to shine upon the just and the wicked; but as mediator and pleader for the emptiness and darkness of sinful hearts, He would deny Himself that primitive gift of light.

The history of God's dealings with man began in the Old Testament when light was made, and history will come to an end in the final judgment, when the sun and moon shall be darkened and the stars withdraw their shining, and all the heavens will be clothed with blackness. In this particular midday, He stood between the light which was created and the ultimate darkness where evil will be condemned. The tensions of history He felt within Himself: The Light came into the darkness but the darkness did not comprehend the Light. As a dying person sometimes sees his whole life summarized, so now He saw all history recapitulated in Himself when the darkness of sin had its moment of triumph. The scapegoat, on which the priests of the Old Law laid their hand and then sent into the wilderness, now became verified in Him Who descended to the very gates of hell. Evil cuts off every thread connecting man with God, setting up barriers against all the avenues that open unto Him and closing all the aqueducts that might strengthen man to go to God. He now felt as if He Himself had severed the cord that bound human life to the Divine. The physical agony of Crucifixion was as nothing compared to this mental agony which He took upon Himself. Children can make crosses, but only sin can make the darkness of soul.

Christ's cry was of abandonment which He felt standing in a sinner's place, but it was not of despair. The soul that despairs never cries to God. As the keenest pangs of hunger are felt not by the dying man who is completely exhausted but by the man battling for his life with the last ounce of strength, so abandonment was felt not only by the ungodly and unholy but by the most holy of men, the Lord on the Cross. The greatest mental agony in the world, and the cause of many psychic disorders, is that minds and souls and hearts are without God. Such emptiness would never have a consolation, if He had not felt all of this as His own. From this point on, no atheist could ever say in his loneliness, He does not know what it is to be without God! This emptiness of humanity through sin, though He felt it as His own, was nevertheless spoken with a loud voice to indicate not despair, but rather hope that the sun would rise again and scatter the darkness.

THE FIFTH WORD

There now came a point in the discourse of the Seven Last Words from the Cross which would seem to indicate that Our Blessed Lord was speaking of Himself, whereas in some of the previous words He was speaking to others. But the facts are not quite so simple. It is, indeed, true that the loss of blood through the sufferings, the unnatural position of the body with the extreme tension on hands and feet, the overstretched muscles, the wounds exposed to air, the headache from the crowning of thorns, the swelling of the blood vessels, the increasing inflammation—all would have produced a physical thirst. It was not surprising that He thirsted; what was surprising was that He said so. He Who threw stars into their orbits and spheres into space, He Who shut up the sea with doors, He Who made waters come out of the rock smitten by Moses, He Who had made all the seas and rivers and fountains, He Who said to the woman of Samaria: "The man who drinks the water I give him will not know thirst any more," now let fall from His lips the shortest of the seven cries from the Cross:

> I thirst. *John 19:28*

When He was crucified, He refused to take a concoction which was offered Him; now He avidly asked for a drink. But there was considerable difference between the two drinks; the first was myrrh and was a stupefying potion to ward off pain; that He refused, in order that His senses might not be dulled. The drink that was now given to Him was vinegar or the sour bad wine of the soldiers.

> A jar stood there full of sour wine; so they soaked a sponge with the wine, fixed it on a javelin, and held it up to his lips. *John 19:29*

He Who had turned water into wine at Cana could have used the same infinite resources to have satisfied His own thirst, except for the fact that He never worked a miracle in His own behalf. But why did He ask for a drink? It was not solely because of the need, great though that must have been. The real reason for the request was the fulfillment of the prophecies:

> Jesus, aware that all had now come to its appointed end, said in fulfillment of Scripture, I thirst. *John 19:28*

All that the Old Testament had foretold of Him had to be fulfilled to the smallest iota. David in the Scriptures had foretold His thirst during His Passion:

> My mouth is dry as a potsherd, and my tongue sticks to my jaw . . .
> They put poison in my food and gave me vinegar when I was thirsty.
> *Psalm 21:16; Psalm 68:21–22*

Thus the soldiers, though they gave Him the vinegar in mockery, for so it is explicitly stated, nevertheless fulfilled the Scriptures. The vinegar was given to Him on a bunch of hyssop, a plant that grew about a

foot and a half high. It was hyssop, too, that was dipped in the blood
of the Paschal Lamb; it was hyssop that was used to sprinkle the lintel
and posts of the Jews in Egypt to escape the avenging angel; it was
hyssop that was dipped in the blood of the bird in cleansing the leper;
it was David himself, after his sin, who said that he would be purged
with hyssop and be made clean.

That which takes place last in the life of men held by intention the
first place in His, for He came to suffer and die. But He would not
give up His life until He had fulfilled details of the Scriptures that
men might know that it was He, the Christ, the Son of God, Who
was dying on the Cross. He was taking out of the Scriptures the idea
that the Messiah of the promise must not accept death as a fate, but
perform it as a deed. Exhaustion was not to put Him to death, as exhaustion accounted not for His thirst. As High Priest and Mediator it
was the prophecies concerning Him that prompted the cry of thirst.
Indeed the Jewish Rabbis had already applied that prophecy to Him;
the Midrash stated: "Come and dip thy morsel in the vinegar—this is
spoken of the Messiah—of His Passion and torments, as is written in
the prophet Isaiah. 'He was wounded for our transgressions, He was
bruised for our iniquities.' "

Since the soldiers mockingly gave Our Blessed Lord the vinegar at
the end of hyssop, it is very likely that they intended to ridicule one
of the Jewish sacred rites. When the blood of the lamb was sprinkled
by the hyssop, the purification through a symbol was now fulfilled as
the hyssop touched the Blood of Christ. St. Paul, dwelling on that
idea, writes:

> But now Christ has come, high priest of good things already in being.
> The tent of his priesthood is a greater and more perfect one, not made
> by men's hands, that is, not belonging to this created world; the blood
> of his sacrifice is his own blood, not the blood of goats and calves; and
> thus he has entered the sanctuary once and for all and secured an
> eternal deliverance. For if the blood of goats and bulls and the sprin-
> kled ashes of a heifer have power to hallow those who have been de-
> filed and restore their external purity, how much greater is the power
> of the blood of Christ; he offered himself without blemish to God, a
> spiritual and eternal sacrifice; and his blood will cleanse our conscience
> from the deadness of our former ways and fit us for the service of the
> living God. *Hebrews 9:12–14*

The bystanders at the Cross who knew well the Old Testament
prophecies were thus given another proof that He was the suffering
Messiah. His fourth word, which expressed His sufferings of Soul, and
His fifth word, which expressed sufferings of Body, were both foretold.
Thirst was the symbol of the unsatisfying character of sin; the pleas-

ures of the flesh purchased at the cost of joy of the spirit are like drinking salt water. The rich man in hell, in the parable, thirsted and begged Father Abraham to ask Lazarus to wet his tongue with but a drop of water. Making complete atonement for sin demanded that the Redeemer now feel the thirst even of the lost before they are lost. But for the saved, too, it was a thirst—a yearning for souls. Some men have a passion for money, others for fame; His passion was for souls! "Give Me to drink" meant "give Me thy heart." The tragedy of Divine love for mankind is that in His thirst men gave Him vinegar and gall.

THE SIXTH WORD

From all eternity God willed to make men in the image of His Eternal Son. Having perfected and achieved this likeness in Adam, He placed him in a garden, beautiful as God alone knows how to make a garden beautiful. In some mysterious way the revolt of Lucifer echoed to earth, and the image of God in man became blurred. The Heavenly Father now willed in His Divine mercy to restore man to his pristine glory, in order that fallen man might know the beautiful image to which he was destined to be conformed. God sent His Divine Son to this earth, not just to forgive sin but to satisfy justice through suffering.

In the beautiful Divine economy of Redemption, the same three things which cooperated in the Fall shared in Redemption. For the disobedient man Adam, there was the obedient new Adam, Christ; for the proud woman Eve, there was the humble new Eve, the Virgin Mary; for the tree of the Garden, there was the tree of the Cross. Looking back on the Divine plan and after having tasted the vinegar which fulfilled the prophecy, He now uttered what in the original is only one word:

It is accomplished. *John 19:30*

It was not an utterance of thanksgiving that His suffering was over and finished, though the humiliation of the Son of Man was now at an end. It was rather that His life from the time of His birth to the time of His death had faithfully achieved what the Heavenly Father sent Him to do.

Three times God used that same word in history: first, in Genesis, to describe the achievement or completion of creation; second, in the Apocalypse, when all creation would be done away with and a new heaven and earth would be made. Between these two extremes of the beginning and the accomplished end, there was the link of the sixth utterance from the Cross. Our Divine Lord in the state of His greatest humiliation, seeing all prophecies fulfilled, all foreshadowings realized, and all things done which were needful for the Redemption of man, uttered a cry of joy: "It is achieved."

The life of the Spirit could now begin the work of sanctification, for the work of Redemption was completed. In creation, on the seventh day, after the heavens and the earth were finished, God rested from all the work that He had done; now the Savior on the Cross having taught as Teacher, governed as King, and sanctified as Priest, could enter into His rest. There would be no second Savior; no new way of salvation; no other name under heaven by which men might be saved. Man had been bought and paid for. A new David arose to slay the Goliath of evil, not with five stones but with five wounds—hideous scars on hands, feet, and side; and the battle was fought not with armor glistening under a noonday sun, but with flesh torn away so the bones could be numbered. The Artist had put the last touch on his masterpiece, and with the joy of the strong He uttered the song of triumph that His work was completed.

There was not a single type from the turtledove to the temple which was not fulfilled in Him. Christ, one with the Eternal Father in the work of creation, had perfected Redemption. There was not a historic foretelling—from Abraham who offered in sacrifice his son, to Jonah who was in the belly of the whale for three days—which was not in Him fulfilled. The prophecy of Zechariah that He should make entrance into Jerusalem on an ass in humility; the prophecy of David that He should be betrayed by one of His own familiars; the prophecy of Zechariah that He should be sold for thirty pieces of silver, and that this price should afterwards be used to buy a field of blood; the prophecy of Isaiah that He would be barbarously treated, scourged, and put to death; the prophecy of Isaiah that He would be crucified between two malefactors, and that He would pray for His enemies; the prophecies of David that they would give Him vinegar to drink and divide His garments among them, that He would be a prophet like Moses, a priest like Melchisedech, a Lamb to be slain, a scapegoat driven out of the city, that He would be wiser than Solomon, more kingly than David, and that He should be the One to Whom Abraham and Moses looked in prophecy—all these wonderful hieroglyphics would have been left unexplained, had not the Son of God Incarnate on His Cross looked back on all the sheep and goats and bullocks who were offered in sacrifice and said: "It is achieved."

It was not after preaching the beautiful Sermon on the Mount that He said that His work was perfected. It was not to teach that He came; it was, as He said, to give His life as a ransom for many. On

His way up to Jerusalem He had told His Apostles that He would be delivered to the Gentiles, would be mocked and spat upon, and would be scourged and put to death; in the garden when Peter lifted his sword, Christ asked if He should not drink the chalice that the Heavenly Father had given Him. At the age of twelve, the first time He spoke in Scripture, He said that He must be about the business of His Father. Now the work which the Father had given Him to do was finished. The Father had sent the Son in the likeness of sinful flesh and by the Eternal Spirit He was conceived in Mary's womb. All this came to pass that He might suffer on the Cross. Thus reparation involved the whole Trinity. What was achieved was Redemption, as Peter himself would say after he received the Spirit, and understood the meaning of the Cross.

> Well you know that it was no perishable stuff, like gold or silver, that bought your freedom from the empty folly of your traditional ways. The price was paid in precious blood, as it were of a lamb without mark or blemish—the blood of Christ. *I Peter 1:18–19*

THE SEVENTH WORD

One of the penalties imposed on man as a result of original sin was that he would die in body. After the exile from the garden, Adam stumbled upon the limp form of his son Abel. He spoke to him, but Abel did not answer. The head was lifted, but it fell back limp; his eyes were cold and staring. Then Adam remembered that death was the penalty for sin. It was the first death in the world. Now the new Abel, Christ, slain by the race of Cain, prepared to go home. His sixth word was earthward; the seventh was Godward. The sixth was the farewell to time, the seventh, the beginning of His glory. The prodigal Son was returning back home; thirty-three years before, He had left the Father's house and gone off into the foreign country of this world. There He began spending His substance, the Divine riches of power and wisdom; in His last hour, His substance of Flesh and Blood was wasted among sinners. There was nothing left to feed upon except the husks and the sneers and the vinegar of human ingratitude. He now entered into Himself and prepared to take the road back home into His Father's house and, as He did so, He let fall from His lips the perfect prayer:

> Father, into thy hands I commit my spirit. *Luke 23:46*

These words were not spoken in an exhausted whisper, as men do as they breathe their last. He had already said that no one would take away His life from Him, but that He would lay it down of Himself.

Death did not lay its hand on His shoulder and give Him a summons to depart; He went out to meet death. In order to show that He would not die from exhaustion, but by an act of will, His last words were spoken:

> Gave a loud cry. *Matthew 27:50*

It is the only instance in history of a Dying One Who was a Living One. His words of departure were a quotation from the Psalms of David:

> I put my trust in the Lord.
> I will rejoice and be glad in thy unfailing love;
>   for thou hast seen my affliction
>   and hast cared for me in my distress.
> Thou hast not abandoned me to the power of the enemy
> but hast set me free to range at will.
> Be gracious to me, O Lord, for I am in distress,
> and my eyes are dimmed with grief. *Psalm 30:6–9*

He was not singing the song of death to Himself; He rather proclaimed the onward march of Divine life. He was not taking refuge in God because He must die; rather His dying was a service to man and the fulfillment of the will of the Father. It is difficult for man, who thinks of dying as the most terrible crisis in his life, to understand the joy that inspired these words of the dying Christ. Man thinks that it is his dying that decides his future state; it is rather his living that does that. Some of the choices he has made, the opportunities that were in his hand, the graces that he accepted or threw away are what decide his future. The peril of living is greater than the peril of dying. So now it was the way He lived, namely, to ransom men, that determined the joy of His dying and His union with the Heavenly Father. As some planets only after a long period of time complete their orbits, as if to salute Him Who sent them on their way, so the Word Incarnate, having completed His earthly mission, now returned again to the Heavenly Father Who sent Him on the work of Redemption.

As these words were spoken, there came from the opposite hill of Jerusalem the sound of thousands of lambs who were being slain in the outer court of the temple that their blood might be offered before the Lord God on the altar, and their flesh might be eaten by the people. Whether there is any truth in the teaching of the Rabbis that it was on the same day that Cain slew Abel that God made the Covenant with Abraham, that Isaac was led up to the mountain for sacrifice, that Melchisedech offered bread and wine to Abraham, and that Esau sold his birthright to Jacob, we know not; but on this day the Lamb of God was slain and all the prophecies were fulfilled. The work of Redemption was finished. There was a rupture of a heart in a rapture of love; the Son of Man bowed His head and willed to die.

50. Seven Words to the Cross

Our Lord spoke seven words *from* the Cross; but there were also seven words spoken *to* Our Lord on the Cross.

THE FIRST WORD TO THE CROSS

Some never remain near the Cross long enough to absorb the mercy which flows from the Crucified. They are known as the "passers-by."

> The passers-by hurled abuse at him: they wagged their heads and cried, You would pull the temple down, would you, and build it in three days? Come down from the cross and save yourself, if you are indeed the Son of God.   *Matthew 27:39,40*

The Lord was no sooner on the Cross than they asked Him to come down. "Come down from the Cross" is the most typical demand of an unregenerate world in the face of self-denial and abnegation: a religion without a Cross. As He, the Son of God, was praying for the executioners, "Father forgive," they sneered: "If Thou art the Son of God." If He had obeyed their taunt "Come down," in whom would they believe? How could Love be Love if it costs not the Lover? If Christ had come down, there would have been the Cross, but not the crucifix. The Cross is contradiction; the Crucifixion is the solution of the contradiction of life and death by showing that death is the condition of a higher life.

The passers-by shamelessly revived the old accusation at the trial that He would destroy the temple of Jerusalem and then make another in three days, though they knew He spoke of the Temple of His Body. It rankled so in their minds they would even revive it when Stephen, the first martyr, was stoned. But mockery is an ingredient of the cup of sorrow, and how else would His followers draw strength in similar trials, if He had not borne it patiently? The cruelty of lips which sneer is part of the heritage of sin as much as the cruelty of hands which nail. On the mountain of temptation, Satan used the same technique when he asked the hungry Lord to change stones into bread. It was so unbecoming the Son of God to be hungry! Now it was so unbecoming for the Son of God to suffer.

Why did the passers-by not have the patience to wait for the "three days" which was implied in their taunts? Skeptics always want miracles such as stepping down from the Cross, but never the greater miracle of forgiveness.

THE SECOND WORD TO THE CROSS

The world has room only for the ordinary; never the very good or the very bad. The good are a reproach to the mediocre and the evil are a disturbance. Hence on Calvary, Goodness is crucified between two thieves. That is His true position: among the worthless and the rejects. He is the right man in the right place. He Who said He would come like a thief in the night is among the thieves; the Physician is among the lepers; the Redeemer is in the midst of the unredeemed.

The good thief, touched by Christ, now spoke to the Savior on the Cross:

Jesus, remember me when you come to your throne. *Luke 23:42*

This was the only word spoken to the Cross that was not a reproach. While passers-by were judging the Divinity of Our Lord by deliverance from pain, the good thief was asking for deliverance from sin. The believer asks no proofs; nor was there a condition: "If Thou art the Son of God." His words implied that certainly He Who could usher him into a Kingdom could assuage his pain and unfasten the nails, if He so willed.

The conduct of everyone around the Cross was the negation of the very faith the good thief manifested; yet he believed when others disbelieved. The penitent thief called Him "Lord" or One Who possessed the right to rule; he ascribed to Him a Kingdom which certainly was not of this world, for He bore no outward mark of kingship. Victim and Lord were to the good thief compatible terms. A dying thief understood it before the Apostles. This is the only deathbed conversion mentioned in the Gospels, but it was preceded by the Cross of suffering. What the good thief asked for was to be remembered. But why be remembered, except that the pardon Christ offered to His executioners could also be offered to him? Nor was there a word of smiting or reproach to the thief, for his heart was already bruised and broken. This was the only word spoken to the Cross that received an answer, and it was the promise of Paradise to the thief that very day.

THE THIRD WORD TO THE CROSS

The third word to the Cross came from the thief on the left:

Are not you the Messiah? Save yourself, and us. *Luke 23:39*

The typical selfish man who is never conscious of having done wrong asks: "Why did God do this to me?" He judges the saving power of God by release from trials. This thief on the left was the first Communist. Long before Marx, he was saying: "Religion is the opiate of the people. If it cannot give relief from trial, what good is it?" A religion that thinks of souls when men are dying, which bids them look to God at the moment when the courts are inflicting injustice, which talks about Paradise or "pie in the sky," when stomachs are empty and bodies racked with pain, which discourses about forgiveness when social outcasts, two thieves and a village carpenter, are dying on a scaffold—such a religion is "the opiate of the people."

The only salvation the thief on the left could understand was not spiritual or moral, but physical: "Save Thyself and us!" "Save what? Our souls? No! Man has no soul! Save our bodies! What good is religion if it cannot stop pain? Step down from a gibbet! Rescue a class! Christianity is either a social gospel or it is a drug." Such was his cry.

Men can be in identical circumstances and react in totally different ways. Both thieves were alike in the depravity of their hearts, and yet each reacted differently to the man in their midst. No external means, no good example, of and by itself, is enough to convert unless the heart itself is changed. This thief was certainly a Jew, for he based his acceptance of the Messiah or Christ solely on His power to take him down from the Cross. But suppose that the Christ did unpinion the nails, dry up the fountains in his hands and feet, restore him to freshness and newness of life, would the rest of his earthly life have been a demonstration of faith in Christ—or a continuation of his life as a thief? If Our Lord were only a man who had to sustain his reputation, He would have had to show his might then and there; but being God, Who knows the secrets of every heart, He kept silence. God answers no man's prayer merely to show His power.

THE FOURTH WORD TO THE CROSS

This word came from the intelligentsia of the time, the chief priests, Scribes, and Pharisees.

> He saved others, but he cannot save himself. King of Israel, indeed! Let him come down now from the cross, and then we will believe him. Did he trust in God? Let God rescue him, if he wants him—for he said he was God's son. *Matthew 27:42,43*

The intelligentsia always know enough about religion to distort it, hence they took each of the three titles which Christ had claimed for Himself—"Savior," "King of Israel," and "Son of God,"—and turned them into ridicule.

"Savior": So He was called by the Samaritans. Now they would admit He had saved others, probably the daughter of Jairus, the son of the widow of Naim, and Lazarus. They could afford to admit it now, for the Savior Himself stood in need of salvation. "He saved others, He cannot save Himself." The conclusive miracle to them was still lacking.

Of course, He could not save Himself! The rain cannot save itself, if it is to bud the greenery. The sun cannot save itself, if it is to light a world; the soldier cannot save himself, if he is to save his country. And Christ cannot save Himself, if He is to save His creatures!

"King of Israel": That title the crowd gave Him after He fed the multitude and fled into the mountains alone. They repeated it again on Palm Sunday, when they strewed branches beneath His feet. Now that title was mocked as they sneered: "If He is the King of Israel, He has but to come down from the Cross."

Must all the kings of earth be seated on golden thrones? Suppose Israel's King decided to rule from a Cross, to be King not of their bodies through power, but of their hearts through love? Their own literature suggested the idea of a King Who would come to glory through humiliation. How foolish then to mock a King because He refused to come down from His throne. And if He did come down, they would be the first to say, as they had before, that He did it through the power of Beelzebub.

Irreligious forces have their holiday in moments of great catastrophe. In wartime, they ask: "Where is thy God now?" Why is it that in time of trouble, God is always put on trial, and not man? Why in war, should the judge and the culprit change places as man asks: "Why does not God stop the war?"

Thus did Christ hear Himself mocked! They did not know they were already lost. They thought He was. Therefore they, the really damned, mock One Whom they believed to be damned. Hell was triumphing in the human! Truly this was the hour of the power of the devils of hell.

They said they would believe if He came down. But they did not believe when they saw Him raise Lazarus from the dead. Nor would they believe when He would rise from the dead. They then would prohibit the Apostles from preaching the Resurrection which they knew to be a fact. No descent from the Cross would have won men. It is human to come down; it is Divine to hang there!

THE FIFTH WORD TO THE CROSS

When there was darkness over the earth, Our Lord let ring out a cry that prompted the fifth word to the Cross:

Eli, Eli, lema sabachthani? Mark 15:35

which meant

> My God, my God, why hast thou forsaken me?

Hearing this, some of those who stood by said:

> Hark, he is calling Elijah . . . Let us see if Elijah will come to take
> him down. *Mark 15:35,36*

Whether there was a willful misinterpretation of the Lord's cry so
that they mistook Eloi for Elijah is not certain. But there was certainly mockery, for it was a belief of the Jews, because prophesied by
Malachi, that Elijah must come before the Lord came. Their words
meant that He certainly could not be the Lord, for Elijah had not yet
come. Thus they made the self-vaunted Messiah appear as if He summoned a man who was to precede His coming. Actually, Elijah had
come in spirit in the person of John the Baptist. Before John was
born, the angel appeared to his father Zachary, saying that the son to
be born of him:

> He will go before him as forerunner, possessed by the spirit and power
> of Elijah. *Luke 1:16*

That the spirit of Elijah rested in John was evident, for the first
sermon the Baptist preached was "Repent." This was the way Malachi
had prophesied the forerunner of the Lord would announce Him.
Furthermore, John's mode of life and dress pointed up his inner
resemblance to the great Thesbite. The Lord was on the Cross; Elijah
had come in spirit. The mockers undoubtedly recalled Our Lord's reference to Elijah during His public life. He was telling the messengers
from John that the reception of any truth He taught depended upon
one's state of will. Hence to accept John as Elijah meant the acceptance of the repentance John was to bring about in souls:

> For all the prophets and the Law foretold things to come until John
> appeared, and John is the destined Elijah, if you will but accept it.
> *Matthew 11:14*

If their consciences were right, He told them, they would have accepted John in the spirit of Elijah. Two years passed, and their consciences were revealed as Christ hung on the Cross. They reproached
John with asceticism and self-denial; they now reproached Jesus for
hanging on the Cross. As the people expected a different Elijah as His
forerunner, so they expected a different Christ. The cry to the Cross,
on the part of those who misinterpreted a word, was typical of many
who think religion always means something other than it actually
does. All through the Crucifixion, the one unifying motif was: "Come

down from the Cross." Satan did not want Him to mount it, Peter was scandalized at the very mention of it. Even those who believe Christ was a human person do not want His Cross. The world is always waiting for Elijah to take Him down. *The uncrucified Christ is the worldling's desire.* The refusal to come down will forever be the reproach to those who want a lily Christ with hands unscarred and white.

THE SIXTH WORD TO THE CROSS

The sixth word to the Cross came from soldiers:

> The soldiers joined in the mockery and came forward offering him their sour wine. If you are the king of the Jews save yourself.
>
> *Luke 23:36,37*

These men were not Jews, nor citizens of conquered Israel; they were proud legionnaires of Rome. Why then did they refer to Him mockingly as the King of the Jews? Because in keeping with the spirit of paganism, they thought all gods were national gods. Babylon had its gods; the Medes and Persians had theirs; the Greeks had theirs; and so did the Romans have their own. The implication was that of all the national gods, none seemed poorer and weaker than the God of Israel Who could not save Himself from a tree. It is likely, too, that the soldiers' ridicule was inspired by the inscription on the Cross in three languages which read:

> Jesus of Nazareth King of the Jews. *John 19:19*

Others had asked Him to come down from the Cross or to save Himself, but the soldiers, like the thief on the left, challenged Him to "save Himself." They, too, were interested in salvation, but only physically, not spiritually. There was a hidden boast in how well they had done their job of execution so that He could not extricate Himself from the Cross.

The soldiers had already shaken dice for His seamless robe. Caiphas rent his priestly robes, but the robes of the High Priest on the Cross were not rent. He left to His military revilers His seamless robe and their belief that He could not save Himself. They would be stationed at the tomb on Easter morning to see how wrong they were and why He would not save Himself.

These soldiers belonged to an Empire where a general who sacrificed thousands of soldiers for temporal glory was held in high repute; but they scorn the Captain of salvation Who Himself died that others might live. This is one of the few passages in the New Testament where soldiers are spoken of unfavorably. Little did they see that His refusal to save Himself was not weakness but obedience to the law of sacrifice. Their lives committed them to the duty of dying, if need be, to save their country. But that same sacrifice lifted above the military plane they could not grasp. They could see events only in succession; but He had ordained all from the beginning. He came to "give His life as a ransom for many." If in obedience to their command He had saved Himself, man would have been left unsaved.

THE SEVENTH WORD TO THE CROSS

When Christ was crucified, the sun hid its light; when He died, the earth shook in grief. In that earthquake, the rocks were rent, graves were opened, and many bodies of the saints that had been asleep rose and came out of the tombs and appeared to many in the Holy City. If the earth gave signs of recognition when God was delivering His people from the slavery in Egypt by the parting of the waters of the sea, with how much greater reason now did it manifest recognition as the Lord liberated man from the slavery of sin. Though the hearts of the people could not be rent, the rocks could.

The centurion, who had charge of the soldiers, noting the earthquake and recalling the manner in which the Man on the central cross had died, began to reflect. Then this sergeant in the Roman army gave testimony, not in the realm of dreams as did Claudia, the other pagan, but with the expression of an honest and reasonable man:

Truly this Man was a son of God. *Mark 15:39*

The Christ Who had been utterly abandoned by His disciples, save one, at the foot of the Cross; Who had not a single voice raised in His defense except that of a woman; and Who had no one to come forward courageously to acknowledge Him—He is finally owned in His death by a battle-scarred soldier who had commanded and presided over the execution. Doubtless the centurion had crucified many before, but he felt there was something mysterious in this Sufferer, Who prayed for His enemies and was so strong in His last breath, as to prove that He was Master of the life He was surrendering. Seeing all nature become animated and vocal, his mind saw the refutation of the foul calumnies and the innocence of the righteous man; aye, even more, he proclaimed His Divinity.

The Cross was beginning to bear fruit: a Jewish thief had already asked for and received salvation; and now a soldier of Caesar bowed in adoration of the Divine Sufferer. That strange combination which was everywhere in the public life of Our Lord is now manifested on the Cross: humiliation and power. While others condemned Him of blasphemy, the centurion worshiped Him as the Son of God.

51. *The Rending of the Veil of the Temple*

Our Blessed Lord had called His Body the Temple because the fullness of Divinity dwelt in it. The earthly temple of Jerusalem was only a symbol of Himself. In that temple of stone there were three great divisions. Beyond the court of entrance was a place that was called "holy," and beyond it a place more secret still, which was called "the Holy of Holies." The court was separated from the holy place by a veil, and a great veil also divided the holy place from the Holy of Holies.

The very moment that Our Blessed Lord willed His death:

> At that moment the curtain of the temple was torn in two from top to bottom. *Matthew 27:51*

The very fact that it was torn from top to bottom was to indicate that it was not done by the hand of man, but by the miraculous Hand of God Himself, Who had ordained that, as long as the Old Law should endure, the veil should hang before the Holy of Holies. Now He decreed that it should be torn asunder at His death. That which of old was sacred now remained opened and manifest before their eyes, uncovered like any common and ordinary thing, while before them on Calvary, as a soldier pierced His heart, was revealed the new Holy of Holies containing the ark of the New Testament and the treasures of God. The death of Christ was the deconsecration of the earthly temple, for He would raise up the new Temple in three days. Only one man, once a year, could enter into that old Holy of Holies; now that the veil was rent which separated holiness from the people, and separated the Jew from the Gentile, both would have access to the new Temple, Christ the Lord.

There is an intrinsic connection between the soldier piercing the Heart of Christ on the Cross, which drew forth Blood and water, and the rending of the veil of the temple. Two veils were rent: one, the purple veil of the temple which did away with the Old Law; the other, the veil of His Flesh which opened the Holy of Holies of Divine love tabernacled among us. In both instances, what was holy was made manifest; one, the Holy of Holies, which had been only a figure; the other, the true Holy of Holies, His Sacred Heart, which opened to the guilty access to God. The veil in the ancient temple signified that heaven was closed to all until the High Priest sent by the Father would rend the veil and open its gates to all. St. Paul told how the high priest of old, only once a year, and then not without an offering of blood for his own faults and those of the people, was permitted to enter the Holy of Holies. The Epistle to the Hebrews explains this mystery:

> By this the Holy Spirit signifies that so long as the earlier tent still stands, the way into the sanctuary remains unrevealed. All this is symbolic, pointing to the present time. The offerings and sacrifices there prescribed cannot give the worshipper inward perfection. It is only a matter of food and drink and various rites of cleansing—outward ordinances in force until the time of reformation.
> But now Christ has come, high priest of good things already in being. The tent of his priesthood is a greater and more perfect one, not made by men's hands, that is, not belonging to this created world; the blood of his sacrifice is his own blood, not the blood of goats and calves; and thus he has entered the sanctuary once and for all and secured an eternal deliverance. *Hebrews 9:1–12*

Then, comparing the veil of the flesh and the veil of the temple, the Epistle adds:

> The blood of Jesus makes us free to enter boldly into the sanctuary by the new, living way which he has opened for us through the curtain, the way of his flesh. *Hebrews 10:19,20*

A thousand years before, David, looking forward to the Messiah, wrote:

> If thou hadst asked for whole-offering and sin-offering
> I would have said, Here I am.
> My desire is to do thy will, O God,
> and thy law is in my heart.
> In the great assembly I have proclaimed what is right,
> I do not hold back my words,
> as thou knowest, O Lord. *Psalm 39:7–10*

As the Psalmist looked back on the sacrifices of slain beasts, the burnt offerings to attain Divine favor, and the sin offerings to make reparation for wrong, his mind dwelt upon them only to cast them aside. For he well knew that these slaughtered bulls, goats, and sheep could not really affect man's relationship with God. He saw in a future day God having His Divinity enshrined in a human Body as in a temple, and coming with only one purpose, namely, to surrender His life in accordance with the Divine will. David proclaimed that the Divine Incarnation would be the perfection of the sacrifices and the priesthood of the Jewish Law. Now the figure was fulfilled as the spotless Lamb of God offered Himself to His Heavenly Father. The old promise made to Israel in Egypt still held good and could be claimed, in a higher sense, by all who invoked the Blood poured out on the Cross:

> As for you, the blood will be a sign on the houses in which you are: when I see the blood I will pass over you; the mortal blow shall not touch you, when I strike the land of Egypt. *Exodus* 12:13

Levi's House of priesthood was now dismissed. The Order of Melchisedech became the law in the House of Levi. The "no admittance" sign before the Holy of Holies of the earthly temple was removed. When Christ came into the world to be the fulfillment of the order of Melchisedech, the House of Levi denied Him welcome. In fact, Levi had exacted tithes of Him just a few weeks before His death in demanding temple taxes. But, as the veil of the temple was torn, the priesthood of Melchisedech came into its own, and with it the true Holy of Holies, the true Ark of the New Covenant, the true Bread of Life—the Christ, the Son of the Living God.

52. The Piercing of the Side

When Our Savior breathed His last, the bones of the thieves were crushed to hasten their death. The Law had commanded that the body of one who was crucified, and therefore accursed of God, should not remain on the cross during the night. Furthermore, with the Sabbath of Paschal week nigh, it was urgent upon the followers of the Law to kill the thieves and bury all who were crucified. But there was a prophecy yet to be fulfilled concerning the Messiah. The fulfillment came when:

> One of the soldiers stabbed his side with a lance, and at once there was a flow of blood and water. *John 19:13*

The Divine Miser had hoarded up a few precious drops of His Blood to pour forth after He gave up His spirit, to show that His love was stronger than death. Blood and water came forth; Blood, the price of Redemption and the symbol of the Eucharist; water, the symbol of regeneration and baptism. St. John, who witnessed the scene of the soldier piercing the Heart of Christ, wrote about it later:

> This is he who came with water and blood: Jesus Christ. He came, not by water alone, but by water and blood. *I John 5:6*

There was something more than a natural phenomenon here inasmuch as John gave it a mysterious and sacramental significance. Water stood at the beginning of Our Lord's ministry when He was baptized, Blood stood at the close of it when He offered Himself as a spotless oblation. Both became the ground of faith, for at the baptism, the Father declared Him to be His Son, and the Resurrection witnessed again to His Divinity.

The messenger from the Father was impaled with the message of love written on His Own Heart. The thrust of the lance was the last profanation of God's Good Shepherd. Though He was spared the brutality that was arbitrary, such as the breaking of His legs, nevertheless, there was some mysterious Divine purpose in the opening of the Sacred Heart of God. John, who leaned on His breast the night of the Last Supper, fittingly recorded the opening of the Heart. At the Deluge Noah made a door in the side of the ark, by which the animals entered, that they might escape the flood; now a new door is opened into the heart of God into which men might escape the flood of sin. When Adam slept, Eve was taken from his side and was called the mother of all living. Now as the second Adam inclined His head and slept on the Cross under the figure of Blood and water there came from His side His bride, the Church. The open heart fulfilled His words:

> I am the door; anyone who comes into the fold through me shall be safe. *John 10:9*

St. Augustine and other early Christian writers wrote that Longinus, the soldier who opened the treasures of His Sacred Heart, was cured of an affliction of blindness; later Longinus died as a bishop and a martyr of the Church, his feast being kept on the fifteenth of March. When John saw the action, his mind went back to the prophecy of Zechariah, six centuries before:

> They shall look on him whom they pierced. *John 19:37*

Sorrow does not come first, then the look at the Cross; rather sorrow for sins springs from a vision of the Cross. All excuses are cast aside when the vileness of sin is most poignantly revealed. But the arrow of sin that wounds and crucifies brings the balm of forgiveness that heals. Peter saw the Master, and then went out and wept bitterly. As those who looked on the brazen serpent were healed of the poison bite; now the figure passes into reality, and those who looked at One Who seemed like a sinner, but was not, were healed of sin.

All must look whether they like it or not. The pierced Christ stands emblazoned at the crossroads of the world. Some look and are softened to penitence; others look and go away regretfully but not sorrowfully, as did that mob on Calvary "who went home beating their breasts." The beating of the breasts here was a sign of impenitence; it was their refusal to look on Him Whom they had pierced. The *mea culpa* is the beating of the breast that saves.

Though the executioners pierced His side, they did not break a bone of His Body as was also prophesied. Exodus had said that the Paschal Lamb was not to have a bone of its body broken. This lamb was only a type of the literal fulfillment of the Lamb of God:

> This happened in fulfillment of the text of Scripture: No bone of his shall be broken. *John 19:36*

This prophecy was accomplished in spite of His enemies, who asked for the contrary. As the physical Body of Christ had external wounds, bruises, and scars, and yet the inner structure was left untouched, so there seemed to be a foretelling that though His Mystical Body, the Church, would have its moral wounds and scars of scandals and disloyalties, nevertheless, not a bone of its body would ever be broken.

53. *The Night Friends of Christ*

The body of the Savior hung limp upon the Cross—anybody's property, but it belonged to the mother especially. No one in all the world, except Mary, could pronounce His words at the Last Supper as she could, though she was not a priestess. Since no one but the Blessed Mother had given Him body and blood, the Holy Spirit overshadowing, only she could say: "This is my body; this is my blood." She alone gave Him that by which He redeemed; she alone made Him possible; she alone made Him the new Adam. There was no human counterpart; only the Spirit of Love.

Mary claimed Him as her own through the services of two rich men. One was Nicodemus, the secret disciple who made his appearances at night. Nicodemus was a doctor of the law and was looked upon as a master in Israel. From the very beginning, he knew that Our Savior was a teacher come from heaven, yet in order to preserve his authority and not expose himself to the hatred of his countrymen, he always showed up in darkness. The other, Joseph of Arimathea, gave Him the new tomb. The latter had gone to Pilate to ask him for the Body of Our Lord, and Pilate committed It to him. The wealth, rank, and position of these men was noteworthy; one heard the Crucified One tell about His being "lifted up"; the other came from the land of mourning, the site of Rachel's tomb. Isaiah centuries before had foretold that Our Lord would be "rich in death"; He is now given over to the rich man, Joseph of Arimathea.

These two men with a few devout followers prepared to take Our Lord down, to unfasten the nails and take off the crown of thorns. Bending over the figure on which the Blood was hardened, only the eyes of faith could see the marks of royalty there. But with the love that broke through all bounds of calculation, these two latecomers and hidden disciples tried to show their loyalty. It is likely that when the dead Christ was taken down from the Cross, He was laid in the arms of His Blessed Mother. To a mother no child ever grows up. It must have seemed for the moment that Bethlehem had come back again, for He was a Babe in her embrace. But all had changed. He was no longer white as He came from the Father; He was red as He came from the hands of men.

Nicodemus and Joseph anointed the Body with a hundred pounds of myrrh and spices and wound it about with pure linen. The elaborate embalming rather suggested that these secret disciples, as the Apostles themselves, were not expecting the Resurrection. Physically, they were mindful of Him; spiritually, they knew not yet Who He was. Their concern about His burial was a token of their love for Him, not of their faith in Him as the Resurrection and Life.

Now at the place where he had been crucified there was a garden.
John 19:41

The word "garden" hinted at Eden and the fall of man, as it also suggested through its flowers in the springtime the Resurrection from the dead. In that garden was the tomb in which "no man had ever been buried." Born of a virgin womb, He was buried in a virgin tomb, and as Crashaw said: "And a Joseph did betroth them both." Nothing seems more repelling than to have a Crucifixion in a garden, and yet there would be compensation, for the garden would have its Resurrection. Born in a stranger's cave, buried in a stranger's grave, both human birth and death were strangers to His Divinity. Stranger's grave too, because since sin was foreign to Him, so too was death. Dying for others, He was placed in another's grave. His grave was borrowed, for He would give it back on Easter, as He gave back the beast that He rode on Palm Sunday, and the Upper Room which He used for the Last Supper. Burying is only a planting. Paul would later on draw from the fact that He was buried in a garden the law that if we are planted in the likeness of His death, we shall rise with Him in the glory of His Resurrection.

54. The Earth's Most Serious Wound— The Empty Tomb

In the history of the world, only one tomb has ever had a rock rolled before it, and a soldier guard set to watch it to prevent the dead man within from rising: that was the tomb of Christ on the evening of the Friday called Good. What spectacle could be more ridiculous than armed soldiers keeping their eyes on a corpse? But sentinels were set, lest the Dead walk, the Silent speak, and the Pierced Heart quicken to the throb of life. They said He was dead; they knew He was dead; they would say He would not rise again; and yet they watched! They openly called Him a deceiver. But, would He still deceive? Would He, Who "deceived" them into believing they won the battle, Himself win the war for life and truth and love? They remembered that He called His Body the Temple and that in three days after they destroyed It, He would rebuild It; they recalled, too, that He compared Himself to Jonah and said that as Jonah was in the belly of the whale for three days, so would He be in the belly of the earth for three days and then would rise again. After three days Abraham received back his son Isaac, who was offered in sacrifice, for three days Egypt was in a darkness that was not of nature; on the third day God came down on Mount Sinai. Now, once again, there was worry about the third day. Early Saturday morning, therefore, the chief priests and the Pharisees broke the Sabbath and presented themselves to Pilate, saying:

> Your Excellency, we recall how that impostor said while he was still alive, I am to rise after three days. So will you give orders for the grave to be made secure until the third day? Otherwise his disciples may come, steal the body, and then tell the people that he has been raised from the dead; and the final deception will be worse than the first.
>
> *Matthew 27:63,64*

Their request for a guard until the "third day" had more reference to Christ's words about His Resurrection than it did to the fear of the Apostles stealing a corpse and propping it up like a living thing in simulation of a Resurrection. But Pilate was in no mood to see this group, for they were the reason why he had condemned Innocent Blood. He had made his own official investigation that Christ was dead; he would not submit to the absurdity of using Caesar's armies to guard a dead Jew. Pilate said to them:

> You may have your guard, go and make it secure as best you can.
> *Matthew 27:65*

The watch was to prevent violence; the seal was to prevent fraud. There must be a seal, and the enemies would seal it. There must be a watch, and the enemies must keep it. The certificates of the death and Resurrection must be signed by the enemies themselves. The Gentiles were satisfied through nature that Christ was dead; the Jews were satisfied through the Law that He was dead.

> So they went and made the grave secure; they sealed the stone, and left the guard in charge. *Matthew 27:66*

The King lay in state with His guard about Him. The most astounding fact about this spectacle of vigilance over the dead was that the enemies of Christ expected the Resurrection, but His friends did not. It was the believers who were the skeptics; it was the unbelievers who were credulous. His followers needed and demanded proofs before they would be convinced. In the three great scenes of the Resurrection drama, there was a note of sadness and unbelief. The first scene was that of a weeping Magdalen who came to the grave early in the morning with spices, not to greet the Risen Savior, but to anoint His dead Body.

MAGDALEN AT THE GRAVE

In the dim dawn of Sunday morning several women were seen approaching the tomb. The very fact that the women brought spices proved that they did not expect a Resurrection. It seemed strange that such should have been the case after the many references by Our Lord to His death and His Resurrection. But evidently the disciples as well as the women, whenever He predicted His Passion, seemed to remember more His death than His Resurrection. It never occurred to them as a possible thing; it was foreign to their thoughts. When the stone was rolled to the door of the sepulcher, not only was Christ buried but also all of their hopes. The only thought the women had was to anoint the body of the dead Christ—an act that was born of despairing and as yet unbelieving love. Two of them, at least, had witnessed the burial; hence their great concern was the practical act:

> Who would roll away the stone for them from the entrance to the tomb. *Mark 16:3*

It was the cry of hearts of little faith. Strong men had closed the entrance to the tomb by placing this huge stone against it; their worry was how to remove the barrier in order that they might carry out their errand of mercy. The men would not come to the tomb until they were summoned—so little did they believe. But the women came, only because in their grief they sought consolation in embalming the dead. Nothing is more antihistorical than to say that the pious women were expecting Christ to rise from the dead. The Resurrection was something they never expected. Their minds were not made up of the kind of material on which such expectations could grow.

But as they approached, they found the stone rolled back. Before their arrival, there had been a great earthquake, and an angel of the Lord, who descended from heaven, rolled back the stone and sat upon it:

> His face shone like lightning; his garments were white as snow. At the sight of him the guards shook with fear and lay like the dead.
>
> *Matthew 28:4*

When the women came near they saw that the stone, great as it was, had been rolled away already. But they did not immediately jump to the conclusion that His Body had risen. Their conclusion could be that someone had removed the body. Instead of the dead Body of their Master, they saw an angel, whose countenance was as lightning and his raiment as snow and who said to them:

> Fear nothing; you are looking for Jesus of Nazareth, who was cruci-fied. He has been raised again; he is not here; look there is the place where they laid him. But go and give this message to his disciples and Peter: He is going on before you into Galilee; there you will see him, as he told you. *Mark 16:6–8*

To an angel, the Resurrection would not be a mystery, but His death would be. For man, His death was not a mystery, but His Res-urrection would be. What had been natural to the angel, therefore, was now made the subject of the announcement. The angel was one keeper more than the enemies had placed about the Savior's grave, one soldier more than Pilate had appointed.

The angel's words were the first Gospel preached after the Resur-rection, and it is the one that went back to His Passion, for the angel spoke of Him, as "Jesus of Nazareth Who was crucified." These words conveyed the name of His humanity, the humility of His dwell-ing place, and the ignominy of His death; in all three, lowliness, igno-miny, and shame are brought in comparison with His rising from the dead. Bethlehem, Nazareth, and Jerusalem are all made the identi-fying marks of His Resurrection.

The angel's words: "Here is the place where they laid Him," confirmed the reality of His death and the fulfillment of the ancient prophecies. Tombstones bear the inscription: *Hic jacet* or "Here lies." Then follows the name of the dead and perhaps some praise of the one departed. But here in contrast, the angel did not write, but expressed a different epitaph: "He is not here." The angel called on the women to behold the place where their Lord's Body had been laid, as though the vacant tomb was evidence enough of the fact of the Resurrection. They were directed to hasten immediately and give intelligence of the Resurrection. It was to a virgin woman that the birth of the Son of God was announced. It was to a fallen woman that His Resurrection was announced.

Those who saw the empty grave were bidden to go to Peter who had tempted Our Blessed Lord once from the Cross and had three times denied Him. Sin and denial could not choke Divine love. Paradoxical though it was, the greater the sin, the less the belief; and yet the greater the repentance from sin, the greater the belief. It was to the lost sheep panting in the wilderness that He came; it was the publicans and the harlots, the denying Peters and the persecuting Pauls to whom the most persuasive entreaties of love were sent. To the man who was named a Rock and who would have tempted Christ from a Cross, the angel now sent through the women the message, "Go tell Peter."

The same individualizing prominence given to Peter in the public life was continued in the Resurrection. But though Peter was mentioned here with the Apostles of whom he was the head, the Lord appeared to Peter alone before He revealed Himself to the disciples at Emmaus. This was evident from the fact that later on the disciples would say that He appeared to Peter. The glad news of Redemption was thus given to a woman who had fallen and to an Apostle who had denied; but both of whom had repented.

Mary Magdalen, who had in the darkness moved ahead of her companions, noticed that the stone had already been rolled to one side, while the entrance stood wide open. A quick glance revealed that the grave was empty. Her first thought was of the Apostles, Peter and John, to whom she ran in excitement. According to Mosaic Law a woman was ineligible to bear witness. But Mary did not bring them tidings of the Resurrection; she was not expecting it. She assumed that He was still under the power of death, as she told Peter and John:

> They have taken the Lord out of his tomb, and we do not know where they have laid him.   *John 20:2*

Out of all the disciples and followers there were only five "watching": three women and two men, like the five in the parable who awaited the coming of the Bridegroom. All of them were without suspicion of the Resurrection.

In their excitement both Peter and John ran to the sepulcher, thus leaving Mary far behind. John was the better runner of the two, and arrived there first. When Peter arrived, they both went into the sepulcher, where they saw linen cloths lying about, as well as the veil they had put on the head of Jesus; but this was not with the linen cloths; but was wrapped up by itself. What had taken place was done decently and in order, not by a thief nor even a friend. The Body was gone from the tomb; the original bindings around His Body were found in their convolutions. If the disciples had stolen the body, they would not in their haste have unwrapped it and left the linen cloths. Christ had risen out of them by His Divine power. Peter and John

> Until then they had not understood the scriptures, which showed that he must rise from the dead. *John 20:9*

They had the facts and the evidence of the Resurrection; but they did not yet understand its full meaning. The Lord now began the first of His eleven recorded appearances between His Resurrection and Ascension: sometimes to His Apostles, at other times to five hundred brethren at once, at some other times to the women. The first appearance was to Mary Magdalen, who returned to the sepulcher after Peter and John had left it. The idea of the Resurrection did not seem to enter her mind either, though she herself had risen from a tomb sealed by the seven devils of sin. Finding the tomb empty, she broke again into a fountain of tears. With her eyes cast down as the brightness of the early sunrise swept over the dew-covered grass, she vaguely perceived someone near her who asked:

> Why are you weeping? *John 20:13*

She was weeping for what was lost, but His question took away the curse of tears by bidding her to stop her tears. She said:

> They have taken my Lord away, and I do not know where they have laid him. *John 20:14*

There was no terror at seeing the angels, for the world on fire could not have moved her, so much had grief mastered her soul. When she had said this, she turned and saw Jesus standing; and she knew not that it was He. She thought He was the gardener—the gardener of Joseph of Arimathea. Believing this man might know where the Lost One could be found, Mary Magdalen went down on her knees and asked:

> If it is you, sir, who removed him, tell me where you have laid him, and I will take him away. *John 20:15*

Poor Magdalen! Worn from Good Friday, wearied by Holy Saturday, with life dwindled to a shadow and strength weakened to a thread, she would "take Him away." Three times did she speak of "Him" without defining His name. The force of love was such as to suppose no one else could possibly be meant.

Jesus said to her:

Mary!   *John 20:15*

That voice was more startling than a clap of thunder. She had once heard Jesus say that He called His sheep by name. And now to that One, Who individualized all the sin, sorrow, and tears in the world and marked each soul with a personal, particular, and discriminating love, she turned, seeing the red livid marks on His hands and feet, she uttered but one word:

Rabbuni!   *John 20:16*

(which is the Hebrew for "master"). Christ had uttered "Mary" and all heaven was in it. It was only one word she uttered, and all earth was in it. After the mental midnight, there was this dazzle; after hours of hopelessness, this hope; after the search, this discovery; after the loss, this find. Magdalen was prepared only to shed reverential tears over the grave; what she was not prepared for was to see Him walking on the wings of the morning.

Only purity and sinlessness could welcome the all holy Son of God into the world; hence, Mary Immaculate met Him at the door of earth in the city of Bethlehem. But only a repentant sinner, who had herself risen from the grave of sin to the newness of life in God, could fittingly understand the triumph over sin. To the honor of womanhood it must forever be said: A woman was closest to the Cross on Good Friday, and first at the tomb on Easter Morn.

Mary was always at His feet. She was there as she anointed Him for burial; she was there as she stood at the Cross; now in joy at seeing the Master, she threw herself at His feet to embrace them. But He said to her with a restraining gesture:

Do not cling to me, for I have not yet ascended to the Father.
John 20:17

Her tender tokens of affection were directed to Him more as the Son of Man than as the Son of God. Hence He bade her not to touch Him. St. Paul would have to give the Corinthians and Colossians the same lesson:

Even if once they counted in our understanding of Christ, they do so now no longer.   *II Corinthians 5:16*

Let your thoughts dwell on that higher realm, not on this earthly life.
I repeat, you died; and now your life lies hidden with Christ in God.
Colossians 3:2

Her tears, He suggested, were to be dried not because she had seen
Him again, but because He was the Lord of heaven. When He had ascended to the right hand of the Father, which signified the Father's
power; when He would send the Spirit of Truth, Who would be their
new Comforter and His inner Presence, then indeed would she truly
have Him for Whom she yearned—the risen glorified Christ. It was
His first hint, after His Resurrection, at the new relationship He
would have with men, of which He spoke so fluently the night of the
Last Supper. He would have to give the same lesson to His disciples,
who were too preoccupied with His human form, by telling them that
it was expedient for Him to leave. Magdalen wished to be with Him
as she was before the Crucifixion, forgetting that the Crucifixion was
endured for glory and for the sending of His Spirit.

Though the Magdalen was humbled by this prohibition of Our Savior, she nevertheless was destined to feel the exaltation of bearing tidings of His Resurrection. The men had grasped the significance of the
empty tomb, but not its relation to Redemption and victory over sin
and evil. She was to break the precious alabaster box of His Resurrection so that its perfume might fill the world. He said to her:

Go to my brothers, and tell them that I am now ascending to my Father and your Father, my God and your God. *John* 20:17

This was the first time He ever called His Apostles "My Brethren."
Before man could be an adopted son of God, he had to be redeemed
from enmity with God.

In truth, in very truth I tell you, a grain of wheat remains a solitary
grain unless it falls into the ground and dies; but if it dies, it bears a
rich harvest. *John* 12:24

He took the Crucifixion to multiply His Sonship into other sons of
God. But there would be a vast difference between Himself as the natural Son and human beings, who through His Spirit would become
the adopted sons. Hence, as always, He made a rigid distinction between "My Father" and "Your Father." Never once in His life did
He say "Our Father" as if the relationship were the same between
Himself and men; His relation to the Father was unique and incom-
municable; Sonship was by nature His; only by grace and adoption
were men sons of God:

The Son does not shrink from calling men his brothers, when he says,
I will proclaim thy name to my brothers; in full assembly I will sing
thy praise. *Hebrews* 2:11

Nor did He tell Mary to inform the Apostles that He was risen but rather that He would ascend. The Resurrection was implied in the Ascension, which was as yet forty days off. His purpose was not just to stress that He who had died was now alive, but that this was the beginning of a spiritual Kingdom which would become visible and unified when He sent His Spirit.

Obediently, Mary Magdalen hastened to the disciples who were "mourning and weeping." She told them she had seen the Lord and the words He had spoken to her. What reception did her tidings receive? Once again, skepticism, doubt, and unbelief. The Apostles had heard Him speak in figure, symbol, parable, and straightforward speech of the Resurrection which would follow His death, but:

> When they were told that he was alive and that she had seen him they did not believe it. *Mark 16:11*

Eve believed the serpent; but the disciples did not believe the Son of God. As for Mary Magdalen and any other woman who might tell of His Resurrection:

> The story appeared to them to be nonsense, and they would not believe them. *Luke 24:11*

It was a forecast of the way the world would receive the news of Redemption. Mary Magdalen and the other women did not at first believe in the Resurrection; they had to be convinced. Neither did the Apostles believe. Their answer was "You know women! Always imagining things." Long before the advent of scientific psychology, people were afraid of their minds playing tricks on them. Modern incredulity in the face of the extraordinary is nothing compared to the skepticism which immediately greeted the first news of the Resurrection. What modern skeptics say about the Resurrection story, the disciples themselves were the first to say, namely, it was an idle tale. As the original agnostics of Christianity, with one assent the Apostles dismissed the whole story as a delusion. Something very extraordinary must happen, and some very concrete evidence must be presented to all of these doubters, before they overcome their reluctance to believe.

Their skepticism was even more difficult than modern skepticism to overcome, because theirs started from a hope that was seemingly disappointed on Calvary; this was far more difficult to heal than a modern skepticism, which is without hope. Nothing could be further from the truth than to say that the followers of Our Blessed Lord were expecting the Resurrection and, therefore, were ready to believe it or to console themselves for a loss that seemed irreparable. No agnostic has written about the Resurrection anything that Peter and the other Apostles had not already had in their own minds. When Mohammed died, Omar rushed from his tent, sword in hand, and declared that he would kill anyone who said that the Prophet had died. In the case of Christ, there was a readiness to believe that He had died, but a reluctance to believe that He was living. But perhaps they were permitted to doubt, so that the faithful in centuries to come might never be in doubt.

GUARDS AND BRIBERY

After the women had gone to notify the Apostles, the guards, who had been standing about the tomb, and who were witnesses to the Resurrection, came into the city of Jerusalem and told the chief priests all that had been done. The chief priests immediately assembled a meeting of the Sanhedrin, the express purpose of which was to bribe the guards.

> After meeting with the elders and conferring together, the chief priests offered the soldiers a substantial bribe and told them to say, His disciples came by night and stole the body while we were asleep. They added, If this should reach the Governor's ears, we will put matters right with him and see that you do not suffer. So they took the money and did as they were told. This story became widely known, and is current in Jewish circles to this day. *Matthew 28:12-15*

The "rich bribe" contrasted rather strongly with the meagre thirty pieces of silver which Judas received. The Sanhedrin did not deny the Resurrection; in fact, they bore their own unbiased testimony to its truth. And that same testimony they carried to the Gentiles through Pilate. They even gave the money of the temple to the Roman soldiers whom they despised; for they had found a greater hate. The money Judas had returned they would not touch because it was "blood money." But now they would buy a lie to escape the purifying Blood of the Lamb.

The bribery of the guard was really a stupid way to escape the fact of the Resurrection. First of all, there was the problem of what would be done with His Body after the disciples had possession of it. All that the enemies of Our Lord would have had to do to disprove the Resurrection would be to produce the Body. Quite apart from the fact that it was very unlikely that a whole guard of Roman soldiers slept while they were on duty, it was absurd for them to say that what had happened, happened when they were asleep. The soldiers were advised to say they were asleep; and yet they were so awake as to have seen thieves and to know that they were disciples. If all of the soldiers were asleep, they could never have discovered the thieves; if a few of them were awake, they should have prevented the theft. It is equally improbable that a few timid disciples should attempt to steal their Master's Body from a grave closed by stone, officially sealed, and guarded by soldiers without awakening the sleeping guards. The orderly arrangement of the burial cloths afforded further proof that the Body was not removed by His disciples.

The secret removal of the Body would have been to no purpose so far as the disciples were concerned, nor had any of them even thought of it; for the moment, the life of their Master was a failure and a defeat. The crime was certainly greater in the bribers than in the bribed; for, the council was educated and religious; the soldiers were untutored and simple. The Resurrection of Christ was officially proclaimed to the civil authorities; the Sanhedrin believed in the Resurrection before the Apostles. It had bought the kiss of Judas; now it hoped it could buy the silence of the guards.

BROKEN HEARTS AND BROKEN BREAD

On that same Easter Sunday, Our Blessed Lord made another appearance to two of His disciples who were on their way to a village named Emmaus, which was a short distance from Jerusalem. It was not so long ago that their hopes had been burning brightly, but the darkness of Good Friday and the burial in the tomb caused them to lose their gladness. No subject was more in men's minds that particular day than the Person of Christ. As they were discoursing with sad and anxious hearts on the awful incidents of the last two days, a Stranger drew near to them. Their eyes, however, were held fast so that they did not recognize that it was the Risen Savior; they thought Him to be an ordinary traveler. As the story unfolded, it became clear that what blinded their eyes was their unbelief; had they been expecting to see Him, they might have recognized Him. Because they were interested in Him, He vouchsafed His Presence; because they doubted His Resurrection, He concealed the joy and knowledge of His Presence. Now that His Body was glorified, what men saw of Him depended on His willingness to reveal Himself and also on the disposition of their own hearts. Though they did not know Our Lord, they nevertheless were ready to enter into discussion with the Stranger concerning Him. After listening to their long discussion, the Stranger asked:

> What is it you are debating as you walk? They halted, their faces full of gloom. *Luke 24:17*

Obviously, the reason these disciples were sad was because of their bereavement. They had been with Jesus; they had seen Him arrested, insulted, crucified, dead, and buried. Sorrow afflicts a woman's heart when she loses the beloved; but men generally become perplexed in mind rather than heart at a similar loss; theirs was the sorrow of a shattered career.

The Savior with His infinite wisdom did not begin by saying, "I know why you are sad." His technique was rather to draw them out; a sorrowful heart is best consoled when it relieves itself. If their sorrow would have a tongue and speak, He would have an ear and reveal. If they would but show their wounds, He would pour in the oil of His healing.

One of the two, whose name was Cleophas, was the first to speak. He expressed amazement at the ignorance of the Stranger Who was apparently so unfamiliar with the events of the last few days.

> Are you the only person staying in Jerusalem not to know what has happened there in the last few days? *Luke 24:18*

The risen Lord asked:

> What do you mean? *Luke 24:19*

He called their attention to *facts*. They apparently had not gone deeply enough into the facts for proper conclusions. The cure for their sorrow was in the very things that disturbed them, to see them in their right relations. As with the woman at the well, He asked a question, not to get information, but to deepen knowledge of Himself. Then not Cleophas alone but also his companion told Him what had happened. They spoke:

> All this about Jesus of Nazareth, they replied, a prophet powerful in speech and action before God and the whole people; how our chief priests and rulers handed him over to be sentenced to death, and crucified him. But we had been hoping that he was the man to liberate Israel. What is more, this is the third day since it happened, and now some women of our company have astounded us: they went early to the tomb, but failed to find his body, and returned with a story that they had seen a vision of angels who told them he was alive. So some of our people went to the tomb and found things just as the women had said; but him they did not see. *Luke 24:19–24*

These men had hoped great things, but God, they said, had disappointed them. Man draws a blueprint and hopes that God in some way will rubber-stamp it; disappointment is often due to the triviality of human hopes. Original drawings now had to be torn up—not because they were too great, but because in the eyes of God they were too little. The hand that broke the cup of their petty desires offered a richer chalice. They thought that they had found the Redeemer before He was crucified, but actually they had discovered a Redeemer *crucified*. They had hoped for a Savior of Israel, but were not expecting a Savior of the Gentiles as well. They must have heard Him say on many occasions that He would be crucified and rise again, but they could not fit catastrophe into their idea of a Master. They could believe in Him as a Teacher, as a political Messiah, as an ethical reformer, as a savior of the country, a deliverer from the Romans, but they could not believe in the foolishness of the Cross; nor did they have the faith of the thief hanging on the cross. Hence they refused to regard the evidence of which the women had told them. They were not sure even that the women had seen angels. Possibly it was only an apparition. Furthermore, it was the third day which had come and gone, and He had not been seen. But all the while they were walking and talking with Him.

There seemed to be a double purpose in the appearance of Our Savior after His Resurrection, one to show that He Who died had risen, the other, that though He had the same Body, it was now glorified and not subject to physical restrictions. Later on, He would eat with His disciples to prove the first; now, as with the Magdalen whom He forbade to touch Him, He stressed His risen state.

With these disciples as with all of the Apostles, there was no predisposition to accept the Resurrection. The evidence for it had to make its way against doubt and the most obstinate refusals of human nature. They were among the last people in the world to credit such a tale. One might almost say that they were resolved to be miserable, refusing to enquire into the possibility of the truth of the story. Resisting both the evidence of the women and the confirmation of those who had gone to verify their story, the final word was that they had not seen the risen Lord.

Then the risen Savior said to them:

> How dull you are! How slow to believe all that the prophets said! Was the Messiah not bound to suffer thus before entering upon his glory?
>
> *Luke 24:25,26*

They are accused of being foolish and slow of heart, because if they had ever sat down and examined what the prophets had said about the Messiah—that He would be led like a lamb to slaughter—they would have been confirmed in their belief. Credulity toward men and incredulity toward God is the mark of dull hearts; readiness to believe speculatively and slowness to believe practically is the sign of sluggish hearts. Then came the key words of the journey. Previously, Our Blessed Lord had said that He was the Good Shepherd, that He came to lay down His life for the Redemption of many; now in His glory, He proclaimed a moral law that in consequence of His sufferings men would be raised from a state of sin to fellowship with God.

The Cross was the condition of glory. The Risen Savior spoke of a moral necessity grounded on the truth that everything that happened to Him had been foretold. What seemed to them an offense, a scandal, a defeat, a succumbing to the inevitable was actually a dark moment foreseen, planned, and preannounced. Though the Cross seemed to them incompatible with His glory, to Him it was the appointed path thereto. And if they had known what the Scriptures had said of the Messiah, they would have believed in the Cross.

> Then he began with Moses and all the prophets, and explained to them the passages which referred to himself in every part of the scriptures.
>
> *Luke 24:27*

He showed to them all the types and all the rituals and all the ceremonials that were fulfilled in Him. Quoting from Isaiah, He showed the manner of His death and Crucifixion and His Last Words from the Cross; from Daniel, how He was to become the mountain that filled the earth; from Genesis, how the seed of a woman would crush the serpent of evil in human hearts; from Moses, how He would be the brazen serpent that would be lifted up to heal men of evil, and how His side would be the smitten rock from which would come the waters of regeneration; from Isaiah, how He would be Emmanuel, or "God with us"; from Micheas, how He would be born in Bethlehem; and from many other writings He gave them the key to the mystery of God's life among men and the purpose of His coming.

At last they arrived at Emmaus. He made it appear as if He were about to continue His journey along the same road, just as once before when a storm was sweeping the lake, He made it appear as though He would pass by the boat of the Apostles. The two disciples begged Him, however, to stay with them. Those who have good thoughts of God in the day will not readily surrender them at nightfall. They had learned much, but they knew that they had not learned all. They still did not recognize Him, but there was a light about Him which promised to lead to a fuller revelation and dissipate their gloom. Their invitation to be a guest He accepted, but immediately He acted as the Host for:

> When he had sat down with them at table, he took bread and said the blessing; he broke the bread, and offered it to them. Then their eyes were opened, and they recognized him; and he vanished from their sight. *Luke 24:30,31*

This taking of the bread and breaking it and giving it to them was not an ordinary act of courtesy, for it resembled too closely the Last Supper at which He bade His Apostles to repeat the Memorial of His death as He broke the bread which was His Body and gave it to them. Immediately on the reception of the Sacramental Bread that was broken, the eyes of their souls were opened. As the eyes of Adam and Eve were opened to see their shame after they had eaten the forbidden fruit of the knowledge of good and evil, so now the eyes of the disciples were opened to discern the Body of Christ. The scene parallels the Last Supper: in both there was a giving of thanks; in both, a looking up to heaven; in both, the breaking of the bread; and in both, the giving of the bread to the disciples. With the conferring of the bread came a knowledge which gave greater clarity than all the instructions. The breaking of the bread had introduced them into an experience of the glorified Christ. Then He disappeared from their sight. Turning to one another, they reflected:

> Did we not feel our hearts on fire as he talked with us on the road and explained the scriptures to us? *Luke 24:32*

His influence upon them was both affective and intellectual: affective, in the sense that it made their hearts burn with love; and intellectual, inasmuch as it gave them an understanding of the hundreds of pre-announcements of His coming. Mankind is naturally disposed to believe that anything religious must be striking and powerful enough to overwhelm the imagination. Yet this incident on the road to Emmaus revealed that the most powerful truths often appear in the commonplace and trivial incidents of life, such as meeting a fellow traveler on a road. Christ veiled His Presence in the most ordinary roadway of life. Knowledge of Him came as they walked with Him; and the knowledge was that of glory that came through defeat. In His Glorified Life as in His public life, the Cross and glory went together. It was not just His teachings that were recalled; it was His sufferings and how expedient they were for His exaltation.

The disciples immediately returned and went back to Jerusalem. As the woman at the well in her excitement left her water pitcher at the well, so these disciples forgot the purpose of their journey to Emmaus and went back to the Holy City. There they found the eleven Apostles gathered together, and with them other followers and disciples. They recounted all that had happened on the way and how they recognized Him in the breaking of the bread.

55. *The Doors Being Closed*

The two disciples on their return to Jerusalem found the Apostles in varying degrees of unbelief. It is likely that Thomas was with the Apostles in the early part of the evening, but left early. The disciples of Emmaus had seen the Resurrection first with the eyes of the mind and then with the eyes of the body. The Apostles would see it first with the eyes of the body and then with the eyes of the mind.

The place where the disciples were assembled that Easter Sunday evening was the Upper Room; where Our Lord gave the twelve the Eucharist, only seventy-two hours before. Added to the doubts of the disciples was fear which prompted them to close the doors and to bolt them, lest the representatives of the Sanhedrin break in to arrest them on the false charge of stealing the Body. There was also a dread that possibly the people might storm, as they often did, the house of those who were unpopular. Though the doors were shut, suddenly in the midst of them appeared the Risen Lord, greeting them with the words:

Peace be with you. *Luke 24:36*

He bade the women at the grave, who were plunged in grief, to rejoice; but now, having brought about peace by the Blood of the Cross, He came in His own Person to bestow it. Peace is the fruit of justice. Only when the injustice of sin against God had been requited could there be an affirmation of true peace. Peace is the tranquility of order, not tranquility alone; for robbers can be tranquil in the possession of their spoils. Peace also implies order, the subordination of the body to the soul, of the senses to reason, and of the creature to the Creator. Isaiah said there was no peace to the wicked because they are at enmity with themselves, with one another, and with God.

Now the Risen Christ stood among them as the new Melchisedech, the Prince of Peace. Three times after His Resurrection, He gave the solemn benediction of peace. The first was while the Apostles were terrified and frightened; the second, after He gave proof of His Resurrection; and the third, a week later when Thomas was with them.

The Apostles believed at first that they had seen a Spirit; despite the words of the women, the testimony of the disciples of Emmaus, the empty sepulcher, the angelical vision, and the recital of Peter of his interview with the Risen One. His Presence, they admitted to themselves, could be accounted for in no natural way, since the doors were barred. Reproving them for their unbelief, as He did the disciples of Emmaus, He said to them:

> Why are you so perturbed? Why do questionings arise in your minds?
> *Luke 24:38*

He showed them His hands and His feet, which had been pierced with nails on the Cross, then His side, which had been opened with a lance, saying to them:

> Look at my hands and feet. It is I myself. Touch me and see; no ghost has flesh and bones as you can see that I have. *Luke 24:39*

It is very likely that the incredulous Apostles actually touched the Body of Christ; this might explain why Thomas later demanded such a sign; he would not be inferior to others. John, who had leaned on His breast the night of the Last Supper, was particularly interested in the side or heart. He never forgot that touching scene; for, later on he wrote:

> It was there from the beginning; we have heard it; we have seen it with our own eyes; we looked upon it, and felt it with our own hands.
> *I John 1:1*

John too, would remember it when he wrote his Apocalypse where he described the sacred humanity of the Lord enthroned and adored in heaven:

> A Lamb with the marks of slaughter upon him. *Apocalypse 5:6*

It was thus He would be recognized as One Crucified though now in glory, Prince and Lord. It was not that the cruel wounds were to be a reminder of the cruelty of men, but rather that by pain and sorrow, Redemption had been wrought. If the scars had been removed, men might have forgotten that there was a sacrifice, and that He was both Priest and Victim. His argument was that the body that he showed them was the same that was born of the Virgin Mary, nailed to the Cross and laid in a grave by Joseph of Arimathea. But It had properties which It did not possess before.

Peter, James, and John had seen Him transfigured when His garments were whiter than snow, but the rest of the disciples had only seen Him as a Man of Sorrow. This was their first gaze upon a risen and glorious Lord. These nail prints, this pierced side, these were the unmistakable scars of battle against sin and evil. As many a soldier looks upon the wounds he received in battle not as a disfigurement, but as a trophy of honor, so He wore His wounds to prove that love was stronger than death. After the Ascension these scars would become as oratorical mouths of intercession before the Heavenly Father; scars that He would bear on the last day to judge the living and the dead. In an old legend it is said that Satan appeared to a saint and said: "I am the Christ"; the saint confounded him by asking: "Where are the marks of nails?"

If men had been left to themselves to form their own conception of the Risen Christ, they never would have represented Him with the signs and remnants of His shame and agony on earth. Had He risen with no memorials of His Passion, men might have doubted Him with the passing of time. That there might be no doubt of the sacrificial purpose of His coming, He gave them not only the Memorial of His death the night of the Last Supper, asking that it be perpetuated as long as time endured, but He also bore on His Person, as Jesus Christ, the "same yesterday, today and forever," the Memorial of His Redemption. But were the Apostles convinced?

> They were still unconvinced, still wondering, for it seemed too good to be true. So he asked them, Have you anything here to eat?
>
> *Luke 24:41*

So they placed before Him a piece of meat and a honeycomb; He took these and ate in their presence, and He bade them share His meal. It was not a phantom that they were seeing. To some extent they believed in the Resurrection, and that belief gave them joy; but the joy was so great they could hardly believe it. At first they were too frightened to believe; now they were too joyful to believe. But Our Lord would not rest until He had completely satisfied their senses. Eating with them would be the strongest proof of His Resurrection. After raising the daughter of Jairus, He ordered that food should be given her; after the resurrection of Lazarus, Lazarus took food with Him; now, after His own Resurrection, He ate with His Apostles. Thus He would convince them that it was the same living Body which they had seen and touched and felt; but it was at the same time a Body that was glorified. It had no wounds as signs of weakness, but rather as glorious scars of victory. This glorified Body ate not as the plant draws in moisture from the earth because of need but as the sun imbibes the same from power. He had given some indications of what this glorified nature of His would be like in the Transfiguration, when Moses and Elijah spoke with Him about His death. That was a promise and a pledge that corruption would put on incorruption, the mortal would put on immortality, and death be swallowed up in life.

After having proved to His disciples that He had risen by showing them His hands, feet, and side, and by eating before them, He gave to them the second salutation of peace, saying:

> Peace be with you! As the Father sent me, so I send you. Then he breathed on them, saying, Receive the Holy Spirit! *John 20:21*

The first salutation of peace was when they were frightened; now that they were filled with the joy of believing, the second salutation of peace had reference to the world. His concern was not with the world of His public life, but the whole world He had redeemed. A few hours before He had gone to His death He had prayed to His Father:

> As thou hast sent me into the world, I have sent them into the world.
> *John 17:18*

Continuing the idea, He said that He was praying not only for those that would be His representatives upon earth but for everyone throughout history who would believe in Him.

> But it is not for these alone that I pray, but for all those who through their words put their faith in me. *John 17:20*

Thus the night of the Last Supper before going to His death, He was concerned about His mission to the world after His Crucifixion—a mission into a world that had rejected Him. Now, after the Resurrection, He reiterated the same idea to His Apostles, the twelve stones of the foundation of this city of God. In the Old Testament the high priest put stones on the raiment he wore over his breast; now the true High Priest engraved living stones on His heart. His mission and their mission was one. As Christ was sent and through His suffering entered into glory, so now He bequeathed to them His share of the Cross and, after that, His glory.

Our Lord did not say, "As My Father sent Me so also I send you," because there are two entirely different Greek words used in the original for "sent." The first word was used to describe both Our Lord's mission from the Father and the mission of the Holy Spirit; the second word implied rather a commission, and had reference to Christ's authority as an ambassador. Christ came forth from the eternal bosom of the Father in His Incarnation; so now the Apostles would go forth from Him. Just as Our Lord had insisted on the difference between "My Father" and "Your Father"; so now He stressed the difference between the respective missions. Christ was sent to manifest the Father because He was one in nature with the Father; the Apostles, who were the foundation stones of the Kingdom, were to manifest the Son. As He spoke these words they could see the glorious scars on His risen Body. Imprinting them on their mind, they understood that as

the Father had sent Him to suffer in order to save mankind, so the
Son was sending them to suffer persecution. As the love of the Father
was in Him, so the love of the Father and Himself would be in them.
The authority behind the apostolic mission was overwhelming; for its
roots were in the analogy of the Father sending His Son and of the
Son sending them. It was no wonder that He told them that whoever
would reject one of His Apostles would be rejecting Him. Though
Thomas was not there, he nevertheless would partake of the gifts,
even as St. Paul did.

Then Our Lord breathed on them as He conferred some power of
the Holy Spirit. When love is deep, it is always speechless or wordless;
God's love is so deep that it can be expressed humanly by a sigh or a
breath. Now that the Apostles had learned to lisp the alphabet of Redemption, He breathed on them as a sign and an earnest of what was
to come. It was but a cloud that would precede the plenteous rain;
better still, it was the breath of the Spirit's influence and a foretelling
of the rushing wind of Pentecost. As He had breathed into Adam the
breath of natural life, so now He breathed into His Apostles, the
foundation of His Church, the breath of spiritual life. As man became
the image of God in virtue of the soul that was breathed into him, so
now they became the image of Christ as the power of the Spirit was
breathed into them. The Greek word used to express His breathing on
them is employed nowhere else in the New Testament; but it is the
very word which the Greek translators of the Hebrew used to describe
God's breathing a living soul into Adam. Thus there was a new creation as the first fruit of the Redemption.

As He breathed on them, He gave them the Holy Spirit, which
made them no longer servants, but sons. Three times the Holy Spirit
is mentioned with some external sign; as a dove at Christ's baptism
betokening His innocence and Divine Sonship; as fiery tongues on the
day of Pentecost as a sign of the Spirit's power to convert the world;
and as the breath of the Risen Christ with all of its regenerative
power. As the Lord had made clay to anoint the eyes of the blind
man, showing that He was the Creator of man, so now by breathing
the Spirit upon His Apostles did He show that He was the regenerator
of the life of the clay that fell.

When Our Lord was at the Feast of the Tabernacles, watching the
water brought up from the pool, He said that if any man believed in
Him, He would cause fountains of living waters to flow from His
bosom. The Scriptures add:

> He was speaking of the Spirit which believers in him would receive
> later; for the Spirit had not yet been given, because Jesus had not yet
> been glorified. *John 7:39*

At that celebrated feast, He affirmed that He would first have to die and pass into glory, before the Holy Spirit could come. His words now implied that He was already in His state of glory; for He was bestowing the Spirit. He was now associating the Apostles with the life of His Resurrection; at Pentecost, He would associate them with His Ascension.

Next He conferred upon them the power of forgiving sins. There was even to be a distinction between sins that the Apostles would forgive and sins they would not forgive. How they would distinguish between the two would evidently depend on hearing them. He said:

> If you forgive any man's sins, they stand forgiven; if you pronounce them unforgiven, unforgiven they remain. *John 20:23*

As the Jewish priest pronounced who were clean and who were unclean among the lepers, so now Christ conferred the power of forgiving and withholding forgiveness on sinners. Only God can forgive sins; but God in the form of man forgave the sins of Magdalen, of the penitent thief, of the dishonest tax collector, and of others. The same law of the Incarnation would now hold; God would continue to forgive sins through man. His appointed ministers were to be the instruments of His forgiveness, as His own human nature was the instrument of His Divinity in purchasing forgiveness. These solemn words of the Risen Savior meant that sins were to be forgiven through a judicial power authorized to examine the state of a soul and to grant or refuse forgiveness as the case demanded. From that day on, the remedy for human sin and guilt was to be a humble confession to one having authority to forgive. To be humble on one's knees confessing to one to whom Christ gave the power to forgive (rather than prostrate on a couch to hear guilt explained away)—that was one of the greatest joys given to the burdened soul of man.

56. Fingers, Hands, and Nails

The first appearance of Our Lord in the Upper Room was to only ten of the Apostles; Thomas was not present. He was not with the Apostles, but the Gospel assumes that he should have been with them. The reason of his absence is unknown; but likely it was because of his unbelief. In three different passages of the Gospel, Thomas is always portrayed as looking on the darker side of things, as regards both the present and the future. When the news came to Our Lord about the death of Lazarus, Thomas wanted to go and to die with him. Later on, when Our Blessed Lord said that He would return again to the Father and prepare a place for His Apostles, Thomas' doleful answer was that he knew not where the Lord was going, nor did he himself know the way.

Immediately after the other Apostles became convinced of the Resurrection and glory of Our Divine Savior, they brought to Thomas the tidings of the Resurrection. Thomas did not say he refused to believe, but that he was unable to believe until he had some experimental proof of the Resurrection, in spite of their testimony that they had seen the Risen Lord. He enumerated the conditions of his belief:

> Unless I see the mark of the nails on his hands, unless I put my finger into the place where the nails were, and my hands into his side, I will not believe it. *John 20:25*

The disparity between those who believed and those who were unprepared for belief could be seen in the reception that the ten got as they told Thomas of the Resurrection. His refusal to trust the testimony of ten competent companions, who had seen the Risen Christ with their own eyes, proved how skeptical was the gloomy man. His, however, was not the frivolous skepticism of indifference or hostility to truth; he wanted knowledge in order to have faith. It was unlike the self-wise who want knowledge against faith. In one sense, his attitude was that of the scientific theologian who promotes knowledge and intelligence after having banished all doubt.

This is the only passage in Sacred Scripture where the word "nails" is used in connection with Our Savior, and which harkens back to the words of the Psalmist: "They pierced My hands and My feet." Thomas' doubts arose, for the most part, from his despondency and from the depressing influence of sorrow and isolation; for he was a man apart from his fellows. Sometimes a man who misses a meeting misses much. If the minutes of the first meeting were written they would have contained the tragic words of the Gospel: "Thomas was not there." Sunday was beginning to be the Lord's Day; for after eight days the Apostles were again assembled in the Upper Room, and Thomas was with them.

The doors still being closed, the Risen Savior stood in the midst of them and, for the third time, gave the salutation:

> Peace be with you! *John* 20:19

Immediately upon speaking of peace, Our Divine Savior treated the subject on which peace rested, namely, His death and Resurrection. There was not the slightest trace of faultfinding in Our Lord, as there would not be the slightest trace of faultfinding with Peter at a later appearance by the Sea of Galilee. Thomas had asked for a proof based on the senses or the faculties that belong to the animal kingdom; and a proof of the senses would be given him. Our Lord spoke to Thomas:

> Reach your finger here; see my hands. Reach your hand here and put it into my side. Be unbelieving no longer, but believe. *John* 20:27

He had once said that a sinful and adulterous generation seeketh after a sign, and no sign would be given them other than the sign of Jonas the prophet. This was precisely the sign that was given to Thomas. The Lord knew of the skeptical words that Thomas had previously spoken to his fellow Apostles—another proof of His Omniscience. The wound in His side must have been very large, since He asked Thomas to put his hand into it; so also the wounds on His hands must have been large, as Thomas was bidden to substitute a finger for a nail. Thomas' doubts lingered longer than those of the others, and his extraordinary skepticism is an added proof of the reality of the Resurrection.

There was every reason to suppose that Thomas did as he was invited to do, just as there was every reason to suppose that the ten Apostles had done precisely the same on the first Easter evening. The rebuking words of Our Lord to Thomas—to be doubting no longer—also contained an exhortation to believe and to shake off his gloom, which was his besetting sin.

Paul was not disobedient to the heavenly vision; neither was Thomas. The doubter was so convinced by positive proof that he became a worshiper. Throwing himself on his knees, he said to the Risen Savior:

> My Lord and my God! *John* 20:28

In one burning utterance, Thomas gathered up all of the doubts of a depressed humanity to have them healed by the full implications of the exclamation, "My Lord and My God." It was an acknowledgment that the Emmanuel of Isaiah was before him. He, who was the last to believe, was the first to make the full confession of the Divinity of the Risen Savior. But, since it came from evidence of flesh and blood, it was not followed by the blessing which was conferred on Peter when he acknowledged that He was the Son of the Living God. However, the Risen Savior said to Thomas:

> Because you have seen me you have found faith. Happy are they who never saw me and yet have found faith. *John* 20:29

There are some who will not believe even when they see, such as Pharaoh; others believe only when they see. Above both these types the Lord God placed those who had not seen and yet believed. Noah had been warned by God of the things that had not yet come to pass; he believed as he prepared his ark. Abraham went out of his own home not knowing whither he went, but still trusting in the God who promised that he would be the father of a progeny more numerous than the sands of the seas. If Thomas had believed through the testimony of his fellow disciples, his faith in Christ would have been greater; for Thomas had often heard his Lord say that He would be crucified and rise again. He also knew from the Scriptures that the Crucifixion was the fulfillment of a prophecy, but he wanted the additional testimony of the senses.

Thomas thought that he was doing the right thing in demanding the full evidence of sensible proof; but what would become of future generations if the same evidence was to be demanded by them? The future believers, the Lord implied, must accept the fact of the Resurrection from those who had been with Him. Our Lord thus pictured the faith of believers after the apostolic age when there would be none who would have seen it; but their faith would have a foundation because the Apostles themselves had seen the Risen Christ. They saw that the faithful might be able to do so without seeing, believing on their testimony. The Apostles were happy men, not just because they had seen Our Lord and believed; they were far happier when they fully understood the mystery of Redemption and so lived in it, and even had their throats cut for the reality of the Resurrection. Some gratitude must always, however, be credited to Thomas, who touched Christ as a man, but believed in Him as God.

57. *Love as the Condition of Authority*

After the events of the Passover week in Jerusalem, the Apostles returned again to their former haunts and abodes, and particularly to the Sea of Galilee so full of tender memories. It was while they were fishing that the Lord had called them to be "Fishers of Men." Galilee would now be the scene of the Lord's last miracle, as it was the scene of His first, when He turned water into wine. On the first occasion, there was "no wine"; on this last occasion there were "no fish." In both, the Lord uttered a command: at Cana, to fill the waterpots; in Galilee, to cast the nets into the sea. Both resulted in a full supply; Cana had its six water pots of wine with the best wine served at the last; Galilee had its nets full of fish.

The Apostles at the sea on this occasion were Simon Peter, who as usual is mentioned first; next to him, however, is mentioned Thomas, who now after confessing that Christ was the Lord and God remained near to him who was called to be the chief of the Apostles. Nathanael of Cana in Galilee was also there; so were James and John and two other disciples. It is noteworthy that John, who once had a boat of his own, was now in the bark of Peter. Peter, taking the leadership and giving the inspiration to others, said:

> I am going out fishing. We will go with you, said the others.
> *John* 21:3

Though they had labored all the night, they caught nothing. When morning came they saw Our Lord on the shore, but they did not know that it was He. This was the third time that He came near to them as One Unknown in order to draw out their affections. Though they were near enough to the shore to address Him, like the disciples at Emmaus they neither discerned His Person nor recognized His voice, so enveloped was the Risen Body with glory. He was on the shore and they were on the sea. Our Lord spoke to them, saying:

> Friends, have you caught anything? They answered No. He said, Shoot
> the net to starboard, and you will make a catch. *John* 21:5,6

The Apostles must have remembered another such command when Our Lord told them to let down their nets for a draught, not specifying right or left. Then Our Lord was in the boat, now He was on the shore. The tossings of life were over. Immediately, in obedience to the Divine command, they were so successful in their catch that they were unable to draw the nets because of the multitude of fishes. In the first miracle of the catch of fishes during the public life the nets broke; Peter, awed by the miracle, asked Our Lord to depart from him because he was a sinful man. The very abundance of God's mercy made him feel his nothingness. But in this miraculous draught of fishes they were made strong; for immediately John said to Peter:

> It is the Lord! *John* 21:7

Both Peter and John remained true to their characters; as John was the first to reach the empty tomb on Easter morn, so Peter was the first to enter it; as John was the first to believe that Christ was risen, so Peter was the first to greet the Risen Christ; as John was the first to see the Lord from the boat, so Peter was the first to rush to the Lord, plunging into the sea to be first at His feet. Naked as he was in the boat, he cast a coat about him, forgot personal comfort, abandoned human companionship, and eagerly swam the hundred yards to the Master. John had the greater spiritual discernment, Peter the quicker action. It was John who leaned on the Master's breast the night of the Last Supper; he was the one, too, who was nearest the Cross, and to his care the Savior committed His mother; so now he was the first to recognize the Risen Savior on the shore. Once before, when Our Savior had walked on the waves towards the ship, Peter could not wait for the Master to come to him, as he asked the Master to bid him come upon the water. Now he swam to shore after girding himself out of reverence for His Savior.

The other six remained in the boat. When they came to shore, they saw fire, fish laid thereon, and some bread, which the compassionate Savior had prepared for them. The Son of God was preparing a meal for His poor fishermen; it must have reminded them of the bread and fishes He had multiplied when He had announced Himself as the Bread of Life. After they had dragged the net ashore and counted the one hundred and fifty-three fish they had caught, they were well convinced that it was the Lord. The Apostles understood that, as He had called them to be fishers of men, so this great catch symbolized the faithful who would ultimately be brought to the bark of Peter.

At the beginning of His public life, on the banks of the Jordan, Christ had been pointed out to them as the "Lamb of God"; now that He was about to leave them, He applied this title to those who were to believe in Him. He who called Himself the Good Shepherd now gave to others the power to be shepherds. The following scene took place after they had dined. As He gave the Eucharist after the supper and the power to forgive sins after He had eaten with them, so now, after partaking of bread and fish, He turned to the one who had denied Him three times and asked a triple affirmation of love. The confession of love must precede the bestowing of authority; authority without love is tyranny:

> Simon son of John, do you love me more than all else?   *John 21:15*

The query was: "Do you love Me with that truly supernatural love, the mark of a chief shepherd?" Peter had once presumed on the greatness of His love, telling His Master the night of the Last Supper, that even though all others would be offended and scandalized in Him, yet he would not deny. Peter was now addressed as Simon, son of John— Simon being his original name. Our Lord thus reminded Peter of his past as a natural man, but especially of his fall or denial. He had been living by nature rather than grace. The title also had another significance; it must have reminded Peter of his glorious confession when Our Lord said to him, "Blessed art thou Simon, son of John," and made him the Rock on which He would build His Church. In answer to the question about love, Peter said:

> Yes, Lord, you know that I love you. Then feed my lambs, he said.
> *John 21:15*

Peter now no longer claimed any superiority of affection over the other followers of Our Lord, for the other six Apostles were standing about. In the original Greek, the word which Our Blessed Lord used for love was not the same as that which was used by Peter in answer. The word that Peter used implied a rather natural emotion. Peter missed the full significance of Our Lord's words about the highest kind of love. Peter in self-distrust affirmed no more than a natural love. Having made love the condition of service to Him, the Risen Savior now told Peter, "Feed My lambs." The man who had fallen most deeply and learned most thoroughly his own weakness was certainly the best qualified for strengthening the weak and feeding the lambs.

Thrice repeated was the appointment of Peter as the Vicar of Christ on earth. Peter's denial had not changed the Divine decree making him the Rock of the Church; for Our Blessed Savior continued the second and third question:

> A second time he asked, Simon son of John, do you love me? Yes, Lord, you know I love you. Then tend my sheep. A third time he said, Simon son of John, do you love me? Peter was hurt that he asked him a third time, Do you love me? Lord, he said, you know everything; you know I love you.   *John 21:16–17*

The original Greek word used by Our Lord in the second question implied supernatural love, but Peter used the same word as before which signified a natural love. In the third question, Our Lord used the same word that Peter used for love the first time, namely, the word that meant only a natural affection. It was as if the Divine Master was correcting His own words in order to find one more congenial to Peter and his character. Perhaps it was the adoption of Peter's own word in the third question that cut him and grieved him most.

In answer to the third question, Peter left out the affirmation of love, but conceded omniscience to the Lord. In the original Greek, the word which Peter used when he said that Our Lord knew all things implied a knowledge by Divine vision. When Peter said the Lord knew that he loved Him, the Greek word used meant only knowledge by direct observation. As Peter went step by step down the ladder of humiliation, step by step the Lord followed him with the assurance of the work for which he was destined.

Our Lord said of Himself: "I am the Door." To Peter He had given the keys and the function of the doorkeeper. The Savior's function as the visible Shepherd over the visible flock was drawing to an end. He transferred that function to the head shepherd before withdrawing His visible Presence to the Throne of Heaven where He would be the invisible Head and Shepherd.

The Galilean fisherman was promoted to the leadership and the primacy of the Church. He was the first among all the Apostles in every apostolic list. Not only was he always named first but there was also precedence in action; he was the first to bear witness to the Lord's Divinity, and the first of the Apostles to bear witness to Christ's Resurrection from the dead. As Paul himself said, the Lord was first seen by Peter; Peter was the first after the Mission of the Spirit on Pentecost to preach the Gospel to his fellow men. He was first in the infant Church to defy the rage of the persecutor, first among the twelve to welcome the believing Gentiles into the Church, and first about whom it was foretold that he would suffer a death of martyrdom for the sake of Christ.

During the public life, when Our Blessed Lord had told Peter that he was a Rock upon which He would build His Church, He prophesied that He would be crucified and would rise again. Peter then tempted Him away from the Cross. In reparation for that temptation which Our Lord called satanic, He now, having commissioned Peter with full authority to rule over His lambs and sheep, foretold that Peter himself would die upon the Cross. He was almost saying to Peter: "You will have a Cross like the Cross to which they nailed Me, and from which you would have prevented Me from entering into My glory. Now you must learn what it really means to love. My love is a vestibule to death. Because I loved you, they have killed Me; for your love of Me, they will kill you. I once said that the Good Shepherd would give up His life for His sheep; now you are My shepherd in My place; you will, therefore, receive the same reward for your labors as I have received—crossbeams, four nails, and then life eternal."

> And further, I tell you this in very truth: when you were young you fastened your belt about you and walked where you chose; but when you are old you will stretch out your arms, and a stranger will bind you fast, and carry you where you have no wish to go. *John 21:18*

Impulsive and self-willed though he was in the days of his youth, yet in his old age Peter would glorify the Master by a death on the Cross. From Pentecost on, Peter was led where he would not go. He was obliged to leave the Holy City, where imprisonment and the sword awaited him. Next He was led by His Divine Master to Samaria and into the house of the Gentile, Cornelius; then he was led to Rome, the new Babylon, where he was strengthened by the strangers of the dispersion whom Paul had brought into the fold; finally, he was led to a Cross and died a martyr's death on the hill of the Vatican. He was crucified at his own request with his head downwards, deeming it unworthy to die like the Master. Inasmuch as he was the Rock, it was fitting that he himself be laid in the earth as an impregnable foundation of the Church.

Thus the man who was always tempting the Lord away from the Cross was the first of the Apostles to go to it. The Cross that he embraced redounded to the glory of his Savior more than all the zeal and impetuosity of his youth. When Peter did not understand that the Cross implied Redemption from sin, he put his own death before that of the Master, saying that though all others would fail to defend Him, he would not. Now Peter saw that it was only in the light of the Cross of Calvary that the Cross he would embrace had meaning and significance. Toward the end of his life, Peter would see the Cross before him and write:

> I know that very soon I must leave it; indeed our Lord Jesus Christ has told me so. But I will see to it that after I am gone you will have means of remembering these things at all times.
>
> It was not on tales artfully spun that we relied when we told you of the power of our Lord Jesus Christ and his coming. *II Peter 1:14–15*

58. *The Divine Mandate*

Many of the other appearances of the Risen Savior were sudden and startlingly unexpected; but there was one made by appointment before He entered into His agony. He told the Apostles that He would go before them into Galilee. After the Resurrection, first the angel and then the Lord Himself made the same appointment, which set it off as one of extraordinary importance. The exact place of Galilee was not recorded nor is it of importance whether it was on the Mount of the Beatitudes or on the Mount of Thabor. Neither is it known how many were present besides the Apostles, but it is distinctly stated that the eleven were there, indicating the loss of one from the apostolic college that would not be filled up until Pentecost. In the Old Testament, God had made appointments on mountains. Mount Moria was the place of appointment with Abraham; Mount Horeb, the place of appointment with Moses. When the Apostles kept this appointment on the mountain where the Risen Savior had bidden them meet Him:

> They fell prostrate before him.   *Matthew* 28:17

He said to them:

> Full authority in heaven and on earth has been committed to me.
> *Matthew* 28:18

When He said that all power was given to Him in heaven and on earth, He did not mean it as the Son of God, for that belonged already to Him by nature. Rather it was a power that He had merited by His Passion and His death and which was foretold by Daniel, who saw in a prophetic vision the Son of Man having everlasting dominion and glory. The power that was given to Him was foretold in Genesis, namely, that He Who was the seed of a woman would bruise the serpent's head. The kingdoms of the earth which Satan promised Him if He would be a political savior were now declared to be His own. His authority extended over the earth, all souls having been bought by His Blood. This authority as the Son of Man extended not only on earth but also in heaven. His Words combined the Resurrection and the Ascension; as the Resurrection gave Him power upon earth conquering both its sin and its death, so the Ascension gives Him power in heaven to act as mediator between God and man.

Christ's next utterance was a corollary of the first. If all authority was given to Him in heaven and on earth, then He had the right to delegate that authority to whomsoever He pleased. It was important that the authority He delegated be given to those who were contemporaneous with Him in order that He might pass it on to them. An electric wire that is fifteen hundred or two thousand miles away from a dynamo cannot communicate current. Any authority to act in Christ's name must needs be given by Christ Himself and then passed on through the centuries by those who immediately received it.

While on earth He exercised the triple office of Priest, Prophet or Teacher, and King. Now as He prepared to leave them for heaven whence He came, He deputed that triple office to His Apostles: the priestly office in bidding them renew the Memorial of His death and by conferring on them the power to forgive sins; the prophetic or teaching office, by promising to send them the Spirit of Truth Who would recall to their minds all things He had taught them and would keep them one in faith; and the kingly office, by giving them a Kingdom (as His Father had given Him a Kingdom), over which they had the powers of binding and loosing. Leaving no doubt that the purpose of His coming was to prolong His Priesthood, His Truth and His Kingship, He consigned His Apostles to the world:

> Go forth therefore and make all nations my disciples; baptize men everywhere in the name of the Father and the Son and the Holy Spirit, and teach them to observe all that I have commanded you. And be assured, I am with you always, to the end of time. *Matthew 28:19,20*

If this commission were given solely for the time span of the Apostles, it is evident that they could not possibly go to all nations. The dynamism or current that was passed into the Apostles under the headship of Peter was to continue until Christ's Second Coming. No doubt was left concerning the authority and the work of the Church when the Master would leave the earth. That day the Propagation of the Faith came into being. No longer were the Apostles and their successors to consider themselves solely as masters in Israel; from now on the whole world was theirs. Nor were they merely to teach; for He Who gave the commission was not just a teacher. They were to make disciples in every nation; and discipleship implied surrender of heart and will to the Divine Master. The power of His redemptive Cross would be in vain unless His servants used it to incorporate other human natures unto Himself. As Mary gave Him the human nature which was now glorified in His Person, so men were to give their human natures to Him, dying as He died, in order that they might enter into glory.

This incorporation to Himself was to be initiated by baptism, as He told Nicodemus. Unless a man be born of water and the Holy Spirit he could not enter into the Kingdom of God. As being born of the flesh made a man flesh, so being born of the Spirit would make him a participant of His Divine nature. The baptism was to be administered not in "the names" of the three Persons of the Blessed Trinity, since it would imply three gods, rather, it was to be given in the *name* of the Father, Son and Holy Spirit, because the Three Persons are one, having the nature of God. A most imperfect analogy is that our living, our knowing, and our loving are all rooted in human nature; so too the Power of the Father, the Wisdom of the Son, and the Love of the Holy Spirit are all One in the nature of God. As the three angles of a triangle do not make three triangles but one; as ice, water, and steam are different manifestations of the one nature, H_2O, so infinitely beyond all finite comparison the Power, Wisdom, and Love are but one God.

This authority which He gave them and which was to be extended throughout the entire earth might still have left in the minds of the Apostles a doubt concerning His Presence with them. This doubt was straightway cleared up when He assured His Church:

Be assured, I am with you always, to the end of time. *Matthew* 28:20

The promise was without limit; it would endure until the end of the world. God had told Abraham that He would be with him; Moses and Aaron were told that He would be in their mouths; Josue and Moses were promised that God would be with them; and Solomon was assured that God would be with him in the building of His house. Jeremiah, when he pleaded ignorance, was assured that God would put words into his mouth. But in these cases, the Divine Presence lasted only during the lifetime of the persons to whom it was given. No such limitation of Divine Protection and Presence was mentioned in the case of the Apostles. "The Gates of Hell will not prevail against My Church," He told Peter once. Confirmation of that promise was given again in the words: "I am with you through the days that are coming, until the consummation of the world."

59. *Last Appearance in Jerusalem*

Before the expiration of the forty days, the Apostles returned again to Jerusalem, where the Risen Christ had previously appeared to them. There He made it clear that His companionship with them was past; His influence would now be in heaven. But before taking leave, He reiterated the importance of prophesy and history. No one before was ever preannounced; but He was, and the more they would search the Old Testament the more they would understand. From now on, the Church was to draw from its treasury of the Law, the prophets, and the Psalms all that referred to Him.

> Everything written about me in the Law of Moses and in the prophets and psalms was bound to be fulfilled. Then he opened their minds to understand the scriptures. *Luke 24:44,45*

A new light made all things appear different from what they were before; they looked different in the light of the Resurrection from what they were in the previous darkness. It takes more than the light of the sun to read Moses and the prophets and the Psalms; some interior illumination, which is inseparable from good will and love, is also required. Several times Our Lord told His own autobiography, and in each instance without exception it referred to the atonement He would make between God and man. He now summarized His life for the last time, repeating that the Old Testament referred to Him as the Suffering but Conquering Servant.

> This is what is written: that the Messiah is to suffer death and to rise from the dead on the third day. *Luke 24:46*

It is not His Sermon on the Mount that He would have remembered, but His Cross. There would have been no Gospel had there been no Cross; and the death on the Cross would have been useless for the removal of human guilt, if He had not risen from the dead. He said it behooved Him to suffer because He had to show the evil of sin, and evil is most manifest in the Crucifixion of Goodness. No greater darkness would ever descend upon the earth than that which fell upon Him on Calvary. In all other wars, there is generally a gray, or a mixture of good and evil, on both sides; but in the Crucifixion, there was black on one side and white on the other. Evil would never be stronger than it was on that particular day. For the worst thing that evil can do is not to bomb cities and to kill children and to wage wars; the worst thing that evil can do is to kill Goodness. Having been defeated in that, it could never be victorious again.

Goodness in the face of evil must suffer, for when love meets sin, it will be crucified. A God Who wears His Sacred Heart upon His sleeve, as Our Lord did when He became man, must be prepared to have human daws peck at it. But at the same time, Goodness used that very suffering as a condition of overcoming evil. Goodness took all the anger, wrath, and hate, and pleaded: "Forgive"; it took life and offered it for another. Hence to Him it was expedient that He suffer in order to enter glory. Evil, conquered in its full armor and in the moment of its monumental momentum, might in the future win some battles, but it would never win the war.

No hope could be given to a wounded world by a Confucius, Buddha, or even a Christ who taught goodness and then rotted in the grave. No healing can be brought to broken wings by a humanism, which is brotherhood without tears; or by a gentle Christ Who has no source of knowledge distinct from any other teacher, and Who, in the end like them, could not burst the fetters of death, nor prove that truth crushed to earth may rise again.

This summary that Our Lord gave of His life threw down the challenge to men and took Him out of history. What assurance would there be that evil would not triumph over good? Suppose He was only a good man or the greatest moralist the world ever had, then what assurance would there be for the victory of virtue? What inspiration for sacrifice? If He, Who came to this earth to teach the dignity of the human soul, Who could challenge a sinful world to convict Him of sin, Who could at the moment of death forgive His enemies, had no other issue and destiny than to hang on a common tree with common criminals and thieves to make a Roman holiday, then each man may despairingly inquire: "If this is what happens to a good man, then why should one lead a good life?" In that case, the greatest of all injustices would go unredressed and the noblest of all lives would die unvindicated. Pay whatever compliments one may to His teaching, His patience under blows, His meekness before mobs—these eulogies do not make Him the Lord of death and life; they rather make these virtues vain, for they have no reward.

By saying that He had to suffer, Christ glorified His Father. Admire holiness as much as you please, but what is one to think of a God Who would look down on this spectacle of Innocence going to the gallows and not pull out the nails and put a sceptre there? Or a God Who would not send an angel to snatch a crown of thorns and place a garland there? Shall God be a party to saying that the noblest life that ever walked this earth is impotent before the evil deeds of men? What is humanity to think of human nature, if the white flower of a blameless life is trampled under the hobnail boots of Roman executioners, and then destined to decay like crushed flowers? Would it not send forth a greater stench because of its primal sweetness and make us hate not only the God Who had no care for truth and love, but even our fellow men for being a party to His death? If this is the end of goodness, then why be good at all? If this is what happens to justice, then let anarchy reign!

But if Our Lord took the worst the world had to offer, and then by the power of God rose above it; if He, the unarmed, could make war with no other weapon than goodness and pardon, so that the slain had the gain, and they who killed Him lost the day, then who should ever be without hope? Who shall ever despair in any momentary defeat by evil? Who shall fail to trust when he sees walking in the darkness the Risen One with glorious scars on hands and feet and side? The law He gave was clear: life is a struggle; unless there is a Cross in our lives, there will never be an empty tomb; unless there is the crown of thorns, there will never be the halo of light; unless there is a Good Friday, there will never be an Easter Sunday. When He said: "I have conquered the world," He did not mean His followers would be immune from woes, pain, sorrow, and crucifixion. He gave no peace which promised a banishment from strife; for God hates peace in those who are destined for war. If the Heavenly Father did not spare His Son, He, the Heavenly Son, would not spare His disciples. What the Resurrection offered was not immunity from evil in the physical world, but immunity from sin in the soul.

The Divine Savior never said to His Apostles: "Be good and you will not suffer"; but He did say: "In this world you shall have tribulation." He told them also not to fear those that kill the body, but rather to fear those who can kill the soul. Now He told the Apostles that His life was a model for all of His followers; they were encouraged to take the worst this life had to offer with courage and serenity. He said that all sufferings were as the shade of "His hand outstretched caressingly." No talisman was He to promise us security from trials; rather as a Captain He went into battle in order to inspire men to transfigure some of life's greatest pains into the richest gains of the spiritual life. It was the Cross of Christ that raised the questions of life; it was the Resurrection that answered them. Not the feminine but the virile Christ is He Who unfurls before an evil world the pledge of victory in His own Body—the scar-spangled banner of

Salvation. As the poet Edward Shillito has put it: "No false gods, immune from pain and sorrow, could console us in these days."

Jesus of the Scars

If we have never sought, we seek Thee now;
 Thine eyes burn through the dark, our only stars;
We must have sight of thorn-pricks on Thy brow,
 We must have Thee, O Jesus of the Scars.

The heavens frighten us; they are too calm;
 In all the universe we have no place.
Our wounds are hurting us; where is the balm?
 Lord Jesus, by Thy Scars we claim Thy grace.

If when the doors are shut, Thou drawest near,
 Only reveal those hands, that side of Thine;
We know to-day what wounds are, have no fear,
 Show us Thy Scars, we know the countersign.

The other gods were strong; but Thou wast weak;
 They rode, but Thou didst stumble to a throne;
But to our wounds only God's wounds can speak,
 And not a god has wounds, but Thou alone.*
Edward Shillito, 1872–1948

* From the book entitled *Masterpieces of Religious Verse*, edited by James Dalton Morrison (Harper & Brothers, New York). Reprinted by permission.

60. Repentance

After having spoken His own autobiography, Christ wrote the biography of all whom He redeemed; the fruits of His Cross must now be applied to all peoples and all nations:

> In his name repentance bringing the forgiveness of sins is to be proclaimed to all nations. Begin from Jerusalem; it is you who are the witnesses to it all. *Luke 24:47,48*

The first sermon that Christ preached was on the subject of repentance:

> From that day Jesus began to proclaim the message: Repeat; for the kingdom of Heaven is upon you. *Matthew 4:17*

The first sermon of Peter was on repentance; the first sermon of Paul was on repentance; now the last sermon Christ preached before ascending into heaven was the theme of His first. Repentance was to be the burden of the New Testament teaching. Repentance is thus linked up with the fulfillment of the ancient prophecies, but above all with the application of the Redemption won on Calvary. Peter, who heard this message, would be preaching it himself in a short time:

> It is to him that all the prophets testify, declaring that everyone who trusts in him receives forgiveness of sins through his name.
>
> Acts 10:43

Repentance implied a turning away from sin and a turning to God. The first four Beatitudes He preached were a description of this inner and radical change of heart, namely, poverty or humility of spirit, sorrow for sin, meekness, hunger and thirst for love of God. In the parable of the Prodigal Son, Our Lord had drawn a picture of the soul penitent who "entered into himself," as if sin had externalized him, and then returned humbly to the father's house. The Angels of heaven, He said, rejoice more over one sinner doing penance than ninety-nine just who need not penance; the publican in the back of the temple mourning over his sins, He said, went back to his house justified. Now in His farewell discourse before the Ascension, He bade the world repent.

This preaching of repentance was to begin at Jerusalem, for Salvation was first to the Jews. In that city the one great Sacrifice was offered for the sins of the world; there it was that the priesthood was shadowed forth with its rites and oracles. There it was that prophecy announced the Captain of Israel; and it was there as Isaiah said:

> For instruction issues from Zion, and out of Jerusalem comes the word of the Lord. *Isaiah 2:3*

The Divine order to begin preaching Redemption in Jerusalem was a mark of His great compassion; for He was directing the Apostles to go to those who had falsely accused Him and tell them that He was their Advocate; that He would plead their cause from on high; and finally assure them that, though they sourged Him, through His stripes they would be healed.

Having finished His own autobiography, Our Lord reminded them again of the Spirit that He promised the night of the Last Supper and fulfilled partly when He breathed on them and gave them the power to forgive sins.

> I am sending upon you my Father's promised gift; so stay here in this city until you are armed with the power from above. *Luke 24:49*

Thus He promised a manifest increase of the Spirit beyond a breathing; in fact it would be a "power from on high." But to receive it, they must wait ten days after His Ascension. This power would be greater than that given to Moses for his work of guiding Israel; greater than that given to Josue to conquer his enemies; greater than that given to kings and prophets; and it would enable them to proclaim the Redemption. The Apostles did not understand the nature of this power; for to them it meant a kind of restoration of Israel:

> Lord, is this the time when you are to establish once again the sovereignty of Israel? *Acts 1:6*

They were still thinking in the old terms of a political Messiah, and of making Jerusalem what Caesar had presently made Rome. But He warned that it was not for them to know the times or the seasons; a faith in a bright future was not to prompt a presumptuous curiosity. In all things they must wait upon God. The present is the exclusive object of apostolic duty; as regards the future, some will reap where they did not sow.

Power they would have, but not power to restore Israel; it would be a power over living souls to channel into them the forgiveness and grace stored up in the reservoir of Calvary.

> But you will receive power when the Holy Spirit comes upon you; and you will bear witness for me in Jerusalem, and all over Judea and Samaria, and away to the ends of the earth. *Acts 1:8*

They wanted an earthly kingdom; He spoke of a spiritual one. They wanted a return of the old things; He told them they would be "witnesses" of a new thing. And to be a witness meant to be a martyr. The power of His Spirit was consonant with human weakness. They could be humanly weak as Paul was in his preaching but full of power because of the Spirit. They were bound by the idea of a nation: Israel; He included the world in His vision.

Their new power would be a gift; it would not be generated from within by self-confidence, by a subjective belief that one had influence over others or by a psychological trick of believing in oneself. Organized revivals based on commercialized propaganda would draw crowds, but such tricks could no more produce spiritual effects than they could produce thunder and lightning. At this solemn moment when Christ is about to turn over the world itself to His eleven, He returned to the subject of the Last Supper: the Holy Spirit. As He began His public life with the descent of the Holy Spirit, so they were to begin their mission to the world. The Spirit came to Him after His obedience to His mother and foster father in Nazareth; so the Spirit would come to them after their obedience to tarry in Jerusalem as they abided in prayer. When that power would come, they were to be witnesses not to His miracles alone or His prophecies or His moral commands, but to His Person. As on the Mount of the Beatitudes He reaffirmed that there is no doctrine apart from His Person. One could no more choose to believe His words about the lilies and disbelieve His words about hell than to believe in His Body and not His Blood. With this affirmation that Christianity is Christ, He prepared to ascend to His Father.

61. The Ascension

For those forty days after His Resurrection, Our Divine Savior was preparing His Apostles to bear the loss of His Presence through the gain of the Comforter who was to come.

> He showed himself to these men after his death, and gave ample proof that he was alive: over a period of forty days he appeared to them and taught them about the kingdom of God. *Acts 1:3*

It was not a period when He dispensed gifts, but rather one in which He gave out laws and prepared the structure for His Mystical Body, the Church. Moses had fasted days before the giving of the Law; Elijah fasted forty days before the restoration of the Law; and now for forty days the Risen Savior laid the pillars of His Church, and the new Law of the Gospel. But the forties were about to end, and the Apostles were bidden to wait upon the fiftieth day—the day of jubilee.

Christ led them out as far as Bethany, which was to be the scene of the last adieu; not in Galilee but in Jerusalem, where He had suffered, would take place His return to His Heavenly Father. His sacrifice being completed, as He was about to ascend to His Heavenly throne, He raised His hands bearing the imprint of nails. That gesture would be one of the last recollections the Apostles would have, save one. The hands were raised first to heaven and then pulled downward to earth as if to draw down its blessings on men. Pierced hands best distribute benediction. In the Book of Leviticus, after the reading of the prophetical promise of the Messiah, there came the high priestly benediction; so too, after showing that all prophecies were fulfilled in Him, He prepared to enter the heavenly sanctuary. Hands that held the sceptre of authority in heaven and on earth now gave the final blessing:

> Blessed them with uplifted hands; and in the act of blessing he parted from them . . . *Luke 24:51*

> He took his seat at the right hand of God. *Mark 16:19*

> And they returned to Jerusalem with great joy, and spent all their time in the temple praising God. *Luke 24:52,53*

Had Christ remained on earth, sight would have taken the place of faith. In heaven, there will be no faith because His followers will see; there will be no hope, because they will possess; but there will be love for love endureth forever! His leave-taking of the earth combined the Cross and the Crown that governed the smallest detail of His life. The Ascension took place on Mount Olivet at the base of which is Bethany. He led His Apostles out through Bethany, which meant passing through Gethsemane and the very spot where He wept over Jerusalem! Not as from a throne, but from a mountain elevated above the garden with the twisted olive trees crimsoned with His Blood, did He give the final manifestation of His Divine power! His heart was not embittered by His Cross, for the Ascension was the fruit of His Crucifixion. As He said, it was fitting that He suffer in order to enter into His glory.

In the Ascension the Savior did not lay aside the garment of flesh with which He had been clothed; for His human nature would be the pattern of the future glory of other human natures, which would become incorporated to Him through a sharing of His life. Intrinsic and deep was the relation between His Incarnation and His Ascension. The Incarnation or the assuming of a human nature made it possible for Him to suffer and redeem. The Ascension exalted into glory that same human nature that was humbled to the death.

A Coronation upon the earth, instead of an Ascension into heaven, would have confined men's thoughts of Him to the earth. But the Ascension would cause men's minds and hearts to ascend above the earth. In relation to Himself, it was fitting that the human nature which He took as the instrument for teaching, and governing, and sanctifying, should partake of glory as it shared in shame. It was very hard to believe that He, Who was the Man of Sorrows and acquainted with grief, was the beloved Son in Whom the Father was well pleased. It was difficult to believe that He, Who did not come down from a Cross, could ascend into heaven, or that the momentary glory that shone about Him on the Mount of the Transfiguration was a permanent possession. The Ascension put all such doubts away by introducing His human nature into intimate and eternal communion with God.

The human nature which He took was mocked as a Prophet when they blindfolded Him and asked Him to tell who struck Him; He was mocked as a King when they put upon Him a mock-robe of royalty and gave Him a reed of straw for a sceptre; finally He was mocked as a Priest when they challenged Him, Who was offering Himself as a Victim, to come down from the Cross. By the Ascension His triple office of Teacher, King, and Priest was vindicated. But the vindication would be complete when He would come in justice as the Judge of men in the human nature which He took from men. No one to be judged could complain that God knows not the trials to which humans are subject. His very appearance as the Son of Man would prove that He had fought the same battles as men and endured the same temptations as those standing at His bar of justice. His judgment would immediately find an echo in hearts.

Another reason for the Ascension was that He might plead in heaven to His Father with a human nature common to the rest of men. He could now, as it were, show the scars of His glory not only as trophies of victory but also as emblems of intercession. The night He went into the garden He prayed, as if He were already at the right hand of the Father in His heavenly abode; He uttered a prayer that was less that of a dying than that of an exalted Redeemer.

> That the love thou hadst for me may be in them, and I may be in them. *John 17:26*

While in heaven, He would be not only an Advocate of men with the Father but He would also send the Holy Spirit as man's Advocate with Him. The Christ at the right hand of the Father would represent humanity before the Father's throne; the Holy Spirit abiding with the faithful would represent in them the Christ Who went to the Father. In the Ascension, Christ took our necessities to the Father; thanks to the Spirit, Christ the Redeemer would be brought into the hearts of all who would believe in Him.

The Ascension would give Christ the right to intercede powerfully for mortals:

> Since therefore we have a great high priest who has passed through the heavens, Jesus the Son of God, let us hold fast to the religion we profess. For ours is not a high priest unable to sympathize with our weaknesses, but one who, because of his likeness to us, has been tested every way, only without sin. *Hebrews 4:14*

62. *Christ Takes on a New Body*

Ten days after the Ascension, the Apostles were gathered together awaiting the Spirit Who would teach them and reveal to them all that Our Blessed Lord had taught them. During His public life, He told them that He would take on a new Body. It would not be physical like the one He took from Mary. That Body is now glorified at the right hand of the Father. Nor would it be a moral body like a social club which derives its unity from the will of men. Rather, it would be His new social Body that would be bound to Him by His Heavenly Spirit which He would send on leaving this earth. He spoke of His new Body sometimes as a Kingdom, though St. Paul would speak of it as a Body which the Gentiles could understand more readily. He told the Apostles the nature of this new Body. It would assume seven main features:

1 He told them that to be a member of His new Body men would have to be born into it. But it would not be through a human birth, for that made sons of Adam; to be a member of His new Body one would have to be reborn through the Spirit in the waters of baptism which would make adopted sons of God.

2 The unity between this new Body and Him would not be through singing hymns to Him, nor having social teas in His name, nor listening to broadcasts, but through sharing His life:

Dwell in me, as I in you . . . I am the vine, and you the branches.

John 15:5

3 His new Body would be like all living things, small at first—even, as He said, "like a mustard seed"; but it would grow from simplicity to complexity until the consummation of the world. As He put it:

First the blade, then the ear, then full-grown corn in the ear.

Mark 4:28

4 A house expands from the outside in, by the addition of brick to brick; human organizations grow by the addition of man to man, i.e., from the circumference to the center. His Body, He said, would be formed from the inside out, as a living embryo is

formed in the human body. As He received life from the Father, the faithful would receive life from Him. As He put it:

May they all be one: as thou, Father, art in me, and I in thee, so also may they be in us. *John 17:21*

5 Our Lord said that He would have only one Body. It would be a spiritual monstrosity for Him to have many bodies or a dozen heads. To keep it one, it would have one shepherd, whom He appointed to feed His lambs and His sheep.

There will then be one flock, one shepherd. *John 10:16*

6 He said that His new Body would not manifest itself before men until the day of Pentecost when He would send His truth-giving Spirit.

If I do not go, your Advocate will not come. *John 16:7*

Anything that would start, therefore, even twenty-four hours after Pentecost or twenty-four hours ago would be an organization; it might have the human spirit, but it would not have the Divine Spirit.

7 The most interesting observation He made about His Body was that it would be hated by the world, as He was. Anything worldly the world loves. But what is Divine, the world hates.

Because I have chosen you out of the world, for that reason the world hates you. *John 15:20*

The nucleus of this new Mystical Body was His Apostles. They were to be the raw material into which He would send His Spirit to quicken them into His prolonged Self. They would represent Him when He was gone. The privilege of evangelizing the world was reserved to them. This new Body, of which they were the embryo, was to be His posthumous Self, and His prolonged Personality through the centuries.

Until Our Lord sent His Spirit on them fifty days after His Resurrection, the Apostles were like the elements in a chemical laboratory. Science knows up to 100 per cent the chemicals which enter into the constitution of a human body; but it cannot make a human being because of its inability to provide the unifying principle, the soul. The Apostles could not give the Church Divine life any more than chemicals could make human life. They needed God's invisible Divine Spirit to unify their visible human natures.

Accordingly, ten days after the Ascension, the glorified Savior in

Heaven sent upon them His Spirit, not in the form of a book but as tongues of living fire. As cells in a body form a new human life when God breathes a soul into the embryo, so the Apostles appeared as the visible Body of Christ when the Holy Spirit came to make them one. This Mystical Body or the Church is called in tradition and Scripture the "whole Christ" or "the fullness of Christ."

The new Body of Christ then appeared publicly before men. Just as the Son of God took upon Himself a human nature from the womb of Mary, overshadowed by the Holy Spirit, so on Pentecost He took a Mystical Body from the womb of humanity, overshadowed by the Holy Spirit. Just as He once taught, governed, and sanctified through His human nature, so now He would continue to teach, to govern, and to sanctify through other human natures united in His Body or Church.

Because this Body is not physical like a man, nor moral like a bridge club, but heavenly and spiritual because of the Spirit which made it one, it is called a Mystical Body. As a human body is made up of millions and millions of cells, and yet is one because vivified by one soul, presided over by one visible head, and governed by an invisible mind, so this Body of Christ, though made up of millions and millions of persons who are incorporated into Christ by baptism, is one because vivified by the Holy Spirit of God and presided over by one visible head and governed by one invisible Mind or Head Who is the Risen Christ.

The Mystical Body is Christ's prolonged Self. St. Paul came to understand this truth. Perhaps no one has ever lived who hated Christ more than Saul. The early members of Christ's Mystical Body prayed that God would send someone to refute Saul. God heard their prayer; He sent Paul to answer Saul. One day this persecutor, breathing hatred, set out for Damascus to seize the members of Christ's Mystical Body there and bring them back to Jerusalem. The time was only a few years after the Ascension of Our Divine Savior, and Our Lord was now glorified in Heaven. Suddenly a great light shone about Saul, and he fell to the ground. Aroused by a Voice like a bursting sea he heard:

Saul, Saul, why do you persecute me? *Acts 9:4*

Nothingness dared to ask the name of Omnipotence:

Tell me, Lord, who you are?

And the Voice answered:

I am Jesus, whom you are persecuting. *Acts 9:5*

How could Saul be persecuting Our Lord Who was glorified in Heaven? Why should the Voice from Heaven say: "Saul, Saul, why dost thou persecute Me?"

If someone stepped on the foot, would not the head complain because it is part of the body? Our Lord was now saying that in striking His Body, Paul was striking Him. When the Body of Christ was persecuted, it was Christ the Invisible Head Who arose to speak and to protest. The Mystical Body of Christ, therefore, no more stands between Christ and an individual than His physical Body stood between Magdalen and His forgiveness, or His hand stood between the little children and His blessing. It was through His human Body that He came to men in His individual life; it is through His Mystical Body or His Church that He comes to men in His mystical corporate life.

Christ is living now! He is teaching now, governing now, sanctifying now—as He did in Judea and Galilee. His Mystical Body or the Church existed throughout the Roman Empire before a single one of the Gospels had been written. It was the New Testament that came out of the Church, not the Church which came out of the New Testament. This Body had the four distinctive marks of life; it had *unity*, because vivified by one Soul, one Spirit, the gift of Pentecost. As unity in doctrine and authority is the centripetal force which keeps the life of the Church one, *catholicity* is the centrifugal force which enables her to expand and absorb redeemed humanity without distinction of race or color. The third note of the Church is *holiness*, which means that it endures on condition that it keep itself healthy, pure, and free from the disease of heresy and schism. This holiness is not in each member but rather in the whole Church. And because the Holy Spirit is the soul of the Church, it can be the Divine instrument for the sanctification of souls. The sunlight is not polluted because its rays pass through a dirty window; neither do the sacraments lose their power to sanctify because the human instruments of those sacraments may be stained. Finally, there is the work of *apostolicity*. In biology, *Omne vivum ex vivo* or "All life comes from life." So too the Mystical Body of Christ is apostolic, because historically it took its roots in Christ and not from a man separated by centuries from Him. That is why the infant Church met to choose a successor of Judas who had to be a witness of the Resurrection and a companion of the Apostles.

> One of those who bore us company all the while we had the Lord Jesus with us, coming and going, from John's ministry of baptism until the day when he was taken up from us—one of those must now join us as witness to his resurrection. *Acts 1:21–22*

Thus the Christ Who "emptied" Himself in the Incarnation now had His "fullness" on Pentecost. The kenosis or humiliation is one facet of His Being; the pleroma or His continued life in His Bride, Spouse, Mystical Body or Church is the other. As the emptying of the light and heat of the sun cries out for the filling of the earth with its radiant energy, so the downward course of His love finds its completion in what St. Paul calls His "fullness"—the Church.

Many think they would have believed in Him if they had lived in His day. But actually there would have been no great advantage. Those who do not see Him as Divine living in His Mystical Body today would not have seen Him as Divine living in His physical Body. If there are scandals in some cells of His Mystical Body, there were scandals too in His physical Body; both put forward a human appearance which in moments of weakness or Crucifixion require moral strength to see Divinity. In the Galilean days, it required faith supported by motives of credibility to believe in the Kingdom He came to establish or His Mystical Body through which He would sanctify men through His Spirit, after His Crucifixion. In these days, it requires faith supported by the same motives of credibility to believe in the Head, or the Invisible Christ, governing, teaching, and sanctifying through His visible head and His Body the Church. In each case a "lifting-up" was required. To redeem men, Our Lord told Nicodemus that He had to be "lifted up" on the Cross; to sanctify men in the Spirit, He had to be "lifted up" to heaven in the Ascension.

Christ, therefore, still walks the earth, now in His Mystical Body, whereas then in His physical Body. The Gospel was the prehistory of the Church, as the Church is the posthistory of the Gospel. He still is denied inns, as He was in Bethlehem; new Herods with Soviet and Chinese names persecute Him with the sword; other Satans appear to tempt Him to short cuts of popularity away from the Cross and mortification; Palm Sundays of great triumph come to Him, but they are preludes to Good Fridays; new charges (and often from religious people, as of old) are hurled against Him—that He is an enemy of Caesar, is unpatriotic, and would pervert a nation; on the outside He is stoned, on the inside attacked by false brethren; not even Judases who were called to be Apostles are wanting to betray Him and deliver Him over to the enemy; some of His disciples who gloried in His name walk with Him no more, because—like their predecessors—they find His teaching, particularly on the Bread of Life, to be "hard."

But since there is never a death without a Resurrection, His Mystical Body will in the course of history have a thousand deaths and a thousand Resurrections. The bells will always be tolling for His execution, but the execution will be everlastingly postponed. Some final day, in His Mystical Body there will come a universal persecution, when He will go to His death as He did before, "suffering under Pontius Pilate," suffering under the omnipotent power of the State. But in the end, all that was foretold of Abraham and Jerusalem will come to pass in its spiritual perfection, when He will be glorified in His Mystical Body as He was glorified in His physical Body. As John the Apostle described it:

> Come, and I will show you the bride, the wife of the Lamb. So in the Spirit he carried me away to a great high mountain, and showed me the holy city of Jerusalem coming down out of heaven from God. It shone with the glory of God; it had the radiance of some priceless jewel, like a jasper, clear as crystal. It had a great high wall, with twelve gates, at which were twelve angels; and on the gates were inscribed the names of the twelve tribes of Israel. There were three gates to the east, three to the north, three to the south, and three to the west. . . . I saw no temple in the city; for its temple was the sovereign Lord God and the Lamb. And the city had no need of sun or moon to shine upon it; for the glory of God gave it light, and its lamp was the Lamb. By its light shall the nations walk, and the kings of the earth shall bring into it all their splendour. The gates of the city shall never be shut by day—and there will be no night . . . He who gives this testimony speaks: Yes, I am coming soon! Amen. Come, Lord Jesus! The grace of the Lord Jesus be with you all.
>
> *Apocalypse 21:9–14,22–26; 22:20–21*

Index

Index

eternal prehistory of Christ,
20; friend of Bridegroom,
103; greatness of, 56; herald,
55; and Herod Antipas,
127–33; refusal of title, 71;
refusal to baptize Jesus, 57;
spirit of, as animating Christ,
163; Visitation, 24
John the Evangelist, 64, 75,
108, 257, 286, 337, 348; after
arrest of Christ, 328; at
Crucifixion, 371; described,
108–9; at empty tomb, 406;
feast at Cana, 76; at
Gethsemane, 317; interest in
Pierced Side, 417; on Lamb
slain from beginning, 72–73;
at miracle of catch of fishes,
425; "one whom Jesus
loved," 291; on road to
Jerusalem, 171; remaining
true to character, 426; symbol
of Mary's new family, 35, 79;
third word from the Cross,
375–78; and Transfiguration,
158–61
John, 1:1, 53; 1:1–3, 25, 112;
1:3, 53; 1:3–5, 26; 1:7, 237;
1:12, 31; 1:14, 31, 53, 177;
1:29, 71; 1:38, 107; 1:42,
106; 1:45,46, 47, 109;
1:47,48, 109; 1:49–51, 109;
1:51, 90; 2:3, 76; 2:4, 50, 77;
2:5, 79; 2:10, 80; 2:16, 82;
2:17,18, 82; 2:19, 83, 332;
2:21,22, 84; 2:24,25, 226;
3:1, 86; 3:3,4, 87, 88; 3:5–6,
60; 3:5–7, 88; 3:8,9, 89;
3:13, 89, 194; 3:15–16, 90;
3:16, 91, 194, 298, 327;
3:19–21, 227; 3:20,21, 345;
3:39, 103; 3:31, 90; 4:7, 94;
4:9, 94; 4:10, 26, 95;
4:11,12,13,14, 95; 4:16,17,
96; 4:18, 96, 97; 4:19,20, 97;
4:21–24, 97; 4:23, 302;
4:25,26,29, 98;

4:39,40,41,42, 99; 5:6, 213,
398; 5:8,11, 213; 5:17, 214;
5:18, 176, 215; 5:27, 195;
5:28, 252; 5:36, 220; 6:2,5,
134; 6:7, 109; 6:9, 135; 6:15,
69, 261; 6:20, 137; 6:26,27,
138; 6:32, 195; 6:33, 24;
6:35, 24, 139;
6:35–41,48–51, 139; 6:38,
90, 193; 6:38–55, 249; 6:42,
90; 6:44, 94; 6:52–54, 139;
6:58, 140; 6:61, 143; 6:63,
90, 143, 302; 6:64, 302; 6:65,
287; 6:67, 143; 6:68–71, 144;
6:71, 144; 7:5, 176; 7:6, 176,
261; 7:11–13, 177; 7:15, 47,
215; 7:16, 215; 7:20, 215;
7:26, 178; 7:30, 77; 7:33–34,
180; 7:37,38, 178; 7:39, 179,
420; 7:46–49, 180; 7:53, 182;
8:1, 182; 8:4, 183; 8:5, 183;
8:6, 185, 8:8, 158; 8:9, 186;
8:11, 187; 8:12, 139, 179;
8:20, 77; 8:23, 194; 8:28, 92;
8:32, 204; 8:33,34, 204;
8:35, 205; 8:36, 188; 8:42,
216; 8:45–47, 205; 8:46, 152;
8:53, 63–66, 216; 8:55, 195;
9:11, 30, 189; 9:22, 188;
9:33,35,36, 188, 189; 9:37,
190; 10:7–9, 139; 10:7–10,
154; 10:9, 191, 399; 10:10,
191; 10:11, 192; 10:11–14,
139; 10:16, 236, 444; 10:17,
192; 10:18, 192, 193; 10:24,
218; 10:30, 218; 10:31, 219;
10:32, 219; 10:33, 219;
10:39, 219, 251; 11:4, 249;
11:8, 251; 11:9,10, 251;
11:16, 111; 11:22, 252;
11:25, 139, 253;
11:27, 253; 11:33, 196, 253;
11:36, 254; 11:39, 254;
11:40, 250; 11:44, 254;
11:47,48, 255; 11:48,51, 255;
11:51,52, 256; 11:53, 249,
256; 12:4,5, 288; 12:5, 258;

beginning of death, 77–78;
six, on Sabbath, 213–14; tax
money found in fish, 208;
and unbelief, 220–21; unbelief
not always cured by, 239
Miriam, 46
Mission of the Cross, 52; and
mission of Apostles, 419–20
Mockery of Christ, 441; crown
of thorns, 356–57; Herod
Antipas, 347; passersby at
Crucifixion, 388; Pharisees at
Crucifixion, 391; after
religious trial, 335; by Roman
soldiers at Crucifixion,
393–94
Mohammed, 17, 18, 115, 191,
362; alms, 156; death of, 153,
409–10
Money-changers at the temple,
81–82
Moria, Mount, 216, 430
Morrison, James Dalton, 436
Mosaic Law, 115; dedication of
firstborn, 38–39; sprinkled
with Blood of the Lamb, 187;
stoning for adultery, 183–84;
tablets, 185 (See also Old
Testament)
Moses, 61, 64, 132, 191, 270,
418, 438; "baptism" of
Aaron, 58; Covenant, 376;
crowd comparing Christ to,
138; and the face of God,
325; God to be with him,
432; last words, 372; lifting of
serpent, 90, 91; prefigure of
Messiah, 135; shepherd's
stick, 135; on Sinai, 102;
smiting of rock, 178; at
Transfiguration, 159; veil,
158; washing of hands of
guilt, 362
Mother of Men, 79
"Must," Christ's use of word,
51 (See also Obedience)
"My Father," 310–15

"My Father's house," 82
Myrrh, Christ anointed with,
257; crib and Cross related,
44; offered to Christ on
Cross, 370
Mystical Body, 445–48 (See
also Church)
Mystical Rose, 24

Naaman, 212
Nails, 422
Naos, 83
Nathanael, 75, 212, 257, 425;
on Nazareth, 47 (See also
Bartholomew)
Nazarene, 46
Nazareth, 24, 46, 329; Christ as
carpenter in, 52–54; place of
humiliation, 47; Prophet
unhonored in own home,
210–13
Nero, 55, 132
New Testament, Ark of, 396,
397; came out of Church,
446; Last Supper, 276, 277;
persecution of, 45; ratified by
sacrificial death of Lamb,
277; repentance as burden of
teaching, 437
Nicodemus, 42, 86–92, 139,
147, 345, 363; burial of
Christ, 400; first visit to
Jesus, 86; "night character"
of the Gospel, 86; and
spiritual birth, 88
Nineveh, 243, 244–45
Noah, 424
Nobility, in Kingdom of God,
172
Numbers, 39; brazen serpent,
90

Obedience, 51–52, 193; atoning
for pride, 54; at Cana, 78;
Christ's first open confession
of coming Crucifixion, 165;